DAY HIKES AROUND
Monterey
& Carmel

127 GREAT HIKES

Robert Stone

2nd EDITION

Day Hike Books, Inc.
RED LODGE, MONTANA

Published by Day Hike Books, Inc.
P.O. Box 865
Red Lodge, Montana 59068
www.dayhikebooks.com

Distributed by The Globe Pequot Press
246 Goose Lane
P.O. Box 480
Guilford, CT 06437-0480
800-243-0495 (direct order) · 800-820-2329 (fax order)
www.globe-pequot.com

Cover photograph by Joshua Simas
Back cover photograph by Robert Stone
Layout/maps by Paula Doherty

The author has made every attempt to provide accurate information in this book. However, trail routes and features may change—please use common sense and forethought, and be mindful of your own capabilities. Let this book guide you, but be aware that each hiker assumes responsibility for their own safety. The author and publisher do not assume any responsibility for loss, damage, or injury caused through the use of this book.

Cover photo:
Soberanes Canyon Trail, Hike 95

Back cover photo:
McWay Falls, Hike 120

Table of Contents

THE HIKES

Santa Cruz County:
Santa Cruz • Capitola • Aptos • Watsonville

North Monterey County:
Moss Landing • Prunedale • Castroville

Jacks Peak County Park

Fort Ord National Monument

Toro County Park

Carmel Valley:
Garland Ranch Regional Park

Carmel Valley:
Los Padres Reservoir • Tassajara Road

Point Lobos State Reserve

Garrapata State Park

Palo Colorado Road

Old Coast Road

Andrew Molera State Park

Hiking the Monterey and Carmel Area

Monterey County, along the Central California coastline, encompasses some of the most beautiful and diverse scenery in the world. The county has 99 miles of spectacular coastline, stretching from Monterey Bay and Carmel Bay to the rugged Big Sur oceanfront. Mountains backdrop the coast, separating the coastline from the rich agricultural land. Carmel, Monterey, and other picturesque communities dot a landscape abundant with green valleys, beaches, woodlands, parks, natural preserves, and calm bays along the scalloped coastline.

This completely revised and updated edition of *Day Hikes Around Monterey and Carmel* includes 127 great hikes throughout the area. A wide range of scenery and geography accommodates all levels of hiking, from easy beach strolls to strenuous, all-day mountain climbs. The trails have been chosen for their scenery, variety, and ability to be hiked within a day. Highlights along the miles of hiking trails include numerous waterfalls, creeks and canyons, huge stands of redwoods, tidepools, isolated beaches, rugged peninsulas, long-spanning bridges, lighthouses, craggy pinnacles, wildlife viewing sites, walking paths that weave through towns, and incredible views from the coast to the inland valleys.

Use the hikes' statistics and summaries, located at the beginning of each hike, to find a hike that is appropriate to your ability and intentions. The map on page 14 identifies the overall locations of the hikes, major access roads, and the area's larger parks. (The majority of hikes are a short drive from scenic Highway 1.) Many additional overall maps, as well as a map for each hike, provide closer details. Times are calculated for continuous hiking. Allow extra time for exploration.

The selection of hikes begins at the north end of Monterey Bay at Santa Cruz. Hikes 1—11 are located around this beach resort community with a beautiful coastline. The forested foothills of the Santa Cruz Mountains back the city, where many redwood groves are found. The diverse ecosystem ranges from sandy bluff-side beaches to cool, old-growth forests with perennial streams. The variety of trails range from beachfront walkways to undeveloped hillsides with riparian woodlands.

Traveling south down the coastline along Monterey Bay leads to Hikes 12—25. The land levels out and major waterways flow into the ocean. Along this length of Monterey Bay are long stretches of isolated, sandy

beaches and expansive, rolling sand dunes. Coastal wetlands and es-
tuaries attract tens of thousands of migratory birds along the Pacific
Flyway. This area is popular for surfing, fishing, horse riding, and bird
watching.

The oceanfront communities of Monterey, Pacific Grove, Pebble
Beach, and Carmel sit on the Monterey Peninsula at the south end of
the crescent-shaped Monterey Bay. The peninsula is a beautiful meeting of land and sea. It is at the heart of the Monterey Bay National
Marine Sanctuary, the largest marine reserve in the nation. In addition
to its quaint communities and world-class golf courses, the peninsula
is also known for migrating Monarch butterflies, groves of gnarled cypress, Monterey pines, and a jagged shoreline that overlooks tidepools,
beaches, and rock formations. Birds, sea lions, harbor seals, whales, and
other wildlife may be spotted along the shore. Hikes 26—47, on the
Monterey Peninsula, include everything from municipal green space to
trails that wind through dense forests, across coastal bluffs, and along
the undulating shoreline.

The south end of the Monterey Peninsula borders Carmel, a quaint
European-style village with an array of galleries, restaurants, boutiques,
gardens, and courtyards tucked within the tree-lined meandering streets.
The charming hamlet hugs Carmel Bay, with an oceanfront walking path, a
wetland preserve, and the stream-fed Mission Park.

A short distance inland are several county and state parks that cover
thousands of acres. The landscape varies from dry sandstone ridges
to cool canyons dotted with redwoods. Hikes 48—53 are in Jacks Peak
County Park. The park is located along a forested ridge that separates the
Monterey Peninsula from Carmel Valley, offering excellent views from
Monterey to Point Lobos. Hikes 54—58 are found in Fort Ord National
Monument, a former military base. The public land covers 7,200 acres,
some of the last undeveloped land on the Monterey Peninsula. A maze
of 86 miles of multi-use trails crisscrosses the rolling hills. Toro County
Park lies adjacent to Fort Ord. Hikes 59—63 travel through valleys to
ridges and peaks, covering over 20 miles of hiking trails.

Stretching east from the Monterey Peninsula is Carmel Valley. The
Carmel River flows down this verdant valley from the upper reaches
of the Ventana Wilderness. Garland Ranch (Hikes 64—76) rises from the

willow-lined banks of the river. The area crosses meadows and woodlands to the peaks of the Santa Lucia Mountains, with panoramic coastal, mountain, and valley views. Continuing southeast through Carmel Valley leads to Tassajara Road, which accesses trails along a ridge at the northeast end of the Ventana Wilderness (Hikes 77—86). The headwaters of several waterways, including the Carmel River, drain from either side of Tassajara Road. The remote trails along the ridge offer expansive views to the Pacific, while canyon hikes offer forested solitude.

A crown jewel among California's state parks is Point Lobos State Reserve, Hikes 88—94. The 1,276-acre reserve has incredible headlands with sculpted cliffs, coves, inlets, tidepools, isolated beaches, marine terraces, coastal bluffs, large stands of Monterey cypress, and miles of hiking trails. Point Lobos marks the northern end of the Big Sur coast.

The awesome coastline continues southward, a meeting of mountains and sea. Hiking along the Big Sur coast will be unforgettable. Highway 1 winds along the precipitous mountain cliffs with endless views of the Pacific. Stunning bridges span numerous creeks and deep canyons, while other portions of the road cross flat, grassy marine terraces that gently slope to the scalloped coastline and offshore rocks. Hikes 95—121 explore the north end of the amazing Big Sur coastline. State parks along this stretch of coastline include Garrapata State Park, Andrew Molera State Park, Pfeiffer Big Sur State Park, and Julia Pfeiffer Burns State Park. Hikes 105 and 106 follow the Old Coast Road, used before the 714-foot Bixby Creek Bridge was built.

Hikes 122—127 are located inland along the Gabilan Range in Pinnacles National Monument. Arising from the range is a rugged and fantastic landscape of craggy pinnacles, steep volcanic ridges, gorges, and talus caves. The area is one of the few release sites for the California condor. Hikes along the precipitous ledges or through the boulder-filled caves will long be remembered.

When hiking, bring the basic necessities to help ensure an optimum outing. Wear supportive, comfortable hiking shoes and layered clothing. Take along hats, sunscreen, sunglasses, water, snacks, and appropriate outerwear. Be aware that ticks and poison oak may be present. Use good judgement about your capabilities, and allow extra time to enjoy this beautiful area of California.

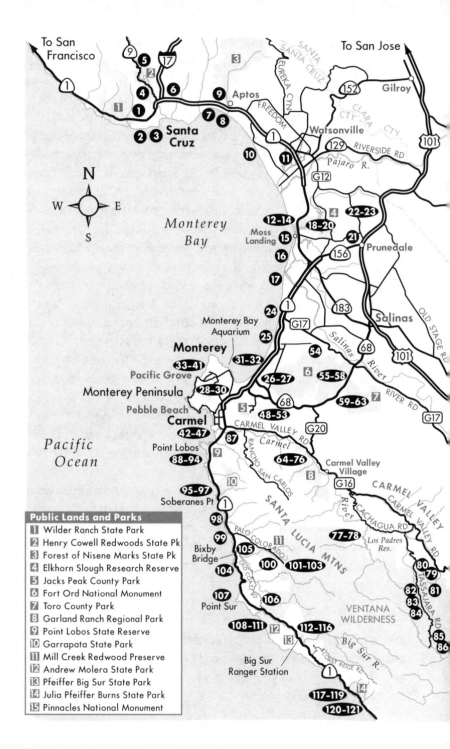

To San Francisco

To San Jose

Gilroy

Aptos

Santa Cruz

Watsonville

Monterey Bay

Moss Landing

Prunedale

Salinas

Monterey Bay Aquarium

Monterey

Pacific Grove

Monterey Peninsula

Pebble Beach

Carmel

Pacific Ocean

Point Lobos

Carmel Valley Village

Soberanes Pt

Bixby Bridge

Point Sur

VENTANA WILDERNESS

Los Padres Res.

SANTA LUCIA MTNS

CARMEL VALLEY

Big Sur Ranger Station

N
W   E
S

Public Lands and Parks

1 Wilder Ranch State Park
2 Henry Cowell Redwoods State Pk
3 Forest of Nisene Marks State Pk
4 Elkhorn Slough Research Reserve
5 Jacks Peak County Park
6 Fort Ord National Monument
7 Toro County Park
8 Garland Ranch Regional Park
9 Point Lobos State Reserve
10 Garrapata State Park
11 Mill Creek Redwood Preserve
12 Andrew Molera State Park
13 Pfeiffer Big Sur State Park
14 Julia Pfeiffer Burns State Park
15 Pinnacles National Monument

Map of the Hikes

MONTEREY and CARMEL AREA

Santa Cruz to Monterey Peninsula
Big Sur Coast to Julia Pfeiffer Burns State Park

Master Map

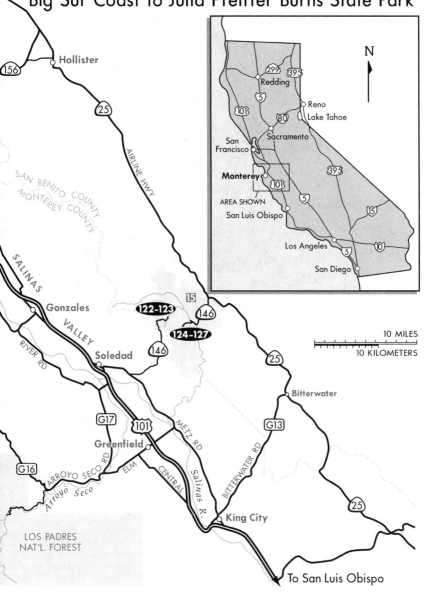

N

Hollister

156

25

AIRLINE HWY

SAN BENITO COUNTY
MONTEREY COUNTY

SALINAS

Gonzales

VALLEY

RIVER RD

Soledad

122-123

146

124-127

146

15

Redding

299   395

5

101

Reno
Lake Tahoe

80

San
Francisco

Sacramento

Monterey

101

395

AREA SHOWN

San Luis Obispo

5

Los Angeles

5

15

10

San Diego

10 MILES

10 KILOMETERS

Bitterwater

25

G17

101

Greenfield

METZ RD

G13

G16

ARROYO SECO RD

ELM

CENTRAL

Arroyo Seco

Salinas R.

BITTERWATER RD

King City

25

LOS PADRES
NAT'L. FOREST

To San Luis Obispo

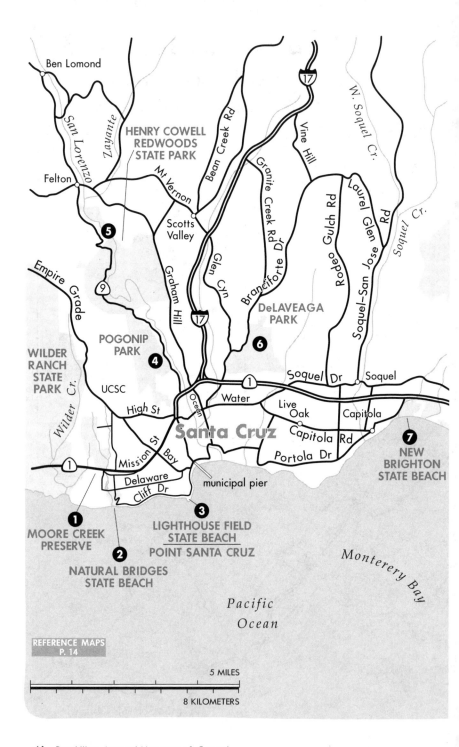

Ben Lomond

San Lorenzo

Zayante

HENRY COWELL
REDWOODS
STATE PARK

Bean Creek Rd

Granite Creek Rd Dr

Vine Hill

W. Soquel Cr.

Mt Vernon

Felton

Scotts
Valley

5

9

Empire Grade

WILDER
RANCH
STATE
PARK

POGONIP
PARK

4

UCSC

Wilder Cr.

High St

Graham Hill

Glen Cyn

Branciforte Dr

Rodeo Gulch Rd

Laurel Glen Rd

Soquel-San Jose Rd

Soquel Cr.

DeLAVEAGA
PARK

6

Soquel Dr   Soquel

Water

Ocean

Live
Oak

Capitola

Mission St

Bay

Delaware

Cliff Dr

Santa Cruz

Capitola Rd

Portola Dr

7

NEW
BRIGHTON
STATE BEACH

municipal pier

1

MOORE CREEK
PRESERVE

2

NATURAL BRIDGES
STATE BEACH

3

LIGHTHOUSE FIELD
STATE BEACH
POINT SANTA CRUZ

Monterery Bay

Pacific
Ocean

REFERENCE MAPS
P. 14

5 MILES

8 KILOMETERS

Santa Cruz to Watsonville

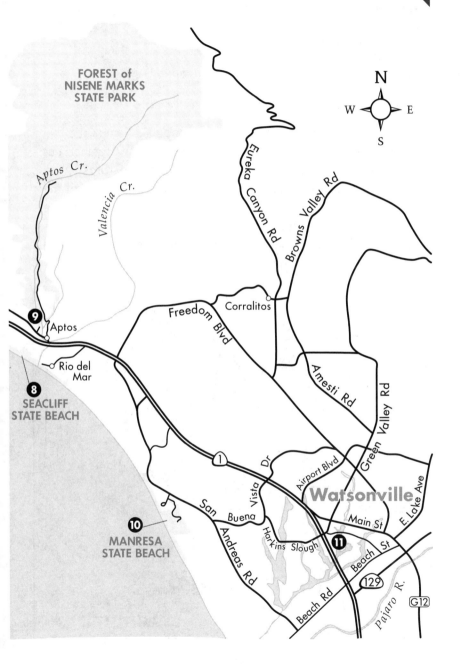

FOREST of
NISENE MARKS
STATE PARK

N
W — E
S

Aptos Cr.

Valencia Cr.

Eureka Canyon Rd

Browns Valley Rd

Freedom Blvd

Corralitos

9 Aptos

Rio del
Mar

Amesti Rd

Green Valley Rd

8
SEACLIFF
STATE BEACH

1

Vista Dr

Airport Blvd

Watsonville

E. Lake Ave

10
MANRESA
STATE BEACH

San Andreas Rd

Buena

Harkins Slough

Main St

11

Beach St

Beach Rd

129

Pajaro R.

G12

1. Moore Creek Preserve

Hiking distance: 2.5 miles round trip
Hiking time: 1.5 hours
Configuration: out-and-back with 2 loops
Elevation gain: 200 feet
Difficulty: easy
Exposure: mix of oak woodland and open, grassy slope
Dogs: not allowed
Maps: U.S.G.S. Santa Cruz · Moore Creek Preserve map

**map
page 20**

Moore Creek Preserve is a 246-acre greenbelt in Santa Cruz that opened to the public in 2003. The undeveloped watershed has a variety of habitats, including wetlands, riparian forests, live oak groves, coastal terrace prairie, and spectacular views of the ocean. Seasonal Moore Creek meanders through the east side of the preserve en route to a seaside lagoon at Natural Bridges State Beach (Hike 2). The creek's headwaters begin just north in the lower foothills of the Santa Cruz Mountains.

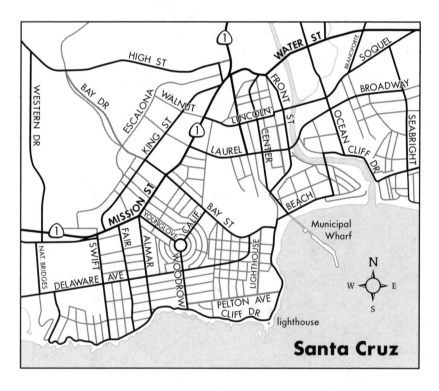

To the trailhead

From the west end of Santa Cruz, take Mission Street (Highway 1) to Western Drive. Drive one mile north on Western Drive to Meder Street. Turn left and park along the curb. Parking is not allowed past this point.

ALTERNATIVE PARKING. At the lower (south) end of the preserve is a trailhead along Highway 1. The posted trailhead is located 0.3 miles west of Western Drive, directly across Highway 1 from Shaffer Road. Parking is available along the highway.

The hike

Walk 0.4 miles west to the posted trailhead at the west end of Meder Street, a narrow, forested lane. Curve right on the East Meadow Trail to a signed junction at 0.1 mile. Bear left on the Moore Creek Trail, and drop into the oak-filled canyon. Traverse the east canyon slope along a rock wall with caves. Zigzag down two switchbacks to the canyon floor, and cross the bridge over seasonal Moore Creek. Ascend the west slope and pass through a trail gate. Leave the oak woodland to rolling grassy slopes and a T-junction. From here the views extend across Monterey Bay to Pacific Grove in Monterey County. The left fork descends 0.7 miles to the alternative trailhead on Highway 1.

Bear right (north) on the Prairie View Trail, and cross the rolling terrain 100 yards to a fork. Begin the loop to the left, staying on the Prairie View Trail to the fenceline bordering a private ranch. Go to the right, skirting the edge of the preserve and walking parallel to the fence. Climb the sloping meadow to the ridge and a trail split. The Terrace Loop Trail, the return route, is on the right. For now, go straight ahead on the Vernal Ridge Trail along the preserve boundary. Curve right along the edge of a thick oak woodland draped with lace lichen. Meander on the B-shaped loop through the wooded draw, returning to the ridge overlooking the bay. Now, go to the left on the Terrace Loop Trail, following the 400-foot ridge east. Curve right, completing the second loop. Veer left 100 yards, returning to the Moore Creek Trail junction. Bear left, back to the trailhead on the same route. ■

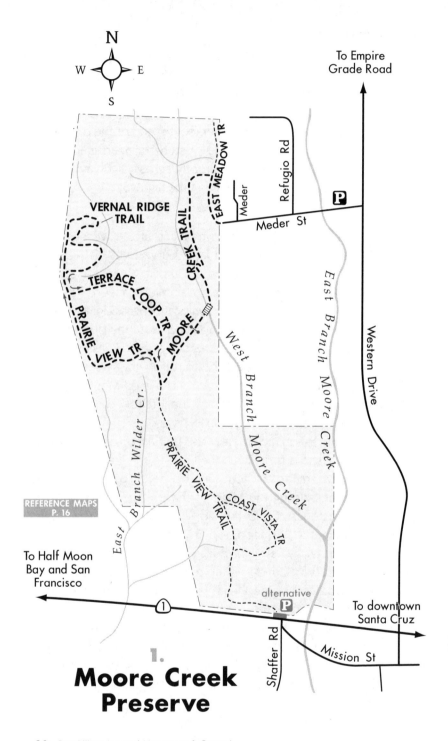

N
W · E
S

To Empire
Grade Road

VERNAL RIDGE
TRAIL

EAST MEADOW TR

Refugio Rd

Meder

P

Meder St

CREEK TRAIL

TERRACE LOOP TR

PRAIRIE

VIEW TR

MOORE

West Branch Moore Creek

East Branch Moore Creek

Western Drive

East Branch Wilder Cr.

PRAIRIE VIEW TRAIL

COAST VISTA TR

REFERENCE MAPS
P. 16

To Half Moon
Bay and San
Francisco

East Branch

alternative
P

1

To downtown
Santa Cruz

Shaffer Rd

Mission St

1.
Moore Creek
Preserve

2. Natural Bridges State Beach

Hiking distance: 1-mile loop
Hiking time: 45 minutes
Configuration: loop
Elevation gain: 50 feet
Difficulty: very easy
Exposure: shaded forest and exposed bluff and beach
Dogs: not allowed
Maps: U.S.G.S. Santa Cruz · Natural Bridges State Beach map

map
page 23

Natural Bridges State Beach overlooks the ocean on the west edge of Santa Cruz. The 54-acre park was named for three picturesque offshore rock formations with water-carved arches. The last of the three natural stone bridges collapsed after the devastating 1989 earthquake, but the gorgeous rock sculptures still remain. Along the shore is a sandy, half-moon beach backed by a large lagoon fed by Moore Creek. At the west end of the beach are rock terraces filled with tidepools in shallow depressions. Near the center of the park is a eucalyptus grove which attracts an annual monarch butterfly migration. The renowned site is home to one of the largest populations of wintering monarch butterflies in the United States (September through February). This hike loops around the state park on an interpretive trail through the diverse habitats.

To the trailhead

From the junction of Beach Street and West Cliff Drive by the wharf (Municipal Pier) in downtown Santa Cruz, head south on West Cliff Drive. Drive 2.7 miles along the oceanfront cliffs, passing the Point Santa Cruz Lighthouse, to the state beach entrance at Swanton Boulevard. Drive straight ahead into the parkland. To the left is the coastal overlook parking lot. Stay to the right and continue 0.4 miles to the parking lot at the visitor center. An entrance fee is required.

The park can also be accessed from the north via Natural Bridges Drive.

The hike

You may wish to pick up an interpretive brochure at the visitor center. The walk starts on the right (east) side of the visitor center at the posted Monarch Trail. Follow the boardwalk path through eucalyptus groves, descending to the floor of the ravine and a junction. The left fork leads 50 yards to the Monarch Resting Area viewing platform. Return to the junction and continue down canyon on the dirt path. Curve left and climb natural rock steps out of the ravine. Follow the ridge north through Monterey pines and eucalyptus groves. Cross the upper end of the park road near Delaware Avenue, and continue on the Moore Creek Trail. Curve south to a junction by seasonal Moore Creek. The right fork leads to Delaware Avenue. Veer left and cross through the riparian corridor on a boardwalk, curving toward the beach. After the boardwalk ends, the trail crosses a series of short bridges through groves of blackberries to the west banks of the Moore Creek estuary. Scramble up the short rocky terrace on the right to a coastal overlook. Descend the hill to the beach between the lagoon and the ocean. Walk 200 yards along the sandy beach to the base of the cliffs, viewing the offshore natural bridge outcroppings. Loop around the lagoon to the wide trail at the back of the beach. Return 30 yards to the parking lot. ■

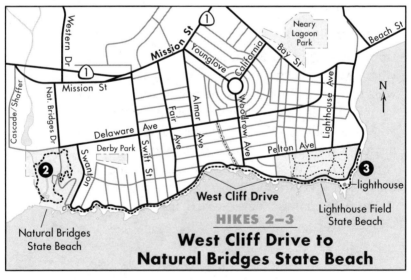

HIKES 2–3
West Cliff Drive to Natural Bridges State Beach

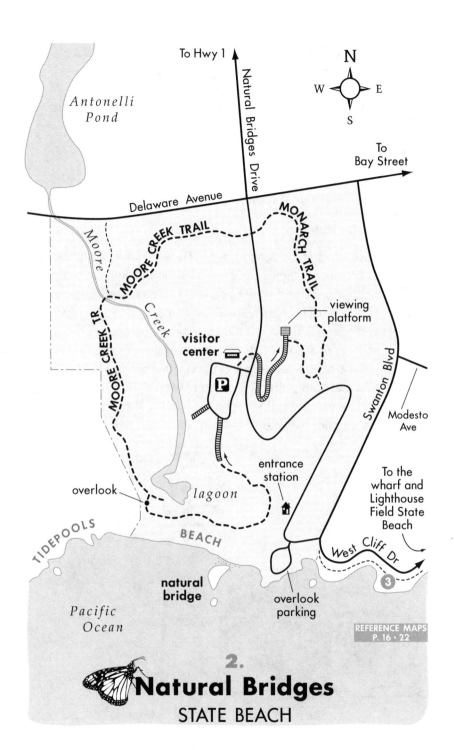

To Hwy 1

Natural Bridges Drive

N
W · E
S

To Bay Street

Antonelli Pond

Delaware Avenue

MOORE CREEK TRAIL

MONARCH TRAIL

Moore

Creek

MOORE CREEK TR

viewing platform

visitor center

P

Swanton Blvd

Modesto Ave

overlook

lagoon

entrance station

To the wharf and Lighthouse Field State Beach

TIDEPOOLS

BEACH

West Cliff Dr

3

natural bridge

Pacific Ocean

overlook parking

REFERENCE MAPS
P. 16 · 22

2.
Natural Bridges
STATE BEACH

3. Lighthouse Trail • Point Santa Cruz
LIGHTHOUSE FIELD STATE BEACH to
NATURAL BRIDGES STATE BEACH

Hiking distance: 4.5 miles round trip
Hiking time: 2.5 hours
Configuration: out-and-back
Elevation gain: level
Difficulty: easy
Exposure: forested pockets and exposed bluffs
Dogs: allowed
Maps: U.S.G.S. Santa Cruz

Lighthouse Field State Beach covers 40 acres atop Point Santa Cruz (also called Lighthouse Point) near downtown Santa Cruz. The point, with a stone lighthouse and surfing museum, defines the northern tip of Monterey Bay. A large, grassy open space with cypress trees lines the coastal terrace, interspersed with picnic areas and informal paths. The dog-friendly park acts as a buffer between the residential area and the oceanfront bluffs. Hugging the 40-foot eroding cliffs is undulating West Cliff Drive. A popular two-mile walking path, known as the Lighthouse Trail, hugs the cliffs parallel to West Cliff Drive. The path links Lighthouse Field State Beach with Natural Bridges State Beach (Hike 2). Along this stretch, the pounding surf has created caves,

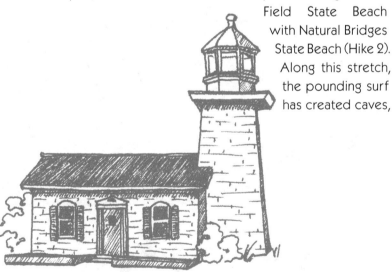

The lighthouse at Point Santa Cruz.

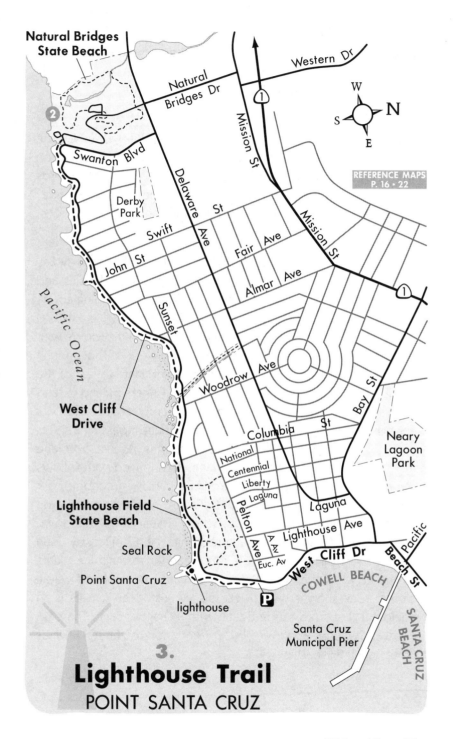

Natural Bridges State Beach

Western Dr

Natural Bridges Dr

Mission St

W N S E

REFERENCE MAPS
P. 16 • 22

Swanton Blvd

Delaware Ave

Derby Park

St

Mission St

Swift

Fair Ave

John St

Almar Ave

Pacific Ocean

Sunset

Woodrow Ave

Bay St

West Cliff Drive

Columbia St

Neary Lagoon Park

National

Centennial

Liberty

Laguna

Laguna

Lighthouse Field State Beach

Pelton Ave

Lighthouse Ave

A Av

Pacific

Seal Rock

Euc. Av

West Cliff Dr

Beach St

Point Santa Cruz

COWELL BEACH

lighthouse

P

Santa Cruz Municipal Pier

SANTA CRUZ BEACH

3.
Lighthouse Trail
POINT SANTA CRUZ

sculpted rock formations, natural bridges, indented cliffs, sheltered coves, and tidepools. The trail passes scenic overlooks with benches and a series of small pocket beaches with stairways accessing the shoreline.

To the trailhead

From the junction of Beach Street and West Cliff Drive by the wharf (Municipal Pier) in downtown Santa Cruz, head south on West Cliff Drive. Drive 0.4 miles on the oceanfront cliffs towards the lighthouse to the first parking lot on the left (ocean side). Parking pullouts are spaced along the road on both sides.

The hike

Take the paved blufftop path south, overlooking Monterey Bay from Point Santa Cruz at the lighthouse to Soquel Point and Pacific Grove. At 0.4 miles, steps lead down to a landing above a beach with large boulders. Across West Cliff Drive is a natural off-leash dog area. The state parkland has open meadows with native grasses, pockets of trees, and a network of meandering paths. At a half mile is the lighthouse at Point Santa Cruz. Off the point is Seal Rock and other outcroppings. Fingers of land extend seaward with natural arches and small, sandy coves. The park ends at 0.8 miles, but the coastal trail continues, passing a series of flat rock ledges and off-shore formations. At just over one mile, cross a seasonal stream drainage. An unpaved path follows the drainage 0.4 miles inland through a narrow greenbelt park, connecting West Cliff Drive with Delaware Avenue. Continue on the coastal path to Sunset Ave, where a stairway leads down to the beach by large rock outcroppings. At 1.7 miles, by John Street, short dirt paths on the left meander through ice plants to the edge of the cliffs. Below are fingers of land and water-carved rock shelves with tidepools. At just over 2 miles is an enclosed U-shaped sandy beach with a shallow cave. The path ends at Swanton Boulevard by the entrance to Natural Bridges State Beach (Hike 2). ■

4. Pogonip Park

Hiking distance: 3.5-mile loop
Hiking time: 2 hours
Configuration: loop connected with quarter-mile trail
Elevation gain: 300 feet
Difficulty: easy
Exposure: shaded forest and open grassland
Dogs: allowed
Maps: U.S.G.S. Santa Cruz and Felton · Pogonip Park map

**map
page 29**

Pogonip Park is a 640-acre expanse in the coastal hills at the north end of Santa Cruz. The park lies between Highway 9, the University of California, and Henry Cowell Redwoods State Park. The dog-friendly park has several diverse habitats that include shady glens with oaks; sycamore, willow, and madrone groves; second-growth stands of redwoods; riparian creekside vegetation along Pogonip Creek and Redwood Creek; and open grassland meadows. A nine-mile network of trails crosses Pogonip Park. This hike explores cool, shady forests and mountain meadows to great views of Monterey Bay and the city of Santa Cruz.

To the trailhead

From River Street (Highway 9) and Highway 1 in Santa Cruz, drive 0.4 miles north on River Street to Golf Club Drive on the left. Turn left and continue 0.1 mile. Park along the road, just before crossing under the train trestle.

The hike

Walk a quarter mile up the narrow, paved road past agricultural gardens to the park entrance. Stroll through rolling grassy meadows with coast live oaks and ocean views, staying on the road. Pass the Pogonip Creek Trail to the historic Pogonip Clubhouse from 1911. Curve left around the structure to the ranger cabins; the Prairie Trail will be on the left. Continue on the road as it narrows to a footpath, entering an oak canopy on the Brayshaw Trail. At the posted junction with the Fern Trail, bear right and walk 100 yards to a Y-fork.

Begin the loop to the right, staying on the Fern Trail. Cross a wooden footbridge over Redwood Creek in a redwood grove. Wind up the shady hillside, crossing through a sloping meadow. Steadily climb to the top in a shaded, lush forest. Cross the hilltop on a level grade along the north end of a meadow to a junction with the Rincon Trail, 0.8 miles from the ranger cabins. The Rincon Trail leads 0.4 miles to Highway 9 and connects to Henry Cowell Redwoods State Park (Hike 5). Bear left on the Spring Trail, and stroll through oaks and redwoods. Glimpses through the trees reveal Santa Cruz and the sea. Pass the Spring Box Trail on the right to the Ohlone Trail on the left. Bear left and descend through meadows and oaks, completing the 1.5-mile loop. Return by retracing your steps to the right. ▪

5. Henry Cowell Redwoods State Park
River Trail—Eagle Creek—Ridge Road Loop

Hiking distance: 4.6 miles
Hiking time: 2.5 hours
Configuration: out-and-back with loop
Elevation gain: 500 feet
Difficulty: easy to slightly moderate
Exposure: mostly shaded forest
Dogs: allowed
Maps: U.S.G.S. Felton · Henry Cowell Redwoods State Park map

**map
page 31**

Henry Cowell Redwoods State Park is tucked into the coastal mountains that run a few miles north of Santa Cruz. The dog-friendly park has a network of more than 15 miles of hiking, biking, and equestrian trails. The huge 4,000-acre parcel of land is divided into two disconnected units. This hike is located in the smaller southern unit, just south of Felton and adjacent to the university and Pogonip Park. The lower 1,800-acre park includes majestic old-growth redwoods up to 1,800 years old; oak, pine and sycamore forests; stream-fed canyons; open grassland meadows; dry chaparral-covered ridges; and the serpentine San Lorenzo River with riparian river gorges and sandy beaches. This loop hike explores all of these ecosystems. The route follows the San

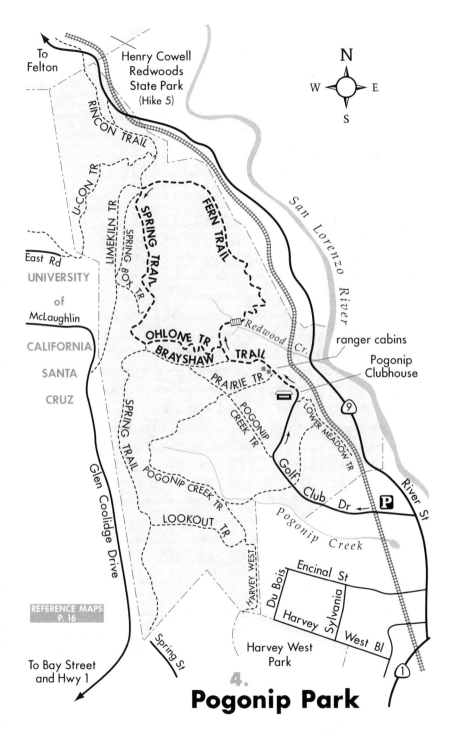

To Felton

Henry Cowell
Redwoods
State Park
(Hike 5)

N
W E
S

RINCON TRAIL

U-CON TR

LIMEKILN TR

SPRING BOX TR

SPRING TRAIL

FERN TRAIL

San Lorenzo River

East Rd
UNIVERSITY
of
McLaughlin
CALIFORNIA
SANTA
CRUZ

OHLONE TR
BRAYSHAW TRAIL
PRAIRIE TR

Redwood Cr.

ranger cabins

Pogonip
Clubhouse

9

SPRING TRAIL

POGONIP CREEK TR

POGONIP CREEK TR

LOOKOUT TR

Glen Coolidge Drive

LOWER MEADOW TR

Golf Club Dr

P

River St

Pogonip Creek

HARVEY WEST

REFERENCE MAPS
P. 16

Spring St

To Bay Street
and Hwy 1

Encinal St

Du Bois

Harvey

Sylvania

West Bl

Harvey West
Park

1

4.
Pogonip Park

Lorenzo River, strolls through moist redwood groves, and climbs to an observation deck at 800 feet, with views of the surrounding mountains and Monterey Bay.

To the trailhead

From River Street (Highway 9) and Highway 1 in Santa Cruz, drive 6 miles north on Highway 9 to the posted state park entrance on the right. Turn right and continue 0.6 miles to the parking lot on the right by the nature store. A parking fee is required.

The hike

The River Trail can be accessed behind the nature store or just west of the visitor center. Take the paved Pipeline Road to the posted River Trail located between the two buildings. Follow the dirt path 20 yards to an elevated overlook of the San Lorenzo River. Bear left and head downstream. The forested Pipeline Road and the bluff-edge River Trail run close together and parallel. The road route allows bikes and dogs. Meander through a forest of maple and redwood groves a half mile to the train trestle, where the two paths merge. Cross under the trestle 100 yards and curve right on the River Trail. Descend to a trail fork. The River Trail crosses Eagle Creek on a bridge, the return route.

Begin the loop to the left on the Eagle Creek Trail. Curve through the shaded forest on the undulating path, and cross a wood bridge over Eagle Creek. Curve right and leave the creek. Climb to a posted junction with the Pine Trail just before reaching the campground. Go right through an oak, pine, and madrone forest, steadily gaining elevation to the 800-foot summit and observation deck atop a knoll at 2.6 miles. The platform has 360-degree vistas from the ocean to the inland mountains. Continue to the right on the Ridge Road, and descend to the west into the dense redwood forest. Cross the Pipeline Road to a T-junction with Rincon Road. Bear right and wind down the hillside. Veer left onto the River Trail to the south edge of Eagle Creek. Cross the bridge over the creek, completing the loop. Return to the left. ∎

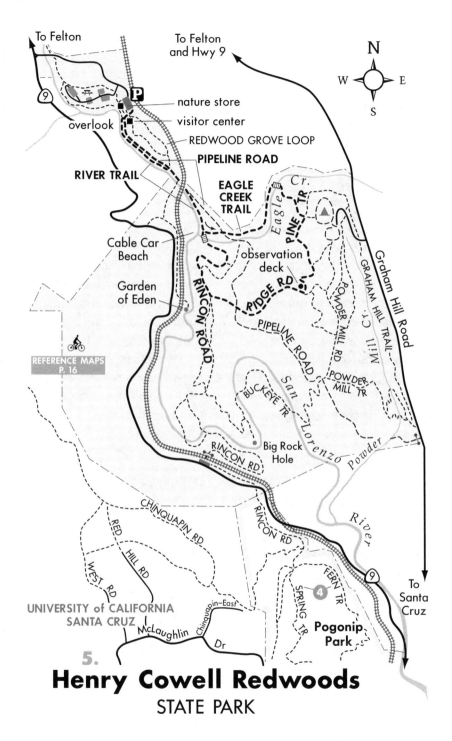

To Felton

To Felton and Hwy 9

N
W · E
S

P

nature store

visitor center

REDWOOD GROVE LOOP

PIPELINE ROAD

RIVER TRAIL

overlook

EAGLE CREEK TRAIL

Eagle Cr.

PINE TR.

Cable Car Beach

observation deck

Garden of Eden

RIDGE RD

GRAHAM HILL TRAIL

Graham Hill Road

POWDER MILL RD

REFERENCE MAPS P. 16

RINCON ROAD

PIPELINE ROAD

POWDER MILL TR.

Mill Cr.

San Lorenzo

BUCKEYE TR.

Powder

RINCON RD.

Big Rock Hole

River

CHINQUAPIN RD.

RINCON RD.

RED HILL RD

WEST RD.

UNIVERSITY of CALIFORNIA SANTA CRUZ

McLaughlin

Chinquapin–East

Dr

SPRING TR.

FERN TR.

4

9

To Santa Cruz

Pogonip Park

5.
Henry Cowell Redwoods
STATE PARK

6. Top of the World
DeLAVEAGA PARK

Hiking distance: 3-mile loop
Hiking time: 1.5 hours
Configuration: loop
Elevation gain: 350 feet
Difficulty: easy
Exposure: shady, forested hillside and exposed ridge
Dogs: allowed
Maps: U.S.G.S. Santa Cruz, Soquel, Felton and Laurel

DeLaveaga Park encompasses 565 acres on the northeast side of Santa Cruz. Jose Vicente DeLaveaga, a San Francisco businessman, owned the land in the late 1800s and willed it to the city in 1894 for recreational use. The dog-friendly park includes a golf course, disc golf course, athletic fields, picnic areas, and hiking/biking trails. Branciforte Creek, a tributary of the San Lorenzo River, flows through the west edge of the park. An unsigned trail system of old dirt roads and single-track footpaths weaves through the wooded hills. This hike begins at the creek and climbs through the shaded forest to the 456-foot La Corona Lookout, locally known as the Top of the World. From the summit are sweeping vistas of Santa Cruz and Monterey Bay.

To the trailhead

From the intersection of Market Street (just east of Ocean Street) and Water Street in Santa Cruz, drive 1.7 miles north on Market Street, crossing under Highway 1, to the posted park entrance on the right. (En route, Market Street becomes Branciforte Drive.) Turn right into DeLaveaga Park, and continue 0.15 miles to the parking lot by the soccer field.

ALTERNATIVE PARKING. A lower trailhead is located 1.1 miles from the Market Street and Water Street junction (0.6 miles before reaching the main park entrance). Park in the long dirt pullout on the right by the gated dirt road (Sand Pit Road) veering uphill.

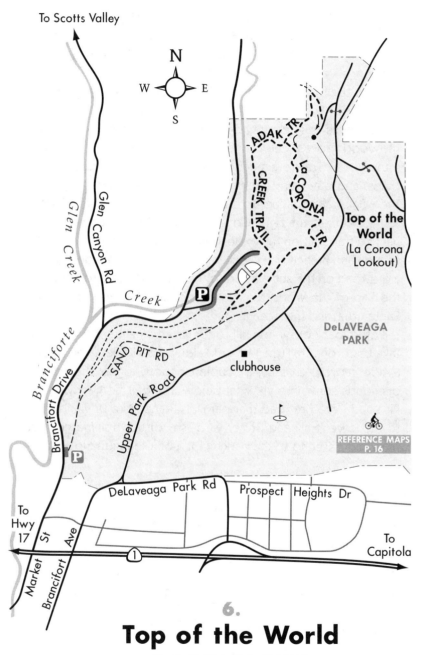

To Scotts Valley

N
W · E
S

Glen Creek

Glen Canyon Rd

Branciforte

ADAK TR

CREEK TRAIL

La CORONA TR

Creek

P

Top of the World
(La Corona Lookout)

DeLAVEAGA PARK

SAND PIT RD

Branciforte Drive

Upper Park Road

clubhouse

REFERENCE MAPS
P. 16

P

DeLaveaga Park Rd

Prospect Heights Dr

To Hwy 17

Market St

Branciforte Ave

1

To Capitola

6.
Top of the World
DeLAVEAGA PARK

The hike

Climb the steps on the southeast side of the park road by the restrooms to a T-junction. Begin the loop and bear left on the footpath, entering the forest. Traverse the hillside, gaining elevation, then descend to the far end of the grassy parkland and baseball field. Follow the Creek Trail to the right along the east side of Branciforte Creek. Climb the hillside and follow the watercourse upstream, weaving through the dense forest with redwood groves. Curve right and zigzag up the hill on the unsigned Adak Trail to a meadow surrounded with coast live oaks, pines, and bay laurel. At the top of the meadow is a junction. The Adak Trail continues to the left and La Corona Trail, the return route, veers to the right. Go left and follow the contours of the hill to a trail split on the exposed ridge overlooking the forested canyon and Branciforte Creek Valley. Bear right and loop back to a dirt road on the summit. Go to the right 60 yards to a bench at the Top of the World summit, overlooking the disc golf course, Santa Cruz, and the ocean.

Return back down the hill to the junction with La Corona Trail. Take La Corona Trail (the left fork) along the hillside. Loop through a side canyon, crossing a couple of footbridges. The baseball diamonds come into view far below. The trail merges with Sand Pit Road—the fire road that parallels Branciforte Drive 0.6 miles to the lower trailhead. Thirty yards shy of this trail merger, bear right and descend to the parking lot, completing the loop. ■

7. New Brighton State Beach

Hiking distance: 1 mile
Hiking time: 45 minutes
Configuration: out-and-back
Elevation gain: 75 feet
Difficulty: easy
Exposure: a mix of shaded forest and grassy bluffs
Dogs: allowed
Maps: U.S.G.S. Soquel · New Brighton State Beach map

map
page 36

New Brighton State Beach stretches for a half mile along the coastline in Capitola just east of Santa Cruz. The beach encompasses 68 acres and is spread out along a forested 75-foot coastal terrace that overlooks Soquel Cove. The west end of the beach, formerly known as China Beach, was named for a village of Chinese fisherman who lived there in the 1870s and 1880s. A campground atop the grassy bluffs is nestled among towering cypress, Monterey pines, and eucalyptus groves, a wintering site for migrating monarch butterflies. Trails weave through the shady glens and down the cliffs to the soft sand beach. The wide beach connects with Seacliff State Beach (Hike 8) in one mile and continues uninterrupted for 15 miles to the town of Moss Landing to the south.

To the trailhead

From Highway 1 in Capitola, exit on Park Avenue. Drive 0.1 mile south to Kennedy Drive and turn left. Continue 0.15 miles to the posted state beach entrance and turn right. Drive 0.3 miles, staying right, to the day use parking lot. An entrance fee is required.

The hike

From the far south end of the parking lot, descend on wood stairs from the China Cove trailhead to the beach. To the west (right) the beach ends in 200 yards where the cliffs jut out into the sea. Go left and follow the wide path above the sandy beach. At 0.2 miles (just past the restrooms), a set of stairs and a sloping walkway lead up the 100-foot cliffs to the forested campground. To the right, a path leads to the amphitheater. Continue straight ahead and cross the campground road. Take the Oak Trail and head north through the oak and pine forest. Pass the ranger station on the left, and descend into a lush forest to the railroad tracks. Walk over the tracks and head downhill, crossing a wooden footbridge over Tannery Gulch to the park entrance station. Return to the railroad tracks and continue 100 yards to wood steps on the right. Climb the steps to the park road, just west of the ranger station. Bear left to the Oak Trail by the ranger station. Retrace your steps to the right, returning to the beach.

To extend the hike, stroll along the beach for just over a mile to Seacliff State Beach and the pier (Hike 8). The remains of the Palo Alto ship extend from the pier's end (see next hike). ■

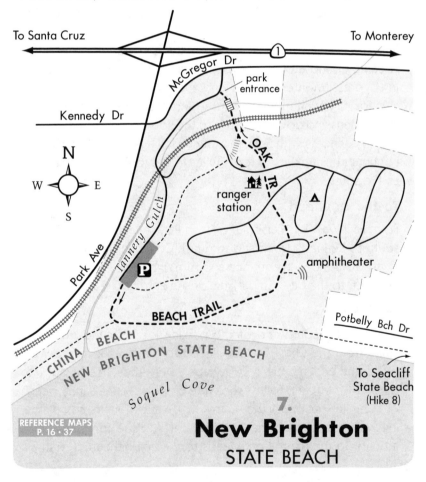

7.
New Brighton
STATE BEACH

8. Seacliff State Beach
from RIO DEL MAR BEACH

Hiking distance: 1.6 miles round trip
Hiking time: 1 hour
Configuration: out-and-back
Elevation gain: 100 feet
Difficulty: easy
Exposure: exposed beachfront
Dogs: allowed
Maps: U.S.G.S. Soquel · Seacliff State Beach map

**map
page 39**

Seacliff State Beach is a long oceanfront park in Aptos. The two-mile stretch of ocean frontage in Soquel Cove is backed by steep, 100-foot sandstone cliffs. For thousands of years it was the village site of the Ohlone Indians. In the heart of the state beach is Seacliff Pier, a 500-foot-long wooden pier. Attached to the end

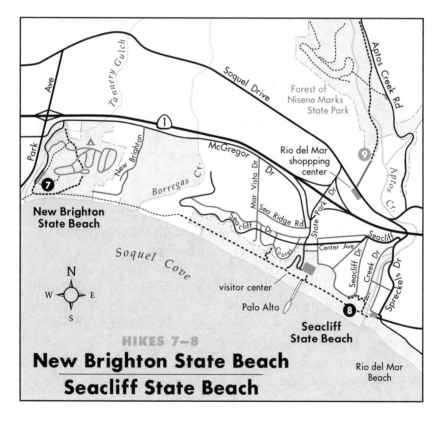

HIKES 7—8
New Brighton State Beach
Seacliff State Beach

of the pier are the remains of the Palo Alto, an old supply ship from World War 1. The historic ship was towed to Seacliff in 1930 and now extends seaward from the end of the pier. For a few years during the early 1930s, the 435-foot ship housed a swimming pool, dance floor, and casino. Since the late 1930s, the converted tanker acts as a popular fishing pier. At the southernmost section of Seacliff State Beach is Rio del Mar Beach, where Aptos Creek empties into the ocean. A beachfront esplanade begins at the beach, crosses Aptos Creek, and strolls along the beachfront walkway to the pier and beyond. Side paths climb the cliffs to coastal overlooks.

To the trailhead

From Highway 1 in Aptos, exit on Rio del Mar Boulevard. Drive 1.3 miles southwest to the beachfront parking lot at the end of the road.

The hike

Walk west on the paved esplanade toward the cliffs. Cross the bridge over Aptos Creek by the lagoon at the mouth of the creek. At the base of the cliffs is a short detour. Follow the west bank of the creek a short distance to the cul-de-sac on Creek Drive. Just before the cul-de-sac, a dirt path on the left climbs wood steps to the upper terrace on Seacliff Drive. One hundred yards to the left is a coastal overlook on the 100-foot cliffs. The views extend across Monterey Bay, from Soquel Point to Moss Landing and Pacific Grove.

Return to the paved esplanade, elevated above the sandy beach, and continue west between the 100-foot cliffs and the wide stretch of sand. Just before reaching the old wood pier, a long flight of wood steps climbs the eroded sandstone cliffs to the parking lot near the main entrance of Seacliff State Beach. Continue past the pier and the park visitor center. A dirt path climbs up the sedimentary cliffs under a canopy of cypress to a beach access on Beachgate Way. Continue northwest on the beachfront path to the end of the trail at a tree-lined rock wall.

To extend the hike, follow the beach strand north to New Brighton State Beach (Hike 7). ∎

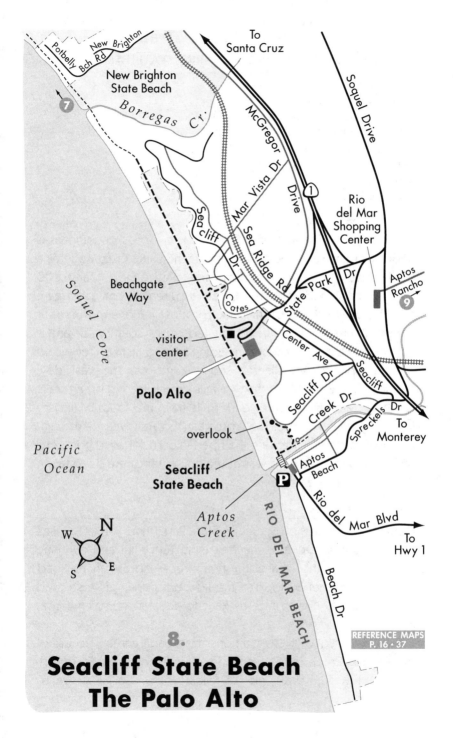

To Santa Cruz

New Brighton State Beach

Potbelly Bch Rd

New Brighton

Borregas Cr.

Soquel Drive

McGregor Drive

Mar Vista Dr

Sea cliff Dr

Sea Ridge Rd

Coates

Rio del Mar Shopping Center

Aptos Rancho

Beachgate Way

State Park Dr

Center Ave

visitor center

Soquel Cove

Palo Alto

Seacliff Dr

Seacliff

overlook

Creek Dr

Spreckels Dr

To Monterey

Pacific Ocean

Seacliff State Beach

Aptos Creek

Aptos Beach

P

RIO DEL MAR BEACH

Rio del Mar Blvd

To Hwy 1

Beach Dr

N
W E
S

REFERENCE MAPS
P. 16 · 37

8.
Seacliff State Beach
The Palo Alto

9. Aptos Rancho Trail
FOREST OF NISENE MARKS STATE PARK

Hiking distance: 4 miles round trip
Hiking time: 2 hours
Configuration: out-and-back with small loop
Elevation gain: 100 feet
Difficulty: easy
Exposure: shaded forest
Dogs: allowed
Maps: U.S.G.S. Soquel and Laurel
The Forest of Nisene Marks State Park map

The Forest of Nisene Marks State Park in Aptos encompasses 10,000 acres on the southern range of the Santa Cruz Mountains. The undeveloped park rises from sea level to more than 2,600 feet at Rosalia Ridge. Aptos Creek, a perennial coastal stream, runs through the heart of the park from Rosalia Ridge to the sea at Rio del Mar Beach. The park has rugged, rolling countryside and is covered with dense forests, including second-growth redwood forests, riparian woodlands, and oak groves. The vast dog-friendly refuge has more than 40 miles of hiking and biking trails. This hike follows the lower park trails from the south boundary to George's Picnic Area. The Aptos Rancho Trail weaves through the creek canyon, following the riparian corridor amid gorgeous redwoods. The preserve was at the epicenter of the devastating 1989 Loma Prieta earthquake.

To the trailhead

From Highway 1 in Aptos, exit on State Park Drive. Drive 0.3 miles north to Soquel Drive at the first light. Turn right and continue 0.1 mile to the light signal at the first street—Aptos Rancho Road. The trailhead is one block to the left, but parking is restricted to residents. Turn right into the Rancho del Mar shopping center and park.

ALTERNATIVE PARKING. Additional trailheads can be accessed from Aptos Creek Road, the main park entrance. From State Park Drive and Soquel Drive, go 0.4 miles east on Soquel Drive to

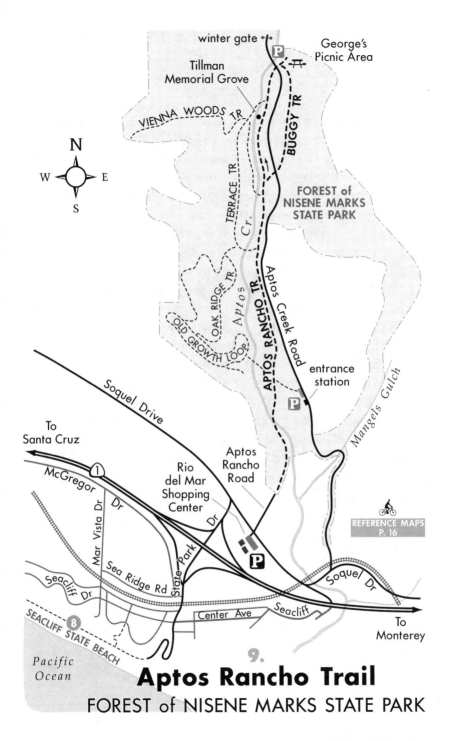

winter gate

George's
Picnic Area

Tillman
Memorial Grove

VIENNA WOODS TR

BUGGY TR

FOREST of
NISENE MARKS
STATE PARK

TERRACE TR

Aptos Cr.

APTOS RANCHO TR

Aptos Creek Road

OAK RIDGE TR

Aptos

OLD GROWTH LOOP

entrance
station

Mangels Gulch

N
W   E
S

Soquel Drive

To
Santa Cruz

McGregor

Mar Vista Dr

Dr

Rio
del Mar
Shopping
Center

Aptos
Rancho
Road

Aptos Rancho Road

Dr

Sea Ridge Rd

State Park

REFERENCE MAPS
P. 16

Seacliff Dr

Center Ave

Seacliff

Soquel Dr

To
Monterey

SEACLIFF STATE BEACH

8

Pacific
Ocean

9.
Aptos Rancho Trail
FOREST of NISENE MARKS STATE PARK

Aptos Creek Road on the left. Turn left and drive 0.8 miles to the park entrance station or 1.9 miles to George's Picnic Area. A parking fee is required at these trailheads.

The hike

Cross Soquel Drive at the signal. Walk 0.1 mile down Aptos Rancho Road to the posted trailhead at road's end. Drop into a dense, mixed forest of redwood, oak, maple, pine, fir, and willow. Wind through the lush riparian habitat on the west slope of Aptos Creek Canyon. At 0.4 miles, rock hop over Aptos Creek beneath a 100-foot vertical wall covered with moss and ferns. Follow the creek upstream, passing the entrance station on Aptos Creek Road and the Old Growth Loop at 0.6 miles. Continue north, parallel to Aptos Creek Road. Drop back into the canyon, and descend to a posted junction with the Terrace Trail by Aptos Creek at 1.1 miles. Stay on the Aptos Rancho Trail, following the creek. Merge briefly with the lower end of the Vienna Woods Trail. Climb a short distance to the Tillman Memorial Grove, a gorgeous redwood grove. Head up the east canyon slope overlooking the creek (passing the north junction with the Terrace Trail) to Aptos Creek Road at 2 miles. Across the road is George's Picnic Area. Pick up the Buggy Trail, and weave through the forest on the hillside parallel to the road. Traverse the hill a half mile, dropping down to the road. Cross the road and head downhill to the Aptos Rancho Trail. Retrace your steps to the left. ■

10. Manresa State Beach

Hiking distance: 1-mile double loop
Hiking time: 45 minutes
Configuration: figure-8 loop
Elevation gain: 100 feet
Difficulty: easy
Exposure: mostly exposed with forested pockets
Dogs: allowed
Maps: U.S.G.S. Watsonville West

map
page 44

Located just south of Aptos, Manresa State Beach is a long stretch of clean white sand backed by steep sandstone cliffs and bordered by blufftop homes. The state beach has two separate access points and feels like two separate parks. The main (northern) section is a narrow two-mile-long beach strand popular with surfers. This hike begins from the Manresa Uplands, the southern portion of the park, by the campground. The campground sits atop a 100-foot coastal terrace with grasslands, tree groves, and sweeping vistas of Monterey Bay. This hike forms a loop from the bluffs to the sandy beach. A steep wooden stairway atop the bluffs leads 170 steps down the cliffs to the beach.

To the trailhead

SEASCAPE. From Highway 1 in Seascape (south of Aptos), exit on San Andreas Road. Drive 3 miles south to Sand Dollar Drive and turn right. Continue a quarter mile to Manresa Beach Road and turn left. Drive 0.3 miles to the Uplands Campground entrance station. Just beyond the entrance, bear right to the beach parking area 200 yards ahead. An entrance fee is required.

HIGHWAY 1. From the Mar Monte Avenue exit off of Highway 1, turn left on Mar Monte Avenue, and drive 0.8 miles to San Andreas Road. Turn left and continue 1.5 miles to Sand Dollar Drive. Turn right and follow the directions above.

The hike

Head south through the picnic area on the posted trail. Follow the blufftop 100 yards to a stairway. The steep staircase descends 100 feet to the sandy beach, the return route. Begin the loop on the bluffs along the perimeter of the campground. Stroll through a dense eucalyptus grove, passing campground connector paths on the left and an amphitheater on the right. Curve right to a paved beach access road on the right. Cross the road and continue on the dirt path. Loop around the forested campground through oaks, pines, and cypress, returning to the paved road. Bear left toward the sea, and follow the road downhill through the draw to the ocean. The hike can be extended along the beach for miles in both directions. For this hike, go to the right, towards the north end of the uplands and the long set of wooden stairs. En route the views extend across Monterey Bay from Santa Cruz Point to the stacks at Moss Landing and Pacific Grove. Climb the 170-step stairway, returning to the blufftop. ■

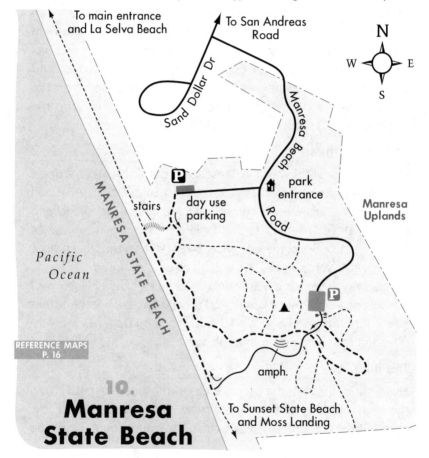

To main entrance
and La Selva Beach

To San Andreas
Road

N

W ←◆→ E

S

Sand Dollar Dr

Manresa Beach

park
entrance

P

stairs

day use
parking

Road

Manresa
Uplands

Pacific
Ocean

MANRESA STATE BEACH

P

▲

REFERENCE MAPS
P. 16

amph.

To Sunset State Beach
and Moss Landing

10.
**Manresa
State Beach**

11. Wetlands of Watsonville

Ohlone Trail • Upper Struve Slough Trail

Hiking distance: 5.4 miles round trip
Hiking time: 3 hours
Configuration: 3 out-and-back trails from a central loop
Elevation gain: near level
Difficulty: easy to slightly moderate
Exposure: exposed
Dogs: allowed
Maps: U.S.G.S. Watsonville West • Wetlands of Watsonville trail map

map page 47

This is not a backcountry hike, but rather a pathway walk through a scenic 800-acre open space adjacent to the neighborhoods of Watsonville. The Wetlands of Watsonville is one of the largest remaining wetlands on the central California coast. This vital, freshwater marshland features six interlinking sloughs which drain the Pajaro Valley watershed. The wetland is on the Pacific Flyway, a resting and nesting spot for migrating birds. It is also a breeding and year-round habitat for over 200 species of waterfowl, raptors, and songbirds. For thousands of years it was home to the Ohlone Indians.

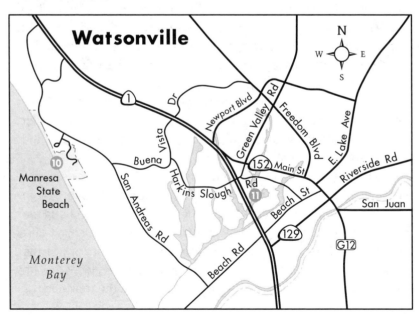

More than five miles of trails with 25 trail entrances line the wetlands throughout town. This hidden gem is popular with locals as a walking, jogging, birding, and biking path. The hike loops around Struve Slough and skirts the edge of Upper Struve Slough.

To the trailhead

From Highway 1 in Watsonville, take the Green Valley Road/Exit 426. Drive 50 yards east to Harkens Slough Road. Turn right and go one block to Westridge Drive. Turn right and continue a quarter mile to the roundabout at the end of the road. Turn right into the West Marine parking lot, and drive 0.2 miles to the far south corner of the lot by the signed trailhead.

The hike

Pass the trailhead map and make a U-bend on the gravel path. Follow the west edge of Struve Slough while overlooking the wetland. At Harkins Slough Road, pass under the road. Continue north along a grove of oak trees to a T-junction. The left fork leads 90 yards to a trailhead access in the Crossroads Square shopping center off of Main Street. Bear right and weave along the edge of the slough to a fork below Main Street. Go left and up to Main Street. Cross at the signal. After crossing, walk 30 yards to the right on the sidewalk, and pick up the Upper Struve Slough Trail on the left. Descend to the greenbelt. Cross a bridge over a water channel to a trail split. The right fork leads 150 yards to a neighborhood access on Montebello Drive, just west of Clifford Avenue. Continue along the east side of the upper slough under a row of willows. Make a right bend up to Clifford Avenue at the north end of the trail.

Retrace your steps back to Main Street. Cross the street and pick up the trail, curving along the east side of Struve Slough. Head south, crossing Harkins Slough Road, and continue along the east border of Struve Slough. Pass a trail access from Heron Court off of Kingfisher Drive. Curve left, following an east fork of the slough. The trail ends at Ohlone Parkway. Return to Harkins Slough Road and cross the bridge. Go left, returning to the trailhead. ∎

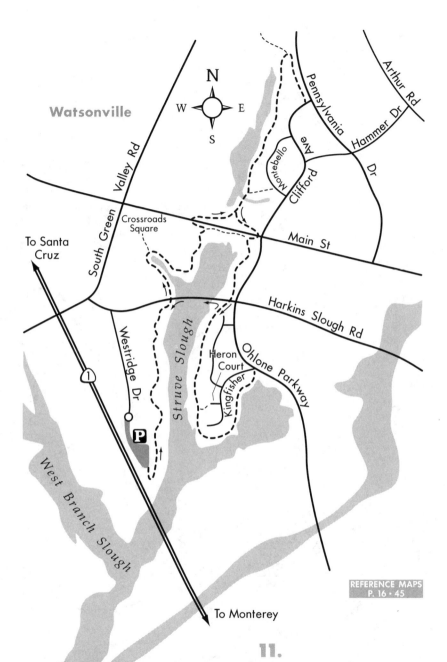

11.
Wetlands of Watsonville
Ohlone Trail • Upper Struve Slough Trail

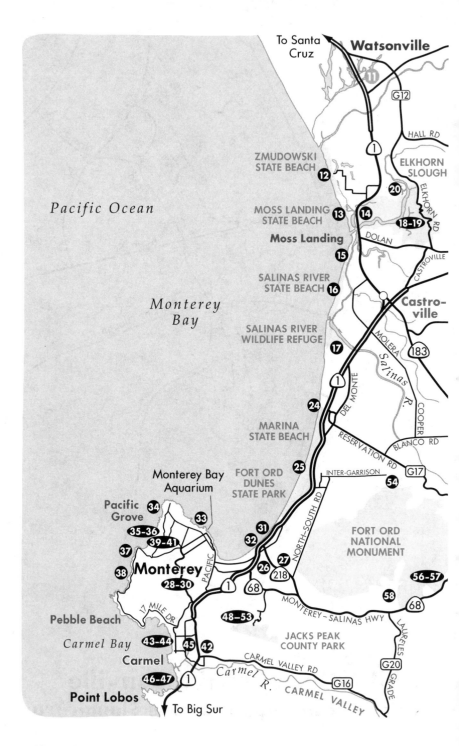

To Santa Cruz

Watsonville

G12

HALL RD

1

ELKHORN SLOUGH

ZMUDOWSKI STATE BEACH **12**

20

ELKHORN RD

MOSS LANDING STATE BEACH **13** **14**

18–19

DOLAN

Moss Landing

15

CASTROVILLE

SALINAS RIVER STATE BEACH **16**

Castro-ville

SALINAS RIVER WILDLIFE REFUGE **17**

MOLERA

Salinas R.

183

COOPER RD

Monterey Bay

Pacific Ocean

1

DEL MONTE

24

RESERVATION RD

BLANCO RD

MARINA STATE BEACH

25

INTER-GARRISON

G17

54

Monterey Bay Aquarium

FORT ORD DUNES STATE PARK

NORTH-SOUTH RD

FORT ORD NATIONAL MONUMENT

Pacific Grove **34**

33

35–36

39–41

31

32

56–57

37

Monterey

38

26 **27**

218

58

68

28–30

PACIFIC

MONTEREY – SALINAS HWY

Pebble Beach

17 MILE DR

1

68

48–53

JACKS PEAK COUNTY PARK

LAURELES GRADE

Carmel Bay

43–44

45 **42**

CARMEL VALLEY RD

G20

Carmel

46–47

1

Carmel R.

CARMEL VALLEY

G16

Point Lobos

To Big Sur

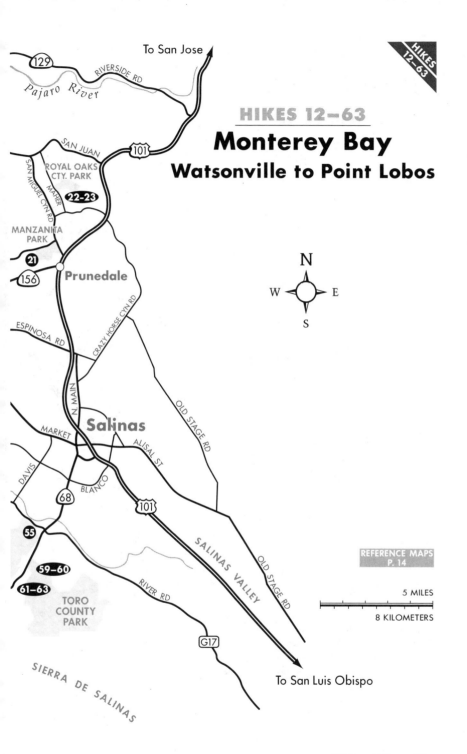

To San Jose

129

RIVERSIDE RD

Pajaro River

SAN JUAN

101

ROYAL OAKS
CTY. PARK

SAN MIGUEL CYN RD

MATHER

22-23

HIKES 12-63
Monterey Bay
Watsonville to Point Lobos

MANZANITA
PARK

21

156

Prunedale

N

W ◇ E

S

ESPINOSA RD

CRAZY HORSE CYN RD

N MAIN

OLD STAGE RD

MARKET

Salinas

ALISAL ST

DAVIS

BLANCO

68

101

55

59-60

61-63

TORO
COUNTY
PARK

RIVER RD

SALINAS VALLEY

OLD STAGE RD

REFERENCE MAPS
P. 14

5 MILES

8 KILOMETERS

G17

SIERRA DE SALINAS

To San Luis Obispo

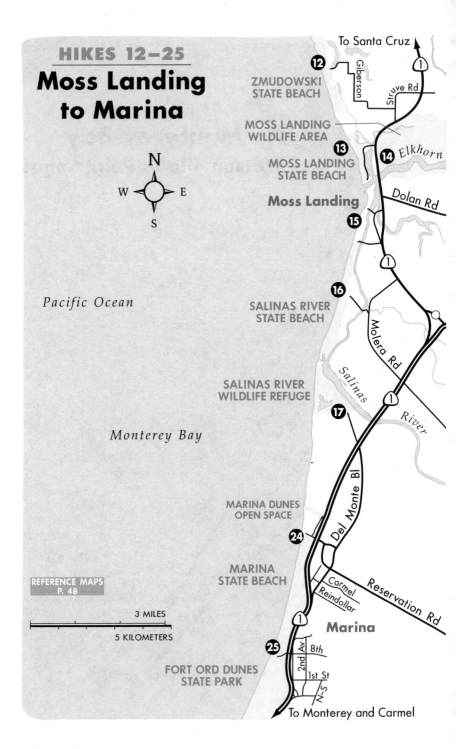

HIKES 12–25
Moss Landing to Marina

To Santa Cruz

⑫

Giberson

Struve Rd

ZMUDOWSKI
STATE BEACH

MOSS LANDING
WILDLIFE AREA ⑬

⑭ Elkhorn

MOSS LANDING
STATE BEACH

Moss Landing

Dolan Rd

⑮

1

Pacific Ocean

⑯

SALINAS RIVER
STATE BEACH

Molera Rd

Salinas

SALINAS RIVER
WILDLIFE REFUGE

River

⑰

1

Monterey Bay

Del Monte Bl

MARINA DUNES
OPEN SPACE

⑳

**REFERENCE MAPS
P. 48**

MARINA
STATE BEACH

Carmel
Reindollar

Reservation Rd

3 MILES

1

Marina

5 KILOMETERS

㉕

2nd Av

8th

1st St

N-S

FORT ORD DUNES
STATE PARK

To Monterey and Carmel

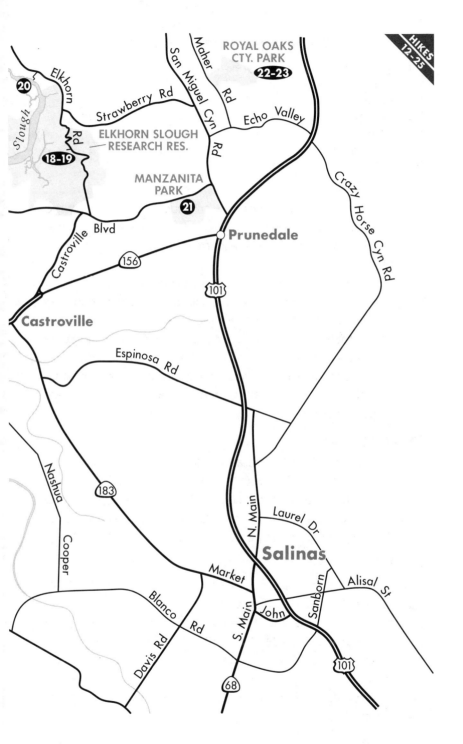

ROYAL OAKS
CTY. PARK
22-23

Elkhorn

20

Slough

Strawberry Rd

San Miguel Cyn Rd

Maher Rd

Echo Valley

Elkhorn Rd

ELKHORN SLOUGH
RESEARCH RES.

18-19

Crazy Horse Cyn Rd

MANZANITA
PARK
21

Castroville Blvd

156

Prunedale

101

Castroville

Espinosa Rd

Nashua

Cooper

183

N. Main

Laurel Dr

Salinas

Market

Blanco Rd

Davis Rd

S. Main

John

Sanborn

Alisal St

101

68

12. Zmudowski State Beach

Hiking distance: 3.2 miles round trip
Hiking time: 1.5 hours
Configuration: out-and-back
Elevation gain: level
Difficulty: easy
Exposure: open coast
Dogs: not allowed
Maps: U.S.G.S. Moss Landing

Zmudowski State Beach (pronounced *mud-OW-ski*) is a wide, isolated beach backed by sand dunes and expansive agricultural fields. It is a popular area for fishermen, equestrians, and bird watchers.

The state beach sits at the northern tip of Monterey County, stretching across 177 acres. The land was donated to the state in 1950 by Watsonville schoolteacher Mary Zmudowski. The Pajaro River forms the boundary between Monterey County and Santa Cruz County, draining into Monterey Bay at Zmudowski State Beach. At the mouth of the river, the estuary has been set aside as a natural preserve. To the south, the state beach ends near Moss Landing State Beach (Hike 13).

To the trailhead

Drive 17 miles north of Monterey on Highway 1 to Moss Landing. Drive 1.3 miles north of the Elkhorn Slough Bridge to Struve Road and turn left. Continue a quarter mile to Giberson Road and turn left. Wind through the agricultural fields and past McClusky Slough for 2 miles to the state beach parking area.

The hike

Take the signed path adjacent to the information board. Walk up and over the dune, dropping onto the hard-packed sand at the oceanfront. Follow the shoreline north (right), parallel to the vegetation-covered dunes. At a half mile, as the dunes flatten out, views open up to the vast agricultural fields with scattered Monterey cypress. At just under one mile, the beach ends at the mouth of the Pajaro River at the county line. The homes across the river are in Santa Cruz County.

Return south to the parking area access. Continue 0.7 miles to the Zmudowski State Beach boundary. The desolate beach continues an additional 1.3 miles to the channel at Elkhorn Slough in Moss Landing State Beach (Hike 13). ■

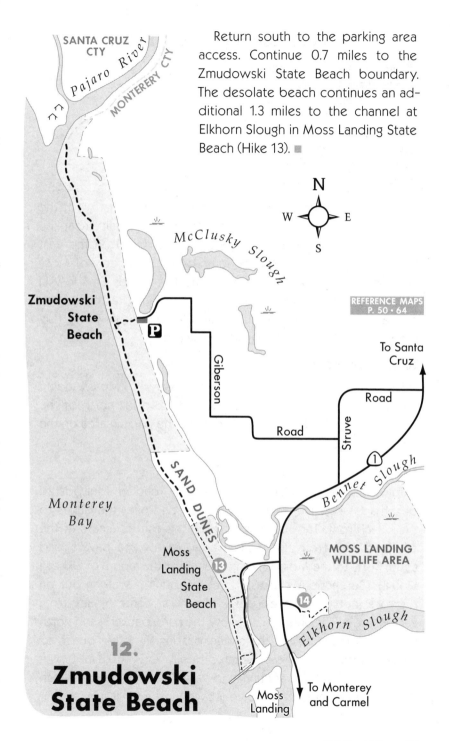

12.
Zmudowski
State Beach

13. Moss Landing State Beach

Hiking distance: 2.6 miles round trip
Hiking time: 1.5 hours
Configuration: out-and-back
Elevation gain: level
Difficulty: easy
Exposure: open coast
Dogs: not allowed
Maps: U.S.G.S. Moss Landing

Moss Landing State Beach (also known as Jetty Beach) is at the north end of Moss Landing, a small fishing community near the middle of Monterey Bay. The beach is bordered on the east by Bennett Slough and on the south by the rock jetty of Moss Landing Harbor. The beach extends north towards Zmudowski State Beach (Hike 12) and is backed by dunes restored with native vegetation. It is a popular beach for surfing, kayaking, fishing, clamming, bird watching, and horse riding.

To the trailhead

Drive 17 miles north of Monterey on Highway 1 to Moss Landing. Turn left (west) on Jetty Road, located 0.6 miles north of the Elkhorn Slough Bridge. Drive 0.6 miles to the parking area on the left.

The hike

Within the short half-mile span along Jetty Road are four posted beach accesses. The accesses cross up and over the dunes to the beachfront. This hike begins from the fourth access at the southern end. From the parking area, follow the paved road south (left) to the Moss Landing Channel at the mouth of Elkhorn Slough. (Be cautious and use careful footing if walking out on the rock jectty.) The views extend across Monterey Bay from Pacific Grove to Santa Cruz. Follow the hard-packed sand north between the dunes and the ocean, passing the other beach accesses. Moss Landing State Beach officially ends at 0.8 miles, but the sandy beachfront continues toward Zmudowski State Beach (Hike 12) at 1.3 miles. Choose your own turn-around spot. ■

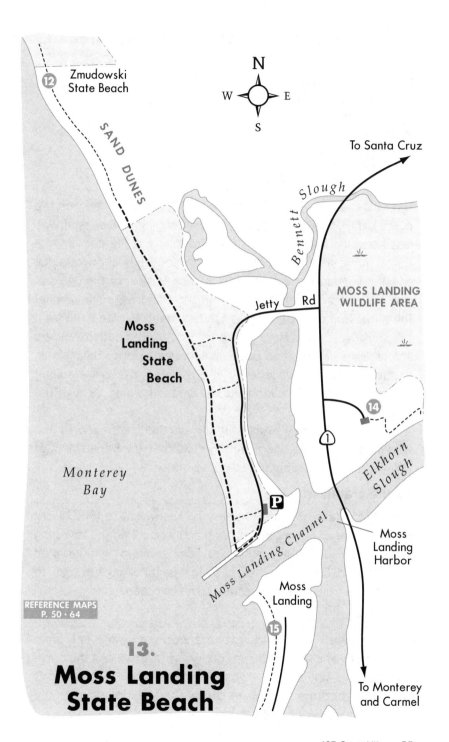

Zmudowski
State Beach

SAND DUNES

N
W E
S

To Santa Cruz

Bennett Slough

Jetty Rd

MOSS LANDING
WILDLIFE AREA

Moss
Landing
State
Beach

Monterey
Bay

1

P

Elkhorn Slough

Moss Landing Channel

Moss
Landing
Harbor

REFERENCE MAPS
P. 50 · 64

Moss
Landing

13.
Moss Landing
State Beach

To Monterey
and Carmel

14. Moss Landing State Wildlife Area

Hiking distance: 0.8 miles round trip
Hiking time: 30 minutes
Configuration: out-and-back
Elevation gain: level
Difficulty: very easy
Exposure: open wetland
Dogs: not allowed
Maps: U.S.G.S. Moss Landing

The Moss Landing Wildlife Area is an 800-acre wetland on the north bank of Elkhorn Slough at Moss Landing. The coastal wetlands and marshes provide protection for wildlife and an area for scientific study. It is along the north-south migration route for coastal birds and a nesting area for snowy plovers. During April and May, harbor seals give birth in the Elkhorn Slough channel. This short trail enters the Moss Landing State Wildlife Area from the southwest corner along Elkhorn Slough. The path meanders across dikes (levees) and past salt harvesting ponds dating back to the 1800s. The ponds were also used for oyster harvesting. Notice the tidal fluctuations in the creeks flowing through the mud flats.

The extensive trail system at the northern entrance of the wildlife area has been permanently closed by the Department of Fish, Wildlife and Game due to public abuse.

To the trailhead

Drive 17.5 miles north of Monterey on Highway 1 to the Elkhorn Slough Bridge at Moss Landing, located just beyond the towering smokestacks. Continue across the bridge and turn right (east) on the dirt road. Drive past the old buildings, following the signs to the wildlife trail and parking area 0.2 miles ahead.

The hike

Walk to the left (east) and cross the wooden bridge. Bear right to the edge of Elkhorn Slough. Follow the levees along the north bank of the slough to an observation platform. The levee is closed beyond the lookout to protect the nesting area for the endangered snowy plover. ■

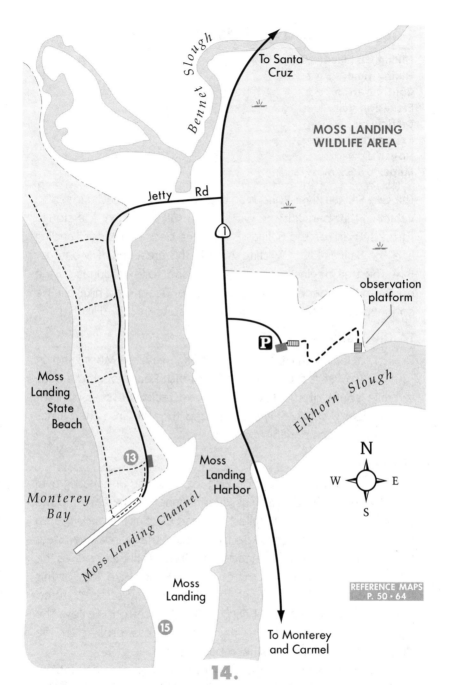

Bennet Slough

To Santa
Cruz

MOSS LANDING
WILDLIFE AREA

Jetty Rd

1

observation
platform

P

Elkhorn Slough

Moss
Landing
State
Beach

13

Moss
Landing
Harbor

N

W ⬥ E

S

*Monterey
Bay*

Moss Landing Channel

Moss
Landing

15

REFERENCE MAPS
P. 50 · 64

To Monterey
and Carmel

14.
Moss Landing Wildlife Area

15. Old Salinas River Road

Hiking distance: 1.5-mile loop
Hiking time: 45 minutes
Configuration: loop
Elevation gain: level
Difficulty: easy
Exposure: open coast
Dogs: allowed
Maps: U.S.G.S. Moss Landing

The Old Salinas River Road is an unpaved walking road (closed to vehicles) that parallels the wide, slow-rolling slough. The slough, formerly part of the Salinas River, runs between Moss Landing and the Salinas River Wildlife Area in the crescent of Monterey Bay. The trail begins in Moss Landing and follows dunes to the northern boundary of Salinas River State Beach. The hike can be continued along the coast through the state beach—Hike 16.

To the trailhead

Drive 17 miles north of Monterey on Highway 1 to Moss Landing. Turn left (towards the coast) on Sandholdt Road, located a quarter mile south of the towering smokestacks. Cross Sandholdt Bridge over the Old Salinas River, and turn left into the Salinas River State Beach parking lot.

The hike

From the south end of the parking lot, take the unpaved gravel road between the Old Salinas River channel on the east and the dunes on the west. At 0.7 miles, the road exits at the parking area at the west end of Potrero Road, located at the Salinas River State Beach boundary. Straight ahead is the Dunes Trail that crosses the state beach to the access off of Molera Road (Hike 16). For this hike, take the trail to the right, crossing over the scrub-covered dunes to the hard-packed sand at the beachfront. Follow the shoreline north, returning to the beach access. Cross over the dunes and back to the trailhead parking lot.

To extend the hike northward, continue along the oceanfront for 0.3 miles to the southern end of the Moss Landing Channel at the mouth of Elkhorn Slough. ■

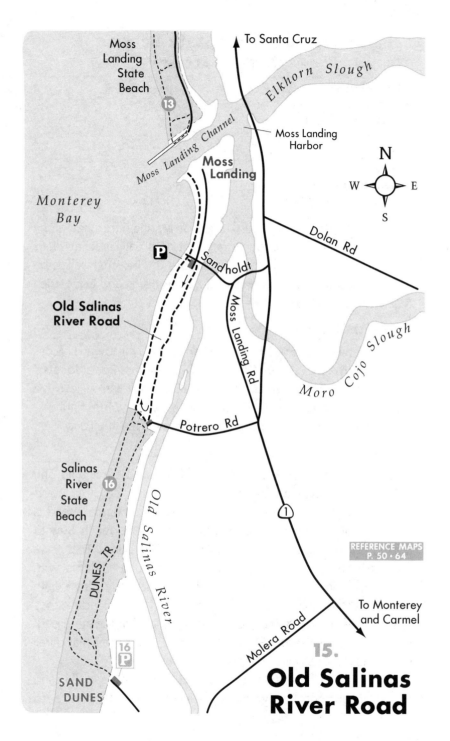

To Santa Cruz

Elkhorn Slough

Moss
Landing
State
Beach

13

Moss Landing Channel

Moss Landing Harbor

**Moss
Landing**

N
W — E
S

Monterey
Bay

Dolan Rd

P

Sand'holdt

Moss Landing Rd

Moro Cojo Slough

**Old Salinas
River Road**

Potrero Rd

Salinas
River
State
Beach

16

Old Salinas River

1

DUNES TR.

REFERENCE MAPS
P. 50 · 64

16
P

To Monterey
and Carmel

SAND
DUNES

Molera Road

**15.
Old Salinas
River Road**

16. Salinas River State Beach
SOUTHERN ACCESS

Hiking distance: 2.2-mile loop
Hiking time: 1.5 hours
Configuration: loop
Elevation gain: near level
Difficulty: easy
Exposure: open coast
Dogs: not allowed
Maps: U.S.G.S. Moss Landing

Salinas River State Beach, just north of Marina, stretches along the coast between the ocean and the Old Salinas River channel. Driftwood is often scattered across the beach, backed by fragile, vegetation-covered sand dunes. A hiking and equestrian trail leads through the rolling dunes.

To the trailhead

Drive 15.5 miles north of Monterey on Highway 1 towards Moss Landing. Turn left (towards the coast) on Molera Road, located 0.9 miles past the turnoff to Highway 183 South/Castroville. Drive 0.8 miles on Molera Road to Monterey Dunes Way. Turn right and continue 0.5 miles to the parking lot at the end of the road.

The hike

Take the signed boardwalk trail 30 yards west to a trail split. The left fork leads over the dune to the beachfront. Begin the loop to the right, leaving the boardwalk. A short distance ahead is another trail split. Again, the left fork leads to the beach. Stay to the right on the Dunes Trail and cross the rolling dunes. The views extend inland over the wetlands and agricultural fields with occasional glimpses of the ocean and the bay. The sandy path meanders through the dunes for a mile, then gradually descends to the Potrero Road parking lot at the north end of the state park. Straight ahead is the Old Salinas River Road, a dirt road that parallels the Old Salinas River to Moss Landing (Hike 15).

Bear left and cross over the dunes to the hard-packed sand at the oceanfront. Follow the shoreline to the left, parallel to the dunes that were just crossed. Watch for the access trail that crosses the dunes to the parking lot. If you reach the Monterey Dunes Colony, you have passed the beach access trail by 100 yards. ■

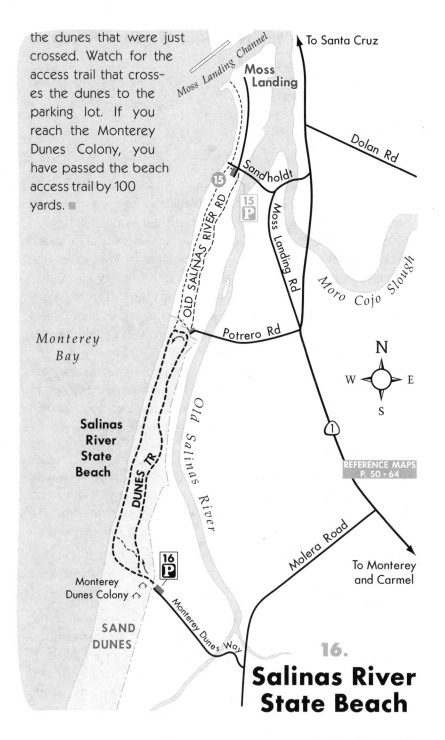

To Santa Cruz

Moss Landing Channel

Moss Landing

Dolan Rd

Sandholdt

15

15 P

Moss Landing Rd

Moro Cojo Slough

OLD SALINAS RIVER RD

Potrero Rd

Monterey Bay

N

W E

S

Old Salinas River

REFERENCE MAPS
P. 50 · 64

1

Salinas River State Beach

DUNES TR

Molera Road

16 P

To Monterey and Carmel

Monterey Dunes Colony ⌃

Monterey Dunes Way

SAND DUNES

16.

Salinas River State Beach

17. Salinas River National Wildlife Refuge

Hiking distance: 4 miles round trip
Hiking time: 2 hour
Configuration: out-and-back
Elevation gain: level
Difficulty: easy
Exposure: open coast
Dogs: not allowed
Maps: U.S.G.S. Marina and Moss Landing

The 518-acre Salinas River National Wildlife Refuge is a protected sanctuary for nesting and migratory birds that was established in 1973. The wildlife refuge is adjacent to Salinas River State Beach and encompasses the estuary where the freshwater of the Salinas River mixes with the salt water of Monterey Bay. During the spring and fall, thousands of migrating birds traveling along the Pacific Flyway seek shelter and food at the estuary. Within the refuge are coastal dunes, beaches, grasslands, salt marshes, saline ponds, and riparian habitats.

This hike, within the boundaries of the preserve, crosses grass-land meadows and undisturbed, vegetation-covered dunes to the isolated, sandy oceanfront. From the trailhead, another path leads a short distance to the banks of the wide Salinas River.

To the trailhead

Drive 13 miles north of Monterey on Highway 1 to the Del Monte Boulevard exit, located between the Reservation Road and Nashua–Molera Road exits. Turn left and drive straight ahead 0.6 miles to the end of the dirt road at the signed trailhead and park-ing area.

The hike

Walk past the metal gate to a trail junction. The right fork is a short side trip on a two-track path to the banks of the Salinas River. The Beach Trail to the left heads west across the flat grassy meadows to the edge of South Marsh, a lagoon and estuary. Bear left towards the coastal dunes. Cross the north edge of the scrub-covered dunes along the south side of the lagoon, reaching the sandy beach at 0.8 miles. At the oceanfront, follow the sandy shoreline

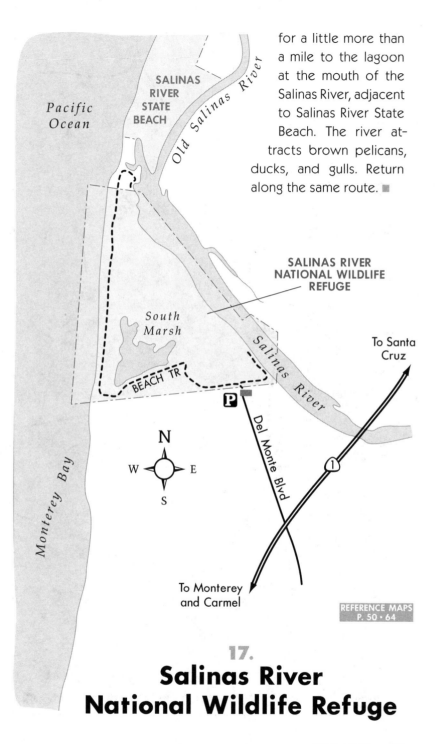

for a little more than a mile to the lagoon at the mouth of the Salinas River, adjacent to Salinas River State Beach. The river attracts brown pelicans, ducks, and gulls. Return along the same route. ∎

SALINAS
RIVER
STATE
BEACH

*Pacific
Ocean*

Old Salinas River

SALINAS RIVER
NATIONAL WILDLIFE
REFUGE

*South
Marsh*

Salinas River

To Santa
Cruz

BEACH TR

P

Del Monte Blvd

①

N

W ⊕ E

S

Monterey Bay

To Monterey
and Carmel

REFERENCE MAPS
P. 50 • 64

17.
Salinas River
National Wildlife Refuge

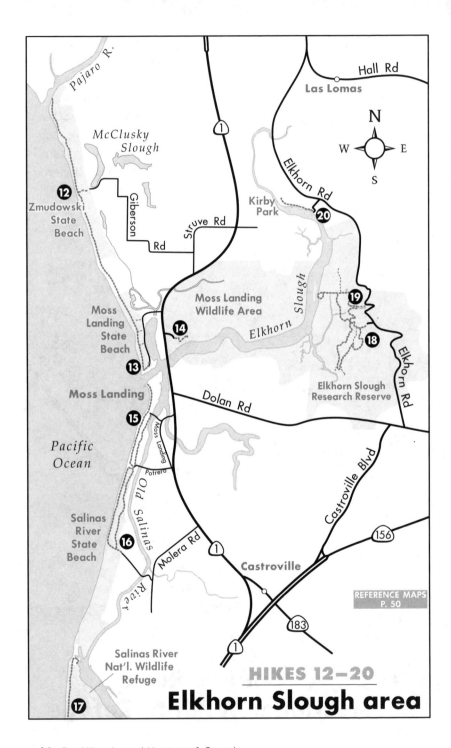

Pajaro R.

McClusky
Slough

Hall Rd

Las Lomas

N

W   E

S

Elkhorn Rd

(1)

12

Zmudowski
State
Beach

Giberson

Rd

Struve Rd

Kirby
Park

20

Moss
Landing
State
Beach

Moss Landing
Wildlife Area

Elkhorn Slough

19

14

Elkhorn

18

13

Elkhorn Rd

Moss Landing

Dolan Rd

Elkhorn Slough
Research Reserve

15

Moss Landing

*Pacific
Ocean*

Potrero

Castroville Blvd

*Salinas
River
State
Beach*

Old Salinas

16

(156)

Molera Rd

(1)

Castroville

River

REFERENCE MAPS
P. 50

17

Salinas River
Nat'l. Wildlife
Refuge

(183)

(1)

HIKES 12—20

Elkhorn Slough area

18. Five Fingers—Long Valley Loop

ELKHORN SLOUGH
NATIONAL ESTUARINE RESEARCH RESERVE

1700 Elkhorn Road · Watsonville
Open Wednesday—Sunday · 9 a.m.—5 p.m.

Hiking distance: 2.3-mile loop
Hiking time: 1.5 hours
Configuration: loop with two short spur trails
Elevation gain: near level
Difficulty: easy
Exposure: mostly exposed with shaded pockets
Dogs: not allowed
Maps: U.S.G.S. Prunedale · Elkhorn Slough Trail Map

map
page 66

Elkhorn Slough is a tidal inlet in Monterey Bay midway between Monterey and Santa Cruz. From Moss Landing, the main channel extends seven miles across 3,000 acres of marshland and tidal flats. The wetland supports more than 250 species of birds, 80 species of fish, and 400 species of invertebrates.

This hike begins in the heart of the slough at the 1,700-acre Elkhorn Slough National Estuarine Research Reserve. The trail leads to the five fingers of Parson's Slough (a smaller side channel), an overlook, and a wildlife blind. Five peninsulas jut out into the water, resembling five fingers for which they are named. The path winds through coastal marshland, meadows, native oak woodlands, and eucalyptus groves.

To the trailhead

Drive 17 miles north of Monterey on Highway 1 to Dolan Road (at the towering smokestacks). Turn right (east) and drive 3.6 miles to Elkhorn Road. Turn left and go 2 miles to the visitor center and parking lot on the left. An entrance fee is required.

The hike

Take the paved path past the visitor center 100 yards to the signed Long Valley Loop Trail. Bear left on the wide grassy path. Cross the meadow and descend through an oak grove to Parson's

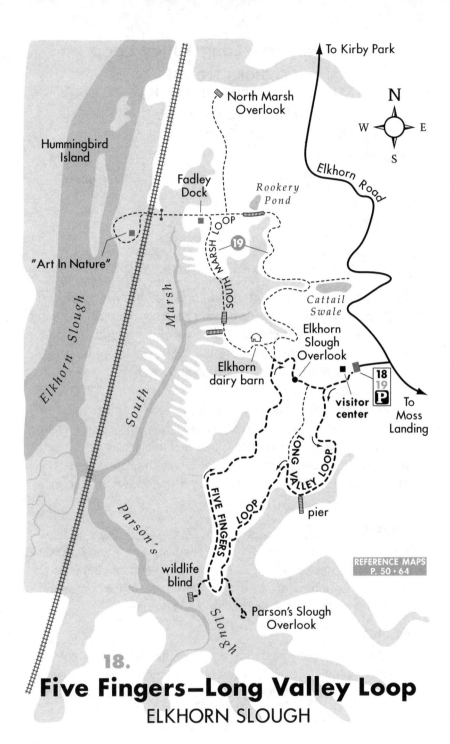

To Kirby Park

N
W   E
S

Hummingbird
Island

Elkhorn Slough

North Marsh
Overlook

Fadley
Dock

*Rookery
Pond*

Elkhorn Road

SOUTH MARSH LOOP

19

"Art In Nature"

Elkhorn Slough

South Marsh

*Cattail
Swale*

Elkhorn
Slough
Overlook

Elkhorn
dairy barn

18
19

P

visitor
center

To
Moss
Landing

LONG VALLEY LOOP

FIVE FINGERS LOOP

Parson's

pier

REFERENCE MAPS
P. 50 · 64

wildlife
blind

Parson's Slough
Overlook

Slough

18.
Five Fingers–Long Valley Loop
ELKHORN SLOUGH

Slough. Follow the north edge of the slough under an oak canopy. A boardwalk pier on the left extends out into the slough. Loop back to the north, and gently climb up the hillside to a posted junction. Bear left on the Five Fingers Loop Trail, and gradually descend to a junction. Detour to the left and walk 0.3 miles to the fenced Parson's Slough Overlook. Return to the junction and continue 100 yards to another trail fork. Take the left fork 130 yards to a long set of stairs. Descend to the wildlife blind on the edge of the slough. Return to the main trail again, and bear left through a eucalyptus grove to a 4-way junction with the South Marsh Loop Trail (Hike 19). Bear right and complete the loop back at the visitor center. ■

19. South Marsh Loop Trail
ELKHORN SLOUGH
NATIONAL ESTUARINE RESEARCH RESERVE
1700 Elkhorn Road · Watsonville
Open Wednesday—Sunday · 9 a.m.—5 p.m.

Hiking distance: 3.3 miles round trip
Hiking time: 1.5 hours
Configuration: out-and-back with large central loop
Elevation gain: near level
Difficulty: easy
Exposure: mostly exposed with shaded pockets
Dogs: not allowed
Maps: U.S.G.S. Prunedale · Elkhorn Slough Trail Map

map
page 69

Elkhorn Slough is an undisturbed 3,000-acre wetland. The marshlands and tidal flats are a resting, nesting, and feeding ground for tens of thousands of migratory birds. This hike begins at the Elkhorn Slough National Estuarine Research Reserve. The trail passes through native oak woodlands and grasslands to overlooks of the marsh and slough, old dairy barns, a heron rookery pond, and an "art in nature" project on the banks of Elkhorn Slough.

To the trailhead

Drive 17 miles north of Monterey on Highway 1 to Dolan Road (at the towering smokestacks). Turn right (east) and drive 3.6 miles to Elkhorn Road. Turn left and go 2 miles to the visitor center and parking lot on the left. An entrance fee is required.

The hike

From the visitor center, take the paved path west. Pass the Long Valley Loop Trail and the Five Fingers Loop Trail on the left (Hike 18) to the Elkhorn Slough Overlook. Descend on the wide, un-paved trail to a 4-way junction near the old abandoned Elkhorn dairy barn. Begin the loop on the left fork of the South Marsh Loop Trail, walking toward the barn. Skirt around the south side of the barn, and pass a wooden boardwalk extending out to the marsh on the left. Cross a footbridge over a channel of South Marsh, and follow the raised path across the wetland to a T-junction.

Take a detour on the left fork. Continue past Fadley Dock towards Hummingbird Island. Walk through a trail gate and cross the railroad tracks, reaching the main channel of Elkhorn Slough in a eucalyptus grove. Bear left along the slough past a row of eucalyptus trees to a small pond and arch at the "art in nature" project. Complete the small loop at the railroad tracks, and return to the South Marsh Loop Trail.

Pass a posted junction to the North Marsh Overlook on the left. Cross a wooden boardwalk along the rookery pond. Curve south through an oak grove while overlooking South Marsh, reaching Cattail Swale at an unsigned trail split. Stay to the right and complete the loop back at the barn. ■

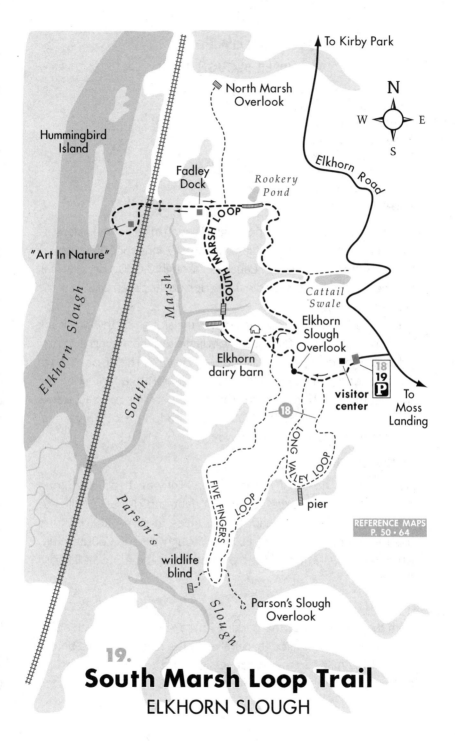

To Kirby Park

N
W   E
S

North Marsh
Overlook

Hummingbird
Island

Elkhorn Road

Fadley
Dock

Rookery
Pond

SOUTH MARSH LOOP

"Art In Nature"

Elkhorn Slough

South Marsh

Cattail
Swale

Elkhorn
Slough
Overlook

Elkhorn
dairy barn

visitor
center

18
19 P

18

To
Moss
Landing

LONG VALLEY LOOP

FIVE FINGERS LOOP

pier

REFERENCE MAPS
P. 50 • 64

Parson's Slough

wildlife
blind

Parson's Slough
Overlook

19.
South Marsh Loop Trail
ELKHORN SLOUGH

20. Kirby Park
UPPER SLOUGH TRAIL

Hiking distance: 1 mile round trip
Hiking time: 30 minutes
Configuration: out-and-back
Elevation gain: level
Difficulty: very easy
Exposure: exposed
Dogs: not allowed
Maps: U.S.G.S. Prunedale and Moss Landing

The main channel of Elkhorn Slough is seven miles long, snaking its way inland from Moss Landing. The tidally influenced waterway, fed by Carneros Creek, meanders through 3,000 acres of salt marshes and mudflats. Endless feeder channels empty into the main waterway.

Kirby Park is located midway down the slough on the east bank. The park is a popular fishing and birding site with a ramp that provides slough access for small boats and kayaks. The Upper Slough Trail is an easy, wheelchair-accessible interpretive trail along the east shore of Elkhorn Slough. The route parallels railroad tracks that were laid in 1872. The trail includes a long footbridge over the marshy banks of the waterway.

To the trailhead

Drive 17 miles north of Monterey on Highway 1 to Dolan Road (at the towering smokestacks). Turn right and drive 3.6 miles to Elkhorn Road. Turn left and go 4.6 miles to Kirby Road. (Kirby Road is 2.6 miles past the Elkhorn Slough Visitor Center.) Turn left and drive 0.2 miles to the parking lot at the edge of Elkhorn Slough.

The hike

From the north end of the parking lot, take the paved path along the edge of Elkhorn Slough, parallel to the railroad tracks on the right. At 0.2 miles are interpretive signs and benches for observing wildlife on the slough. Continue to a 170-foot-long wooden

footbridge. Cross the bridge over the edge of the
slough channel and marshland. After crossing, a
footpath continues a short distance to the end
of the trail at the railroad tracks. ■

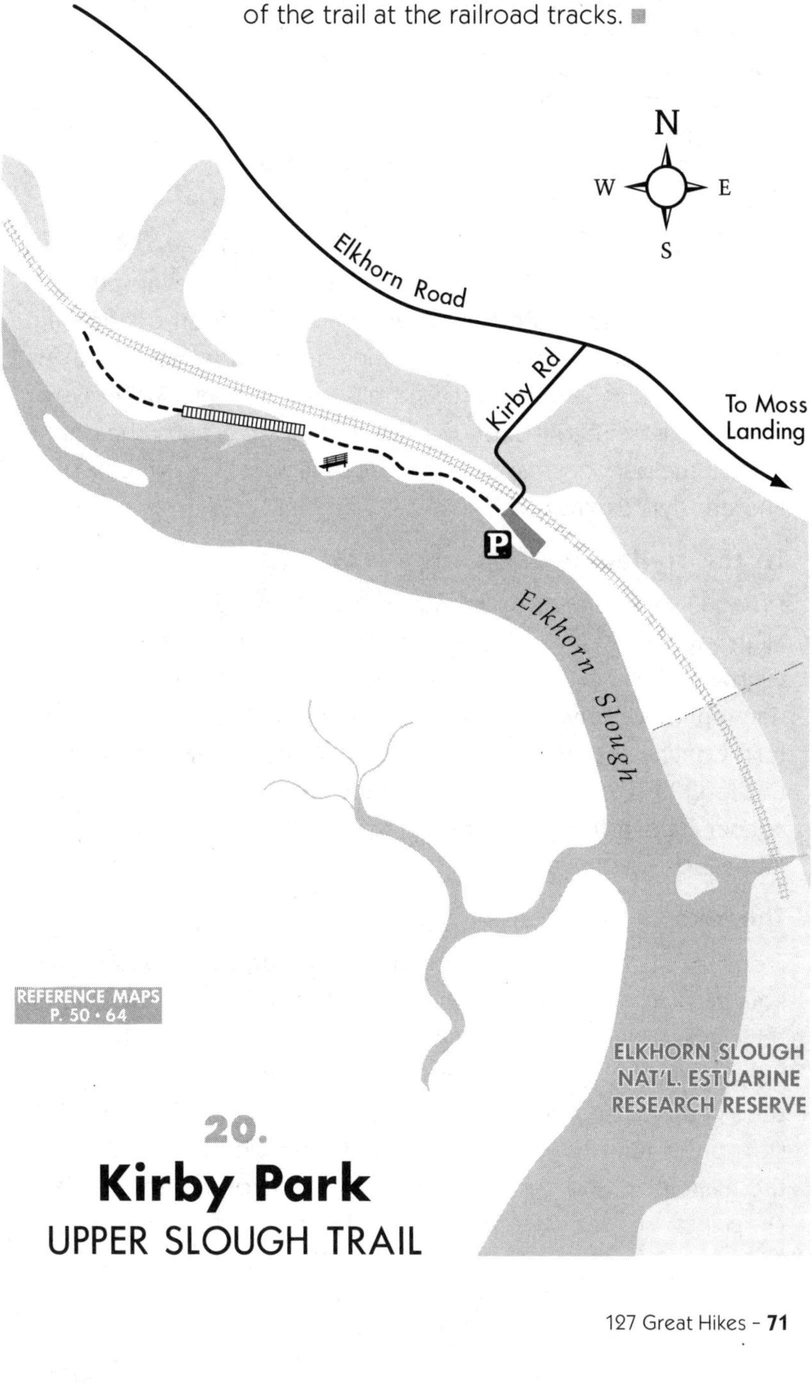

N
W ←◇→ E
S

Elkhorn Road

Kirby Rd

To Moss
Landing

P

Elkhorn Slough

REFERENCE MAPS
P. 50 · 64

ELKHORN SLOUGH
NAT'L. ESTUARINE
RESEARCH RESERVE

20.
Kirby Park
UPPER SLOUGH TRAIL

21. Manzanita Park
17100 Castroville Boulevard · Prunedale

Hiking distance: 3-mile loop
Hiking time: 1.5 hours
Configuration: loop
Elevation gain: 200 feet
Difficulty: easy
Exposure: mix of shaded forest and exposed hillside
Dogs: allowed
Maps: U.S.G.S. Prunedale · Manzanita Park map

Manzanita County Park is a 464-acre park with undeveloped rolling hills adjacent to Prunedale. An 11-acre portion of the park contains athletic fields. The remaining natural area has five miles of hiking, biking, and equestrian trails with spectacular views of North County. This hike follows the outer loop around the perimeter of the park on chaparral-covered hillsides through oak, pine, and eucalyptus groves.

To the trailhead

Drive 13 miles north of Monterey on Highway 1, and exit on Highway 156 East. Continue 6 miles east to Highway 101. Take Highway 101 north 0.7 miles, and turn left onto San Miguel Canyon Road. Drive 0.8 miles to Castroville Boulevard and turn left. Continue 0.7 miles to the signed Manzanita Park turnoff on the left. Turn left and drive 0.2 miles to the parking lot by the soccer field. If the gate is locked, park in the unpaved spaces on either side of the gate.

The hike

From the gate, walk 0.2 miles up the paved park road to the soccer field at the top of the hill on the right. Take the trail to the right along the north edge of the soccer field to a trail fork. Stay to the right on the outer loop, and gradually descend to the northwest corner by two unsigned paths on the right. The side paths lead to locked gates at the park boundary. Stay on the main loop and curve left, passing a canyon trail on the left. Drop into the oak-studded draw, and head through a gorgeous oak canopy to the southwest boundary. Two short connector paths on the right lead to the Dyer Road park access. Curve left to a road split. Stay to the right on the outer loop through tall chaparral, walking parallel to the south boundary and homes on McGuffie Road. Continue uphill through a eucalyptus grove at an overlook of Prunedale. Curve left through a second eucalyptus grove and a connector trail on the right that descends through the forest towards Frisch Road. Stay on the main park trail, with views across Manzanita Park to Moss Landing and the Pacific Ocean. Pass a water tank on the right to a trail split. The right fork leads to a horse trailer parking area. Stay left, passing a vehicle gate, volunteer RV sites, and baseball fields. Complete the loop at the soccer field. ■

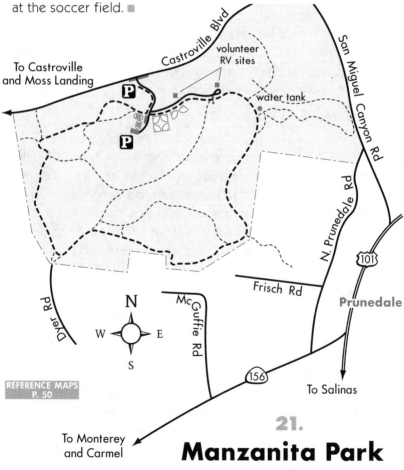

22. Echo—Oak Ridge—Pine Meadow Loop
ROYAL OAKS COUNTY PARK
537 Maher Road · Prunedale

Hiking distance: 1.5 mile-loop
Hiking time: 45 minutes
Configuration: loop
Elevation gain: 200 feet
Difficulty: easy
Exposure: mix of shaded forest and exposed hillside
Dogs: allowed
Maps: U.S.G.S. Prunedale · Royal Oaks County Park map

Royal Oaks County Park encompasses 122 oak studded acres with picnic areas and athletic courts in the valley. The hiking trails are meandering hillside paths that lead from the grassy valley to the cool oak, pine, and cedar woodlands. This hike weaves through the rolling hillside, offering a mix of meadows, oak-dotted slopes, chaparral, and a tree-shaded canopy.

To the trailhead

Drive 13 miles north of Monterey on Highway 1, and exit on Highway 156 East. Continue 6 miles east to Highway 101. Take Highway 101 north 0.7 miles, and turn left onto San Miguel Canyon Road. Drive 1.7 miles to Echo Valley Road and turn right. Go a half mile to Maher Road and turn left. Continue 1.1 mile to Royal Oaks Road. Turn right into the park, and drive 0.2 miles to the tennis courts and park office road on the left. Turn left and park in the lot on the right. An entrance fee is required.

The hike

Walk up the park road past the ranger shop, and curve right on the signed Echo Trail. Follow the park boundary across the oak-dotted grassy slope. Pass the tennis courts on the left to a Y-junction. Begin the loop to the left on the Oak Ridge Trail, bearing right 20 yards ahead. Head uphill through the chaparral and oak into a grassy open field. Views extend across the park to the south park boundary at the ridge. At the east end of the field is a junction with the Hermosa Trail on the right. Bear left, staying on

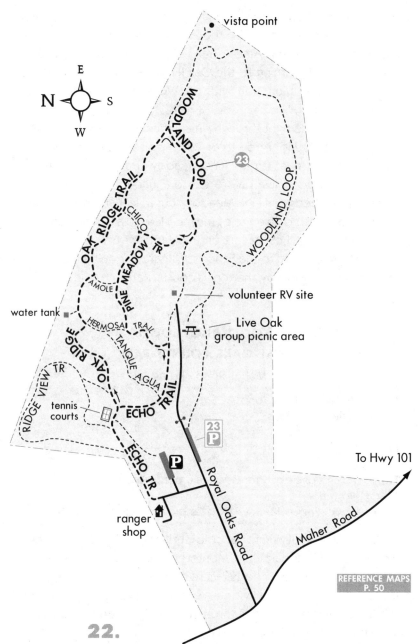

vista point

E
N · S
W

WOODLAND LOOP

23

WOODLAND LOOP

OAK RIDGE TRAIL

CHICO TR

PINE MEADOW TR

AMOLE

water tank

HERMOSA TRAIL

TANQUE AGUA

OAK RIDGE

RIDGE VIEW TR

tennis courts

ECHO TRAIL

ECHO

ECHO TR.

volunteer RV site

Live Oak group picnic area

23 P

P

ranger shop

To Hwy 101

Royal Oaks Road

Maher Road

REFERENCE MAPS P. 50

22.
Echo—Oak Ridge—Pine Meadow Loop
Royal Oaks County Park

the Oak Ridge Trail, and curve right 25 yards ahead by the water tank. Descend to a fork with the Amole Trail on the right. For a short detour, take the Amole Trail through a lush understory of bracken ferns. Returning to the Oak Ridge Trail, continue east to the trail's end at a junction with the Woodland Loop at the far end of the loop (Hike 23).

Descend to the right through a magnificent canopy of twisted oaks with a lush undergrowth of ferns, poison oak, and mint, to a trail fork. Bear right on the Pine Meadow Trail, and wind uphill through the shaded live oak forest to a junction with the Chico Trail at the east edge of Pine Meadow. Curve left and traverse the hillside along the north edge of the meadow to a large open field. Cross the field and curve left on the Hermosa Trail. Descend on the wide grassy path to the Echo Trail. Bear right on the Echo Trail, completing the loop by the tennis courts. Return to the left. ■

23. Woodland Loop
ROYAL OAKS COUNTY PARK
537 Maher Road · Prunedale

Hiking distance: 1-mile loop
Hiking time: 30 minutes
Configuration: loop
Elevation gain: 300 feet
Difficulty: easy
Exposure: mix of shaded forest and exposed hillside
Dogs: allowed
Maps: U.S.G.S. Prunedale · Royal Oaks County Park map

Royal Oaks County Park, an old turkey ranch, lies between Aromas and Prunedale. It is Monterey County's oldest regional park, opened in 1966. The 122-acre park sits in a small grassy valley dotted with coastal live oaks between two forested slopes. The Woodland Loop winds through the oak-covered hillsides to Vista Point, overlooking the valley.

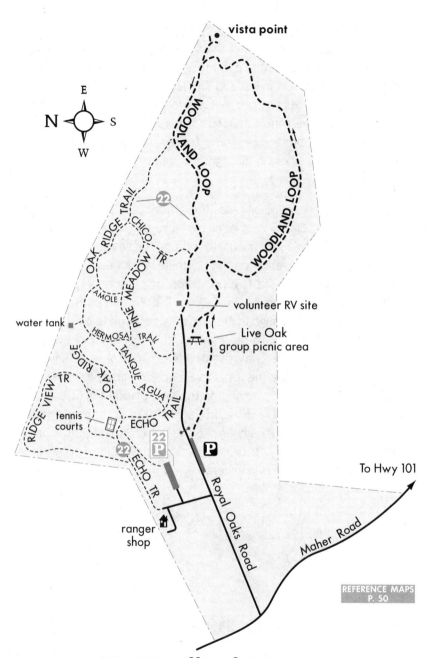

vista point

WOODLAND LOOP

WOODLAND LOOP

OAK RIDGE TRAIL

CHICO TR

PINE MEADOW

AMOLE

HERMOSA TRAIL

TANQUE AGUA

OAK RIDGE TR

RIDGE VIEW TR

ECHO TRAIL

ECHO TR

22

22

22

water tank

volunteer RV site

Live Oak
group picnic area

tennis
courts

P

P

ranger
shop

Royal Oaks Road

To Hwy 101

Maher Road

REFERENCE MAPS
P. 50

23. **Woodland Loop**

Royal Oaks County Park

To the trailhead

Drive 13 miles north of Monterey on Highway 1 and exit on Highway 156 East. Continue 6 miles east to Highway 101. Take Highway 101 north 0.7 miles, and turn left onto San Miguel Canyon Road. Drive 1.7 miles to Echo Valley Road and turn right. Go a half mile to Maher Road and turn left. Continue 1.1 mile to Royal Oaks Road. Turn right into the park, and follow the park road 0.3 miles to the parking spaces on the right. An entrance fee is required.

The hike

Walk up the park road, or cross the grassy parkland to the east end of the Live Oak Group Picnic Area to the signed Woodland Loop trailhead. Take the footpath through the shaded oak forest, steadily gaining elevation on the north-facing hillside. Under the canopy of twisted oaks is a profusion of poison oak, bracken ferns, blackberries, and mushrooms. The forest path weaves across the hillside through the tangle of vegetation to a T-junction. Take a 20-foot detour to the right to Vista Point, elevated on a perch at trail's end. The views stretch west to Monterey Bay.

Return and continue the loop to a junction with the Oak Ridge Trail (Hike 22). Bear left, staying on the Woodland Loop. Descend through the forest of gnarled, dwarfed oaks and atmospheric, tree-filtered sunlight. Pass a junction with the Pine Meadow Trail, returning to the valley floor by a volunteer RV site. Follow the park road back to the parking area. ■

24. Marina State Beach and Marina Dunes Open Space

Hiking distance: 2 miles round trip
Hiking time: 1 hour
Configuration: 3 out-and-back trails
Elevation gain: 100 feet
Difficulty: easy
Exposure: open coast
Dogs: not allowed in Marina State Beach (Access 1 and 3)
      allowed in Marina Dunes Open Space (Access 2)
Maps: U.S.G.S. Marina

map page 81

The 170-acre Marina State Beach is home to huge dunes and sandy cliffs overlooking the Pacific Ocean along Monterey Bay. These three short trails explore the coast along rolling, 80-foot living sand dunes stabilized by thick mats of low-growing vegetation. An interpretive nature trail from Access 1 follows a 2,000-foot-long boardwalk through the dune restoration area. The trail leads to the beach and an observation platform that overlooks Monterey Bay. Interpretive displays describe the rare and endangered vegetation, invasive plants, and creatures living in the dunes. Access 2 leads into the Marina Dunes Open Space and across the crest of a huge dune. Access 3 leads to the edge of 150-foot sand cliffs along a remote stretch of beach. Several trails cross the dunes and cliffs for continued exploration. The state park is also a popular hang gliding launch site.

To the trailhead

ACCESS 1: Drive 8 miles north of Monterey on Highway 1 to Marina, and take the Reservation Road exit. Turn left and drive 0.3 miles into the Marina State Beach parking lot, just past Dunes Drive.

ACCESS 2: Marina Dunes Open Space: From Reservation Road, head north on Dunes Drive a half mile to the signed trailhead at the end of the road.

ACCESS 3: The southern access to Marina State Beach is off of Del Monte Boulevard at the intersection of Lake Drive and Lake Court.

The hike

ACCESS 1: The Marina State Beach parking lot—at the west end of Reservation Road—is perched above the ocean with unobstructed views of the bay. After enjoying the wide vistas, walk to the signed trailhead by the entrance road. The path winds south through the dunes on a wooden boardwalk. Numerous benches and interpretive displays line the trail. The dune path exits on the sandy beachfront at just under a half mile. Return via the beach or retrace your steps.

ACCESS 2: The trail through Marina Dunes Open Space—at the north end of Dunes Drive—is a 0.7-mile round trip walk. The wide, hard-packed sand path begins at the display panels and heads west to the crest of the huge dune. Gradually descend towards the ocean in the softer sand to the interpretive displays on the low bluffs overlooking the bay. The rolling dunes can be explored on a variety of distinct paths.

ACCESS 3: From the southern access to Marina State Beach—off Lake Drive—walk past the trailhead display. Climb up the steep, scrub-covered dune on a wide sand path to the ridge. Sharply descend to the edge of the sandy cliffs overlooking the isolated oceanfront. Towering 150-foot, wind-sculpted sand cliffs, the tallest along Monterey Bay, back the remote beach. ■

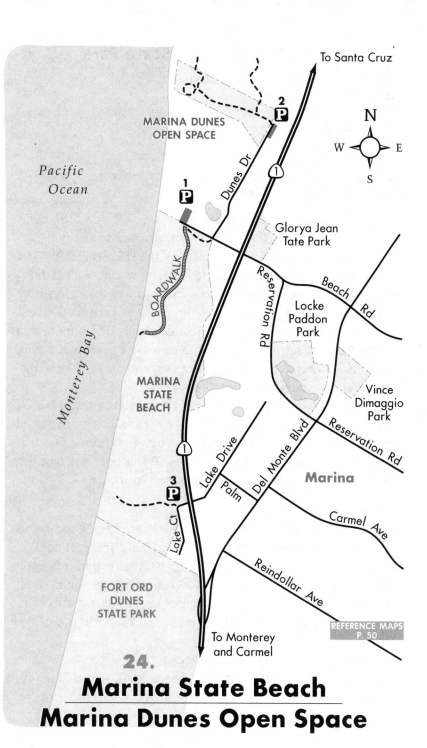

To Santa Cruz

N
W ✦ E
S

MARINA DUNES
OPEN SPACE

Pacific
Ocean

Dunes Dr

①

2 P

Glorya Jean
Tate Park

Reservation Rd

Beach Rd

Locke
Paddon
Park

1 P

BOARDWALK

Monterey Bay

MARINA
STATE
BEACH

Vince
Dimaggio
Park

Reservation Rd

①

Lake Drive

Del Monte Blvd

Marina

3 P

Palm

Carmel Ave

Lake Ct

Reindollar Ave

FORT ORD
DUNES
STATE PARK

REFERENCE MAPS
P. 50

To Monterey
and Carmel

24.
Marina State Beach
Marina Dunes Open Space

25. Fort Ord Dunes State Park

Hiking distance: up to 7 miles round trip
Hiking time: up to 4 hours
Configuration: out-and-back
Elevation gain: near level
Difficulty: easy
Exposure: exposed
Dogs: allowed on paved road but not allowed on beach
Maps: U.S.G.S. Marina and Seaside

Fort Ord Dunes State Park encompasses 979 acres of dune-covered oceanfront. The coastal park, opened to the public as a state park in 2009, was occupied by the U.S. Army until 1994. It was used as a training center for beach combat, with 15 firing ranges and 12 ammunition bunkers. The land was restricted from the public for many decades. A four-mile stretch of undeveloped shoreline is backed by vegetated dunes. The remote and isolated beach is open and vast. The state park has miles of trails overlooking Monterey Bay. It is popular with hikes, bikers, runners, bird watchers, and photographers.

This hike begins at the north end of the state park in Marina and heads south into Seaside. En route the trail passes old firing ranges, faded bunkers, abandoned buildings, and side paths that lead through the dunes to the ocean. Throughout the hike are sweeping coastal views of Monterey and Pacific Grove.

To the trailhead

Drive 8 miles north of Monterey on Highway 1 to Seaside, and take the Light Fighter Drive exit. Drive 0.3 miles east to 2nd Avenue. Turn left and go 0.3 miles to 1st Street. Turn left again and continue a quarter mile to 1st Avenue. (Straight ahead is the trail access under the 1st Street underpass. Parking is also available here to access the trail a half mile from the north end of the trail.)

To continue to the northern trailhead, turn right on 1st Avenue, and go another quarter mile to the state park sign on the left. Turn left and drive one block to a T-junction. Turn right and go

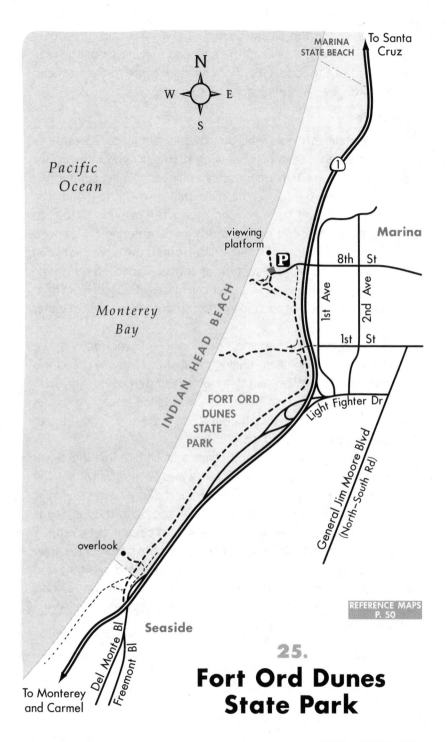

N
W · E
S

Pacific
Ocean

Monterey
Bay

INDIAN HEAD BEACH

To Santa
Cruz

MARINA
STATE BEACH

Marina

1

viewing
platform

P

8th St

1st Ave

2nd Ave

1st St

FORT ORD
DUNES
STATE
PARK

Light Fighter Dr

General Jim Moore Blvd
(North–South Rd)

overlook

Seaside

Del Monte Bl

Freemont Bl

To Monterey
and Carmel

REFERENCE MAPS
P. 50

25.
Fort Ord Dunes
State Park

0.2 miles to the 8th Street Overpass. Turn left and cross over Highway 1. Drive 0.3 miles to the trailhead parking lot on the right at the end of the road. (The extra turns en route to the trailhead are due to gated streets.)

The hike

From the trailhead kiosk, the boardwalk path leads 70 yards to the right to an oceanfront viewing platform with interpretive panels describing its former use as a military training center.

To begin the hike, take the main trail to the left (south) on an old paved road to a junction by a small canyon. Detour to the right and descend on the sandy path, entering the canyon. Follow the draw along the canyon bottom to the ocean at Indian Head Beach. This remote section of coastline, backed by towering dunes, is well-known as a clothing-optional beach. From here, the isolated beach offers uninterrupted hiking for miles in either direction.

Return to the old road and continue to a T-junction with the paved hiking/biking path running parallel to Highway 1 and the railroad tracks. At the gated 1st Street underpass on the left, bear right on the old military road towards the ocean. At the far west end of the road, take the sandy path up, over, and through the dunes to the isolated beach.

Return to the main trail and climb a small hill. Top the slope to coastal views, including Monterey and Pacific Grove. At the south end of Fort Ord Dunes State Park is a three-way trail split, where the paved path turns to dirt. On the right, the trail leads 0.2 miles through the vegetated dunes to an oceanfront overlook atop the bluffs. Straight ahead, the sandy path parallels the train tracks 0.4 miles to the Fremont Boulevard/Del Monte Boulevard freeway exit. To the left, the paved path crosses the railroad tracks and continues south between the tracks and Highway 1. Choose your own turn-around spot. ■

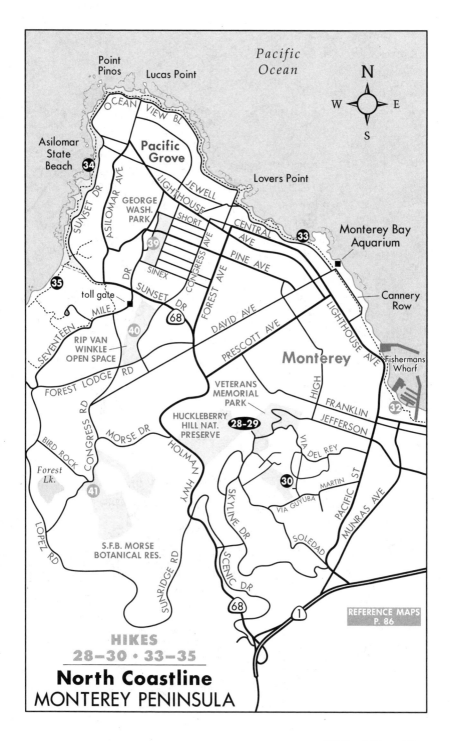

Point
Pinos
Lucas Point

Pacific Ocean

N
W — E
S

Asilomar
State
Beach

34

OCEAN VIEW BL

Pacific Grove

Lovers Point

Monterey Bay
Aquarium

Cannery
Row

SUNSET DR

ASILOMAR AVE

LIGHTHOUSE

JEWELL

GEORGE
WASH.
PARK

SHORT

39

CENTRAL
AVE

33

PINE AVE

CONGRESS AVE

FOREST AVE

SINEX

35

toll gate

SUNSET DR

68

40

DAVID AVE

PRESCOTT AVE

Monterey

LIGHTHOUSE AVE

Fishermans
Wharf

RIP VAN
WINKLE
OPEN SPACE

SEVENTEEN MILE

FOREST LODGE RD

VETERANS
MEMORIAL
PARK

HIGH

FRANKLIN

JEFFERSON

32

CONGRESS RD

MORSE DR

HUCKLEBERRY
HILL NAT.
PRESERVE

28-29

VIA DEL REY

BIRD ROCK

HOLMAN HWY

30

MARTIN

PACIFIC ST

MUNRAS AVE

Forest
Lk.

41

VIA GUYUBA

SKYLINE DR

SOLEDAD

LOPEZ RD

SUNRIDGE RD

S.F.B. MORSE
BOTANICAL RES.

SCENIC DR

68

1

REFERENCE MAPS
P. 86

HIKES
28–30 · 33–35
North Coastline
MONTEREY PENINSULA

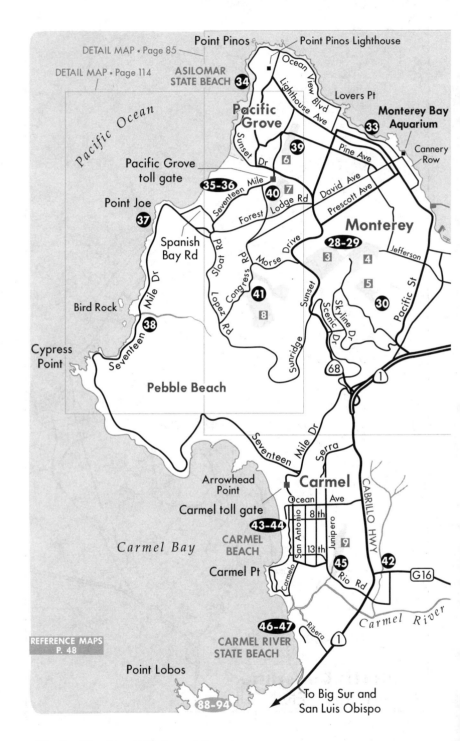

DETAIL MAP • Page 85

DETAIL MAP • Page 114

Point Pinos

Point Pinos Lighthouse

ASILOMAR
STATE BEACH **34**

Lovers Pt

Ocean View Blvd

Lighthouse Ave

**Pacific
Grove**

**Monterey Bay
Aquarium**

33

Cannery
Row

Pine Ave

39

6

Pacific Grove
toll gate

35-36

Sunset Dr

Seventeen Mile

40 7

Forest Lodge Rd

David Ave

Prescott Ave

Monterey

Point Joe

37

Spanish
Bay Rd

Sloat Rd

Congress Rd

Morse Drive

28-29

3

4

Jefferson

5

41

Bird Rock

38

Seventeen Mile Dr

Lopez Rd

8

Sunset

Scenic Dr

Skyline Dr

30

Pacific St

Cypress
Point

Sunridge

68

1

Pebble Beach

Pacific Ocean

Seventeen Mile Dr

Serra

Carmel

Arrowhead
Point

Carmel toll gate

43-44

Carmel Bay

CARMEL
BEACH

Carmel Pt

Ocean Ave

San Antonio

Carmelo

8th

13th

Junipero

9

Juni pero

45

Rio Rd

CABRILLO HWY

42

G16

46-47

CARMEL RIVER
STATE BEACH

Ribera

1

Carmel River

Point Lobos

88-94

To Big Sur and
San Luis Obispo

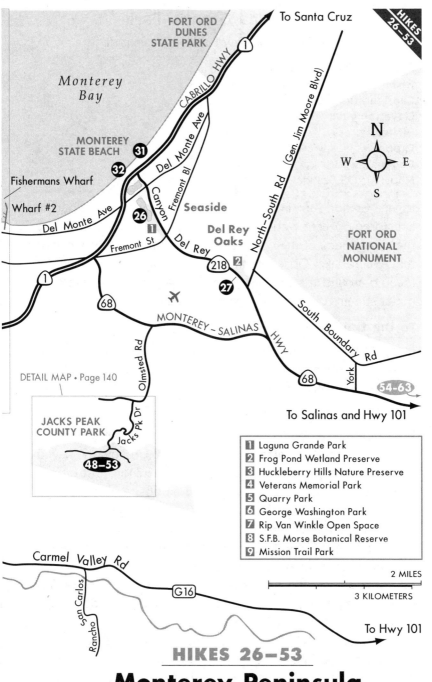

HIKES 26-53

To Santa Cruz

HIKES 26-53

Monterey Bay

FORT ORD DUNES STATE PARK

MONTEREY STATE BEACH 31

32

Fishermans Wharf

Wharf #2

Del Monte Ave

CABRILLO HWY

Del Monte Ave

Fremont Bl

Canyon

26

1

Fremont St

Seaside

Del Rey Oaks

Del Rey

218

2

27

(Gen. Jim Moore Blvd)

North-South Rd

FORT ORD NATIONAL MONUMENT

N
W   E
S

68

MONTEREY – SALINAS Hwy

South Boundary Rd

York

68

54-63

To Salinas and Hwy 101

DETAIL MAP • Page 140

Olmsted Rd

Jacks Pk Dr

JACKS PEAK COUNTY PARK

Jacks Pk Dr

48-53

1	Laguna Grande Park
2	Frog Pond Wetland Preserve
3	Huckleberry Hills Nature Preserve
4	Veterans Memorial Park
5	Quarry Park
6	George Washington Park
7	Rip Van Winkle Open Space
8	S.F.B. Morse Botanical Reserve
9	Mission Trail Park

Carmel Valley Rd

San Carlos

Rancho

G16

2 MILES

3 KILOMETERS

To Hwy 101

HIKES 26–53
Monterey Peninsula

26. Laguna Grande Park

1249 Canyon Del Rey Boulevard · Seaside

Hiking distance: 1.3-mile loop
Hiking time: 40 minutes
Configuration: loop with optional spur trail
Elevation gain: level
Difficulty: easy
Exposure: mostly exposed
Dogs: allowed
Maps: U.S.G.S. Seaside · The Thomas Guide—Monterey Bay

Laguna Grande Park, in the town of Seaside, is a 35-acre park in a restored 60-acre wetland. Laguna Grande, a freshwater lake, is the centerpiece of the park. A hiking and biking pathway circles the 12-acre lake. Observation platforms for bird watching are located around the perimeter. Footbridges cross the inlet and outlet streams over the marshland habitat.

To the trailhead

From Highway 1 in the Monterey area, take the Highway 218/ Canyon Del Rey Boulevard exit. Drive a half mile through Seaside to the signed Laguna Grande Park parking lot on the right.

The hike

The loop trail can be hiked in either direction. This route begins to the right, heading north towards Highway 1. Follow the paved path north along the east shore of Laguna Grande. Just before reaching the Holiday Inn, curve left to an observation deck on the left that overlooks the lake. Cross a footbridge over an outlet stream at the north end of the lake. Head south on the wide, meandering gravel path past an entrance trail from Virgin Avenue. Stay left, picking up the paved path again by another observation platform. Cross a footbridge over the southeast end of Laguna Grande. The paved path returns to the hillside parking lot through a eucalyptus grove by the Eastern Orthodox Church.

To extend the hike, take the unpaved footpath at the southeast footbridge. Parallel the stream south into the canyon through groves of eucalyptus and oak. Just before reaching Freemont

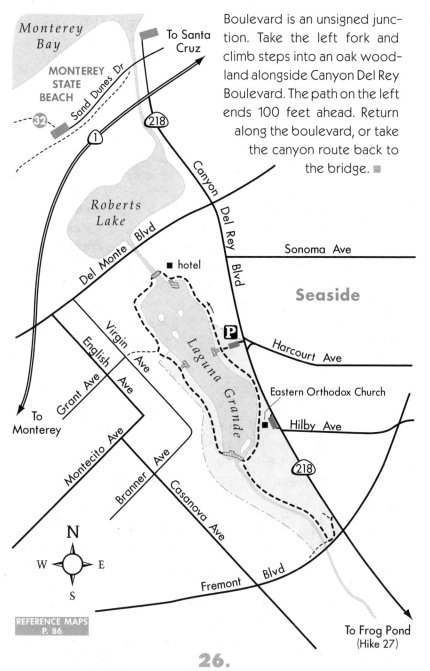

Boulevard is an unsigned junction. Take the left fork and climb steps into an oak woodland alongside Canyon Del Rey Boulevard. The path on the left ends 100 feet ahead. Return along the boulevard, or take the canyon route back to the bridge. ▪

Monterey Bay

MONTEREY STATE BEACH

Sand Dunes Dr

32

1

218

To Santa Cruz

Canyon Del Rey Blvd

Roberts Lake

Del Monte Blvd

▪ hotel

Sonoma Ave

Seaside

P

Harcourt Ave

Virgin Ave

English Ave

Grant Ave

To Monterey

Montecito Ave

Branner Ave

Laguna Grande

Eastern Orthodox Church

Hilby Ave

218

Casanova Ave

N

W E

S

Fremont Blvd

REFERENCE MAPS
P. 86

To Frog Pond
(Hike 27)

26.

Laguna Grande Park

27. Frog Pond Wetland Preserve

Hiking distance: 1-mile loop
Hiking time: 30 minutes
Configuration: loop
Elevation gain: level
Difficulty: easy
Exposure: a mix of shaded forest and open wetland
Dogs: allowed
Maps: U.S.G.S. Seaside · Plants of the Frog Pond Natural Area

The Frog Pond Wetland Preserve is a 17-acre wildlife habitat in Del Rey Oaks. The preserve has a freshwater pond, grassland meadows, marshland, and coastal live oak woodlands. The tranquil wetland is a habitat for the tiny Pacific tree frog and a large variety of resident and migratory birds. The trail circles the perimeter of the reserve through several diverse plant communities—riparian willows, seasonal wetlands, oak woodlands, redwoods, Monterey pine, grasslands, and coastal sage scrub. Five varieties of mushrooms can be spotted in the oak woodlands.

To the trailhead

From Highway 1 in the Monterey area, take the Highway 218/Canyon Del Rey Boulevard exit. Drive 1.9 miles, through Seaside into Del Rey Oaks, to the signed wetland preserve trailhead on the left, across from Via Verde. Parking is limited to small roadside pullouts on both sides of the road. (En route, Canyon Del Rey Boulevard becomes Canyon Del Rey Road.)

The hike

Descend the steps at the signed preserve entrance. Take the right fork through the marshland on the narrow, sandy path. Continue southeast, parallel to Canyon Del Rey Road. Pass a cut-across path on the left. Curve left past an entrance trail from North-South Road (General Jim Moore Boulevard), and head across a footbridge. Follow the eastern boundary of the preserve past a few massive oaks. Cross grasslands with oak and willow groves. Curve left along the north boundary, crossing a boardwalk and bridge over an inlet stream to Frog Pond. A wooden observation

platform overlooks the pond. Cross two
more bridges, completing the loop at the
preserve entrance. ■

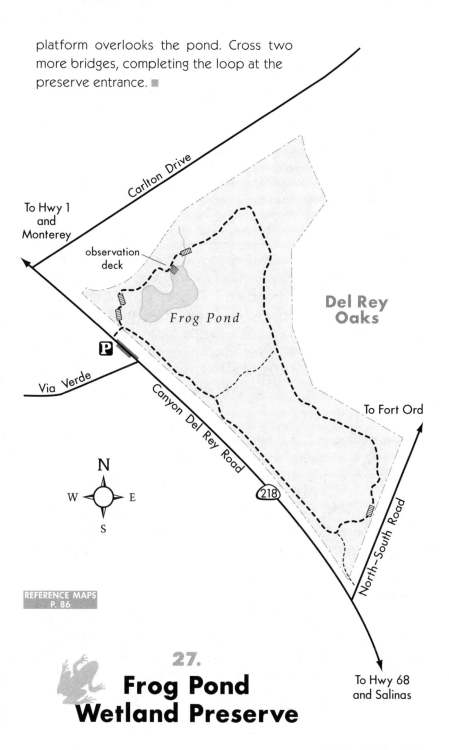

Carlton Drive

To Hwy 1
and
Monterey

observation
deck

Frog Pond

**Del Rey
Oaks**

P

Via Verde

Canyon Del Rey Road

To Fort Ord

(218)

North–South Road

N
W · E
S

REFERENCE MAPS
P. 86

To Hwy 68
and Salinas

27.
Frog Pond
Wetland Preserve

28. Presidio View—Bear Track—Scenic Trail Loop

HUCKLEBERRY HILL NATURE PRESERVE

Hiking distance: 1.5 miles round trip
Hiking time: 1 hour
Configuration: out-and-back with large loop
Elevation gain: 300 feet
Difficulty: easy
Exposure: a mix of shaded forest and open hillside
Dogs: allowed
Maps: U.S.G.S. Monterey · Huckleberry Hill Nature Preserve map

The Huckleberry Hill Nature Preserve surrounds a steep mountain knoll on the Monterey Peninsula between Monterey and Pacific Grove. The 81-acre open space is a hidden gem tucked into the hills, overlooking the peninsula and the ocean. The forested preserve offers sweeping coastal views, including the long, crescent curve of Monterey Bay. The trails, shaded by Monterey pines, form a web-like pattern to the 720-foot summit. This hike leads to the preserve's interior to a vista point atop the knoll.

To the trailhead

From Pacific Street in downtown Monterey, drive 1.2 miles west on Jefferson Street, winding through Veterans Park, to the small parking lot on the right by the flagpole.

From Highway 1, take Highway 68 west 0.8 miles to Skyline Forest Drive. Turn right and go 0.2 miles to the end of the road at Skyline Drive. Turn left and continue 1 mile to Veterans Drive. Turn right and quickly turn left into the signed Veterans Park parking lot.

The hike

From Veterans Memorial Park, take the signed trail north along the west edge of the campground to the posted Presidio View Trail. Bear left on the access trail between two fencelines. Climb 185 steps into the Huckleberry Hill Nature Preserve. Continue uphill through the forest, passing Scenic Road and Water Tank Road on the right. At the top of the ridge is a junction with Summit

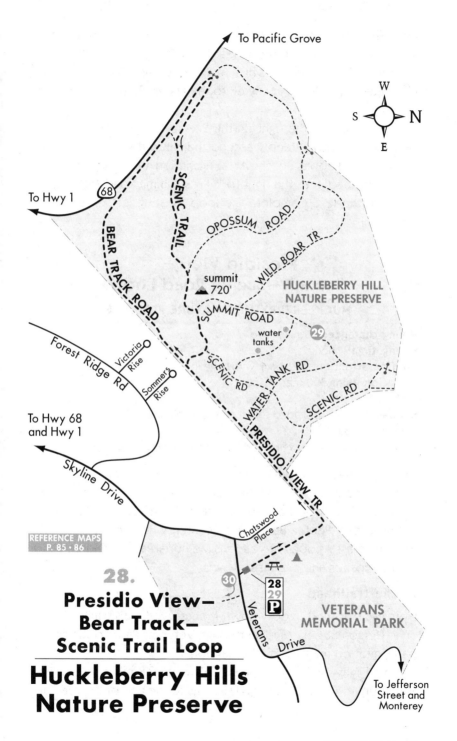

To Pacific Grove

W · N · E · S (compass)

To Hwy 1

68

SCENIC TRAIL

BEAR TRACK ROAD

OPOSSUM ROAD

WILD BOAR TR.

summit
720'

HUCKLEBERRY HILL
NATURE PRESERVE

SUMMIT ROAD

water
tanks

29

Forest Ridge Rd

Victoria Rise

Sommers Rise

SCENIC RD.

WATER TANK RD.

SCENIC RD.

PRESIDIO VIEW TR.

To Hwy 68
and Hwy 1

Skyline Drive

REFERENCE MAPS
P. 85 · 86

Chatswood Place

30

28
29
P

Veterans Drive

VETERANS
MEMORIAL PARK

To Jefferson
Street and
Monterey

28.
Presidio View—
Bear Track—
Scenic Trail Loop
Huckleberry Hills
Nature Preserve

Road (Hike 29). Continue straight, descending on the Bear Track Road along the southern boundary. Curve right and follow the western park boundary, which includes vistas of the ocean at Moss Beach. Parallel Highway 68 to the end of Bear Track Road at a fire access gate.

Bear sharply to the right on the Scenic Trail, heading into the preserve's interior. Steeply ascend the hill to magnificent coastal views of Pebble Beach. At a T-junction with the unsigned Opossum Road, take the right fork. Pass Summit Road and Scenic Road on the left. Complete the loop, bearing left on Presidio View Trail. ■

29. Presidio View— Summit—Scenic Road Loop
HUCKLEBERRY HILL NATURE PRESERVE

Hiking distance: 1.5-mile loop
Hiking time: 1 hour
Configuration: out-and-back with large loop
Elevation gain: 300 feet
Difficulty: easy
Exposure: a mix of shaded forest and open hillside
Dogs: allowed
Maps: U.S.G.S. Monterey · Huckleberry Hill Nature Preserve map

This loop hike in the Huckleberry Hill Nature Preserve, centered around a mountain knoll on the Monterey Peninsula, climbs to the top of the 720-foot knoll. From the summit are vistas of Monterey, Pacific Grove, Pebble Beach, and Monterey Bay. The hike begins from the grassy slopes of Veterans Memorial Park, a 50-acre park with campsites and expansive lawns.

To the trailhead

From Pacific Street in downtown Monterey, drive 1.2 miles west on Jefferson Street, winding through Veterans Park, to the small parking lot on the right by the flagpole.

From Highway 1, take Highway 68 west 0.8 miles to Skyline Forest Drive. Turn right and go 0.2 miles to the end of the road at

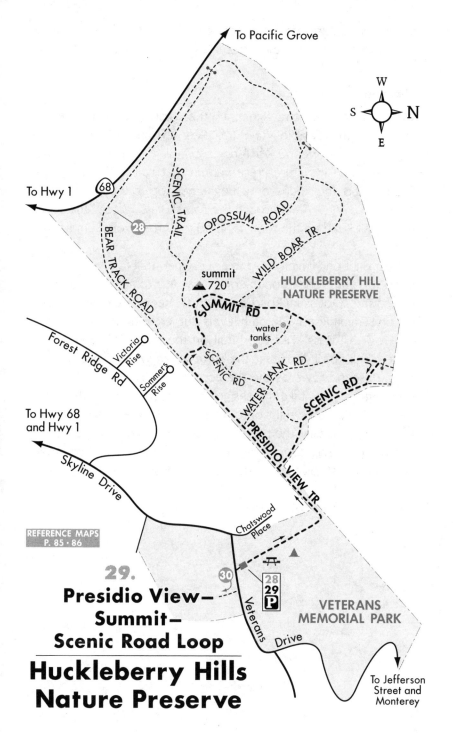

To Pacific Grove

W
S ✦ N
E

To Hwy 1

68

28

SCENIC TRAIL

OPOSSUM ROAD

WILD BOAR TR

BEAR TRACK ROAD

summit
720'

SUMMIT RD

HUCKLEBERRY HILL
NATURE PRESERVE

water
tanks

Forest Ridge Rd

Victoria Rise

Sommers Rise

SCENIC RD

WATER TANK RD

SCENIC RD

PRESIDIO VIEW TR

To Hwy 68
and Hwy 1

Skyline Drive

Chatswood Place

REFERENCE MAPS
P. 85 · 86

29.
**Presidio View–
Summit–
Scenic Road Loop**

Huckleberry Hills
Nature Preserve

30

28
29
P

Veterans Drive

VETERANS
MEMORIAL PARK

To Jefferson
Street and
Monterey

Skyline Drive. Turn left and continue 1 mile to Veterans Drive. Turn right and quickly turn left into the signed Veterans Park parking lot.

The hike

Walk past the trailhead sign along the west edge of the campground to the Presidio View Trail. Bear left and follow the narrow access between two fences, climbing 185 steps into the Huckleberry Hill Nature Preserve. On the right is the unsigned Scenic Road, the return route. Begin the loop to the left, staying on Presidio View Trail through the forest. Pass Water Tank Road to Summit Road on the top of the ridge, across from Sommerset Rise.

Bear right on Summit Road to an unsigned trail fork with Scenic Road 100 yards ahead on the right. Stay left to a Y-junction with the posted Opossum Road on the left. Veer to the right, staying on Summit Road. The path levels out, crossing the top of the 720-foot hill. Pass Wild Boar Trail on the left, and descend to Water Tank Road, just past the large green water tanks on the right. Descend towards the fire access gate. Fifty yards before reaching the gate, take the unsigned connector trail on the right. Descend and curve right onto Scenic Road, parallel to the east boundary fence. At the footpath, bear left, following the fenceline downhill and completing the loop at the top of the steps. Descend the steps and return to the trailhead. ▪

30. Quarry Park to Veterans Park

Via Del Pinar · Monterey

Hiking distance: 1.3 miles round trip
Hiking time: 40 minutes
Configuration: out-and-back
Elevation gain: 100 feet
Difficulty: easy
Exposure: mostly forested
Dogs: allowed
Maps: U.S.G.S. Monterey

**map
page 98**

Quarry Park is a forested ten-acre park with towering pines and oaks and a lush box canyon. The natural, undeveloped park is tucked into a quiet neighborhood in the heart of residential Monterey. Quarry Park is connected to Veterans Memorial Park, a short distance to its north, via a hiking trail. This short but scenic hike meanders through Quarry Park to the small canyon. The trail then weaves through the hills, skirting homes into Veterans Park. To add distance to the hike, Veterans Memorial Park continues into Huckleberry Hill Nature Preserve (Hikes 29–30).

To the trailhead

From Pacific Street, head west on Martin Street. Drive 0.3 miles to Via Gayuba and turn right. Continue 0.2 miles to Via Del Pinar and turn right (north). Go 0.1 mile to the signed park on the left. The park is located between Stephen Place and Herrmann Drive.

The hike

Pass the trailhead sign and enter Quarry Park. At 100 yards is a signed junction with the Veterans-Quarry Park Trail, our main route. For now, continue straight ahead, staying on the canyon floor. Parallel the stream on the right while strolling under the canopy of towering pines and oaks. At 0.2 miles, the path ends at the base of a vertical-walled box canyon.

Return to the junction and take the Veterans-Quarry Park Trail up the north wall of Quarry Canyon and behind the homes on Dorey Way. At the top is a grassy flat overlooking the canyon. Veer right up a few steps and follow the trail sign. Wind through the greenbelt corridor, with views of Monterey, the bay, and the surrounding mountains. The trail ends at the Veterans Memorial Park parking lot by the campground on the left. The park entrance and Skyline Drive are 250 yards to the left. Just before the entrance, on the north side of the road, is the Huckleberry Hill Nature Preserve trailhead (Hikes 28–29). Return along the same path. ■

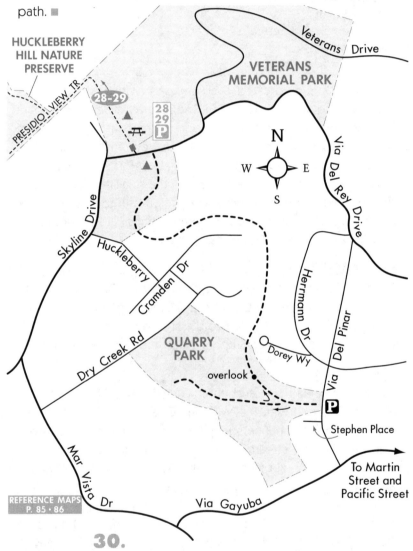

30.
Quarry Park to Veterans Park

31. Seaside Beach
(Del Monte Beach)
MONTEREY STATE BEACH

Hiking distance: 1.5 miles round trip
Hiking time: 1 hour
Configuration: loop
Elevation gain: 50 feet
Difficulty: easy
Exposure: exposed beachfront
Dogs: not allowed
Maps: U.S.G.S. Seaside

Monterey State Beach takes in two separate plots of land along a continuous stretch of beach. The southern unit is a narrow, 14-acre beach extending east from Monterey's Wharf #2 (Hike 33). This hike takes in the northern unit, located in the town of Sand City. The northern stretch is known as both Seaside Beach and Del Monte Beach. The hike begins adjacent to the Best Western Hotel on the restored but fragile vegetated dunes. A short boardwalk loops around the low dunes to the north.

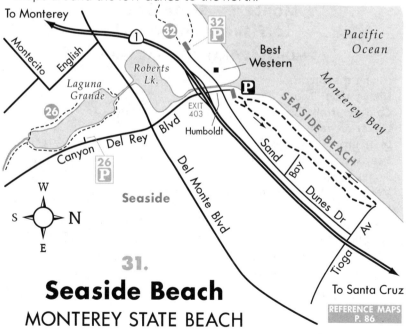

Seaside Beach
MONTEREY STATE BEACH

To the trailhead

Drive 1.5 miles north of Monterey on Highway 1 and take the Seaside/Del Rey Oaks exit #403. Turn left, under the highway on Humboldt Street, and drive 0.1 mile into the Monterey State Beach parking lot, just past Sand Dunes Drive. If the lot is full, head 0.2 miles south on Sand Dunes Drive to a second parking area.

The hike

From the information kiosk, take the sandy path and curve right. Head north and parallel the coastline through the ocean-front dunes. Weave up and across the rolling dunes stabilized with low-growing vegetation. Along the way are great views of Monterey Bay, Monterey, and Pacific Grove. At 0.4 miles, the serpentine path connects with Bay Street, then Tioga Avenue at 0.7 miles. The path ends at Tioga Avenue on the 40-foot-high cliffs. Descend the cliffs and return along the sandy beachfront. ■

32. Monterey State Beach to Fishermans Wharf
MONTEREY BAY COASTAL TRAIL

Hiking distance: 4.7-mile loop
Hiking time: 3 hours
Configuration: loop with optional out-and-back trail
Elevation gain: 50 feet
Difficulty: easy to slightly moderate
Exposure: exposed beachfront
Dogs: allowed
Maps: U.S.G.S. Seaside and Monterey · AAA Monterey Peninsula Guide

Monterey State Beach takes in two separate plots of land on a continuous stretch of beach. The southern unit, known locally as "Windows on the Bay," is a narrow, 14-acre beach extending east from Monterey's Wharf #2. The pier was built in 1870 for commercial fishing and is now a popular tourist spot with restaurants and shops.

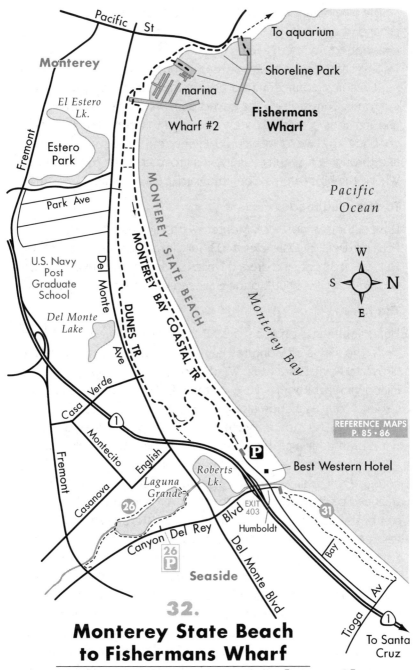

Pacific St

Monterey

To aquarium

Shoreline Park

marina

Fishermans Wharf

Wharf #2

El Estero Lk.

Estero Park

Fremont

Park Ave

Pacific Ocean

U.S. Navy Post Graduate School

Del Monte

MONTEREY STATE BEACH

MONTEREY BAY COASTAL TR

DUNES TR

Del Monte Lake

Ave

Monterey Bay

W

S — N

E

Casa Verde

Fremont

Montecito

English

1

Casanova

Laguna Grande

26

Roberts Lk.

P

REFERENCE MAPS
P. 85 · 86

Best Western Hotel

EXIT 403

Humboldt

Blvd

31

Bay

Canyon Del Rey

26
P

Seaside

Del Monte Blvd

Tioga

1

Av

To Santa Cruz

32.
Monterey State Beach to Fishermans Wharf
Monterey Bay Coastal Trail

The hike begins adjacent to the Best Western Hotel and loops around the beach to Fishermans Wharf. The trail follows the abandoned Southern Pacific Railroad and is part of the Rails-to-Trails system, a nationwide network of trails created from former rail lines and connecting corridors. The trail is also part of the California Coastal Trail. The paved path winds through the dunes and includes panoramic views across Monterey Bay. The route continues between manicured lawns, the broad sandy beach, and through a towering eucalyptus grove en route to Fishermans Wharf. The hike returns along the hard-packed beach.

To the trailhead

Drive 1.5 miles north of Monterey on Highway 1 and take the Seaside/Del Rey Oaks exit #403. Turn left, under the highway on Humboldt Street, and drive 0.1 mile to Sand Dunes Drive. Turn left and go 0.2 miles south to the trailhead parking lot on the right.

The hike

Head southwest on the signed Dunes Trail, a paved beachfront path. The views of Monterey Bay span from Point Pinos in Pacific Grove to Point Santa Cruz. Wind through the low dunes, with an inland view of Roberts Lake on the left. Descend into a looping U-bend to a T-junction alongside Del Monte Avenue. Bear right and parallel Del Monte Avenue. Cross Casa Verde Way, and continue on the hiking/biking path, passing Del Monte Lake on the left. Walk through a eucalyptus-lined corridor. At the naval school entrance, the trail veers right, away from Del Monte Avenue by a trailhead parking lot. Walk across Park Avenue and pass a couple of coastal access paths on the right. El Estero Lake and Estero Park can be seen across the road. At 2.4 miles, the trail reaches Fishermans Wharf, the return point for a loop.

To extend the hike, the trail continues into Fishermans Shoreline Park and follows the oceanfront bluffs. When you are ready to head back to the return loop, walk along the marina back to the municipal wharf and a beach access. Go to the left onto the sandy beach. Follow the curvature of the shoreline on the hard-packed sand. Complete the loop at the trailhead parking lot, just shy of the oceanfront Best Western Hotel. ■

33. Monterey Bay Aquarium to Point Pinos
MONTEREY BAY COASTAL TRAIL

Hiking distance: 4.6 miles round trip
Hiking time: 2 hours
Configuration: out-and-back
Elevation gain: level
Difficulty: easy
Exposure: exposed beachfront
Dogs: allowed
Maps: U.S.G.S. Monterey

map
page 104

The Monterey Bay Coastal Recreation Trail stretches 18 miles from Castroville to Pacific Grove. The paved path follows the coast along the abandoned Southern Pacific Railroad right-of-way. The old railroad was transformed into this popular hiking, biking, and jogging trail in 1986.

This hike follows the beautiful rocky coastline along the blufftop in Pacific Grove on the Monterey Peninsula. Beginning at the Monterey Bay Aquarium, the trail threads through several parks en route to the northern tip of Pacific Grove at Point Pinos. Parklands surround the entire peninsula on the coastal side of Ocean View Boulevard, which parallels the trail. The coastal route passes dramatic rock formations, tidepools, small beach coves, and overlooks. The waters surrounding the peninsula are part of the Pacific Grove Marine Gardens Fish Refuge, a national marine sanctuary.

To the trailhead

The hike begins by the Monterey Bay Aquarium in Monterey, located at the intersection of Ocean View Boulevard and David Avenue. From Highway 1, take the Monterey exit and follow the signs to the aquarium.

The hike

From the aquarium, take the paved path northwest, parallel to Ocean View Boulevard. Follow the coastline past beautiful rock formations and small pocket beaches. Stay to the right of the

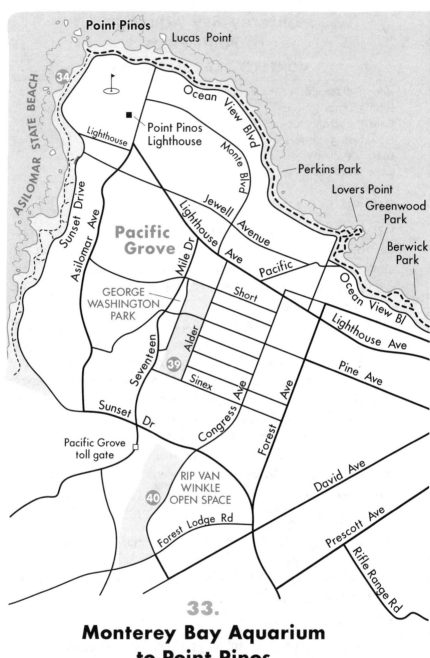

33.
Monterey Bay Aquarium
to Point Pinos
Monterey Bay Coastal Trail

paved bike path. Continue past Victorian homes and benches along the trail. At Berwick Park, a side path meanders to the right, rejoining the main trail a short distance ahead. At one mile, Ocean View Boulevard and the trail turn right at Lovers Point. Explore the rocky, granite headland jutting out into the ocean. Stairways descend from the grassy picnic area to the sandy beaches of Otter Cove, Lovers Point Beach, and Pacific Grove Beach. For a 2-mile round-trip hike, turn around here.

To continue to Point Pinos, follow the cliffside trail past the promontory. Weave through Perkins Park, a landscaped park with stairways, to small beach pockets. The trail overlooks the marine refuge, past continuous rocky coves and tidepools, to Point Pinos at the north tip of Pacific Grove. Return by retracing your steps. ∎

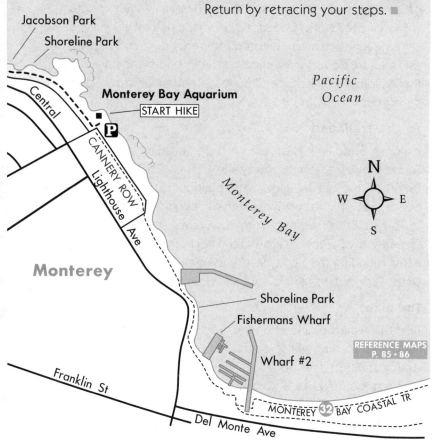

34. Asilomar State Beach and Coast Trail
PACIFIC GROVE • MONTEREY PENINSULA

Hiking distance: 2.4 miles round trip
Hiking time: 1.5 hours
Configuration: out-and-back
Elevation gain: level
Difficulty: easy
Exposure: exposed coast with forested pockets
Dogs: allowed
Maps: U.S.G.S. Monterey

Asilomar State Beach (meaning "refuge by the sea") encompasses 107 acres at the windswept, southwest corner of Pacific Grove on the Monterey Peninsula. The state park has a one-mile strip of sandy beach, an exposed rocky headland with spectacular views of the Pacific Ocean, tidepools, a natural dune preserve, cove beaches, a wind-sculpted Monterey pine and cypress forest, sheltered overlooks, and boardwalk paths. The park includes the Asilomar Conference Grounds, a national historic landmark dating back to 1913.

To the trailhead

Asilomar State Park is on the western coastline in Pacific Grove. From Highway 1, take Highway 68 West (which becomes Sunset Drive) to the ocean. Park in the pullouts on the left along the ocean side of Sunset Drive, south of Jewell Avenue.

To reach the trailhead from downtown Pacific Grove, follow Ocean View Boulevard around the northern tip of Monterey Bay. After rounding the tip, Ocean View Boulevard becomes Sunset Drive. Park in the pullouts south of Jewell Avenue.

The hike

Take the signed trailhead on the gravel paths leading toward the shoreline. To the right is a covered overlook. Follow the meandering trail left (south) above the rocky coves and tidepools, crossing boardwalks and bridges. Numerous connector trails along Sunset Drive join the main path. The trail connects with the Links Nature Walk (Hike 35) at the south end of the state park by the sandy shoreline adjacent to Asilomar Beach (also known as North Moss Beach) in Spanish Bay. Across Sunset Drive, a boardwalk crosses the dunes and weaves through a forest of Monterey pines to the Asilomar Conference Grounds. Return along the same route. ■

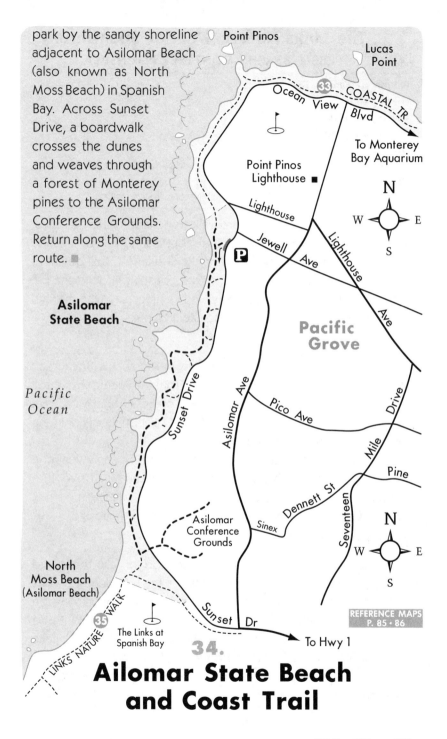

Ailomar State Beach and Coast Trail

35. The Links Nature Walk at Spanish Bay
PEBBLE BEACH • MONTEREY PENINSULA

Hiking distance: 1.3-mile loop
Hiking time: 1 hour
Configuration: loop
Elevation gain: 150 feet
Difficulty: easy
Exposure: a mix of exposed coast and shaded forest
Dogs: allowed
Maps: U.S.G.S. Monterey • Pebble Beach Nature Trails booklet

The Links Nature Walk is a boardwalk trail that crosses the wind-swept dunes between the Del Monte Forest and the broad, sandy North Moss Beach on the Monterey Peninsula. The trail begins at The Inn at Spanish Bay and follows the coastline around the perimeter of The Links at Spanish Bay Golf Course, returning through a forest of Monterey pines and coastal live oaks.

To the trailhead

PEBBLE BEACH. Access to the trail is from the scenic Seventeen Mile Drive, a toll road in Pebble Beach. From the Pacific Grove toll gate off of Sunset Drive, drive 0.3 miles on Seventeen Mile Drive to the turnoff on the right for The Inn at Spanish Bay. Park in the lot near the entrance to the lodge.

CARMEL. From the Carmel toll gate off of Ocean Avenue in downtown Carmel, drive 0.2 miles to Seventeen Mile Drive. Turn left and continue 9 miles to the turnoff on the left for The Inn at Spanish Bay. Park in the lot near the entrance to the lodge.

The hike

The trail begins on the ocean side of the lodge. Take the paved path right to the signed boardwalk trail on the left. Head towards the ocean, weaving through the golf course to a boardwalk on the right. Bear right, crossing the dunes to the oceanfront at a T-junction. The left fork is the Bay Nature Walk (Hike 36). Take the right fork on the Links Nature Walk, following the boardwalk north along the coastline. Pass rock outcroppings, tidepools, and a beach access on the left at the south border of North Moss

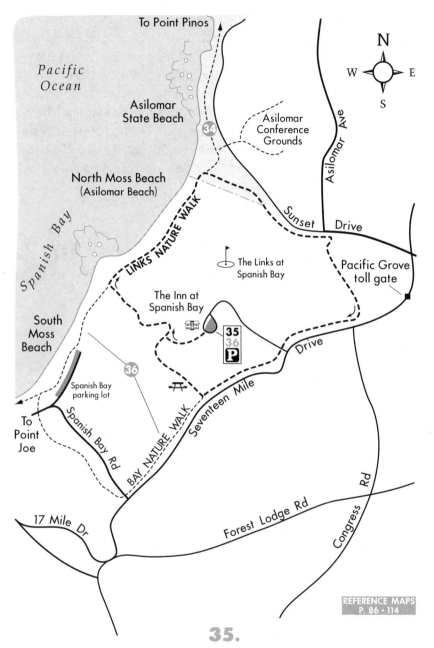

To Point Pinos

Pacific Ocean

Asilomar State Beach

Asilomar Conference Grounds

34

Asilomar Ave

Sunset Drive

North Moss Beach
(Asilomar Beach)

LINKS NATURE WALK

Spanish Bay

The Links at Spanish Bay

Pacific Grove toll gate

The Inn at Spanish Bay

35
36
P

South Moss Beach

36

Drive

Spanish Bay parking lot

BAY NATURE WALK

Seventeen Mile

To Point Joe

Spanish Bay Rd

17 Mile Dr

Forest Lodge Rd

Congress Rd

N
W   E
S

REFERENCE MAPS
P. 86 · 114

35.

The Links Nature Walk
SPANISH BAY

Beach (Asilomar Beach). Continue north for a short distance along Asilomar Beach. Curve inland, crossing over scrub-covered dunes, bordered by the golf course on the right and Sunset Drive to the left. Cross a wooden footbridge over a stream, parallel to Sunset Drive. Pick up the signed trail on the right and head south-east, away from the road. Wind through a Monterey pine forest to Seventeen Mile Road. Parallel the road on the forested path, crossing the entrance road to The Inn at Spanish Bay. Continue to a junction with the Bay Nature Walk. Bear right past a picnic area, completing the loop at the inn.

To extend the hike by one mile, continue with Hike 36. ■

36. The Bay Nature Walk at Spanish Bay
PEBBLE BEACH • MONTEREY PENINSULA

Hiking distance: 1-mile loop
Hiking time: 30 minutes
Configuration: loop
Elevation gain: 120 feet
Difficulty: easy
Exposure: a mix of exposed coast and shaded forest
Dogs: allowed
Maps: U.S.G.S. Monterey • Pebble Beach Nature Trails booklet

The Bay Nature Walk and the Links Nature Walk (Hike 35) are two short, pleasant loop trails at Spanish Bay in Pebble Beach. This hike along the Bay Nature Walk begins at The Inn at Spanish Bay between the Del Monte Forest and North Moss Beach, a broad white sand beach. The trail crosses the windswept dunes along a boardwalk to the Spanish Bay shoreline. The path returns through the dunes and weaves through a forest of Monterey pines and coastal live oaks.

To the trailhead

PEBBLE BEACH. Access to the trail is from the scenic Seventeen Mile Drive, a toll road in Pebble Beach. From the Pacific Grove toll gate off of Sunset Drive, drive 0.3 miles on Seventeen Mile Drive to the turnoff on the right for The Inn at Spanish Bay. Park in the lot near the entrance to the lodge.

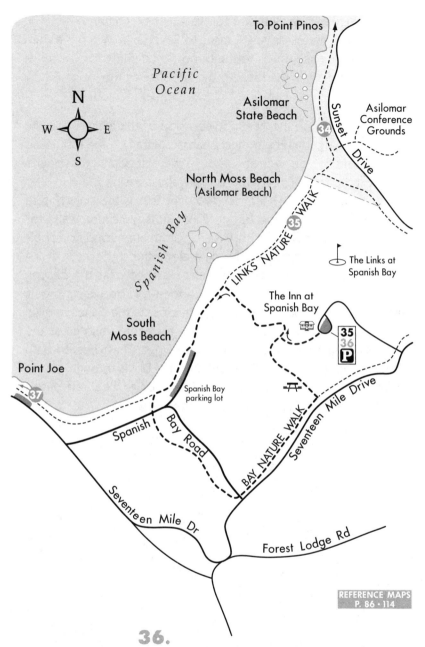

To Point Pinos

Pacific Ocean

N
W   E
S

Asilomar State Beach

Asilomar Conference Grounds

34 Sunset Drive

North Moss Beach
(Asilomar Beach)

Spanish Bay

35 LINKS NATURE WALK

The Links at Spanish Bay

The Inn at Spanish Bay

South Moss Beach

35
36
P

Point Joe

37

Spanish Bay parking lot

Spanish Bay Road

BAY NATURE WALK

Seventeen Mile Drive

Seventeen Mile Dr

Forest Lodge Rd

REFERENCE MAPS
P. 86 · 114

36.
The Bay Nature Walk
SPANISH BAY

CARMEL. From the Carmel toll gate off of Ocean Avenue in downtown Carmel, drive 0.2 miles to Seventeen Mile Drive. Turn left and continue 9 miles to the turnoff on the left for The Inn at Spanish Bay. Park in the lot near the entrance to the lodge.

The hike

The trail begins on the ocean (west) side of the lodge. Take the paved path right to the signed boardwalk trail on the left. Head towards the ocean, weaving through the golf course to a boardwalk on the right. Follow the boardwalk, crossing the dunes to the oceanfront at a T-junction. The right fork is the Links Nature Walk (Hike 35). Take the left fork on the Bay Nature Walk, following the boardwalk south. Pass rock formations and tidepools along Spanish Bay. Stay to the right along the shoreline, skirting the Spanish Bay parking lot. A short distance past the parking lot, cross Spanish Bay Road to a wooden footbridge on the inland side of the road. The sandy path crosses the dunes parallel to Spanish Bay Road. Curve left at the restrooms, and cross the road again just before Seventeen Mile Drive. The forested path follows the west side of Seventeen Mile Drive through groves of Monterey pines to a junction near the lodge. Bear left past a picnic area, completing the loop at the inn. ■

37. Point Joe to Bird Rock
PEBBLE BEACH · MONTEREY PENINSULA

Hiking distance: 3.4 miles round trip
Hiking time: 2 hours
Configuration: out-and-back
Elevation gain: level
Difficulty: easy
Exposure: open coastal bluffs
Dogs: allowed
Maps: U.S.G.S. Monterey

**map
page 115**

Point Joe is a rocky point at the southwest end of Spanish Bay. This hike follows the coastal terrace from Point Joe to Bird Rock and Seal Rock, large granite outcroppings carved by waves and wind. The trail includes scenic vistas, promontories, and beach coves along the Monterey Peninsula. This stretch of coastline is an excellent whale watching location from December through March, when gray whales make their way from Baja California to Alaska. Interpretive displays are at Point Joe and Bird Rock.

To the trailhead

PEBBLE BEACH. Access to the trail is from the scenic Seventeen Mile Drive, a toll road in Pebble Beach. From the Pacific Grove toll gate, located off of Sunset Drive, drive 1.7 miles on Seventeen Mile Drive to the Point Joe parking lot on the right, at the south end of Moss Beach.

CARMEL. From the Carmel entrance gate, off of Ocean Avenue in downtown Carmel, drive 0.2 miles to Seventeen Mile Drive. Turn left and continue 7.6 miles to the Point Joe parking lot on the left.

The hike

From the bluffs at Point Joe, savor the views north, overlooking South Moss Beach, Spanish Bay, and the jagged coastline. Head south along the granite rock point, parallel to Seventeen Mile Drive and the ocean cliffs. The meandering path passes sculpted granite outcroppings and tidepools. As you pass a sandy pocket beach surrounded by boulders, Bird Rock (the destination) can be seen offshore. The path reaches Bird Rock at 1.9 miles. To the south are views of Fan Shell Beach and Cypress Point. To the north are views back to Point Joe and Spanish Bay. Continue to an overlook of Seal Rock, where sea otters, sea lions, and harbor seals can be observed. Return along the same trail.

To extend the hike by one mile, the trail to Indian Village—Hike 38—begins here. ■

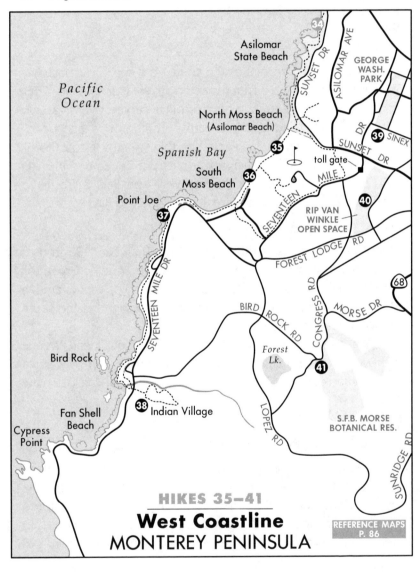

Pacific Ocean

Asilomar State Beach

GEORGE WASH. PARK

North Moss Beach (Asilomar Beach)

Spanish Bay

South Moss Beach

Point Joe

toll gate

RIP VAN WINKLE OPEN SPACE

FOREST LODGE RD

BIRD ROCK RD

CONGRESS RD

MORSE DR

Forest Lk.

Bird Rock

Fan Shell Beach

Indian Village

Cypress Point

LOPEZ RD

S.F.B. MORSE BOTANICAL RES.

SUNRIDGE RD

SEVENTEEN MILE DR

SUNSET DR

ASILOMAR AVE

SINEX

HIKES 35–41
West Coastline
MONTEREY PENINSULA

REFERENCE MAPS P. 86

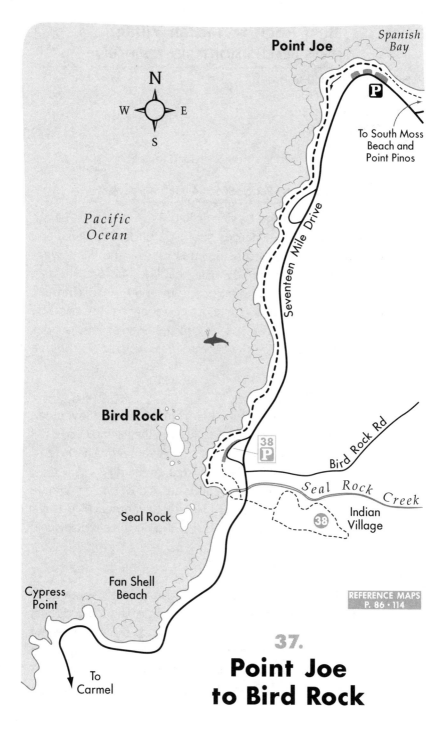

Point Joe

Spanish Bay

N
W   E
S

To South Moss
Beach and
Point Pinos

Pacific Ocean

Seventeen Mile Drive

Bird Rock

Bird Rock Rd

38
P

Seal Rock Creek

Seal Rock

38

Indian
Village

REFERENCE MAPS
P. 86 · 114

Fan Shell
Beach

Cypress
Point

To
Carmel

37.
Point Joe
to Bird Rock

38. Bird Rock to Indian Village
PEBBLE BEACH • MONTEREY PENINSULA

Hiking distance: 1-mile loop
Hiking time: 30 minutes
Configuration: loop
Elevation gain: 50 feet
Difficulty: easy
Exposure: a mix of coastal bluffs and shaded forest
Dogs: allowed
Maps: U.S.G.S. Monterey · Pebble Beach Nature Trails booklet

The hike to Indian Village begins at Bird Rock, a large offshore rock that is home to numerous shoreline birds, sea lions, and harbor seals. A self-guided nature trail follows the windswept coastline and rocky shore towards Seal Rock before crossing the dunes into the Del Monte Forest. The path winds through Monterey pines to Indian Village, a site thought to be used by the Costanoan Indians as a spa before the Spanish missionaries arrived in the 1700s. It is now a large, grassy picnic area with a log cabin.

To the trailhead

PEBBLE BEACH. Access to the trail is from the scenic Seventeen Mile Drive, a toll road in Pebble Beach. From the Pacific Grove toll gate off of Sunset Drive, drive 3 miles on Seventeen Mile Drive to the signed Bird and Seal Rock Picnic Area on the right.

CARMEL. From the Carmel entrance gate, off of Ocean Avenue in downtown Carmel, drive 0.2 miles to Seventeen Mile Drive. Turn left and continue 6.2 miles to the Bird and Seal Rock Picnic Area on the left.

The hike

After marveling at Bird Rock and the coastline, walk south (left) to the signed trail. Continue following the coastline towards Seal Rock. Cross Seventeen Mile Drive and pick up the trail, heading inland. A boardwalk leads through the fragile dunes. Climb the stairs at the east end of the dunes, and enter the shady forest to an unsigned junction. Bear left, following the south banks of

Seal Rock Creek. Pass a natural spring on the right, reaching Indian Village in a meadow and picnic area. For the return loop, bear right on the gravel road. Just before reaching the "Gingerbread House" on the right, watch for the trail on the right . Bear right to the junction, completing the loop. Recross the dunes back to the trailhead. ▪

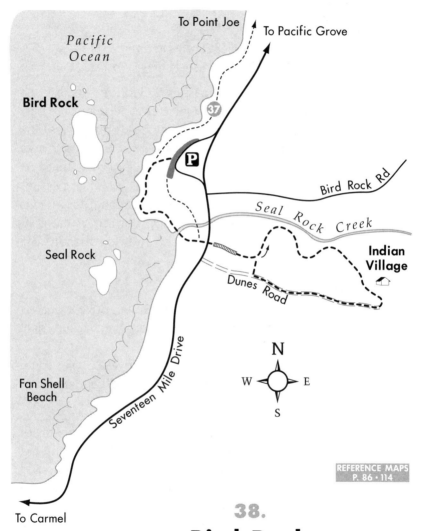

REFERENCE MAPS
P. 86 • 114

38.
Bird Rock to Indian Village

39. George Washington Park

PACIFIC GROVE

Hiking distance: 1 mile round trip
Hiking time: 30 minutes
Configuration: interconnecting loops
Elevation gain: level
Difficulty: easy
Exposure: shaded forest
Dogs: allowed (with off-leash area at park's north end)
Maps: U.S.G.S. Monterey · The Thomas Guide—Monterey Bay

George Washington Park, encompassing 22 wooded acres, is the largest park in Pacific Grove. From October to February, the park plays host to thousands of migrating monarch butterflies. The developed south end of the park has a playground, picnic area, and baseball field. The rest of the six-block-long park has remained in its natural state, with a thick forest of Monterey pines and towering oaks. A network of interconnecting trails winds through the wooded parkland. The north portion of the park, between Pine Avenue and Short Street, is a dog-friendly, off-leash area.

To the trailhead

From Sunset Drive/Highway 68 in Pacific Grove, drive a quarter mile north on Seventeen Mile Drive to Sinex Avenue. Turn right and park.

From Lighthouse Avenue in Pacific Grove, drive 0.6 miles south on Seventeen Mile Drive to Sinex Avenue. Turn left and park.

The hike

The hike can start from nearly any point along the perimeter of the park. This route begins at the south end of the park by the playground area. Walk north past the playground and baseball diamond. Footpaths lead into the shaded groves of Monterey pine and coastal oak. Interconnecting paths weave a mosaic of trails through the forest. The rectangular-shaped park is bordered by roads, eliminating any chance of getting lost. The paths reach Pine Avenue at 0.3 miles. Pick up the trail across the street, and enter the forest at the off-leash area of the park. The winding paths end at Short Street on the north end of the park. ■

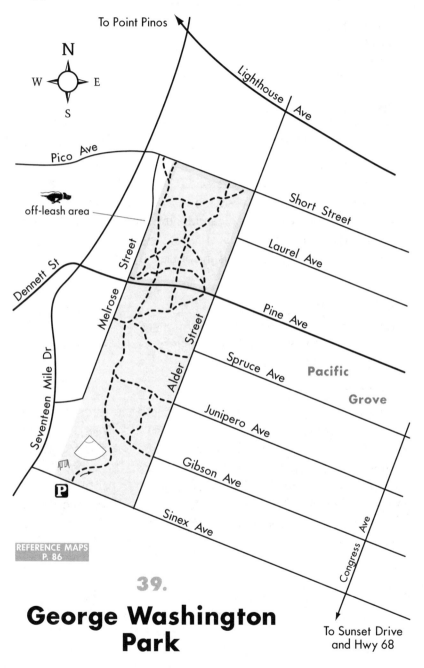

To Point Pinos

N
W — E
S

Lighthouse Ave

Pico Ave

off-leash area

Dennett St

Short Street

Melrose Street

Laurel Ave

Alder Street

Pine Ave

Spruce Ave

Pacific

Grove

Seventeen Mile Dr

Junipero Ave

Gibson Ave

P

Sinex Ave

Congress Ave

REFERENCE MAPS
P. 86

39.

George Washington Park

To Sunset Drive
and Hwy 68

40. Rip Van Winkle Open Space
PACIFIC GROVE

Hiking distance: 1 mile round trip
Hiking time: 30 minutes
Configuration: interconnecting loops
Elevation gain: level
Difficulty: easy
Exposure: shaded forest
Dogs: allowed (off-leash park)
Maps: U.S.G.S. Monterey · The Thomas Guide—Monterey Bay

The Rip Van Winkle Open Space is in Pacific Grove on the border of Pebble Beach. The forested 20-acre parkland, owned by the Pebble Beach Company, sits on stabilized dunes on a coastal terrace. A network of trails meanders through the undeveloped park in a dense forest canopy of Monterey pines, Monterey cypress, and coast live oak. It is a popular jogging and off-leash dog walking park.

To the trailhead

From Sunset Drive/Highway 68 and Congress Avenue in Pacific Grove, drive 0.4 miles south on Congress Avenue to the parking area on the right.

The hike

From the parking area, three paths lead into the forested open space. This route begins on the left (south) fork. Walk past three wooden posts and signpost 16 through the oak and Monterey pine forest to a junction and another sign post. The left fork ends a short distance ahead by an entrance gate into Pebble Beach at Forest Lodge Road. Take the right fork into the forest canopy to another junction. Curve right and follow a path of your choice. The paths interconnect and weave through the rich forest. ■

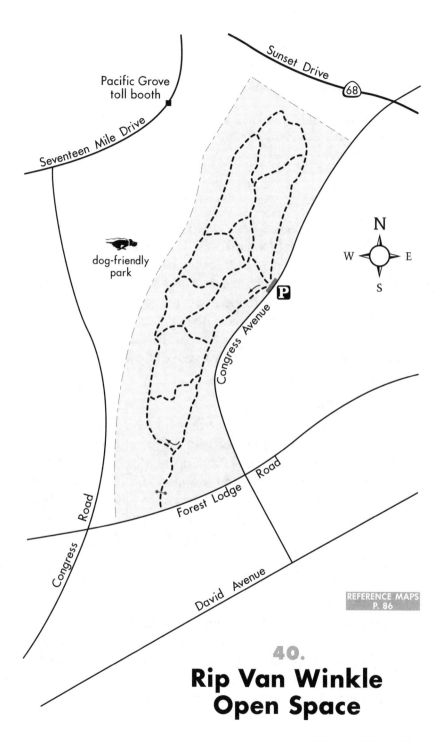

Pacific Grove
toll booth

Sunset Drive

68

Seventeen Mile Drive

dog-friendly
park

N

W · E

S

P

Congress Avenue

Congress Road

Forest Lodge Road

David Avenue

REFERENCE MAPS
P. 86

40.

Rip Van Winkle
Open Space

41. S.F.B. Morse Botanical Reserve
PEBBLE BEACH

Hiking distance: 1.8-mile loop
Hiking time: 1 hour
Configuration: loop, with optional interconnecting trails
Elevation gain: 300 feet
Difficulty: easy
Exposure: shaded forest
Dogs: allowed
Maps: U.S.G.S. Monterey · Pebble Beach Nature Trails booklet

The S.F.B. Morse Botanical Reserve is an 86-acre woodland oasis in the hills of the Del Monte Forest in Pebble Beach. Nearly a dozen fire roads, originally built for the old Pebble Beach Quarry, weave like a maze through the forested acres. This undulating loop trail follows old fire roads across the ancient marine terraces of Huckleberry Hill, the highest point in Pebble Beach. The trail passes through groves of coast live oak, Bishop pine, Monterey pine, Monterey cypress, a pygmy forest of Gowen cypress, and creekside redwoods.

To the trailhead

Access to the botanical reserve is from a toll road in Pebble Beach. From the country club entrance gate on Forest Lodge Road in Pacific Grove, drive 0.1 mile west to Congress Road (the first left). Turn left and continue 1.1 mile to the signed S.F.B. Morse Botanical Reserve entrance on the left, just before the junction with Bird Rock Road. Park in the wide pullout on the right.

From the S.F.B. Morse entrance gate off of Highway 68 West, drive 0.6 miles on S.F.B. Morse Drive and curve left on Congress Road. The signed reserve entrance is 0.3 miles ahead on the left.

The hike

Take the signed footpath into the lush forest, quickly reaching a trail split. Stay to the left, heading up the small canyon on the north-facing hillside. Curve left, crossing the drainage through a dense understory of ferns and vines to an unpaved fire road at a half mile. Bear left on the road, and immediately bear left again, following the trail sign. The trail follows the north ridge of the canyon to a trail split at signposts 2 and 5. Stay to the right through a pine forest. Curve left down a lush draw to a 4-way junction. Walk through the junction 20 yards to signpost 13. Follow the trail sign to the left into an open forest to a 3-way trail split on a flat. Bear left past signpost 3, and descend into the forested canyon. At the canyon floor, leave the road and head down canyon on the signed footpath to the right. Cross a small stream to a Y-fork. Stay left along the canyon floor, returning to Congress Road. Bear left on the road, completing the loop a quarter mile ahead. ∎

41.
S.F.B. Morse Botanical Reserve

42. Hatton Canyon

Hiking distance: 3 miles round trip
Hiking time: 1.5 hours
Configuration: out-and-back
Elevation gain: 100 feet
Difficulty: easy
Exposure: equal mix of shaded canyon and open grassland
Dogs: allowed
Maps: U.S.G.S. Monterey

Hatton Canyon is a charming, hidden canyon close to Carmel. The 160-acre open space canyon parallels Highway 1, north of Carmel Valley Road. The mountains and forest isolate the canyon, which gives the hike more of a back-country feel than the location would indicate. The undeveloped area is a neighborhood favorite, but few people know it is there.

The 1.5-mile-long canyon is a rich wildlife habitat with several diverse habitats. The canyon begins in a broad grassland with cottonwoods, willows, and wetland meadows. Mid-way up the canyon is Hatton Creek (a perennial stream), lined with Monterey pines and oak groves. The upper canyon is a V-shaped gorge with a dense Monterey pine forest.

To the trailhead

The Hatton Canyon Trail is located in Carmel on the east side of Highway 1 between Carmel Valley Road and Rio Road. From Highway 1, head a couple blocks east on either Carmel Valley Road or Rio Road, and turn into "The Barnyard" shopping center. Park in the spaces nearest to Highway 1.

The hike

Walk behind the mall buildings towards Highway 1 to the paved hiking/biking path. Head north (right) and walk through the tunnel under Carmel Valley Road. Curve right, then left onto the natural two-track trail. Follow the tree-lined path into Hatton Canyon. Gently gain elevation beneath towering pines and lichen-draped oaks. Pass a faint trail coming in from the right by an intersecting side canyon. This path leads 100 yards to gated private land. Continue straight, staying in Hatton Canyon, to a horseshoe-shaped left bend at 1.4 miles. Climb the west canyon wall to the end of the trail by a gate on Canyon Drive, 150 yards east of Flanders Drive. Return by retracing your route. ■

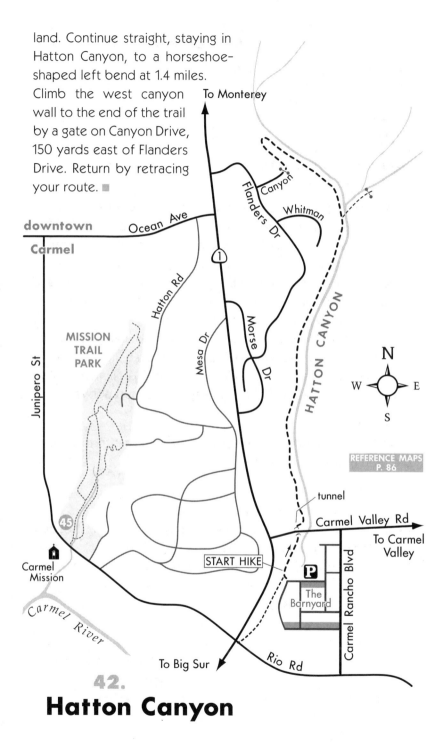

42.
Hatton Canyon

43. Carmel Beach

Hiking distance: 2.4 miles round trip
Hiking time: 1.5 hours
Configuration: out-and-back
Elevation gain: level
Difficulty: easy
Exposure: open coastline
Dogs: allowed and encouraged
Maps: U.S.G.S. Monterey

Fronting the heart of downtown Carmel lies Carmel Beach, an arc of white sand between Pebble Beach and Carmel Point. The crescent-shaped beach is backed by twisted, wind-swept Monterey cypress perched on a large sand dune. Behind the dune are erosion-sculpted bluffs. Granite rock outcroppings and tidepools lie at the north end of the beach. Dog-friendly Carmel permits dogs to run free on the beach.

This hike follows the shoreline of Carmel Beach between Carmel Point and Arrowhead Point. The Scenic Bluff Pathway— Hike 44—parallels the beach along the blufftop. Numerous stairways link the beach with the pathway on the bluff above.

To the trailhead

From downtown Carmel, take Ocean Avenue west to the end of the road at the beachfront.

The hike

The west end of Ocean Avenue opens up to the wide sandy beach. Walk down the steep sand dune to the shoreline. Heading north, the beach extends 0.4 miles, passing several pocket coves to the craggy rock cliffs and tidepools near Arrowhead Point. Heading south, the white sand beach extends 0.7 miles. Along the way, numerous stairways lead up the rocky bluffs to the Scenic Bluff Pathway along Scenic Road. At the south end of Carmel Beach, as the bluffs curve west to Carmel Point, the beach strand ends. A stairway leads up the rocky bluffs to the residential area near the point. Return by following the beach strand back, or take one of the stairways up the bluffs, and return along the tree-lined Scenic Bluff Pathway. ■

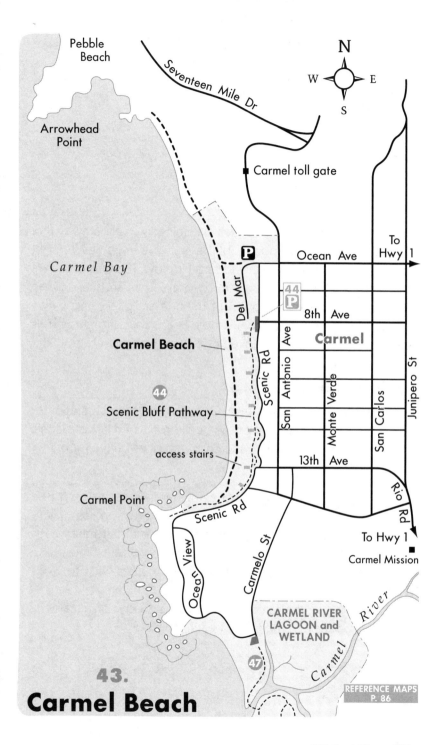

Pebble Beach

Seventeen Mile Dr

N
W   E
S

Arrowhead Point

Carmel toll gate

To Hwy 1

P

Ocean Ave

Carmel Bay

Del Mar

8th   Ave

44
P

Carmel

San Antonio   Ave

Carmel Beach

Scenic Rd

Monte Verde

San Carlos

Junipero St

44
Scenic Bluff Pathway

access stairs

13th   Ave

Carmel Point

Scenic Rd

Rio Rd

To Hwy 1

Carmel Mission

Ocean View

Carmelo St

CARMEL RIVER LAGOON and WETLAND

Carmel River

47

43.
Carmel Beach

REFERENCE MAPS
P. 86

44. Scenic Bluff Pathway at Carmel Beach

Hiking distance: 1.4 miles round trip
Hiking time: 45 minutes
Configuration: out-and-back
Elevation gain: level
Difficulty: easy
Exposure: shaded blufftop
Dogs: allowed and encouraged
Maps: U.S.G.S. Monterey

The Scenic Bluff Pathway is a well maintained gravel pathway that parallels Scenic Road on the bluffs above Carmel Beach. Eight stairways access the white sand beach below. The trail meanders through the shade of Monterey cypress and landscaped gardens to Carmel Point. Throughout the hike are panoramic views of the jagged coastline, from Pebble Beach to Point Lobos. This easy stroll is especially enjoyable for watching sunsets over the Pacific Ocean.

To the trailhead

From downtown Carmel, take Ocean Avenue west to Scenic Road, located a block east of the oceanfront. Turn left on Scenic Road, and drive 2 blocks to the parking spaces on the right.

The hike

Take the gravel path south above the sandy beach strand. The path meanders through the shade of Monterey cypress. Every block has a stairway leading down the rocky cliffs to the beach below (Hike 43). At 0.8 miles, the trail jogs a few times, then ends near Ocean View Avenue as the bay curves west towards Carmel Point.

To return, take the same path back, or descend on a stairway and loop back along the sandy beach strand. ∎

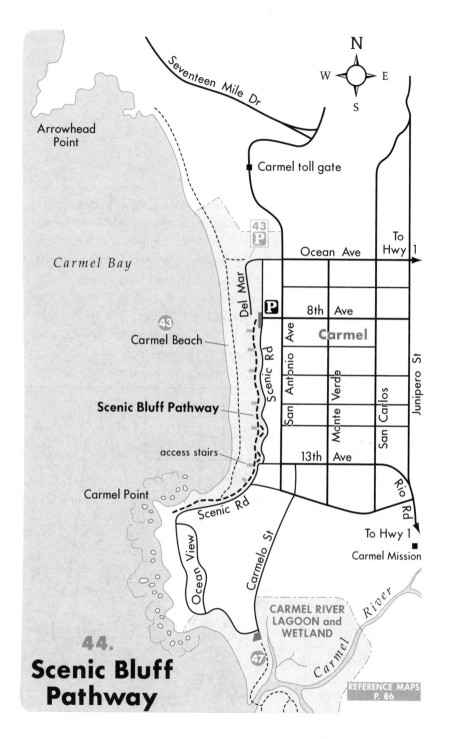

N
W   E
S

Seventeen Mile Dr

Arrowhead Point

Carmel toll gate

43 P

Ocean Ave

To Hwy 1

Carmel Bay

P

8th Ave

Carmel

43

Carmel Beach

Del Mar

San Antonio Ave

Monte Verde

San Carlos

Junipero St

Scenic Bluff Pathway

Scenic Rd

access stairs

13th Ave

Carmel Point

Scenic Rd

Rio Rd

To Hwy 1

Carmel Mission

Ocean View

Carmelo St

Carmel River

CARMEL RIVER LAGOON and WETLAND

47

44.
Scenic Bluff Pathway

REFERENCE MAPS
P. 86

45. Mission Trail Park

Hiking distance: 1.5-mile loop
Hiking time: 1 hour
Configuration: loop
Elevation gain: 100 feet
Difficulty: easy
Exposure: mostly shaded
Dogs: allowed
Maps: U.S.G.S. Monterey · Mission Trail Park map

Mission Trail Park, encompassing 35 acres, is Carmel's largest park. The designated nature park has five miles of well-maintained trails that meander up a forested stream-fed canyon and along the hillsides. The trails wind through native vegetation and grasslands, stands of oaks, pines, eucalyptus, willows, and redwoods. Within the park boundaries are Flanders Mansion, built in 1924, and the one-acre Lester Rowntree Native Plant Garden. The walled, hillside garden has an exhibit of native California trees, shrubs, and plants. The vistas include Carmel and Point Lobos.

The park has four entrances via residential streets, providing

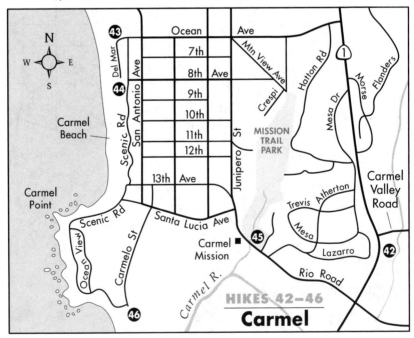

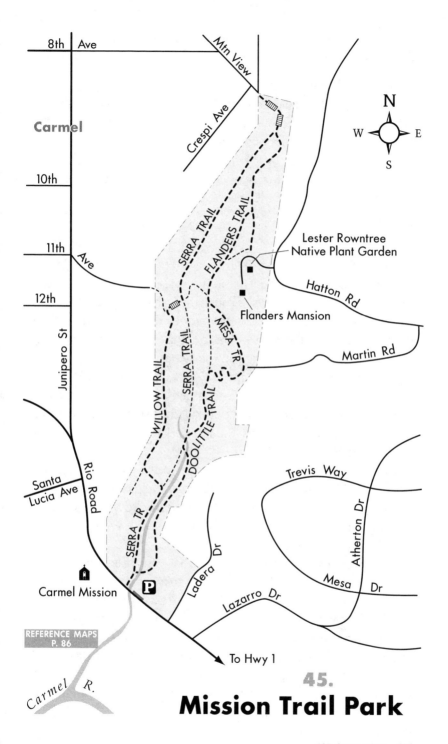

8th Ave

Mtn View

Crespi Ave

Carmel

10th

11th Ave

12th

Junipero St

N
W E
S

SERRA TRAIL

FLANDERS TRAIL

Lester Rowntree
Native Plant Garden

Hatton Rd

Flanders Mansion

MESA TR

Martin Rd

WILLOW TRAIL

SERRA TRAIL

DOOLITTLE TRAIL

Santa
Lucia Ave

Rio Road

SERRA TR

Trevis Way

Atherton Dr

Ladera Dr

Mesa Dr

Carmel Mission

P

Lazarro Dr

REFERENCE MAPS
P. 86

To Hwy 1

Carmel R.

45.
Mission Trail Park

easy access to the trails. This hike begins at the south end of the park, across the street from the Carmel Mission off of Rio Road.

To the trailhead

From Highway 1 and Rio Road in Carmel, drive 0.5 miles west on Rio Road to the signed Mission Trail Nature Preserve on the right (north). Park in the pullouts on the right.

From Ocean Avenue in downtown Carmel, drive 0.8 miles south on Junipero Street to the signed trail on the left (north), across from the Carmel Mission. (En route, Junipero Street becomes Rio Road.)

The hike

Enter the park on the Serra Trail, a service road. Immediately bear right on the posted Doolittle Trail, crossing a trickling stream. Ascend the east canyon wall through the lush vegetation. Traverse the hillside and gradually descend back to the stream on the canyon floor. Cross the stream and follow the wide Serra Trail to the right for a short distance. Pick up the signed Doolittle Trail on the right, and ascend the hillside to a Y-fork. Take the Mesa Trail to the right. Zigzag up the hillside to a flat, grassy mesa that overlooks the forested canyon. The path rejoins the Doolittle Trail and continues north to a junction. The left fork returns to the canyon floor at the Willow Trail bridge.

Take the Flanders Trail up the hillside to the right, and cross a bridge to an unsigned junction. The right fork is the shorter but steeper route to Flanders Mansion and Lester Rowntree Garden. Stay left on the Flanders Trail to a junction with a wide path. The right fork leads to the native plant garden.

After viewing the mansion and garden, return back the path to the Flanders Trail. Continue descending to the canyon floor. After reaching the Serra Trail, head up the narrowing canyon through the forest canopy. Cross two long, wooden footbridges, and emerge from the park at Mountain View and Crespi Avenues. Return down canyon to a footbridge on the right. Cross a bridge to the west side of the canyon at Willow Trail. The right fork exits the park at 11th Street. Bear left on the Willow Trail to a trail split. Curve left, back to the Serra Trail. Return to the right. ■

46. Carmel River Lagoon and Wetlands Natural Preserve

CARMEL RIVER STATE BEACH

Hiking distance: 1 mile round trip
Hiking time: 30 minutes
Configuration: out-and-back
Elevation gain: 50 feet
Difficulty: easy
Exposure: open coast
Dogs: allowed
Maps: U.S.G.S. Monterey

**map
page 135**

The Carmel River Lagoon and Wetlands is a protected sanctuary for migrating birds and shorebirds within Carmel River State Beach. The brackish lagoon sits at the mouth of the Carmel River. A sandbar interrupts the river's flow to the sea, filling the lagoon and forming a marshy wetland area. The sandbar breaks away during rainstorms, emptying the lagoon into the ocean. The sanctuary is fringed with eucalyptus and Monterey cypress groves. This hike begins on the north bank of the Carmel River, then climbs a hillside to scenic views. The path continues to the Portola-Crespi Cross, the historic site where a cross was erected in 1769 to signal passing ships.

To the trailhead

From downtown Carmel, take Ocean Avenue west to Scenic Road, located a block east of the oceanfront. Turn left (south) on Scenic Road, and follow the winding blufftop road 1.4 miles to Carmelo Street. Turn right into the signed Carmel River State Beach parking lot.

The hike

Head left (eastward) to the edge of the lagoon and past the interpretive displays. Follow the shoreline to the sandbar near the oceanfront. Cross the sandbar to the south shore of the Carmel River. If the river is flowing into the ocean, wade across. Climb a few steps to a T-junction. The right fork follows the lower ocean terrace to Middle Beach. Take the left fork and follow the river upstream on the terraced ledge. Gradually gain elevation, overlooking the wetland preserve. Views extend inland up Carmel Valley. The path ends on the hilltop at the Portola Cross. Scenic views stretch across Carmel Bay to Point Lobos and the surrounding mountains.

To continue walking, descend the hill to the south, and take the cliffside footpath to Middle Beach and Monastery Beach (Hike 47). ■

47. Carmel Meadows to Monastery Beach
CARMEL RIVER STATE BEACH

Hiking distance: 2.2 miles round trip
Hiking time: 1.5 hours
Configuration: loop with spur trails at both ends
Elevation gain: 150 feet
Difficulty: easy
Exposure: open coastal bluffs
Dogs: allowed
Maps: U.S.G.S. Monterey

map
page 137

This hike combines beach and bluff trails along Carmel River State Beach at the south end of Carmel. The Carmel River flows through the north end of this 106-acre state beach, forming a lagoon and bird sanctuary. The beach is bordered on the south by Point Lobos State Reserve (Hikes 88—94). The hike connects Carmel Meadows, in the grassland bluffs, to San Jose Creek Beach, locally known as Monastery Beach (named after the Carmelite Monastery in the hills above). A short side trip leads to Portola-Crespi Cross, the site where the Portola-Crespi Expedition erected a cross to signal passing ships in 1769. From the cross are panoramic views of Carmel Bay, the bird sanctuary, the surrounding mountains, and Point Lobos. The walk can be extended north into the lagoon and wetlands—Hike 46.

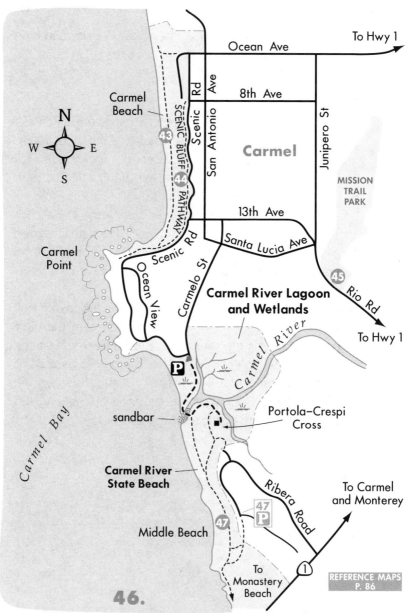

Carmel River Lagoon and Wetlands Natural Preserve
CARMEL RIVER STATE BEACH

To the trailhead

From Highway 1 and Rio Road in Carmel, drive 0.9 miles south on Highway 1 to Ribera Road. Turn right and continue 0.7 miles to the trailhead at the end of the road.

The hike

Take the hilltop trail south past rock outcroppings through grasslands and brush. Follow the blufftop path 0.2 miles to a junction. The right fork descends down steps to a lower path. For now, continue along the hilltop above Middle Beach. The path descends to the lower trail and down to the tidepools and rock formations at the beachfront. Continue following the beach south, reaching San Jose Creek, which pools into a small lagoon near Monastery Beach. The serrated cliffs of Point Lobos extend west out into the ocean. (Point Lobos State Reserve can be accessed by crossing San Jose Creek.)

Return back to the tidepools, and now take the lower trail, passing below a few cliffside homes to a junction at the base of a hill. The right fork is the return route. First, bear left up the hill for a short detour to Portola Cross and a scenic vista point. Return to the junction at the base of the hill, and head up the paved path to Calle La Cruz. Walk one block to Ribera Road. Go right a quarter mile to the trailhead at the end of the road. ▪

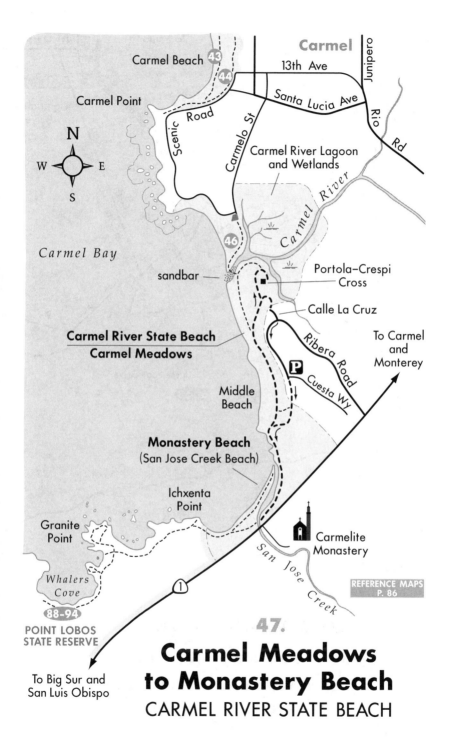

Carmel

Carmel Beach

13th Ave

Carmel Point

Santa Lucia Ave

Scenic Road

Carmelo St

Junipero

Rio Rd

Carmel River Lagoon
and Wetlands

N
W E
S

Carmel River

Carmel Bay

sandbar

Portola–Crespi
Cross

Calle La Cruz

Carmel River State Beach
Carmel Meadows

Ribera Road

To Carmel
and
Monterey

P

Cuesta Wy

Middle
Beach

Monastery Beach
(San Jose Creek Beach)

Ichxenta
Point

Granite
Point

Carmelite
Monastery

San Jose Creek

REFERENCE MAPS
P. 86

Whalers
Cove

88-94

POINT LOBOS
STATE RESERVE

1

To Big Sur and
San Luis Obispo

47.

Carmel Meadows
to Monastery Beach
CARMEL RIVER STATE BEACH

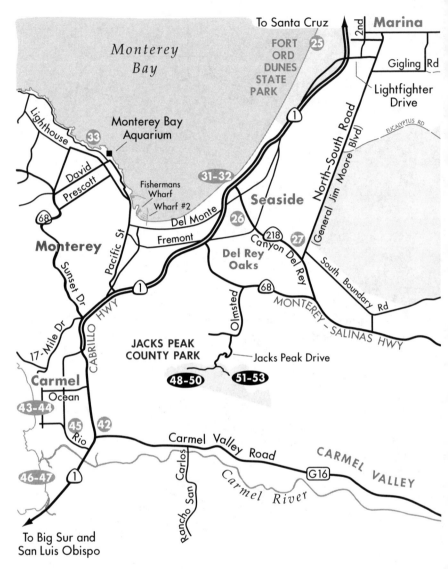

Inland Monterey

Jacks Peak County Park
Fort Ord National Monument
Toro County Park

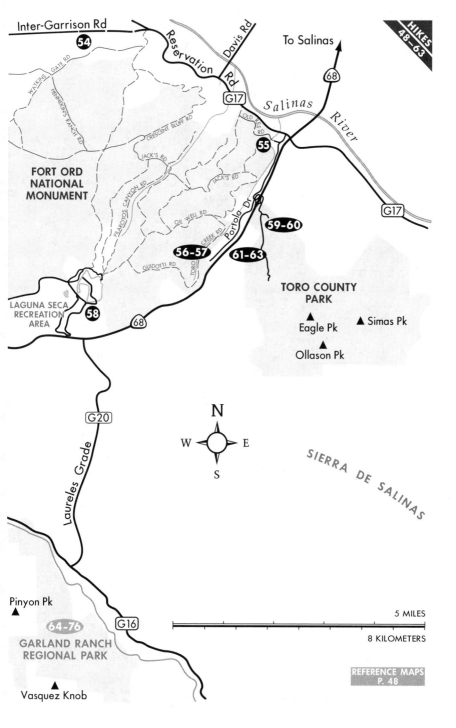

Inter-Garrison Rd

54

Reservation Rd

Davis Rd

To Salinas

68

WATKINS GATE RD

HENNEKEN'S RANCH RD

CRESCENT BLUFF RD

JACK'S RD

PILARCITOS CANYON RD

G17

Salinas River

OLD RES RD

55

**FORT ORD
NATIONAL
MONUMENT**

JACK'S RD

OIL WELL RD

CREEK RD

Portola Dr

59-60

56-57

61-63

GUIDOTTI RD

TORO

58

68

G17

**LAGUNA SECA
RECREATION
AREA**

**TORO COUNTY
PARK**

▲ Eagle Pk   ▲ Simas Pk

▲ Ollason Pk

N

W ✦ E

S

G20

Laureles Grade

SIERRA DE SALINAS

Pinyon Pk
▲

64-76

G16

**GARLAND RANCH
REGIONAL PARK**

▲
Vasquez Knob

5 MILES

8 KILOMETERS

REFERENCE MAPS
P. 48

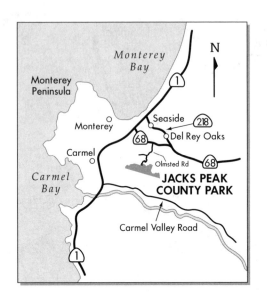

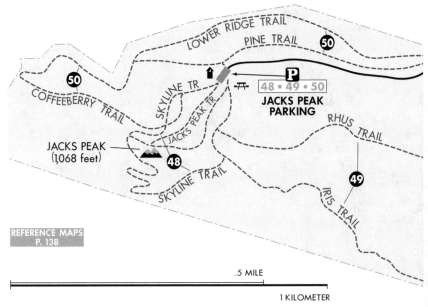

REFERENCE MAPS
P. 138

.5 MILE

1 KILOMETER

Jacks Peak County Park

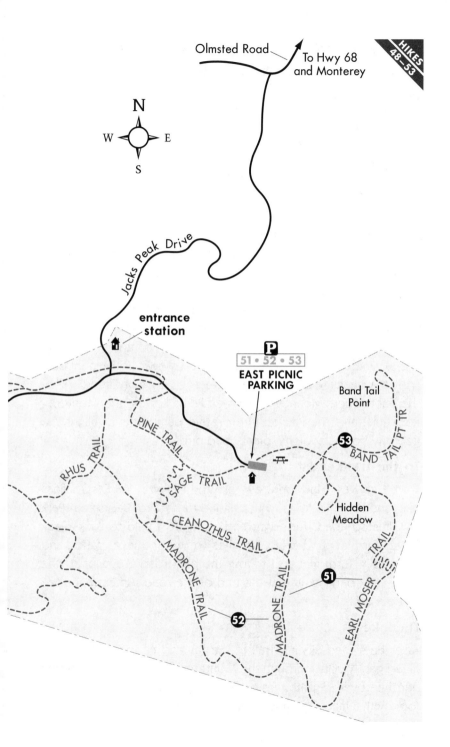

Olmsted Road

To Hwy 68
and Monterey

N
W E
S

Jacks Peak Drive

**entrance
station**

P
51 • 52 • 53
**EAST PICNIC
PARKING**

Band Tail
Point

BAND TAIL PT TR

PINE TRAIL

RHUS TRAIL

SAGE TRAIL

CEANOTHUS TRAIL

Hidden
Meadow

EARL MOSER TRAIL

MADRONE TRAIL

51

52

53

MADRONE TRAIL

48. Skyline Trail and Jacks Peak
JACKS PEAK COUNTY PARK

Hiking distance: 1.2-mile loop
Hiking time: 40 minutes
Configuration: loop
Elevation gain: 200 feet
Difficulty: easy
Exposure: mix of shaded forest and open hillside
Dogs: allowed
Maps: U.S.G.S. Seaside and Monterey · Jacks Peak County Park map

Jacks Peak County Park sits on a wooded ridge that separates the Monterey Peninsula from Carmel Valley. The 525-acre ridgetop preserve has 11 interconnecting hiking and equestrian trails that cover over 8.5 miles.

The Skyline Trail, a self-guided nature trail set amid native Monterey pines, traverses Jacks Peak to its 1,068-foot summit. Jacks Peak is the highest point on the Monterey Peninsula. The Skyline Trail offers some of the best views of the peninsula. From the peak are picturesque bird's-eye views of Carmel Valley, the Santa Lucia Mountains, Carmel, Point Lobos, the Monterey Peninsula, and the Pacific. Interpretive pamphlets highlight the geology, forest ecology, plants, and birds.

To the trailhead

From Highway 1 in Monterey, take the Highway 68 East/Salinas exit, and drive 1.6 miles to the signed turnoff for Jacks Peak Park at Olmsted Road. Turn right and continue 1 mile to Jacks Peak Drive. Turn left and drive 1.2 miles to the entrance station and road split. Turn right and follow the park road 0.6 miles to the Jacks Peak parking area at the end of the road. An entrance fee is required.

The hike

Take the signed Skyline Trail at the far end of the parking area. Head gently uphill through the Monterey pine forest on the soft, needle-covered path. Traverse the hillside to a scenic overlook with a map highlighting landmarks in Monterey Bay. A short distance ahead, cross the Coffeeberry Trail, then continue past a wall of aguajito shale on the left, a whitish rock with marine fossils. At a junction with the Jacks Peak Trail, detour left about 60 yards to the bench on a round grassy knoll at Jacks Peak. From the peak, the Jacks Peak Trail returns directly to the parking area.

For this hike, return to the Skyline Trail and continue south, walking down steps. Bear left and traverse the southern slope while overlooking Carmel Valley. Switchbacks descend through the forest. Curve left, leaving the upper slopes of Carmel Valley to a T-junction with the Iris Trail. Take the left fork, passing the Rhus Trail on the right. Complete the loop on the south side of the parking area. ■

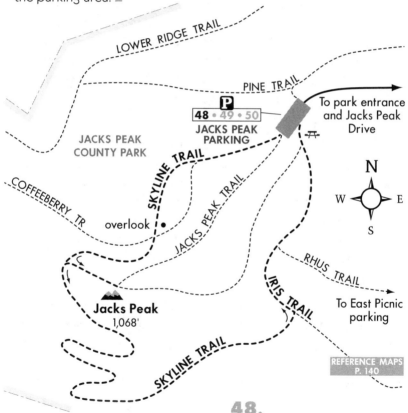

48.
Skyline Trail and Jacks Peak
JACKS PEAK COUNTY PARK

49. Iris—Rhus Loop
JACKS PEAK COUNTY PARK

Hiking distance: 1.8-mile loop
Hiking time: 1 hour
Configuration: loop
Elevation gain: 350 feet
Difficulty: easy
Exposure: mostly shaded forest
Dogs: allowed
Maps: U.S.G.S. Seaside · Jacks Peak County Park map

The Iris and Rhus Trails make a loop through the center of Jacks Peak County Park, offering views of Monterey Bay from the park's ridge. The quiet, away-from-the-crowds trail winds along the forested eastern slopes of Jacks Peak, the highest point on the Monterey Peninsula. The trail then returns through Monterey pine and coastal oak groves. A mat of spongy pine needles carpets the path through the cool, pastoral surroundings.

To the trailhead

From Highway 1 in Monterey, take the Highway 68 East/Salinas exit, and drive 1.6 miles to the signed turnoff for Jacks Peak Park at Olmsted Road. Turn right and continue 1 mile to Jacks Peak Drive. Turn left and drive 1.2 miles to the entrance station and road split. Turn right and follow the park road 0.6 miles to the Jacks Peak parking area at the end of the road. An entrance fee is required.

The hike

From the center of the parking area, walk south into the meadow past the picnic area on the Iris Trail. The path soon reaches a trail fork with the Rhus Trail. Begin the loop to the right, staying on the Iris Trail, and pass a junction with the Skyline Trail on the right (Hike 48). The serpentine path, covered with a soft carpet of pine needles, dips and rises through the lush forest. Parallel the fence along the park's south boundary.

At the trail's east end, round the horseshoe bend left and begin the return. Continue winding through the pastoral forest to a

Y-fork with the Rhus Trail. Take the Rhus Trail to the left. Gradually gain elevation all the way back to the Iris Trail, completing the loop. Bear right, returning to the trailhead. ■

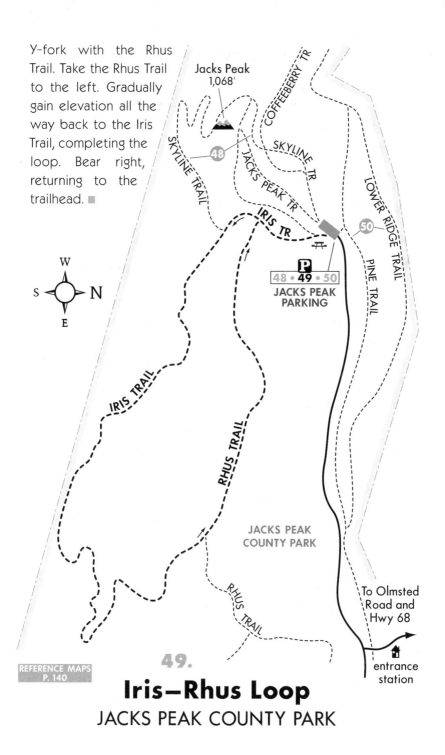

Jacks Peak
1,068'

COFFEEBERRY TR

SKYLINE TRAIL

48

SKYLINE TR

JACKS PEAK TR

LOWER RIDGE TRAIL

IRIS TR

50

PINE TRAIL

W
S ✦ N
E

P
48 • **49** • 50
**JACKS PEAK
PARKING**

IRIS TRAIL

RHUS TRAIL

JACKS PEAK
COUNTY PARK

RHUS TRAIL

To Olmsted
Road and
Hwy 68

entrance
station

REFERENCE MAPS
P. 140

49.

Iris–Rhus Loop
JACKS PEAK COUNTY PARK

50. Coffeeberry—Lower Ridge— Pine Loop

JACKS PEAK COUNTY PARK

Hiking distance: 2.2-mile loop
Hiking time: 1 hour
Configuration: loop
Elevation gain: 350 feet
Difficulty: easy
Exposure: mostly shaded forest with exposed hilltops
Dogs: allowed
Maps: U.S.G.S. Seaside and Monterey · Jacks Peak County Park map

This long, narrow loop descends on the northern slope of Jacks Peak to the county park's north boundary. The hike begins on the Skyline Trail, passing a scenic overlook. The views span across Monterey Peninsula to the bay. The trail then traverses the Coffeeberry Trail to the Lower Ridge Trail, an old ranch road. The trail skirts the boundary on the lush cliffside, dense with ferns and vines. Embedded fossils can be seen in the shale.

To the trailhead

From Highway 1 in Monterey, take the Highway 68 East/Salinas exit, and drive 1.6 miles to the signed turnoff for Jacks Peak Park at Olmsted Road. Turn right and continue 1 mile to Jacks Peak Drive. Turn left and drive 1.2 miles to the entrance station and road split. Turn right and follow the park road 0.6 miles to the Jacks Peak parking area at the end of the road. An entrance fee is required.

The hike

Begin the hike on the signed Skyline Trail at the far southwest end of the parking lot. Head uphill on the spongy, needle-covered path, passing the scenic vista overlook and a map of Monterey Bay. Just beyond the overlook is a 4-way junction with the Coffeeberry Trail. Take the right fork, descending the mountain slope into the canyon. The 0.4-mile descent ends by a home and trail junction at the west park boundary. Bear sharply to the right on the Lower Ridge Trail. Parallel the park boundary through the forest, with views of the peninsula and bay. Continue on the easy uphill grade, passing a cut-off path on the right that leads directly back to the parking area. Look for fossils embedded in a wall of white shale rock that lines the inland side of the trail. The shady cliff-side path reaches the park road at a posted junction with the Pine Trail. Turn sharply right on the Pine Trail. Follow the path—parallel to the park road—through an evergreen forest. The trail often veers away from and dips below the road. Complete the loop at the northeast end of the park-ing area. ■

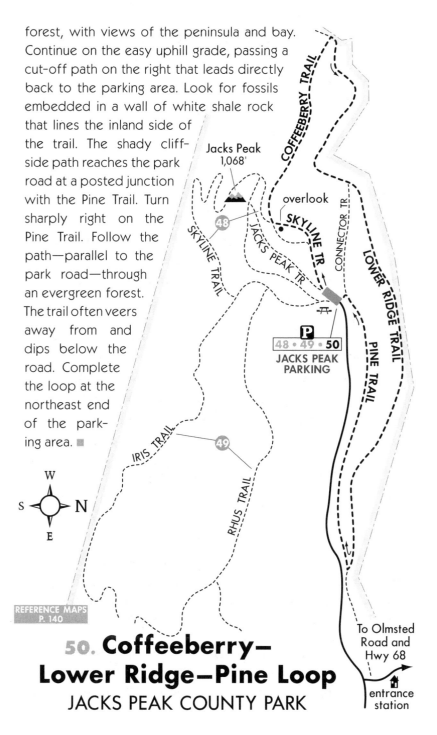

Jacks Peak
1,068'

overlook

COFFEEBERRY TRAIL

SKYLINE TR

CONNECTOR TR.

LOWER RIDGE TRAIL

SKYLINE TRAIL

JACKS PEAK TR

48

P

48 • 49 • 50
**JACKS PEAK
PARKING**

PINE TRAIL

IRIS TRAIL

49

RHUS TRAIL

W
S — N
E

To Olmsted
Road and
Hwy 68

entrance
station

REFERENCE MAPS
P. 140

**50. Coffeeberry–
Lower Ridge–Pine Loop**
JACKS PEAK COUNTY PARK

51. Earl Moser—Madrone Loop
JACKS PEAK COUNTY PARK

Hiking distance: 2-mile loop
Hiking time: 1 hour
Configuration: loop
Elevation gain: 200 feet
Difficulty: easy
Exposure: shaded forest and open meadows
Dogs: allowed
Maps: U.S.G.S. Seaside · Jacks Peak County Park map

The Earl Moser Trail, at the far east end of Jacks Peak County Park, was built in 1981 as a tribute to Earl Moser for his many years of community service and help in acquiring land for the park. The trail loops around the east boundary and follows the mesa-like ridge past several viewing benches. The vistas extend across Carmel Valley to Point Lobos. The Madrone Trail, the return route, meanders through a lush draw filled with wildflowers in a garden-like setting.

To the trailhead

From Highway 1 in Monterey, take the Highway 68 East/Salinas exit, and drive 1.6 miles to the signed turnoff for Jacks Peak Park at Olmsted Road. Turn right and continue 1 mile to Jacks Peak Drive. Turn left and drive 1.2 miles to the entrance station and road split. Turn left and follow the park road 0.4 miles to the East Picnic parking area at the end of the road. An entrance fee is required.

The hike

Take the signed Earl Moser Trail on the north side of the parking area across from the restrooms. Head east past the picnic area on the right and views of Monterey Bay on the left. Follow the wide path, cushioned with a mat of pine needles, to a 5-way junction. The Band Tail Point Trail is to the left. The Madrone Trail, the right fork, is the return route.

Take the narrow Earl Moser Trail, the second path to the left, and begin the loop. Head up the hill through the pine forest.

Curve right at the east park boundary, and parallel the fence to the south. Climb a few short, steep switchbacks to the ridge at a small meadow. Continue along the ridge past viewing benches to an unsigned trail split. Stay to the right, traversing the hillside just below the ridge. Descend into the ravine at the southeast park boundary. Follow the draw deeper downhill to a signed T-junction with the Madrone Trail. Take the right fork on the wide, grassy path. Pass a junction with the Ceanothus Trail on the left. Climb the short hill, completing the loop at the 5-way junction. Return to the trailhead on the left. ▪

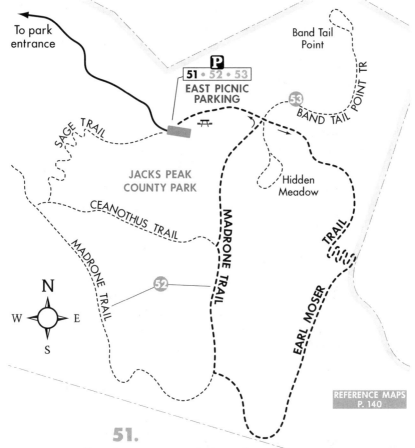

51.
Earl Moser–Madrone Loop
JACKS PEAK COUNTY PARK

52. Sage—Madrone—Ceanothus Loop
JACKS PEAK COUNTY PARK

Hiking distance: 2 miles round trip
Hiking time: 1 hour
Configuration: out-and-back with large loop
Elevation gain: 350 feet
Difficulty: easy
Exposure: shaded forest and open meadows
Dogs: allowed
Maps: U.S.G.S. Seaside · Jacks Peak County Park map

This forested loop trail begins from the park's east trailhead and drops down the hillside into a lush ravine. The trail circles the meadowland through a profusion of vegetation and wildflowers. The hike offers a quiet, contemplative walk through a cool forest. It is an excellent area for bird watching.

To the trailhead

From Highway 1 in Monterey, take the Highway 68 East/Salinas exit, and drive 1.6 miles to the signed turnoff for Jacks Peak Park at Olmsted Road. Turn right and continue 1 mile to Jacks Peak Drive. Turn left and drive 1.2 miles to the entrance station and road split. Turn left and follow the park road 0.4 miles to the East Picnic parking area at the end of the road. An entrance fee is required.

The hike

Take the signed Sage Trail from the southwest end of the parking area. The hillside path descends to a junction with the Pine Trail. Bear left, staying on the Sage Trail, and zigzag down the hillside to a T-junction at a half mile. Begin the loop to the left on the Ceanothus Trail. The path meanders through the lush forest of pine and oak with numerous small dips and rises. The trail ends at a junction with the Madrone Trail at 0.8 miles. Bear right and stroll along the level path through the forest with a thick understory of vegetation. Pass the Earl Moser Trail (Hike 51) on the left, and wind through the forest, looping back to the west. At the next trail junction, the Madrone Trail continues straight. Instead, take

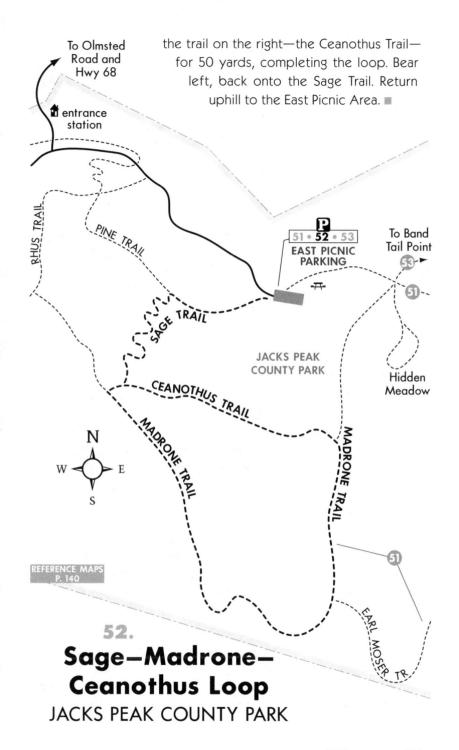

the trail on the right—the Ceanothus Trail—
for 50 yards, completing the loop. Bear
left, back onto the Sage Trail. Return
uphill to the East Picnic Area. ■

To Olmsted
Road and
Hwy 68

entrance
station

RHUS TRAIL

PINE TRAIL

SAGE TRAIL

CEANOTHUS TRAIL

MADRONE TRAIL

MADRONE TRAIL

P
51 • **52** • 53
**EAST PICNIC
PARKING**

To Band
Tail Point

53

51

JACKS PEAK
COUNTY PARK

Hidden
Meadow

N
W   E
S

51

REFERENCE MAPS
P. 140

EARL MOSER TR.

52.
Sage–Madrone–
Ceanothus Loop
JACKS PEAK COUNTY PARK

53. Band Tail Point and Hidden Meadow
JACKS PEAK COUNTY PARK

Hiking distance: 1.6 miles round trip
Hiking time: 45 minutes
Configuration: two out-and-back trails with small loops
Elevation gain: 150 feet
Difficulty: easy
Exposure: shaded forest and open meadow
Dogs: allowed
Maps: U.S.G.S. Seaside · Jacks Peak County Park map

This hike offers two short, easy destinations from the east trail-head at Jacks Peak County Park. The trail to the north leads to Band Tail Point, a vista point that overlooks the Monterey Peninsula. A trail in the opposite direction leads to Hidden Meadow, an isolated meadow in a sea of Monterey pines. The park is home to one of the last remaining stands of Monterey pines in the United States.

To the trailhead

From Highway 1 in Monterey, take the Highway 68 East/Salinas exit, and drive 1.6 miles to the signed turnoff for Jacks Peak Park at Olmsted Road. Turn right and continue 1 mile to Jacks Peak Drive. Turn left and drive 1.2 miles to the entrance station and road split. Turn left and follow the park road 0.4 miles to the East Picnic parking area at the end of the road. An entrance fee is required.

The hike

Begin the hike on the signed Earl Moser Trail across from the rest-rooms. Pass the picnic area and head east, overlooking Monterey Bay. A soft padding of pine needles carpet the path to a 5-way junction. The routes to both Band Tail Point and Hidden Meadow begin from this crossroad.

To begin, take the far left path towards Band Tail Point. The wide path descends gradually. As the trail curves left, ascend a short, steep eroded hill to a trail split. The split forms a small loop that circles the point. The views of the bay can be spotted through the trees. Complete the loop and return to the 5-way junction.

From this direction, three trails head to the left. (The return trail is on the right.) Take the wide middle left fork up the hill to a trail split. Again, a small loop circles the area. Hidden Meadow is on the east side of the loop. To return, retrace your steps. ■

To entrance station

JACKS PEAK COUNTY PARK

Band Tail Point

EARL MOSER TR

BAND TAIL POINT TR

SAGE TRAIL

P
51 • 52 • 53
EAST PICNIC PARKING

Hidden Meadow

CEANOTHUS TRAIL

MADRONE TRAIL

TRAIL

N
W — E
S

EARL MOSER

51

52

MADRONE TRAIL

REFERENCE MAPS
P. 140

53.

Band Tail Point and Hidden Meadow
JACKS PEAK COUNTY PARK

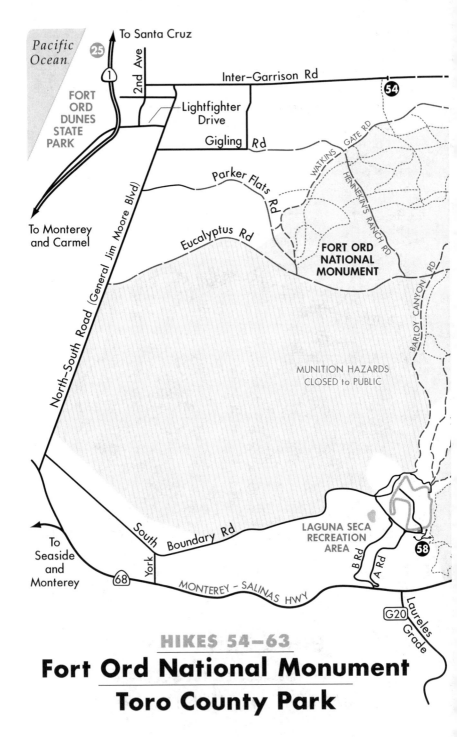

Pacific Ocean

To Santa Cruz

To Monterey and Carmel

FORT ORD DUNES STATE PARK

2nd Ave

Inter-Garrison Rd

54

Lightfighter Drive

Gigling Rd

WATKINS GATE RD

HENNEKIN'S RANCH RD

Parker Flats Rd

Eucalyptus Rd

FORT ORD NATIONAL MONUMENT

North-South Road (General Jim Moore Blvd)

BARLOY CANYON RD

MUNITION HAZARDS CLOSED to PUBLIC

LAGUNA SECA RECREATION AREA

South Boundary Rd

To Seaside and Monterey

68

York

B Rd

A Rd

58

MONTEREY – SALINAS HWY

G20

Laureles Grade

HIKES 54–63

Fort Ord National Monument
Toro County Park

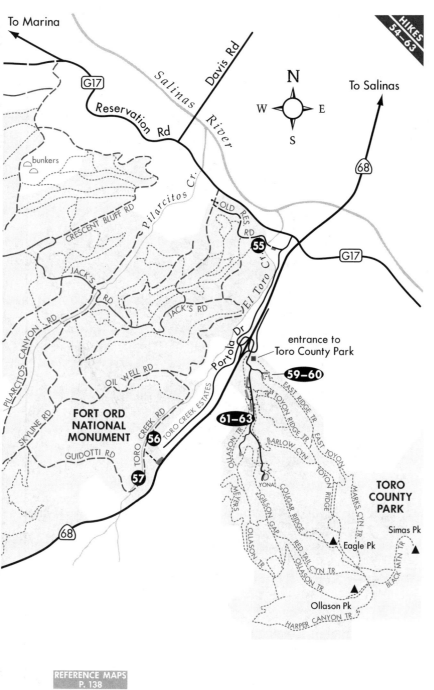

To Marina

G17

Salinas River

Davis Rd

Reservation Rd

N
W — E
S

To Salinas

68

bunkers

CRESCENT BLUFF RD

Pilarcitos Cr.

OLD RES. RD

55

G17

JACK'S RD

JACK'S RD

El Toro Cr.

PILARCITOS CANYON RD

SKYLINE RD

OIL WELL RD

Portola Dr

entrance to
Toro County Park

59-60

EAST RIDGE TR.

EAST TOYON RIDGE TR.

EAST TOYON RIDGE

MARKS CYN. TR.

61-63

FORT ORD
NATIONAL
MONUMENT

TORO CREEK RD

TORO CREEK ESTATES

56

GUIDOTTI RD

57

OLLASON TR.

MEYERS

BARLOW CYN.

YONA

COUGAR RIDGE

GILSON GAP

RED TAIL CYN. TR.

OLLASON TR.

OLLASON TR.

TORO
COUNTY
PARK

BLACK MTN TR.

Simas Pk

Eagle Pk

Ollason Pk

HARPER CANYON TR.

68

REFERENCE MAPS
P. 138

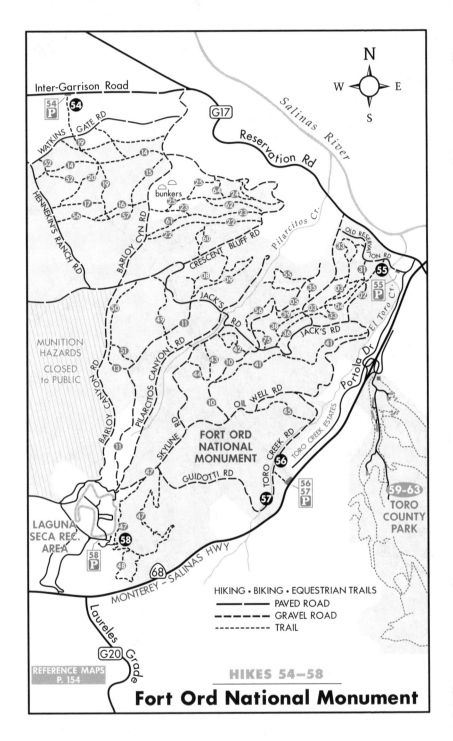

N
W E
S

Inter-Garrison Road

54 P 54

G17

Salinas River

Reservation Rd

WATKINS GATE RD

19

52 14
52 20 19
17 16
56 57

HENNEKIN'S RANCH RD

BARLOY CYN RD

14

15

bunkers
25
25 23
61
22

25
64
62
23
22

60

CRESCENT BLUFF RD

08 09

JACK'S

50

49 11

RD

Pilarcitos Cr.

33

OLD RESERVATION RD

31

55 P

55

55
35
92
03
56 04
38
75
36 JACK'S RD
41

05
03
03

MUNITION
HAZARDS
CLOSED
to PUBLIC

BARLOY CANYON RD

51

13

PILARCITOS CANYON RD

43
44

12

10

41

El Toro Cr.

Portola Dr.

10

OIL WELL RD

45

11

SKYLINE RD

47

FORT ORD
NATIONAL
MONUMENT

GUIDOTTI RD

TORO CREEK RD

TORO CREEK ESTATES

56

56
57 P

47

47

LAGUNA
SECA REC.
AREA

58

58 P

48

68

MONTEREY – SALINAS HWY

59-63
TORO
COUNTY
PARK

HIKING • BIKING • EQUESTRIAN TRAILS
———————— PAVED ROAD
– – – – – – GRAVEL ROAD
········· TRAIL

Laureles Grade

G20

REFERENCE MAPS
P. 154

HIKES 54–58

Fort Ord National Monument

54. Jerry Smith Access Corridor
NORTH TRAILHEAD
FORT ORD NATIONAL MONUMENT

Hiking distance: 1—8 miles round trip
Hiking time: 30 minutes—5 hours
Configuration: several inter-connecting trails
Elevation gain: 100 to 400 feet
Difficulty: easy to moderate
Exposure: mostly exposed rolling hills
Dogs: allowed
Maps: U.S.G.S. Marina and Salinas · Fort Ord public lands map

map
page 159

Fort Ord was a U.S. Army post established in 1917. It was primarily used as a maneuvering area and artillery training field. In 1994, the base was closed and set aside for conservation, becoming a nature reserve. At the time, the fort was the largest U.S. base to be closed. Many of the abandoned military buildings still remain. In 2012, Fort Ord was designated as a national monument.

The public lands offer 86 miles of trail that crisscross over 7,200 acres. The acreage is some of the last undeveloped land on the Monterey Peninsula. The multi-use parkland is open to hikers, bikers, and equestrians. It is also popular with wildlife and nature photographers. The road and trail system throughout the Fort Ord land is closed to vehicles.

This hike begins from the northern end of the undeveloped open space on the Jerry Smith Access Corridor. The half-mile dirt path leads to a maze of trails looping through the natural wildlands. The hike follows mostly single-track trail through chaparral-covered rolling hills and oak woodlands.

To the trailhead

MONTEREY. Drive 8 miles north of Monterey on Highway 1 to Seaside and take the Light Fighter Drive exit. Drive 0.3 miles east to 2nd Avenue. Turn left (north) and go 0.5 miles to Inter-Garrison Road (formerly 3rd Street). Turn right and continue 2.8 miles east to the trailhead and parking area at the end of the road.

MARINA. From Marina, take the Reservation Road exit. Drive 2.9 miles east to Imjin Road and turn right. Continue 0.6 miles to Abrams Drive and turn left. Drive 0.9 miles to a T-junction with Inter-Garrison Road. Turn left and go a half mile east to the trailhead and parking area at the end of the road.

SALINAS. From Highway 101 in Salinas, take the Monterey Peninsula/Highway 68 exit. Drive 4.5 miles to Reservation Road and turn right. Take Reservation Road west to Imjim Road and turn left. Continue 0.6 miles to Abrams Drive and turn left. Drive 0.9 miles to a T-junction with Inter-Garrison Road. Turn left and go a half mile to the trailhead and parking area at the end of the road.

The hike

Pass the trailhead kiosk and take the signed Jerry Smith Access Corridor. Head south on the sandy path, passing closed trails on both the left and right. Cross the open grassland and shaded oak forest. At a half mile, the trail ends at the paved Watkins Gate Road. Cross the road to an information kiosk.

From here is a mosaic of looping trails that offer endless hiking options. The branching trails include frequent intersections. Some junctions are signed, others are not. What the Bureau of Land Management map shows as trail numbers and road names is not always consistent with what is encountered while hiking. To eliminate confusion, an exact route through the maze of trails is not included in these directions. Although it can seem perplexing, it would be difficult to get lost. The myriad of connecting trails that are accessible from this trailhead generally lie between Watkins Gate Road, Hennekin's Ranch Road (both paved), and Barloy Canyon Road (gravel). Most of the trails are single track. ∎

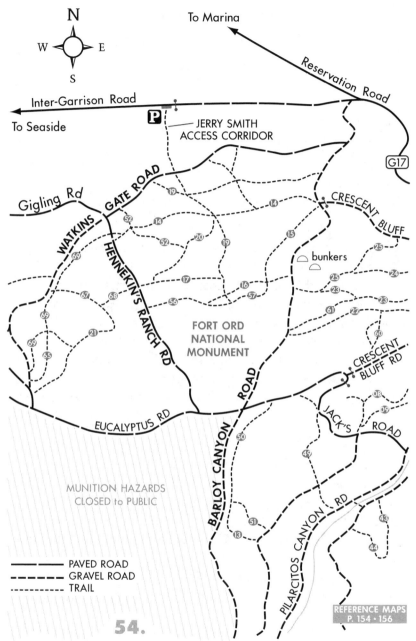

N
W E
S

To Marina

Reservation Road

Inter-Garrison Road

To Seaside

P

JERRY SMITH
ACCESS CORRIDOR

G17

Gigling Rd

WATKINS GATE ROAD

CRESCENT BLUFF

19

52
14
14
20
19
15
25

69

HENNEKIN'S RANCH RD

52

bunkers

17
16
57
56

25
23
24
23

67
68
61
21
60

69
21
CRESCENT BLUFF RD

69
55

FORT ORD
NATIONAL
MONUMENT

BARLOY CANYON ROAD

08
09

EUCALYPTUS RD

JACK'S ROAD

50

49

MUNITION HAZARDS
CLOSED to PUBLIC

PILARCITOS CANYON RD

51

43

13

44

PAVED ROAD
GRAVEL ROAD
TRAIL

REFERENCE MAPS
P. 154 · 156

54.

Jerry Smith Access Corridor
FORT ORD NATIONAL MONUMENT

55. Old Reservoir—
Engineer Canyon Loop
FORT ORD NATIONAL MONUMENT

Hiking distance: 4.6-mile loop
Hiking time: 2.5 hours
Configuration: loop
Elevation gain: 300 feet
Difficulty: easy to moderate
Exposure: open grassland and forested draws
Dogs: allowed
Maps: U.S.G.S. Spreckels and Salinas · Fort Ord public lands map

For thousands of years, the Fort Ord land was inhabited by the Ohlone Indians. The area is now a recreational parkland and wildlife habitat managed by the Bureau of Land Management. The area includes thousands of acres of rolling grasslands, oak forests, and seasonal wetlands. Deer, bobcats, and small mammals can be observed year-round.

This hike makes a loop through a maze of trails in the northeast end of the parklands. The route follows old gravel roads into a grove of old coast oaks and across open, rolling hillsides, offering eastward views of Salinas Valley and the Sierra de Salinas ridge.

To the trailhead

MONTEREY. From Highway 1 in Monterey, take the Highway 68 East/Salinas exit. Drive 13 miles to Reservation Road. Turn left and drive one block to Portola Drive. Turn left again and continue 0.4 miles to the parking area on the left at the end of the road.

SALINAS. From Highway 101 in Salinas, take the Monterey Peninsula/Highway 68 exit. Drive 4.5 miles to Reservation Road and turn right. Drive one block to Portola Drive. Turn left and continue 0.4 miles to the parking area on the left at the end of the road.

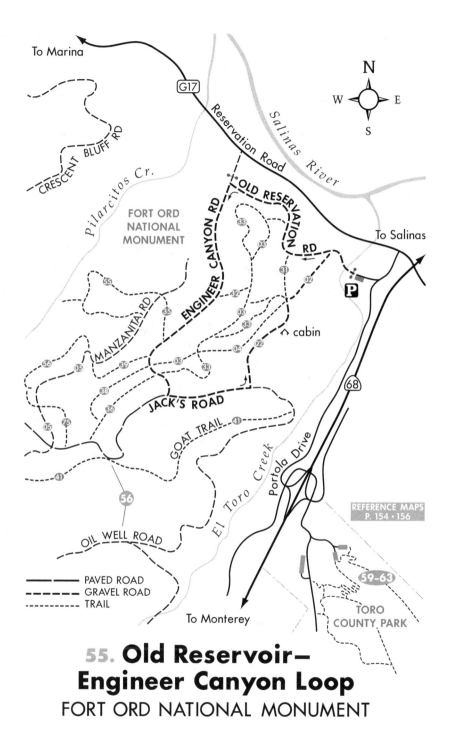

To Marina

G17

Reservation Road

Salinas River

N
W E
S

CRESCENT BLUFF RD

Pilarcitos Cr.

OLD RESERVATION

RD

FORT ORD
NATIONAL
MONUMENT

ENGINEER CANYON RD

To Salinas

55

33

03

31

02

P

42

35

03

33

04

02

↑ cabin

MANZANITA RD

56

05

39

03

33

38

36

JACK'S ROAD

05

75

GOAT TRAIL

41

68

41

56

OIL WELL ROAD

El Toro Creek

Portola Drive

REFERENCE MAPS
P. 154 · 156

——— PAVED ROAD
------- GRAVEL ROAD
········· TRAIL

To Monterey

59-63

TORO
COUNTY PARK

55. **Old Reservoir–**
Engineer Canyon Loop
FORT ORD NATIONAL MONUMENT

The hike

Walk past the trailhead gate at the end of the road, and follow Old Reservation Road, curving into the folded, hilly terrain. Pass the Trail 30 cut-across on the right to Trail 02 on the left. Begin the loop to the right, staying on Old Reservation Road through the rolling hills and tree-filled canyons. Caves can be seen on the hilltops to the left. Crest a small hill to panoramic views of Salinas Valley. Trail 30 rejoins the main trail and descends to a signed junction at the gated park boundary. Bear left on the unpaved Engineer Canyon Road, and wind up the canyon into the hilly interior of the park. Oak trees form a mosaic pattern on the grassy hillsides. Stroll through a grove of live oaks, passing Trail 32. Climb out of the canyon, curving left past Trail 39 to a 5-way junction. Views extend across the valley to Toro County Park.

Descend to a T-junction with Jack's Road. To the right, Jack's Road is paved. Bear left on the unpaved road, heading down the open valley. Just before reaching the pond, which can be seen to the right, is a Y-junction. Leave Jack's Road and take Trail 02 to the left. Wind uphill through oak groves to a large grassy meadow and trail split. Stay to the right, following the east edge of the meadow. Pass an old log cabin on the right to a 4-way junction with Trails 31 and 34 on a saddle. Curve right, staying on Trail 02, and sharply descend through oak trees to complete the loop on Old Reservation Road. Return to the right. ■

56. Oil Well Road—Goat Trail Loop
FORT ORD NATIONAL MONUMENT

Hiking distance: 6-mile loop
Hiking time: 3 hours
Configuration: out-and-back with large loop
Elevation gain: 500 feet
Difficulty: moderate
Exposure: a mix of open slopes and forested pockets
Dogs: allowed
Maps: U.S.G.S. Spreckels · Fort Ord public lands map

map
page 164

The Fort Ord trail system winds through rolling hills, seasonal wetlands, coastal live oak forests, and sandstone ridges. Views extend from the Salinas River Valley to Monterey Bay. This 6-mile loop through the heart of the parkland begins from Highway 68 (Monterey-Salinas Highway) and explores the varied landscapes, including overlooks, oak groves, and a pond.

To the trailhead

MONTEREY. From Highway 1 in Monterey, take the Highway 68 East/Salinas exit. Drive 10 miles to the unsigned (but large) Fort Ord trailhead parking area on the left. The parking area is 2.7 miles east of Laureles Grade.

SALINAS. From Highway 101 in Salinas, take the Monterey Peninsula/Highway 68 exit. Drive 7.5 miles to the trailhead parking area on the right at the west end of Toro Creek Estates. The parking area is 1.5 miles west of Toro County Park.

The hike

Follow the signed Fort Ord trail a short distance to a junction with Toro Creek Road. Take the right fork, parallel to Toro Creek Estates and the El Toro Creek streambed. Just past the baseball fields, cross the streambed to the open grasslands. Cross the south edge of the pasturelands, and curve left into the hills. Climb over the lower hill to a posted junction with Oil Well Road.

Begin the loop to the left, steadily gaining elevation up the draw. Pass the upper end of Trail 45 on the left to the signed Trail 10 on the right. Bear right on Trail 10, traversing the hillside.

Pass an eroded drainage to a fork with Trail 41 (Goat Trail) at 2.5 miles. Take Trail 41 to the right, traversing the oak-dotted draw. The footpath weaves through folds in the hills to a Y-fork. The left fork connects with the paved Jack's Road, and the right fork continues on Goat Trail. Either route can be taken, as the trails reconnect up ahead. (Jack's Road is the shorter, easier route. Goat Trail is a gorgeous, serpentine rollercoaster route, winding through shady oak groves with scenic overlooks.) Goat Trail ends by a pond at a junction with Jack's Road. Take the road to the right, which becomes Oil Well Road. Follow the contours of the hills on the lower slopes, overlooking homes on the left. Complete the loop at the Toro Creek Road junction. Bear left and retrace your route. ■

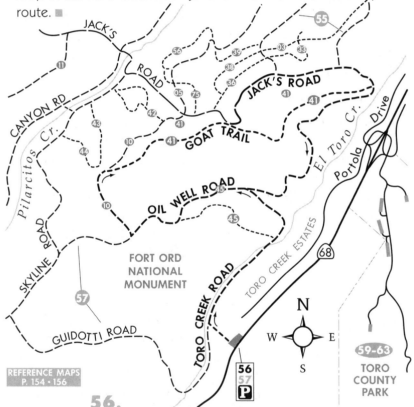

56.
Oil Well Road–Goat Trail Loop
FORT ORD NATIONAL MONUMENT

57. Guidotti—Skyline—Oil Well Loop
FORT ORD NATIONAL MONUMENT

Hiking distance: 6-mile loop
Hiking time: 3 hours
Configuration: loop
Elevation gain: 600 feet
Difficulty: moderate
Exposure: open rolling hills with forested pockets
Dogs: allowed
Maps: U.S.G.S. Spreckels · Fort Ord public lands map

**map
page 166**

This 6-mile loop hike begins from Highway 68 and follows wide, sandy paths through a cross-section of habitats along the former army base land. The hike includes rolling grasslands, sandstone rock outcroppings, a canyon, and a seasonal streambed.

To the trailhead

MONTEREY. From Highway 1 in Monterey, take the Highway 68 East/Salinas exit. Drive 10 miles to the unsigned (but large) Fort Ord trailhead parking area on the left. The parking area is 2.7 miles east of Laureles Grade.

SALINAS. From Highway 101 in Salinas, take the Monterey Peninsula/Highway 68 exit. Drive 7.5 miles to the trailhead parking area on the right at the west end of Toro Creek Estates. The parking area is 1.5 miles west of Toro County Park.

The hike

Walk through the Fort Ord trail gate, and take the wide path to a T-junction. Begin the loop to the left on Toro Creek Road. Cross the rolling grasslands dotted with eucalyptus, oak, and maple trees. The sandy path parallels Highway 68 for a half mile, then curves north on Guidotti Road. Cross an old concrete bridge, built in 1911, and head up the rolling hills. Climb the grade to the ridge and curve north. From the ridge are views of Toro County Park and Salinas. Follow the undulating ridge, passing Trail 47 on the left, to the posted Skyline Road at 2.4 miles.

Take the Skyline Road to the right on the ridge above Pilarcitos Canyon. At the signed Y-fork, the Skyline Trail curves left and descends into Pilarcitos Canyon. Bear right on Oil Well Road, and begin the long and gradual descent. Sandstone rock outcroppings line the hilltop on the left. The winding road passes Trail 10 on the left to Trail 45 on the right. Leave the road and take the footpath to the right, crossing the grassy slopes. Descend along the ridge to a pond at a T-junction on the valley floor. Bear right, crossing the El Toro Creek streambed. The path skirts the north edge of Toro Creek Estates through tree groves, completing the loop. ■

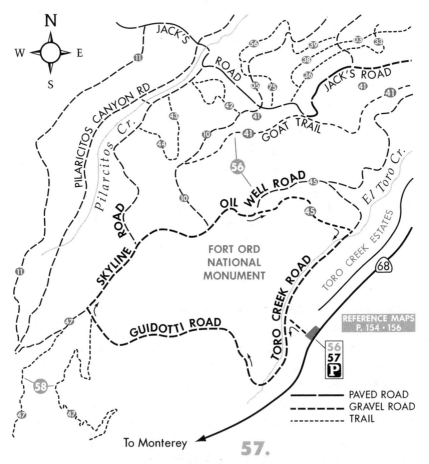

Guidotti–Skyline–Oil Well Loop
FORT ORD NATIONAL MONUMENT

58. Laguna Seca Loop
FORT ORD NATIONAL MONUMENT

Hiking distance: 4 miles round trip
Hiking time: 2 hours
Configuration: loop
Elevation gain: 350 feet
Difficulty: easy to moderate
Exposure: mostly exposed grassland
Dogs: allowed
Maps: U.S.G.S. Spreckles · Fort Ord public lands map

map
page 169

Laguna Seca Raceway is an auto and motorcycle race track adjacent to the south end of Fort Ord National Monument. (Laguna Seca means *dry lake* in Spanish.) It was originally constructed in 1957 on a small portion of the U.S. Army's Fort Ord land. In 1974, the Fort Ord property was deeded over to the Monterey County Parks Department. In 2012, it was designated as a national monument.

This hike begins from a campground in Laguna Seca and forms a loop through the undeveloped wildlands to the west of the raceway course. The hike meanders through the natural reserve on rolling hills and oak-dotted slopes, ranging from the valley floor to the ridges. Along the way are views that span from Salinas to the ocean.

To the trailhead

MONTEREY. From Highway 1 in Monterey, take the Highway 68 East/Salinas exit. Drive 6.5 miles to the posted Laguna Seca Recreation Area turnoff on the left. (The turnoff is 0.3 miles prior to the Laureles Grade junction.) Turn left and immediately turn right. Wind one mile up the hill to a stop sign and junction. Turn right and continue 0.15 miles to a dirt parking lot on the left that is signed "BLM Trail Access Parking." It is located directly across from the restrooms on the right. Turn left and park. An entrance fee is required.

SALINAS. From Highway 101 in Salinas, take the Monterey Peninsula/Highway 68 exit. Drive 11 miles to the posted Laguna Seca Recreation Area turnoff on the right. (The turnoff is 0.3

miles after the Laureles Grade junction.) Turn right and immediately turn right again. Wind one mile up the hill to a stop sign and junction. Turn right and continue 0.15 miles to a dirt parking lot on the left, signed "BLM Trail Access Parking." It is located directly across from the restrooms on the right. Turn left and park. An entrance fee is required.

Additional trail accesses are at 1.6 miles on the right (with parking on the left) and at 1.7 miles (at the end of the access road). Turn right and park by the imposing black tower.

The hike

From the first parking lot, walk 70 yards up the road to the left bend. Veer right by the trail kiosk and into the Grand Prix Campground. Continue 60 yards and curve right, following the trail signs, then curve left to the end of the campground road to the trailhead by campsite 139. Pass through the fence to an overlook of the valley, the open rolling hills, and the surrounding mountains. Walk 40 yards to a junction with Trail 47.

Begin the loop to the left, hiking clockwise. Traverse the oak-dotted slope to a narrow dirt road on the ridge. The left fork leads to an access trail by a pedestrian bridge over the motorway. Bear right and follow the near-level ridge northeast, with a view across Salinas all the way to Moss Landing and the ocean. Drop down to a junction with Skyline Road. Stay to the right while enjoying the 360-degree panoramas. Continue a short distance to a junction with Guidotti Road at an east-running ridge. Bear right on Guidotti Road and walk 80 yards. Go to the right on Trail 47. Follow the ridge on a downward slope. Make a looping right bend, dropping into the valley. Cross the valley floor and loop back to the left. Wind down to an adjacent canyon bottom, then weave up the hillside to another ridge. Loop right and follow the ridge to the west. Climb up the hillside and complete the loop. Go left 40 yards, returning to the trailhead in the campground. ■

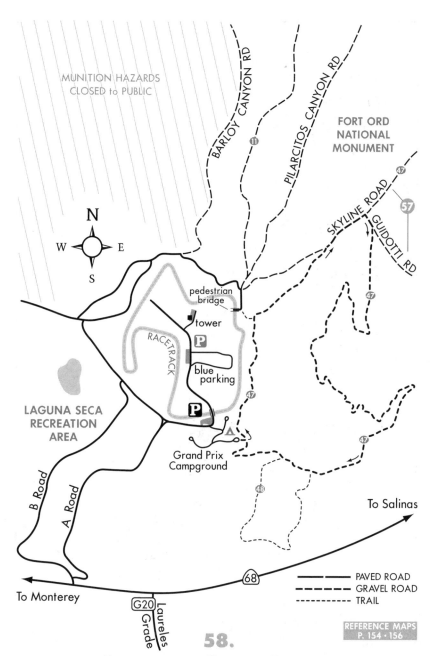

MUNITION HAZARDS
CLOSED to PUBLIC

BARLOY CANYON RD

11

PILARCITOS CANYON RD

FORT ORD
NATIONAL
MONUMENT

SKYLINE ROAD

47

57

GUIDOTTI RD

N
W E
S

pedestrian
bridge

tower

RACETRACK

P

blue
parking

47

47

47

P

LAGUNA SECA
RECREATION
AREA

Grand Prix
Campground

48

B Road

A Road

To Salinas

68

To Monterey

G20

Laureles
Grade

PAVED ROAD
GRAVEL ROAD
TRAIL

REFERENCE MAPS
P. 154 · 156

58.

Laguna Seca Loop
FORT ORD NATIONAL MONUMENT

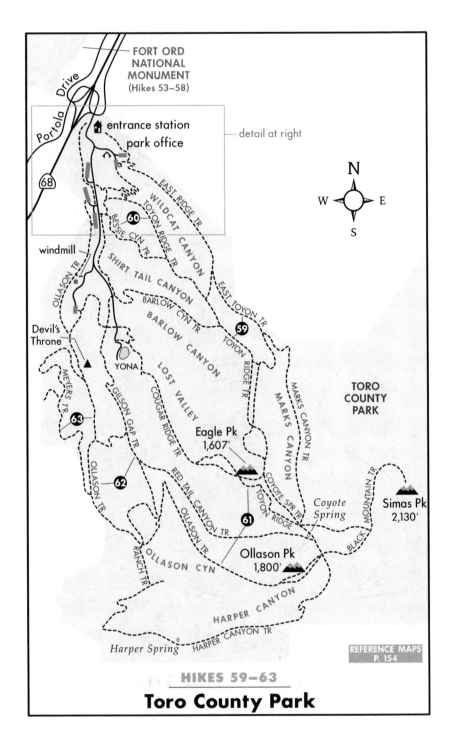

FORT ORD
NATIONAL
MONUMENT
(Hikes 53–58)

Portola Drive

entrance station
park office

detail at right

68

EAST RIDGE TR

WILDCAT CANYON

TOYON RIDGE TR

BESSIE CYN TR

60

windmill

OLLASON TR

SHIRT TAIL CANYON

BARLOW CYN TR

EAST TOYON TR

BARLOW CANYON

59

TOYON RIDGE TR

Devil's
Throne

YONA

LOST VALLEY

MARKS CANYON TR

MARKS CANYON

TORO
COUNTY
PARK

MEYERS TR

63

GILSON GAP TR

COUGAR RIDGE TR

Eagle Pk
1,607'

COYOTE SPR TR

TOYON RIDGE

Coyote
Spring

BLACK MOUNTAIN TR

Simas Pk
2,130'

62

OLLASON TR

RED TAIL CANYON TR

OLLASON TR

61

Ollason Pk
1,800'

RANCH TR

OLLASON CYN

HARPER CANYON

Harper Spring

HARPER CANYON TR

REFERENCE MAPS
P. 154

N
W E
S

HIKES 59–63

Toro County Park

59. Eagle Peak
East Ridge—Eagle Peak—Toyon Ridge Loop
TORO COUNTY PARK

Hiking distance: 6.4-mile loop
Hiking time: 3 hours
Configuration: loop
Elevation gain: 1,400 feet
Difficulty: moderate to strenuous
Exposure: shaded oak woodlands; open ridges and meadows
Dogs: allowed
Maps: U.S.G.S. Spreckels · Toro County Park map

**map
page 173**

Eagle Peak is a grassy, 1,607-foot knoll at the top of Cougar Ridge in Toro County Park. From the peak are 360-degree panoramas that extend from Salinas Valley to Monterey Bay. This long and narrow loop hike leads through oak woodlands, chaparral ridges, and grassland meadows with wildflowers. En route to Eagle Peak are overlooks of the forested canyons.

To the trailhead

MONTEREY. From Highway 1 in Monterey, take the Highway 68 East/Salinas exit, and drive 11.6 miles to the signed turnoff for

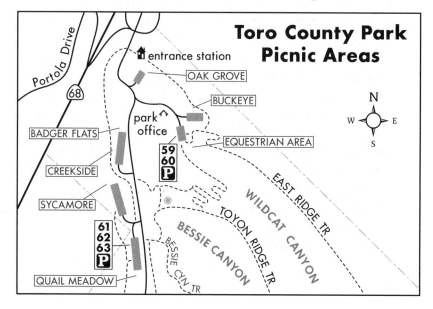

Toro Park on Portola Drive. Turn right and continue a short distance to the park entrance station. Follow the park road 0.1 mile to the park office turnoff by the flagpole. Turn left and continue 0.1 mile to a road split. Park in the lot on the right. An entrance fee is required.

SALINAS. From Highway 101 in Salinas, take the Monterey Peninsula/Highway 68 exit. Drive 6 miles to Portola Drive, and follow the signs to the park entrance.

The hike

Take the footpath or equestrian trail east up the oak-covered hillside, where the two trails join. Emerge to the scrub-covered ridge overlooking Wildcat Canyon. Follow the ridge along the northeastern park boundary. At the head of the canyon is a posted junction. The right fork climbs to a junction with the Toyon Ridge Trail for a shorter 2.8-mile loop.

Instead, take the left fork on the East Toyon Trail, dropping down into the next drainage. Cross the oak-filled valley floor to a large grassy meadow and trail fork. The left fork—the Marks Canyon Trail—leads to Black Mountain and Marks Canyon. Stay to the right, climbing up the east-facing hillside above Marks Canyon to a T-junction with the Toyon Loop. For a shorter 4.2-mile loop, take the right fork 20 yards to the Toyon Ridge Trail and bear right, heading northwest back to the parking lot.

To continue to Eagle Peak, bear left on the cliffside path to a signed junction. The right fork is the return route. For now, continue straight, above Barlow Canyon. Walk through the trail gate, and curve left around the knoll to the ridge. Follow the ridge to the right through oak-dotted grasslands, passing the Coyote Spring Trail on the left. Climb the treeless knoll to Eagle Peak.

After enjoying the views, return along the same route to the signed junction. Take the left fork and descend on Toyon Ridge between Marks Canyon and Barlow Canyon. Pass the Bessie Canyon Trail to a signed junction. Leave the ridge to the right, zigzagging down into wooded Wildcat Canyon. Head down canyon and pass a horse corral, returning to the parking area. ■

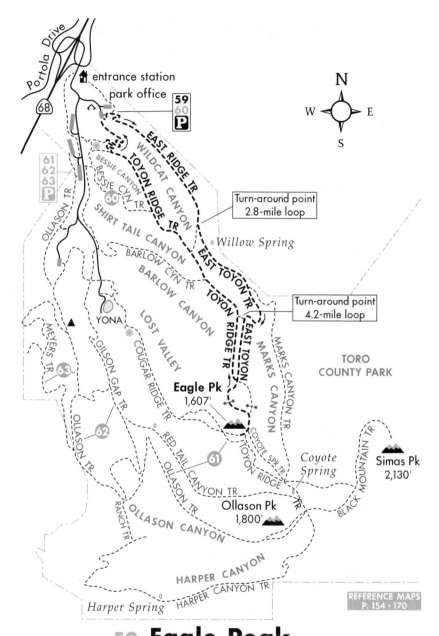

Portola Drive

68

♿ entrance station
park office

59
60
P

N
W   E
S

61
62
63
P

EAST RIDGE TR

WILDCAT CANYON

TOYON RIDGE TR

OLLASON TR

BESSIE CANYON
BESSIE CYN TR
60

SHIRT TAIL CANYON

BARLOW CYN TR

BARLOW CANYON

Turn-around point
2.8-mile loop

Willow Spring

EAST TOYON TR

Turn-around point
4.2-mile loop

YONA

LOST VALLEY

MEYERS TR

63

GILSON GAP TR

COUGAR RIDGE TR

62

OLLASON TR

RED TAIL CANYON TR

61

TOYON RIDGE TR

EAST TOYON

MARKS CANYON TR

MARKS CANYON

COYOTE SPR TR

Eagle Pk
1,607'

TORO
COUNTY PARK

Simas Pk
2,130'

*Coyote
Spring*

BLACK MOUNTAIN TR

OLLASON TR

RANCH TR

OLLASON CANYON

Ollason Pk
1,800'

TOYON RIDGE TR

HARPER CANYON

Harper Spring

HARPER CANYON TR

REFERENCE MAPS
P. 154 • 170

59. **Eagle Peak**
East Ridge–East Toyon–Toyon Ridge Loop
TORO COUNTY PARK

60. Toyon Ridge—Bessie Canyon Loop
TORO COUNTY PARK

Hiking distance: 2.5 miles round trip
Hiking time: 1.5 hour
Configuration: out-and-back with loop
Elevation gain: 550 feet
Difficulty: easy
Exposure: open ridges and wooded hills
Dogs: allowed
Maps: U.S.G.S. Spreckels · Toro County Park map

This short loop hike in Toro Park leads through oak woodlands in Wildcat Canyon to Toyon Ridge, which overlooks both Wildcat and Bessie Canyons. The trail returns down Bessie Ridge above Shirt Tail Canyon.

To the trailhead

MONTEREY. From Highway 1 in Monterey, take the Highway 68 East/Salinas exit, and drive 11.6 miles to the signed turnoff for Toro Park on Portola Drive. Turn right and continue a short distance to the park entrance station. Follow the park road 0.1 mile to the park office turnoff by the flagpole. Turn left and continue 0.1 mile to a road split. Park in the lot on the right. An entrance fee is required.

SALINAS. From Highway 101 in Salinas, take the Monterey Peninsula/Highway 68 exit. Drive 6 miles to Portola Drive, and follow the signs to the park entrance.

The hike

Take the path at the far end of the parking area. Pass the corral and head up Wildcat Canyon through the oak woodland. Switchbacks ascend the hillside to a junction on Toyon Ridge. Take the wide trail to the left, following the ridge that separates Wildcat and Bessie Canyons. At just under one mile is a signed junction with the Bessie Canyon Trail.

Leave the Toyon Ridge Trail, and bear right on the Bessie Canyon Trail. Descend along the ridge between Bessie Canyon on the right and Shirt Tail Canyon on the left. As you near the bottom, wind through the eucalyptus trees towards the park road. On the right—30 yards before reaching the park road—take the unpaved road that winds up the hillside. Pass a water tank on the left, and complete the loop at the Toyon Ridge Trail. Bear left into the wooded canyon, and return along the canyon floor. ▪

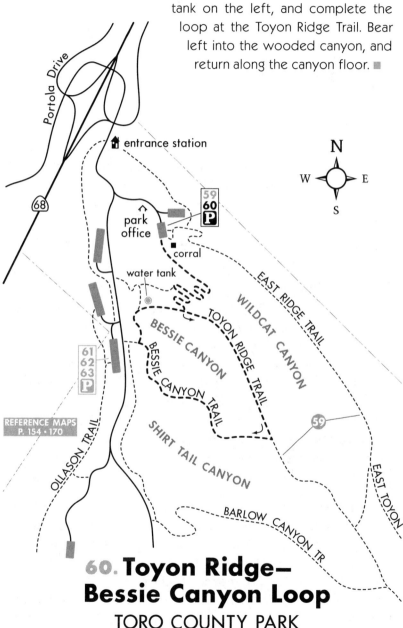

60. Toyon Ridge–Bessie Canyon Loop
TORO COUNTY PARK

61. Ollason Peak
Ollason Trail—Cougar Ridge Loop
TORO COUNTY PARK

Hiking distance: 8-mile loop
Hiking time: 4.5 hours
Configuration: loop
Elevation gain: 1,600 feet
Difficulty: strenuous
Exposure: open ridges and wooded hills
Dogs: allowed
Maps: U.S.G.S. Spreckels · Toro County Park map

Ollason Peak is a bare, 1,800-foot knoll on the higher ridges of Toro Park. From the peak, the views extend from Salinas Valley to Monterey Bay. En route to Ollason Peak, this loop hike passes Eagle Peak and travels through a variety of landscapes, including wooded hillsides, open ridges, and grassy meadows with scattered oaks and wildflowers.

To the trailhead

MONTEREY. From Highway 1 in Monterey, take the Highway 68 East/Salinas exit, and drive 11.6 miles to the signed turnoff for Toro Park on Portola Drive. Turn right and continue a short distance to the park entrance station. Follow the park road 0.5 miles, and turn right and a quick left into the Quail Meadow Picnic Area parking lot. An entrance fee is required.

SALINAS. From Highway 101 in Salinas, take the Monterey Peninsula/Highway 68 exit. Drive 6 miles to Portola Drive, and follow the signs to the park entrance.

The hike

From the far end of the parking lot, cross the footbridge to a T-junction. Bear left through groves of eucalyptus, oak, sycamore and bay trees. Head up the canyon on the unmarked Ollason Trail, passing a windmill on the left. Cross another bridge to an unpaved ranch road. Take the road to the right, and in a short distance, cross through a trail gate. Ascend the oak-dotted grasslands past a junction with the Gilson Gap Connector Trail on the

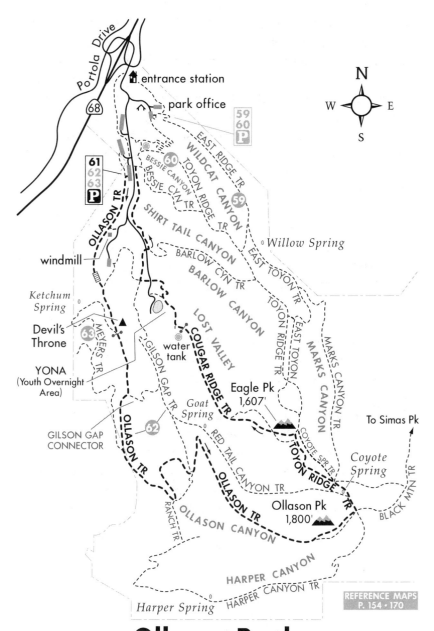

Portola Drive

entrance station

park office

N
W · E
S

59
60
P

61
62
63
P

EAST RIDGE TR

WILDCAT CANYON

60

BESSIE CANYON

BESSIE CYN TR

BESSIE CYN TR

TOYON RIDGE

59

OLLASON TR

SHIRT TAIL CANYON

windmill

BARLOW CYN TR

BARLOW CANYON

Willow Spring

EAST TOYON TR

TOYON RIDGE TR

Ketchum Spring

Devil's Throne

63

MEYERS TR

LOST VALLEY

water tank

COUGAR RIDGE TR

YONA
(Youth Overnight Area)

GILSON GAP TR

GILSON GAP CONNECTOR

62

OLLASON TR

Goat Spring

RED TAIL CANYON TR

EAST TOYON TR

MARKS CANYON TR

MARKS CANYON

Eagle Pk
1,607'

TOYON RIDGE TR

COYOTE SPR TR

To Simas Pk

Coyote Spring

BLACK MTN TR

OLLASON TR

RANCH TR

OLLASON CANYON

Ollason Pk
1,800'

HARPER CANYON

HARPER CANYON TR

Harper Spring

REFERENCE MAPS
P. 154 · 170

61. Ollason Peak
Ollason Trail–Cougar Ridge Loop
TORO COUNTY PARK

left. Cross the open meadows to a Y-junction with the Meyers Trail. Stay left to a junction with the Ranch Trail to Harper Spring. Bear left on the main trail, passing another junction on the left with the Gilson Gap Trail. At the sharp right bend, begin a steeper ascent to a ridge overlooking Harper Canyon. Follow the treeless ridge to a trail split. The left fork ascends the hill to Ollason Peak. The right fork skirts around the south side of the 1,800-foot peak. Both paths rejoin in a saddle and a 4-way junction to the east of the peak. From the junction, the middle fork leads east up to Simas Peak.

Take the Toyon Ridge Trail to the left (north). Pass eroded formations and descend through an oak canopy to a 5-way junction. Continue straight ahead on the signed Toyon Ridge Trail, and traverse the hillside to a posted junction with the Coyote Spring Trail. Curve left 100 yards to the Cougar Ridge Trail. Continue another 40 yards and bear right to the treeless summit of Eagle Peak. Descend from the peak on Cougar Ridge to a saddle. Follow the grassy ridge to a second saddle. Curve right through a fence opening, and wind through an oak grove. Cross through a trail gate by a water tank to a camping area and the YONA pond (Youth Overnight Area). Just before reaching the pond, the Cougar Ridge Trail bears right and zigzags down the hill to the campground road. (You may also pass the pond and walk down the road.) Cross the road and follow the trail 100 yards to the Gilson Gap Trail. Head down the canyon on the right, returning to the park road. Follow the road back or take the parallel trail on the right side of the road, returning to Quail Meadow Picnic Area. ■

62. Ollason Trail—Gilson Gap Loop
TORO COUNTY PARK

Hiking distance: 4.5-mile loop
Hiking time: 2.5 hours
Configuration: loop
Elevation gain: 800 feet
Difficulty: moderate
Exposure: forested valley and open meadows
Dogs: allowed
Maps: U.S.G.S. Spreckels · Toro County Park map

map
page 181

The Ollason-Gilson Gap loop leads up a forested valley floor to oak-dotted grasslands covered with wildflowers. The hike returns on the Gilson Gap Ridge through oak groves and meadows with panoramic mountain views. This route is a less strenuous option than the hike to Ollason Peak (Hike 61).

To the trailhead

MONTEREY. From Highway 1 in Monterey, take the Highway 68 East/Salinas exit, and drive 11.6 miles to the signed turnoff for Toro Park on Portola Drive. Turn right and continue a short distance to the park entrance station. Follow the park road 0.5 miles, and turn right and a quick left into the Quail Meadow Picnic Area parking lot. An entrance fee is required.

SALINAS. From Highway 101 in Salinas, take the Monterey Peninsula/Highway 68 exit. Drive 6 miles to Portola Drive, and follow the signs to the park entrance.

The hike

From the far end of the parking lot, walk over the footbridge to the unmarked Ollason Trail. Bear left along the west edge of the valley floor on the shady path. Pass a windmill on the left, and cross a footbridge over a streambed as the canyon narrows. Curve right and head up to an unpaved ranch road. Take the road to the right, and in a short distance, cross through a trail gate. Cross the oak-studded grasslands past a signed junction with the Gilson Gap Connector Trail on the left. Continue up the rolling grasslands, passing the Meyers Trail on the right, to a junction with the Ranch Trail to Harper Spring. Bear left on the main trail, and head uphill to an old ranch fenceline at the signed Gilson Gap Trail. To the right, the Ollason Trail leads up to Ollason Peak (Hike 61).

Leave the main trail and take the footpath on the left—the Gilson Gap Trail—through an oak grove. Cross through an opening in the fenceline, heading downhill and overlooking the valley. Pass the other end of the connector trail in an open meadow. Continue straight on the Gilson Gap Trail, following the ridge across oak-dotted meadows. Cross through a trail gate, and descend two switchbacks into a forested canyon. Near the valley floor, pass a junction with the Cougar Ridge Trail on the right. Parallel and merge with the campground road. Follow the road back or take the parallel trail on the right side of the road, returning to Quail Meadow Picnic Area. ■

63. Ollason—Meyers Loop
TORO COUNTY PARK

Hiking distance: 4.5 miles round trip
Hiking time: 2.5 hours
Configuration: out-and-back with loop
Elevation gain: 500 feet
Difficulty: moderate
Exposure: forested valley and open meadows
Dogs: allowed
Maps: U.S.G.S. Spreckels · Toro County Park map

map
page 183

The Ollason Trail meanders up the valley floor in Toro Park through groves of oak, sycamore, bay, and eucalyptus trees. A loop on the Meyers Trail winds up a small side canyon to vistas of Devil's Throne (a distinctive rock outcropping) and the upper peaks of Toro Park and Salinas Valley. The return route descends through rolling pasture land dotted with oaks.

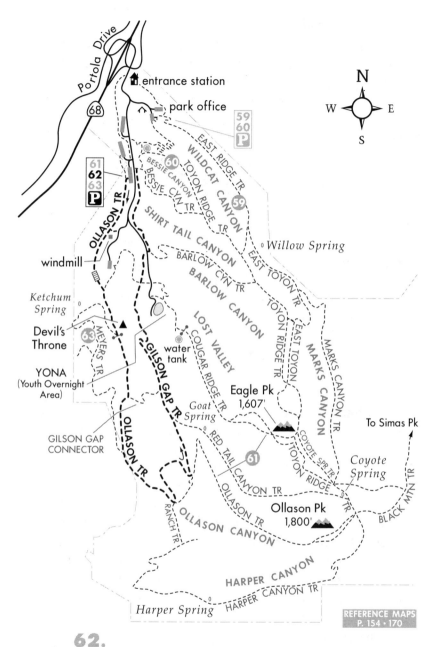

62.
Ollason Trail–Gilson Gap Loop
TORO COUNTY PARK

To the trailhead

MONTEREY. From Highway 1 in Monterey, take the Highway 68 East/Salinas exit, and drive 11.6 miles to the signed turnoff for Toro Park on Portola Drive. Turn right and continue a short distance to the park entrance station. Follow the park road 0.5 miles, and turn right and a quick left into the Quail Meadow Picnic Area parking lot.

SALINAS. From Highway 101 in Salinas, take the Monterey Peninsula/Highway 68 exit. Drive 6 miles to Portola Drive, and follow the signs to the park entrance.

The hike

From the far end of the parking lot, cross the wooden footbridge to the unmarked Ollason Trail. Bear south (left) along the west side of the valley floor through the forested grove. The path travels along the base of the hill, parallel to a streambed on the left. Follow the west edge of the valley past a windmill on the left. As the canyon narrows, cross a footbridge over the seasonal stream to an unpaved ranch road. Take the road to the right, and in a short distance, pass through a trail gate at an unsigned junction. The Ollason Trail continues straight.

Take the unsigned Meyers Trail sharply to the right, veering back to the north through an oak forest. Curve left up a side canyon to the fenced west park boundary. A horseshoe bend to the left leads up to the high point of the trail, with panoramic views of the 669-foot rock mass of Devil's Throne and the upper reaches of Toro Park. Descend and merge with another old ranch road. Follow the near-level grade of the road through the rolling grasslands dotted with oaks. Descend again through pasture land to a junction back with the Ollason Trail. The right fork continues up to Ollason Peak (Hike 61). Go left, heading down the valley. Pass the Gilson Gap Connector Trail on the right, and complete the loop at the trail gate. Cross through the gate and return along the same route. ■

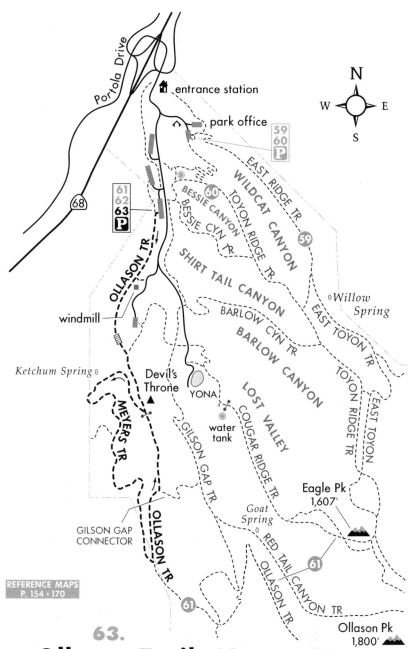

Portola Drive

entrance station

park office

N
W E
S

59
60
P

WILDCAT CANYON

EAST RIDGE TR

60

BESSIE CANYON

TOYON RIDGE TR

BESSIE CYN TR

68

61
62
63
P

OLLASON TR

SHIRT TAIL CANYON

EAST TOYON TR

59

⁰Willow
Spring

windmill

BARLOW CYN TR

BARLOW CANYON

TOYON RIDGE TR

EAST TOYON

Ketchum Spring ⁰

Devil's
Throne

YONA

LOST VALLEY

water
tank

COUGAR RIDGE TR

MEYERS TR

GILSON GAP TR

Eagle Pk
1,607'

Goat
Spring ⁰

GILSON GAP
CONNECTOR

OLLASON TR

RED TAIL CANYON TR

61

OLLASON TR

61

REFERENCE MAPS
P. 154 · 170

Ollason Pk
1,800'

63.
Ollason Trail–Meyers Loop
TORO COUNTY PARK

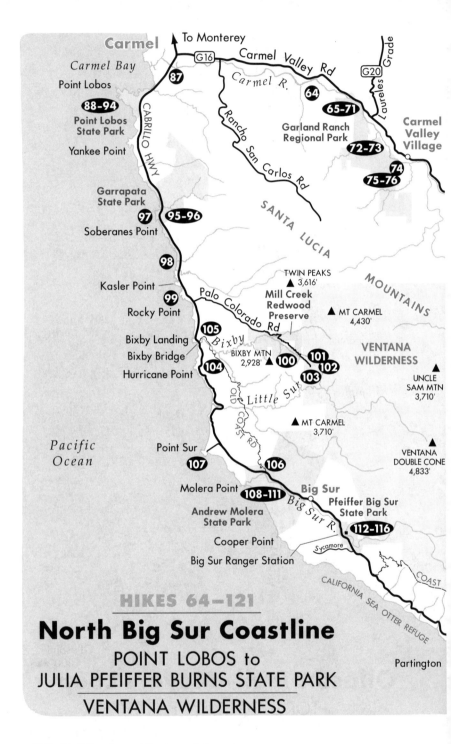

Carmel

To Monterey

G16

Carmel Valley Rd

G20

Laureles Grade

Carmel Bay

Point Lobos

87

Carmel R.

88-94

64

65-71

Point Lobos
State Park

Rancho San Carlos Rd

Garland Ranch
Regional Park

Carmel
Valley
Village

Yankee Point

72-73

74

75-76

CABRILLO HWY

SANTA

LUCIA

Garrapata
State Park

97

95-96

Soberanes Point

98

MOUNTAINS

TWIN PEAKS
▲ 3,616'

Kasler Point

Palo Colorado Rd

Mill Creek
Redwood
Preserve

▲ MT CARMEL
4,430'

99

Rocky Point

Bixby

VENTANA
WILDERNESS

Bixby Landing

105

BIXBY MTN
2,928' ▲

100

101
102

▲
UNCLE
SAM MTN
3,710'

Bixby Bridge

104

103

Hurricane Point

OLD COAST RD

Little Sur

Pacific
Ocean

Point Sur

107

106

▲ MT CARMEL
3,710'

VENTANA
DOUBLE CONE
4,833'

▲

Molera Point

108-111

Big Sur

Big Sur R.

Pfeiffer Big Sur
State Park

Andrew Molera
State Park

112-116

Cooper Point

Sycamore

Big Sur Ranger Station

CALIFORNIA SEA OTTER REFUGE

COAST

HIKES 64-121

North Big Sur Coastline

POINT LOBOS to
JULIA PFEIFFER BURNS STATE PARK

Partington

VENTANA WILDERNESS

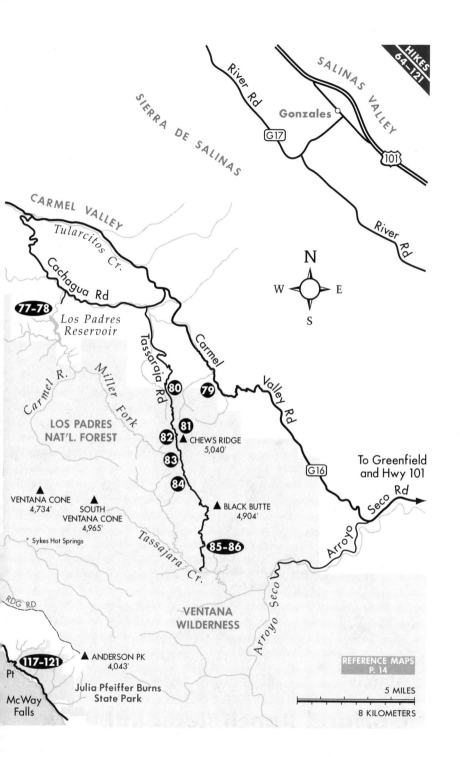

SALINAS VALLEY

River Rd

Gonzales

G17

101

SIERRA DE SALINAS

River Rd

CARMEL VALLEY

Tularcitos Cr.

Cachagua Rd

N

W   E

S

77-78

Los Padres Reservoir

Tassajara Rd

Carmel

Carmel R.

Miller Fork

80

79

Valley Rd

LOS PADRES NAT'L. FOREST

81

82   ▲ CHEWS RIDGE 5,040'

83

84

G16

To Greenfield and Hwy 101

Seco Rd

▲ VENTANA CONE 4,734'

▲ SOUTH VENTANA CONE 4,965'

Sykes Hot Springs

Tassajara Cr.

▲ BLACK BUTTE 4,904'

85-86

Arroyo

RDG RD

VENTANA WILDERNESS

Arroyo Seco

117-121

Pt

McWay Falls

▲ ANDERSON PK 4,043'

Julia Pfeiffer Burns State Park

REFERENCE MAPS P. 14

5 MILES

8 KILOMETERS

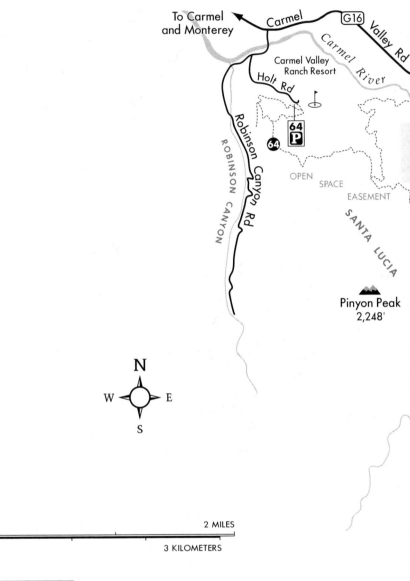

To Carmel
and Monterey

Carmel

G16

Valley Rd

Carmel River

Carmel Valley
Ranch Resort

Holt Rd

Robinson Canyon Rd

ROBINSON CANYON

64 P

64

OPEN SPACE

EASEMENT

SANTA LUCIA

Pinyon Peak
2,248'

N
W E
S

2 MILES

3 KILOMETERS

REFERENCE MAPS
P. 184

HIKES 64–76
Garland Ranch Regional Park

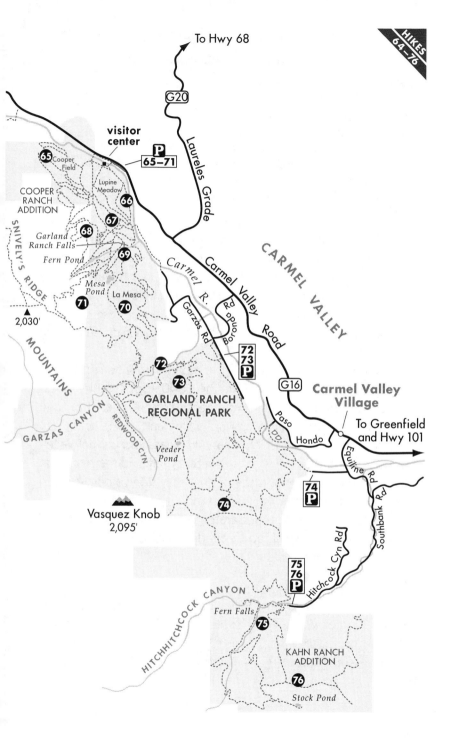

To Hwy 68

G20

visitor center

P
65–71

Laureles Grade

CARMEL VALLEY

65 Cooper Field

COOPER RANCH ADDITION

Lupine Meadow

66

67

68

Garland Ranch Falls

Fern Pond

69

Carmel R.

Carmel Valley Road

Boronda Rd

Garzas Rd

SNIVELY'S RIDGE

Mesa Pond

71

La Mesa

70

▲ 2,030'

MOUNTAINS

72
73
P

G16

Carmel Valley Village

72

73

GARLAND RANCH REGIONAL PARK

GARZAS CANYON

REDWOOD CYN

Veeder Pond

To Greenfield and Hwy 101

Paso Hondo

Equiline Rd

Vasquez Knob 2,095'

74

74
P

Southbank Rd

75
76
P

Hitchcock Cyn Rd

HITCHHITCHCOCK CANYON

Fern Falls

75

KAHN RANCH ADDITION

76

Stock Pond

64. Snively's Ridge Trail
GARLAND RANCH REGIONAL PARK

Hiking distance: 5.6 miles round trip
Hiking time: 3 hours
Configuration: out-and-back
Elevation gain: 1,730 feet
Difficulty: moderate to somewhat strenuous
Exposure: exposed hillsides and forested pockets
Dogs: allowed
Maps: U.S.G.S. Seaside and Mount Carmel
Garland Ranch Regional Park map

Garland Ranch Regional Park stretches from the willow-lined Carmel River to the crest of the Santa Lucia Range. The 3,464-acre park lies along the northern tip of the range. Over 50 miles of trails offer many options for hiking. The multi-use trails criss-cross through the beautiful area, from the Carmel River valley to the highest point of the park along the 2,000-foot summit of Snively's Ridge.

This hike begins from the northern park entrance off of Holt Road and follows Snively's Ridge, the 1,600-foot mountain crest on the northernmost wall of the Santa Lucia Range. The ridge forms the southwest rim of Carmel Valley and offers breathtaking panoramas across the Ventana Wilderness and Carmel Valley. The views extend all the way to Monterey Bay and the peninsula. Snively's Ridge Trail follows the open grassy ridge along an open space easement at the northwest end of the park. The scenic trail is a steady climb at a moderate grade along the contours of the slope. The trail winds up to overlooks of Garland Ranch and its mosaic of trails.

To the trailhead

From Highway 1 and Carmel Valley Road in Carmel, drive 6.1 miles east on Carmel Valley Road to Robinson Canyon Road on the right. Turn right and drive 0.3 miles to Holt Road. Turn left and go 0.6 miles to the end of road at the gate. Park in the pullout on the left.

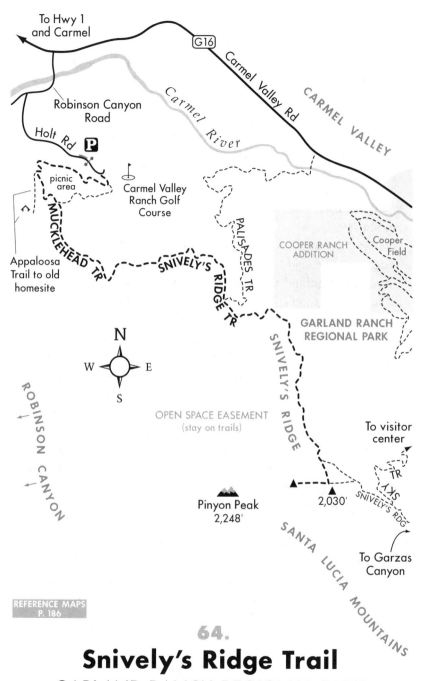

To Hwy 1
and Carmel

G16

Carmel Valley Rd

CARMEL VALLEY

Carmel River

Robinson Canyon
Road

Holt Rd

P

picnic
area

MUCKLEHEAD TR

Carmel Valley
Ranch Golf
Course

PALISADES TR

COOPER RANCH
ADDITION

Cooper
Field

Appaloosa
Trail to old
homesite

SNIVELY'S RIDGE TR

GARLAND RANCH
REGIONAL PARK

N
W   E
S

ROBINSON CANYON

OPEN SPACE EASEMENT
(stay on trails)

SNIVELY'S RIDGE

To visitor
center

SKY TR

SNIVELY'S RDG

Pinyon Peak
2,248'

2,030'

To Garzas
Canyon

SANTA LUCIA MOUNTAINS

REFERENCE MAPS
P. 186

64.
Snively's Ridge Trail
GARLAND RANCH REGIONAL PARK

The hike

Pass through the trail gate, and walk one block down residential Holt Road. At the left bend in Holt Road, bear right onto the trail. Skirt the edge of Carmel Valley Ranch Golf Course to the posted entrance of Garland Ranch Regional Park by a trail fork. Curve right and head up the slope surrounded by lichen-draped oaks and views across Carmel Valley. Steadily walk uphill on an easy grade on the narrow old ranch road to a Y-split. To the right, the Appaloosa Trail leads 200 yards to an old homesite and shed. Stay to the left on the Horseshoe Trail, and continue uphill to a second fork. The left branch leads 50 yards to a picnic area among stately oaks.

Take the signed Mucklehead Trail to the right, and follow the wide path through tall brush. The path quickly opens up and curves left, becoming the Snively's Ridge Trail. Traverse the north-facing slope perched on the mountain cliff. Continue uphill as panoramic views spread out below, from Monterey Bay to Santa Cruz. Just shy of a sweeping left bend is the posted Palisades Trail on the left at 1.5 miles. Continue straight ahead, climbing to vistas into the heart of Garland Ranch Regional Park (on the left), the surrounding mountains, and into Robinson Canyon (on the right). Wind through the open ridgetop meadows studded with madrone and oak groves. Follow the ridge, noticing a close-up view of the fire lookout crowning Pinyon Peak. Near the summit is a trail split. Snively's Ridge Trail descends to the left. Stay to the right to the knoll, the high point of the hike at 2,030 feet. To the left, a footpath rejoins Snively's Ridge Trail. To the right, the narrow path follows the ridgeline south to another knoll with oak trees and a bench. This is the turn-around spot. Return by retracing your route.

To extend the hike, the Snively's Ridge Trail continues southeast, connecting with the Sky Trail (Hike 71) in another half mile and Garzas Canyon Trail (Hike 72) in 1.5 miles. ■

65. Rancho Loop
COOPER RANCH ADDITION
GARLAND RANCH REGIONAL PARK

Hiking distance: 3 mile-loop
Hiking time: 1.5 hours
Configuration: one large loop plus one small loop
Elevation gain: 350 feet
Difficulty: easy to slightly moderate
Exposure: shaded forest and open grassy meadow
Dogs: allowed
Maps: U.S.G.S. Seaside and Mt. Carmel · Garland Ranch Regional Park map

map
page 193

The most widely used trailhead for Garland Ranch Regional Park is at the park's northeast end, directly off of Carmel Valley Road. A visitor center, ranger station, and museum are located near the entrance. Hikes 65—71 begin from this trailhead.

The Cooper Ranch addition, at the northwest end of Garland Ranch Park, is one of two sections of the park that are open to mountain biking. (The Kahn Ranch addition, at the south end of the park, is also open to biking.) The ranch is bordered by a forested wildlife habitat reserve and a large eucalyptus grove to the north. The Santa Lucia Mountains lie to the south. The Rancho Loop circles Cooper Field, a large grassy meadow at the base of the towering mountains, then climbs into the forested foothills.

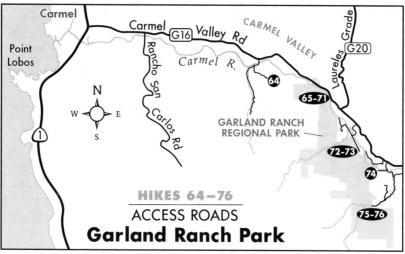

HIKES 64—76
ACCESS ROADS
Garland Ranch Park

To the trailhead

From Highway 1 and Carmel Valley Road in Carmel, drive 8.6 miles east on Carmel Valley Road to the Garland Ranch Regional Park parking lot on the right.

The hike

Follow the gravel path to the right. Bear left at the bridge, crossing over the Carmel River to a trail junction. The visitor center is to the left. Take the Cooper Trail to the right across the flat grasslands to a posted junction. Begin the loop to the right on the Rancho Loop. Follow the north edge of the meadow to a junction by a eucalyptus grove. The main trail skirts the meadow. The right fork weaves through the towering eucalyptus grove. Both trails rejoin at the west end of Cooper Field. Loop back from the west end along the base of the mountains to a trail fork.

Bear right on the Cooper Trail into the oak-studded forest. Ascend the hillside and take the Acorn Trail to the right (near the ranger cabin). Continue climbing and cross a wooden bridge over a gully to an unsigned trail split. Switchback left through the coastal oak forest to the end of the trail at a junction. The left fork is the return route.

The short, half-mile loop starts here. Take the right fork steadily uphill to a 3-way split at the Live Oak Trail. Begin the small loop path to the right, and climb to the high point of the trail. Panoramic views extend across Carmel Valley. Cross the open slope to a junction. The right fork leads to Maple Canyon (Hike 68). Bear left, staying on the Live Oak Trail, and complete the half-mile upper loop. Return downhill to the main loop at the Acorn Trail junction.

Curve right and head down the shaded hillside to a trail split. Veer left on the posted Orchard Trail, and quickly curve right, heading back to the Live Oak Trail. Bear left and curve left again, staying on the Live Oak Trail. Pass the old homestead barns and outbuildings to the Cooper Trail. Cross the east end of Cooper Field, completing the loop and returning to the Carmel River. ▪

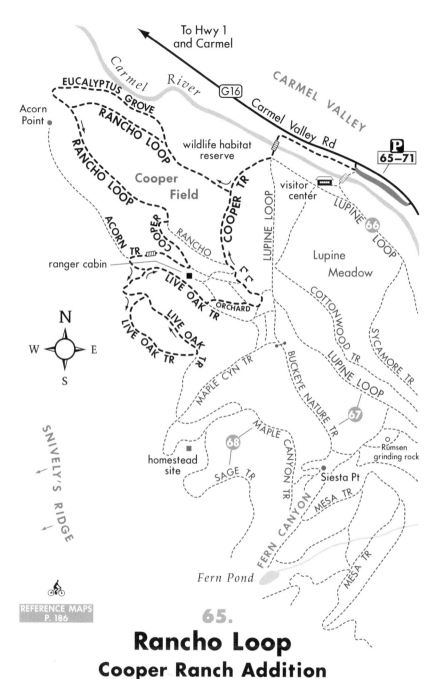

To Hwy 1 and Carmel

Carmel River

G16

CARMEL VALLEY

Carmel Valley Rd

P 65–71

EUCALYPTUS GROVE

RANCHO LOOP

Acorn Point

RANCHO LOOP

Cooper Field

wildlife habitat reserve

COOPER TR

visitor center

LUPINE LOOP

66

Lupine Meadow

ACORN TR

ranger cabin

COOPER

RANCHO

LIVE OAK TR

ORCHARD

LIVE OAK

LIVE OAK TR

COTTONWOOD TR

LUPINE LOOP

SYCAMORE TR

N
W   E
S

MAPLE CYN TR

BUCKEYE NATURE TR

67

Rumsen grinding rock

SNIVELY'S RIDGE

68

MAPLE CANYON TR

SAGE TR

homestead site

Siesta Pt

MESA TR

FERN CANYON

MESA TR

REFERENCE MAPS P. 186

Fern Pond

MESA TR

65.
Rancho Loop
Cooper Ranch Addition
GARLAND RANCH REGIONAL PARK

66. Lupine Loop
GARLAND RANCH REGIONAL PARK

Hiking distance: 1.4-mile loop
Hiking time: 45 minutes
Configuration: loop
Elevation gain: 100 feet
Difficulty: easy
Exposure: open meadows
Dogs: allowed
Maps: U.S.G.S. Seaside and Mt. Carmel · Garland Ranch Regional Park map

The Lupine Loop is an easy hike that circles Lupine Meadow. The riverside meadow is covered in grasses and wildflowers and is dotted with cottonwoods, oaks, sycamores, and pines. The willow-lined banks of the Carmel River border the east side of the meadow. The Sycamore and Cottonwood Trails meander through the meadow, offering variations to the route.

To the trailhead

From Highway 1 and Carmel Valley Road in Carmel, drive 8.6 miles east on Carmel Valley Road to the Garland Ranch Regional Park parking lot on the right.

The hike

Follow the gravel path to the right. Bear left at the bridge, crossing over the Carmel River to a trail junction. Begin the loop to the left on the Lupine Loop, heading southeast past the visitor center. Stroll through the grassy meadows dotted with trees to a junction with the Sycamore Trail. The Lupine Loop follows the perimeter of the meadow, and the Sycamore Trail weaves through the meadow. Take either route, as they rejoin a short distance ahead. At the junction with the Waterfall Trail on the left, curve right, staying in the meadow past a junction with the Cottonwood Trail on the right. (The Cottonwood Trail is a cut-across route that remains in the meadow.) Continue on the left fork—the Lupine Loop—and gently climb the hill through oak groves. The path loops back on an elevated rise above the meadow. Pass the Mesa Trail on the left, and continue above the meadow to a fenceline at the Buckeye and Live Oak junction. Curve right, following the fenceline downhill and returning to the meadow. At the Cottonwood Trail junction, an unmarked diagonal path leads directly to the visitor center. Stay left, following the perimeter of the meadow. Complete the loop at the bridge crossing the Carmel River. ∎

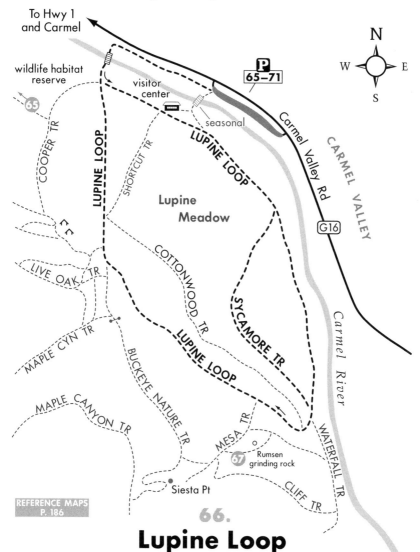

66.
Lupine Loop
GARLAND RANCH REGIONAL PARK

67. Buckeye Nature Trail
GARLAND RANCH REGIONAL PARK

Hiking distance: 2 miles round trip
Hiking time: 1 hour
Configuration: out-and-back with large loop
Elevation gain: 250 feet
Difficulty: easy
Exposure: mostly shaded forest
Dogs: allowed
Maps: U.S.G.S. Seaside and Mt. Carmel · Garland Ranch Regional Park map

The Buckeye Nature Trail is an interpretive trail through cool, moist woods lined with ferns, fungi, and poison oak in a forest of buckeye, oak, and bay laurel trees. Information stations describe plants used by Native Americans and settlers, including those used for medicine, food seasonings, fishing, and musical instruments. The trail returns by the Rumsen Grinding Rock, two flat, high boulders with bedrock mortars. The holes were worn into the rock by native people grinding acorns into edible meal.

To the trailhead

From Highway 1 and Carmel Valley Road in Carmel, drive 8.6 miles east on Carmel Valley Road to the Garland Ranch Regional Park parking lot on the right.

The hike

Follow the gravel path to the right. Bear left at the bridge, crossing over the Carmel River to a trail junction. To the left is the visitor center, and to the right is the Cooper Trail. Continue straight ahead along the west edge of the meadow to the Cottonwood Trail on the left. Begin the loop to the right, climbing out of the meadow to a 4-way junction in an oak grove. The Live Oak Trail bears right, and the Lupine Loop continues to the left. Continue straight towards the Buckeye Nature Trail, passing the Maple Canyon Trail on the right. Enter the Buckeye Nature Trail through a fence gate, and wind through the oak grove past interpretive stations to a trail split with the Siesta Trail on the right. A short detour on the Siesta Trail climbs to a rocky perch overlooking Carmel Valley.

Back at the junction, continue on the Buckeye Nature Trail, and head past a large sandstone formation on the right. Descend steps to a T-junction with the Mesa Trail. Bear left 35 yards, and pick up the Buckeye Trail on the right. Take the narrow hillside footpath past fern-covered sandstone cliffs to a large outcropping on the left and the Rumsen Grinding Rock. After the rock, pass through a trail gate to a T-junction. Go to the left 40 yards, returning to the Mesa Trail. Bear right another 40 yards to a junction with the Lupine Loop (Hike 66). Take the right fork, descending through an oak canopy into Lupine Meadow. Follow the Cottonwood Trail along the south edge of the meadow and complete the loop. Return to the right. ∎

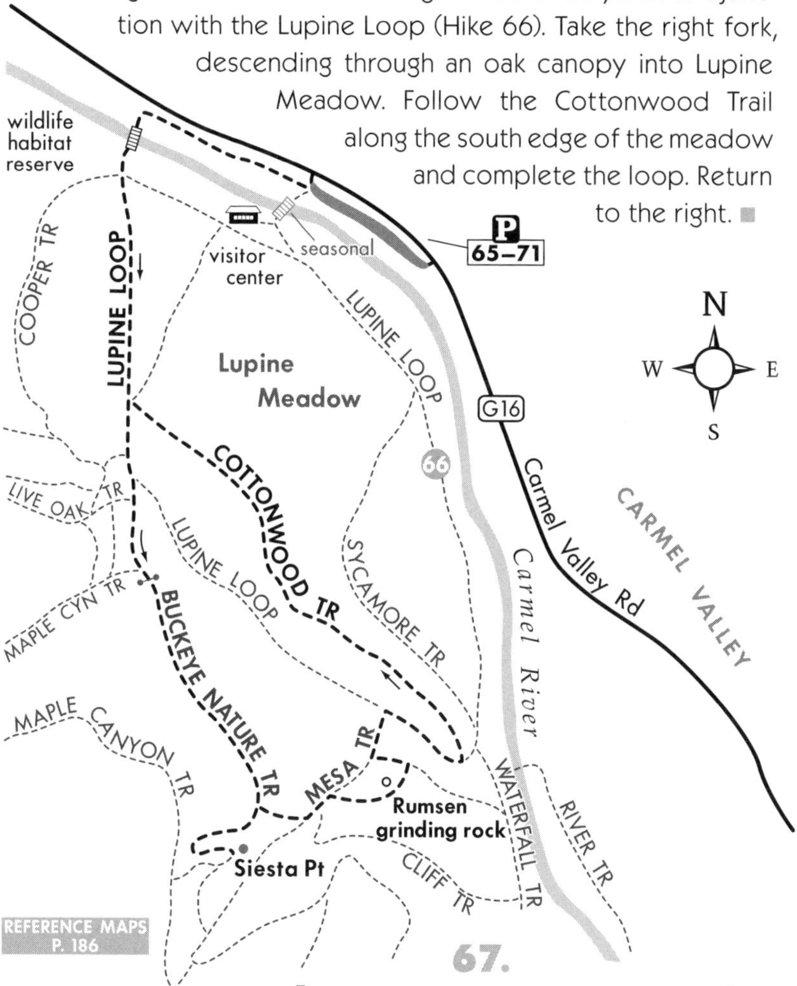

wildlife
habitat
reserve

COOPER TR

LUPINE LOOP

visitor
center

seasonal

LUPINE LOOP

Lupine
Meadow

P
65-71

N
W E
S

G16

66

COTTONWOOD TR

LIVE OAK TR

LUPINE LOOP

Carmel Valley Rd

CARMEL VALLEY

MAPLE CYN TR

BUCKEYE NATURE TR

SYCAMORE TR

Carmel River

MAPLE CANYON TR

MESA TR

Rumsen
grinding rock

WATERFALL TR

RIVER TR

Siesta Pt

CLIFF TR

REFERENCE MAPS
P. 186

67.

Buckeye Nature Trail
GARLAND RANCH REGIONAL PARK

68. Maple Canyon—Fern Canyon Loop
GARLAND RANCH REGIONAL PARK

Hiking distance: 4 miles round trip
Hiking time: 2 hours
Configuration: out-and-back with loop
Elevation gain: 800 feet
Difficulty: easy to somewhat moderate
Exposure: shaded canyon and open meadow
Dogs: allowed
Maps: U.S.G.S. Seaside and Mt. Carmel · Garland Ranch Regional Park map

Garland Ranch Regional Park is home to several different habitats. This hike includes a sampling of several ecosystems. The hike begins at the Carmel River and crosses Lupine Meadow into a shady canyon. The trail then climbs the foothills of the Santa

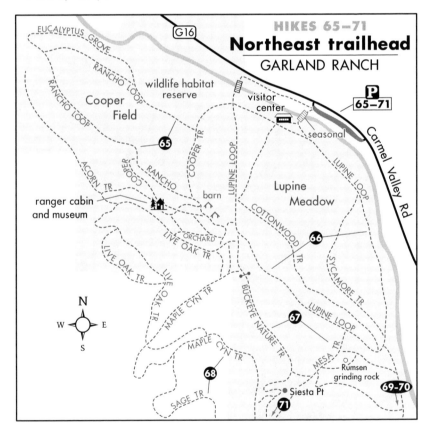

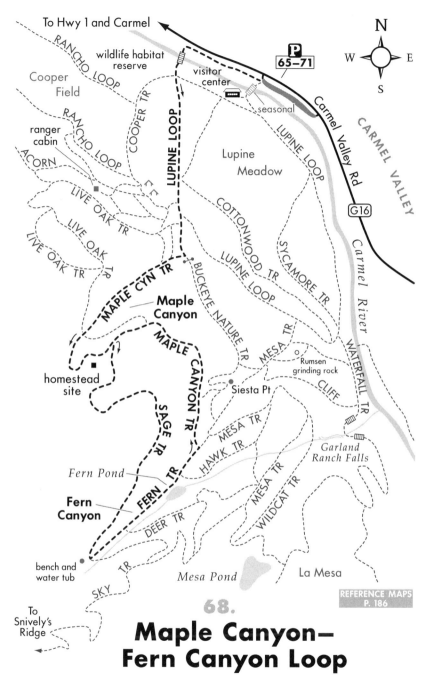

To Hwy 1 and Carmel

N
W   E
S

P
65-71

wildlife habitat reserve

Cooper Field

visitor center

seasonal

Carmel Valley Rd

CARMEL VALLEY

RANCHO LOOP

ranger cabin

RANCHO LOOP

ACORN

LIVE OAK TR

LIVE OAK TR

LIVE OAK TR

COOPER TR

LUPINE LOOP

LUPINE LOOP

Lupine Meadow

COTTONWOOD TR

LUPINE LOOP

SYCAMORE TR

G16

Carmel River

MAPLE CYN TR

Maple Canyon

BUCKEYE NATURE TR

MAPLE CANYON TR

MESA TR

Rumsen grinding rock

CLIFF

WATERFALL TR

homestead site

SAGE TR

Siesta Pt

MESA TR

HAWK TR

Garland Ranch Falls

Fern Pond

FERN TR

Fern Canyon

DEER TR

MESA TR

WILDCAT TR

La Mesa

bench and water tub

SKY TR

Mesa Pond

REFERENCE MAPS
P. 186

To Snively's Ridge

68.

Maple Canyon–
Fern Canyon Loop
GARLAND RANCH REGIONAL PARK

Lucia Mountains through oak groves and open chaparral to an old homestead site. The return route winds through a lush, narrow canyon to Fern Pond, a circular pond rimmed with trees and a variety of ferns.

To the trailhead

From Highway 1 and Carmel Valley Road in Carmel, drive 8.6 miles east on Carmel Valley Road to the Garland Ranch Regional Park parking lot on the right.

The hike

Follow the gravel path to the right. Bear left at the bridge, crossing over the Carmel River to a signed trail split. To the left is the visitor center, and to the right is the Cooper Trail. Continue straight ahead along the west edge of Lupine Meadow towards the mountains. Follow the fenceline, past the Cottonwood and Live Oak Trails, to the signed Maple Canyon and Buckeye Nature Trail junction. Bear right on the Maple Canyon Trail, and steadily climb up the lush, picturesque canyon. Pass the Live Oak Trail, and cross the canyon drainage at a horseshoe bend to the homestead site. The old homestead sits in a small grassy clearing rimmed with trees. A short distance ahead is the Sage Trail junction.

Begin the loop to the right on the Sage Trail, temporarily leaving the lush canyon to the exposed sage and chaparral hillside. Traverse the east-facing hillside, overlooking Fern Canyon and Carmel Valley. Continue to a water trough, bench, and a junction with the Fern Trail. Take the Fern Trail to the left and steeply descend through the narrow, shady canyon. Pass the Deer Trail on the right to Fern Pond, surrounded by aspen, oak, and an abundance of ferns. By the pond is another junction. Take the Maple Canyon Trail to the left, and regain elevation past the Siesta Point Trail, soon after completing the loop. Continue straight ahead—past the homestead site—and retrace your steps. ■

69. Garland Ranch Falls—Mesa Loop
GARLAND RANCH REGIONAL PARK

Hiking distance: 3.5 miles round trip
Hiking time: 1.5 hours
Configuration: out-and-back with large loop
Elevation gain: 600 feet
Difficulty: easy to slightly moderate
Exposure: shaded canyon and open meadow
Dogs: allowed
Maps: U.S.G.S. Seaside and Mt. Carmel · Garland Ranch Regional Park map

**map
page 202**

This loop hike visits Garland Ranch Falls, a 70-foot cataract off a sandstone cliff in an enclosed, fern-filled canyon. The hike is enjoyable year-round, but to experience the cascade of the ephemeral waterfall, plan your hike after a rain. Beyond the falls, the forested trail continues to La Mesa, a flat river terrace and wildlife habitat pond perched in a saddle above the valley floor.

To the trailhead

From Highway 1 and Carmel Valley Road in Carmel, drive 8.6 miles east on Carmel Valley Road to the Garland Ranch Regional Park parking lot on the right.

The hike

Follow the gravel path to the right. Bear left at the bridge, crossing over the Carmel River to a trail junction. Bear left again, passing the visitor center on the Lupine Loop. Walk southeast through the meadow to a posted junction with the Waterfall Trail. Go to the left on the Waterfall Trail, following the rocky riverbed. Ascend the hillside and enter the tree-shaded slopes, passing the Cliff Trail on the right. Traverse the cliffside up the gulch, and cross a footbridge into the steep-walled box canyon at the base of the transient waterfall. After crossing the tributary, climb steps and cross another footbridge, leaving the canyon and emerging into an oak woodland with a lush understory of ferns and moss. Pass through a trail gate to a junction with the Vaquero Trail on the left. Continue straight ahead, steadily gaining elevation to a large grassy mesa with benches and a 4-way junction at 1.6 miles. The right fork, the Mesa Trail, is the return route.

First, continue 125 yards to La Mesa Pond. After enjoying the pond, return to the junction, and take the Mesa Trail to the north, now on your left. The trail gently winds down the hillside, passing junctions with the Sky Trail, Hawk Trail, and Fern Trail. Cross a trickling stream in the fern-covered drainage to a T-junction with the Lupine Loop above the meadow. Bear right, drop into the meadow, and complete the loop. ■

To Hwy 1 and Carmel

wildlife habitat reserve

Cooper Field

RANCHO LOOP

visitor center

seasonal

P
65–71

ranger cabin

RANCHO

COOPER TR

LUPINE LOOP

Lupine Meadow

LUPINE LOOP

Carmel Valley Rd

Carmel River

CARMEL VALLEY

LIVE OAK TR

LIVE OAK

LIVE OAK TR

COTTONWOOD TR

SYCAMORE TR

G16

MAPLE CYN TR

LUPINE LOOP

BUCKEYE NATURE TR

MESA TR

N
W · E
S

MAPLE CANYON TR

Siesta Point

Rumsen grinding rock

WATERFALL TR

CLIFF

RIVER TR (easement)

SAGE TR

MESA TR

Garland Ranch Falls

MESA TR

Fern Pond

HAWK TR

FERN TR

MESA TR

WILDCAT TR

VAQUERO TR

DEER TR

SKY TR

REFERENCE MAPS
P. 186

Mesa Pond

GARZAS CYN TR

La Mesa

MESA TR

69.

Garland Ranch Falls–Mesa Loop
GARLAND RANCH REGIONAL PARK

70. Lupine Meadow to La Mesa
GARLAND RANCH REGIONAL PARK

Hiking distance: 4.5 miles round trip
Hiking time: 2.5 hours
Configuration: out-and-back with loop
Elevation gain: 800 feet
Difficulty: moderate
Exposure: open meadow and shaded canyon
Dogs: allowed
Maps: U.S.G.S. Seaside and Mt. Carmel · Garland Ranch Regional Park map

**map
page 205**

This hike begins at Lupine Meadow by the Carmel River and climbs to La Mesa, a large grassy terrace with a wildlife habitat pond. En route to La Mesa, the trail passes ephemeral Garland Ranch Falls, then climbs to the Oakview Trail, perched on a mountain cliff overlooking Garzas Canyon. The stream-fed canyon bisects Garland Ranch. The trail follows the hillside 500 feet above Garzas Canyon and returns through a grove of stately oaks.

To the trailhead

From Highway 1 and Carmel Valley Road in Carmel, drive 8.6 miles east on Carmel Valley Road to the Garland Ranch Regional Park parking lot on the right.

The hike

Follow the gravel path to the right. Bear left at the bridge, crossing over the Carmel River to a trail junction. Go left and continue past the visitor center. Head southeast through the flat grassy meadow, passing the Sycamore Trail on the right, to a signed junction with the Waterfall Trail at 0.5 miles. Take the Waterfall Trail to the left, and ascend the hillside in a shady woodland. Head up the ravine, crossing a wooden footbridge into a steep-walled grotto at the base of Garland Ranch Falls, the seasonal waterfall. Cross a second footbridge, leaving the canyon and entering an oak grove. Pass through a trail gate to a signed junction.

To begin the loop, bear left on the Vaquero Trail up the forested path. Near the top, the path widens and views open up of the Carmel Valley. The trail ends at a T-junction with the Mesa Trail at the east end of the large, open meadow. Go left on the old ranch road to the Oakview Trail on the right. Take the Oakview Trail, overlooking Garzas Canyon. Pass both junctions with the Oakview Loop, climbing steeply to the ridge. Follow the level ridge to a junction with the Garzas Canyon Trail on the left. Stay right for 30 yards to a junction with Snively's Ridge Trail. Take the Garzas Canyon Trail to the right, gently descending through stately oaks. Emerge from the woodland on the grassy mesa by La Mesa Pond. Past the pond is a 4-way junction. Take the middle fork—the Waterfall Trail—and descend to the Vaquero Trail junction, completing the loop. Return on the Waterfall Trail, following the same route back. ▪

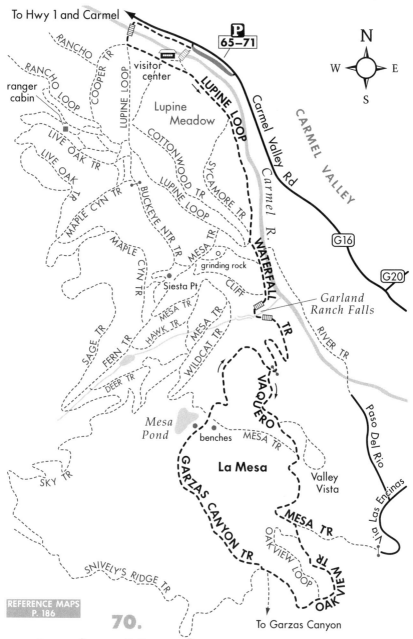

To Hwy 1 and Carmel

P
65–71

visitor center

ranger cabin

RANCHO
RANCHO LOOP
COOPER TR
LUPINE LOOP

Lupine Meadow

LUPINE LOOP

Carmel Valley Rd

Carmel R.

CARMEL VALLEY

N
W · E
S

LIVE OAK TR
LIVE OAK TR

COTTONWOOD TR
SYCAMORE TR
LUPINE LOOP

MAPLE CYN TR

BUCKEYE NTR TR

MESA TR

grinding rock

Siesta Pt.

MAPLE CYN TR

CLIFF

WATERFALL TR

Garland Ranch Falls

G16

G20

RIVER TR

SAGE TR
FERN TR
HAWK TR
MESA TR
MESA TR
WILDCAT TR

DEER TR

VAQUERO

Mesa Pond

benches

MESA TR

La Mesa

Valley Vista

Paso Del Rio

SKY TR

GARZAS CANYON TR

MESA TR

OAKVIEW LOOP

OAK VIEW TR

Via Las Encinas

SNIVELY'S RIDGE TR

REFERENCE MAPS
P. 186

70.

To Garzas Canyon

Lupine Meadow to La Mesa
GARLAND RANCH REGIONAL PARK

71. Lupine Meadow to Snively's Ridge
GARLAND RANCH REGIONAL PARK

Hiking distance: 6 miles round trip
Hiking time: 3 hours
Configuration: out-and-back with large loop
Elevation gain: 1,600 feet
Difficulty: moderate to strenuous
Exposure: shaded hillside and exposed ridge
Dogs: allowed
Maps: U.S.G.S. Seaside and Mt. Carmel · Garland Ranch Regional Park map

Garland Park stretches from the willow-lined Carmel River to the crest of the Santa Lucia Range. This hike begins at the river and climbs through oak woodlands to Snively's Ridge at the mountain crest, stretching 1,600 feet above Carmel Valley. From the ridge are sweeping, unobstructed bird's-eye views of Carmel Valley, the Monterey Peninsula, Salinas, and the interior Santa Lucia Mountains. Portions of the Snively's Ridge Trail are tirelessly steep and require frequent rest stops.

To the trailhead

From Highway 1 and Carmel Valley Road in Carmel, drive 8.6 miles east on Carmel Valley Road to the Garland Ranch Regional Park parking lot on the right.

The hike

Follow the gravel path to the right. Bear left at the bridge, crossing over the Carmel River to a signed trail split. Bear left, passing the visitor center on the Lupine Loop. Follow the tree-dotted meadow, passing the Sycamore Trail on the right, to a junction with the Waterfall Trail at 0.5 miles. Stay on the Lupine Loop. Pass the Cottonwood Trail and climb a small rise to a bluff above the meadow. At the signed junction, bear left on the Mesa Trail. Head up the lush drainage and cross a trickling stream. The winding path passes the Buckeye Trail, Siesta Point, Fern Trail, Hawk Trail, and Sky Trail, all on the right.

At Sky Trail, begin the loop to the left, staying on the Mesa Trail. Emerge onto La Mesa, a huge grassy terrace at a 4-way junction.

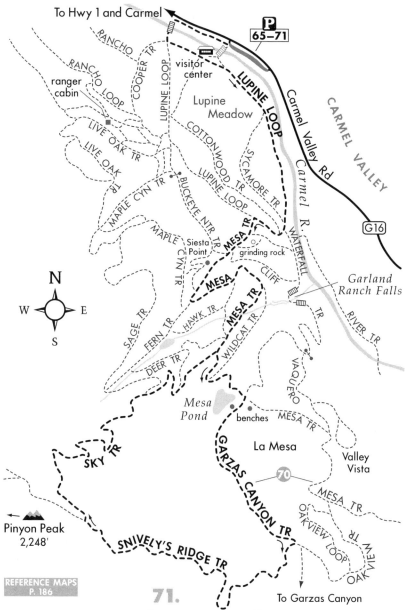

To Hwy 1 and Carmel

P
65–71

RANCHO COOPER TR

RANCHO LOOP

ranger cabin

visitor center

Lupine Meadow

LUPINE LOOP

LUPINE LOOP

Carmel Valley Rd

Carmel R.

CARMEL VALLEY

LIVE OAK TR

LIVE OAK TR

COTTONWOOD TR

LUPINE LOOP

SYCAMORE TR

G16

MAPLE CYN TR

BUCKEYE NTR TR

MESA TR

MESA TR

WATERFALL

N
W · E
S

MAPLE CYN TR

Siesta Point

grinding rock

CLIFF

TR

Garland Ranch Falls

MESA

RIVER TR

SAGE TR

FERN TR

HAWK TR

MESA TR

WILDCAT TR

DEER TR

VAQUERO

Mesa Pond

benches

MESA TR

La Mesa

Valley Vista

SKY TR

GARZAS CANYON TR

70

MESA TR

OAKVIEW LOOP

OAK VIEW TR

Pinyon Peak
2,248'

SNIVELY'S RIDGE TR

REFERENCE MAPS
P. 186

To Garzas Canyon

71.

Lupine Meadow
to Snively's Ridge
GARLAND RANCH REGIONAL PARK

Take the Garzas Canyon Trail on the right. Pass La Mesa Pond, a wildlife habitat pond, and continue into the shady grove of stately oaks at the base of the mountain. Curve left and climb the mountain slope to the ridge and a junction with Snively's Ridge Trail. Begin a very steep ascent to the right on Snively's Ridge. Climb through oak groves and small meadows on the east-facing cliffs above Garzas Canyon. The eroded path mercifully levels out at a fenceline by Snively's Corral, a bench, and a junction.

After resting, descend on the winding Sky Trail to an elevated perch overlooking La Mesa Pond and the network of trails below. Stay to the right past the Sage Trail and Deer Trail, completing the loop at the Mesa Trail. Bear left on the Mesa Trail, retracing your steps back to the trailhead. ▪

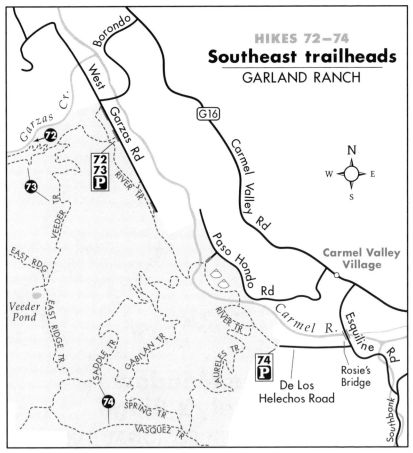

HIKES 72-74
Southeast trailheads
GARLAND RANCH

72. Garzas Canyon to Redwood Canyon
GARLAND RANCH REGIONAL PARK

Hiking distance: 3.6-mile loop
Hiking time: 2 hours
Configuration: loop with short spur trail
Elevation gain: 800 feet
Difficulty: easy to moderate
Exposure: mostly shaded canyon
Dogs: allowed
Maps: U.S.G.S. Seaside and Mt. Carmel · Garland Ranch Regional Park map

**map
page 211**

Garzas Canyon is a stream-fed canyon bisecting Garland Ranch Regional Park. The beautiful Garzas Canyon Trail heads up the lush garden-like canyon past rock-lined pools and numerous creek crossings. A short spur trail leads into Redwood Canyon, a remote side canyon with clusters of towering redwoods. The loop hike returns on a cliffside path above Garzas Canyon.

To the trailhead

From Highway 1 and Carmel Valley Road in Carmel, drive 10.3 miles east on Carmel Valley Road to Boronda Road on the right. The turnoff is 1.7 miles past the signed Garland Ranch parking lot. Turn right on Boronda Road and drive 0.6 miles, crossing over the Carmel River to the end of the road. Turn left on East Garzas Road, and continue 0.2 miles to the signed trail on the right. Park alongside the road.

Additional parking, and a signed connector trail into Garzas Canyon, begins a quarter mile ahead at the end of the road.

The hike

Hike into the shady oak grove, passing the River Trail. Head up the forested slope past the Veeder Trail on the left (Hike 73) to the signed junction with the Terrace Trail, the return route.

Begin the loop to the right on the Garzas Canyon Trail. Switchbacks descend to Garzas Creek at the canyon floor. Head up canyon and cross a long wooden footbridge over the creek. The path climbs numerous small rises, then dips back to the floor and a junction. The Garzas Canyon Trail leads up the canyon wall to La Mesa, a huge, grassy terrace to the north. Stay to the left on the creekside path. Cross another footbridge over the creek to a junction with the East Ridge Trail. (For a shorter hike, the East Ridge Trail connects with the Terrace Trail.) Go to the right and pass through a trail gate on the Redwood Canyon Trail. Continue up canyon, crossing the creek four more times. At the fourth crossing, leave Garzas Creek and veer left up Redwood Canyon. Pass clusters of large redwoods in the narrow side canyon. A half mile up the canyon, a bridge crosses the stream at a junction. This is the return route.

First, continue up Redwood Canyon through the forest, rich with ferns and magnificent redwoods. The canyon splits in a wide flat area covered with redwoods. The trail follows the right canyon and soon fades away.

Return to the bridge and cross, heading up the east canyon wall. Pass through a trail gate to a Y-junction with the East Ridge Trail. Take the left fork fifty yards to a signed junction. Bear right on the Terrace Trail. Traverse the narrow cliffside path above Garzas Canyon, following the contours of the mountain. Climb the steps and complete the loop at the Garzas Canyon Trail. Return to the right. ■

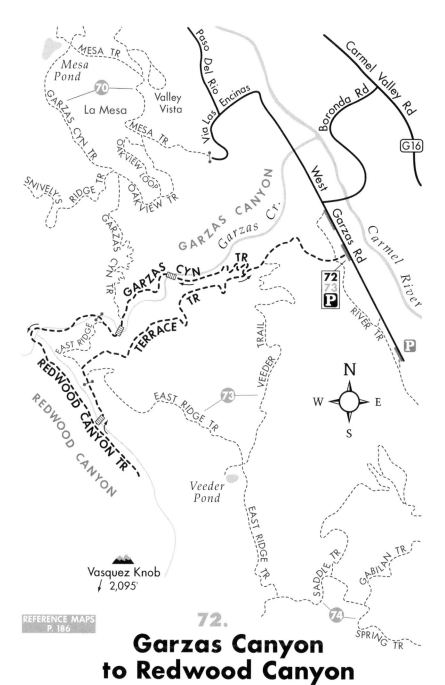

MESA TR

Mesa
Pond

La Mesa

GARZAS CYN TR

Valley
Vista

MESA TR

OAKVIEW LOOP

OAKVIEW TR

SNIVELY'S RIDGE TR

GARZAS CYN TR

GARZAS CYN TR

Paso Del Rio

Via Las Encinas

GARZAS CANYON

Garzas Cr.

GARZAS CYN TR

TR

TR

TERRACE

EAST RIDGE

REDWOOD CANYON TR

REDWOOD CANYON

EAST RIDGE TR

73

VEEDER TRAIL

Veeder
Pond

EAST RIDGE TR

Carmel Valley Rd

Boronda Rd

G16

West Garzas Rd

Carmel River

RIVER TR

72
73
P

P

N
W — E
S

SADDLE TR

GABILAN TR

74

SPRING TR

Vasquez Knob
↓ 2,095'

REFERENCE MAPS
P. 186

72.
Garzas Canyon
to Redwood Canyon
GARLAND RANCH REGIONAL PARK

73. Veeder—East Ridge—Terrace Loop
GARLAND RANCH REGIONAL PARK

Hiking distance: 3.5-mile loop
Hiking time: 2 hours
Configuration: loop
Elevation gain: 1,300 feet
Difficulty: moderate to somewhat strenuous
Exposure: shaded forest and open meadow
Dogs: allowed
Maps: U.S.G.S. Carmel Valley, Mt. Carmel and Seaside
  Garland Ranch Regional Park map

This loop hike climbs hundreds of feet to an overlook in a mountain meadow. The panoramic views include Garzas Canyon, Redwood Canyon, Snively's Ridge, Carmel Valley, and the ocean at Monterey Bay. The trail winds through oak woodlands and traverses a narrow, cliffside path above Garzas Canyon.

To the trailhead

From Highway 1 and Carmel Valley Road in Carmel, drive 10.3 miles east on Carmel Valley Road to Boronda Road on the right. The turnoff is 1.7 miles past the signed Garland Ranch parking lot. Turn right on Boronda Road and drive 0.6 miles, crossing over the Carmel River to the end of the road. Turn left on East Garzas Road, and continue 0.2 miles to the signed trail on the right. Park alongside the road.

Additional parking, and a signed connector trail into Garzas Canyon, begins a quarter mile ahead at the end of the road.

The hike

Take the signed Garzas Trail through the oak woodland. Cross the River Trail and head up the slope to a signed junction on the left with the Veeder Trail. Bear left on the Veeder Trail—the beginning of the loop—and wind up the oak-studded hill past ferns and poison oak. Steadily climb the east-facing hillside while overlooking Carmel Valley. Curve right up the side canyon to a bench in a clearing with views of Garzas Canyon and Snively's Ridge to the northwest. Beyond the bench, climb to a ridge, passing

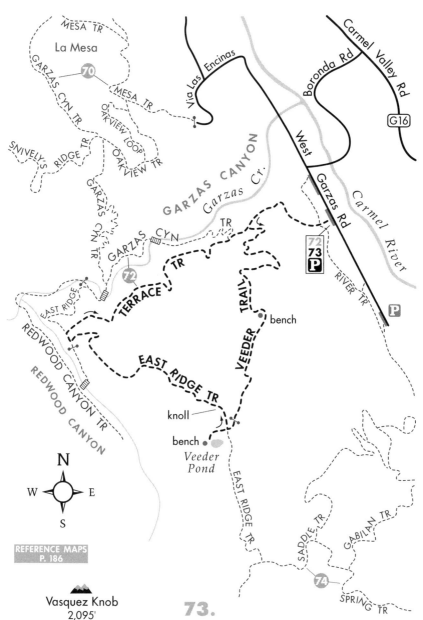

MESA TR

La Mesa

GARZAS CYN TR

70

MESA TR

OAKVIEW LOOP

OAKVIEW TR

SNIVELY'S RIDGE TR

GARZAS CYN TR

GARZAS CYN TR

Via Las Encinas

GARZAS CANYON

Garzas Cr.

GARZAS CYN TR

72

West

Garzas Rd

Boronda Rd

Carmel Valley Rd

G16

Carmel River

72
73 P

RIVER TR

P

TERRACE TR

EAST RIDGE

REDWOOD CANYON TR

REDWOOD CANYON

VEEDER TRAIL

bench

EAST RIDGE TR

knoll

bench
Veeder Pond

EAST RIDGE TR

SADDLE TR

GABILAN TR

74

SPRING TR

N
W E
S

REFERENCE MAPS
P. 186

Vasquez Knob
2,095'

73.

Veeder–East Ridge–
Terrace Loop
GARLAND RANCH REGIONAL PARK

through a trail gate to a saddle and a signed junction with the East Ridge Trail. The left branch climbs up to Vasquez Knob. Before taking the right fork (the continuation of the loop), descend into the open meadow to a bench at Veeder Pond, a vernal pool.

Return to the junction and continue west (left) on the loop. Ascend the small hill to a knoll, the highest point on the hike. The 360-degree vistas extend to the ocean and Monterey Bay. Descend to the west, overlooking Redwood Canyon and the towering trees. The path quickly drops down the north wall of Redwood Canyon to a junction. The left fork leads up Redwood Canyon (Hike 72). Take the right fork 50 yards to a junction with the Terrace Trail on the right. Head right, traversing the cliffs on the narrow path above the canyon. Weave in and out of ravines along the contours of the canyon. Climb some steps to a junction with the Garzas Canyon Trail. Bear to the right, completing the loop at the Veeder Trail. Return on the same route. ▪

74. Vasquez Ridge

Laureles–Vasquez–Spring Loop

GARLAND RANCH REGIONAL PARK

Hiking distance: 5.5 miles round trip
Hiking time: 3 hours
Configuration: out-and-back with loop
Elevation gain: 1,700 feet
Difficulty: strenuous
Exposure: shaded canyon and exposed ridge
Dogs: allowed
Maps: U.S.G.S. Carmel Valley and Mt. Carmel
Garland Ranch Regional Park map

map
page 217

This loop hike lies at the southeast end, and lightly hiked area, of Garland Ranch Regional Park. The trail steeply ascends the mountain to Vasquez Ridge at an overlook with a bench and panoramic views. The path follows the ridge, overlooking Hitchcock Canyon and Carmel Valley, then returns through an oak-filled and spring-fed canyon beneath the ridge.

To the trailhead

From Highway 1 and Carmel Valley Road in Carmel, drive 11.9 miles east on Carmel Valley Road to Esquiline Road on the right. The turnoff is just past Carmel Valley Village. Turn right and drive 0.2 miles, crossing Rosie's Bridge over the Carmel River, to De Los Helechos Road. Turn right and park at the end of the street.

The hike

From the end of De Los Helechos Road, walk through the Lazy Oaks right-of-way past a few homes to the Garland Park entrance. Follow the path through oak groves to a posted trail split. Curve left, quickly reaching a second junction. The right fork follows the River Trail. Curve left on the Laureles Trail, and ascend the forested hillside. Climb through the oak woodland to magnificent valley views. Continue climbing through the forest, emerging on the grassy Vasquez Ridge at 1.3 miles. On the ridge is a bench, a junction, and magnificent views. A detour to the left leads 0.2 miles through oak-dotted meadows to the fenced park boundary.

Return to the junction and take the Vasquez Trail 40 yards to a posted trail fork. Begin the loop to the left, staying on the Vasquez Trail. Follow the ridge up the meadow along the south boundary, overlooking Hitchcock Canyon. At the Y-junction, another short detour left leads to the hilltop summit at the park boundary. The right fork heads downhill on the Saddle Trail, crossing the head of Redwood Canyon. Pass a junction on the left with the East Ridge Trail, and skirt around the left side of the knoll. Steadily descend to a Y-fork. Take the Spring Trail to the right, and head downhill into the oak-filled canyon beneath Vasquez Ridge. Pass the narrow Gabilan Trail on the left to a trough, spring, and water tank on the canyon floor. Curve left down canyon, then ascend the hillside, completing the loop on the ridge. Retrace your footsteps on the Laureles Trail. ∎

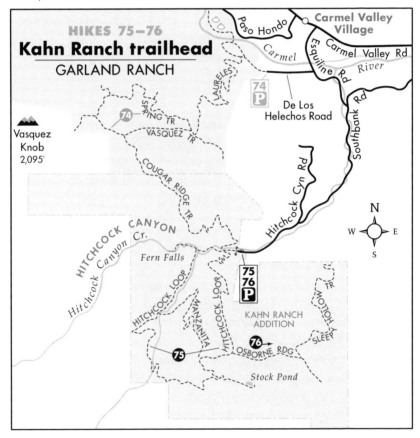

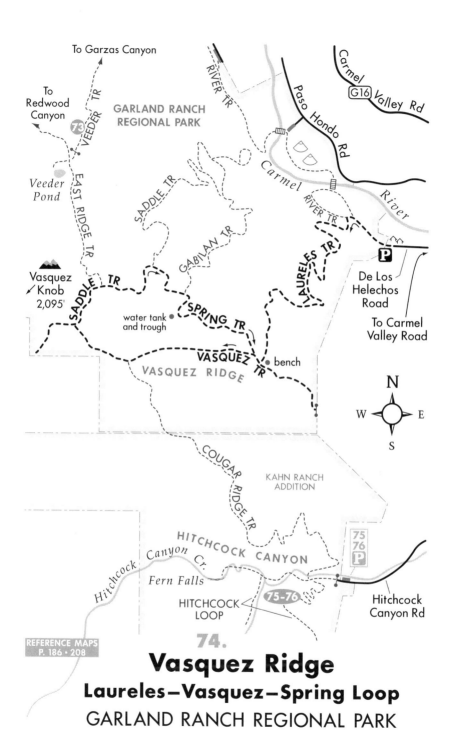

To Garzas Canyon

To Redwood Canyon

Carmel Valley Rd

G16

RIVER TR

Paso Hondo Rd

GARLAND RANCH REGIONAL PARK

VEEDER TR

73

Veeder Pond

EAST RIDGE TR

SADDLE TR

Carmel

RIVER TR

River

Vasquez Knob 2,095'

SADDLE TR

GABILAN TR

LAURELES TR

P

De Los Helechos Road

To Carmel Valley Road

water tank and trough

SPRING TR

VASQUEZ TR

bench

VASQUEZ RIDGE

N

W — E

S

COUGAR RIDGE TR

KAHN RANCH ADDITION

HITCHCOCK CANYON

Hitchcock Canyon Cr.

Fern Falls

75 76 P

HITCHCOCK LOOP

75-76

Hitchcock Canyon Rd

REFERENCE MAPS P. 186 • 208

74.
Vasquez Ridge
Laureles–Vasquez–Spring Loop
GARLAND RANCH REGIONAL PARK

75. Hitchcock Loop

KAHN RANCH ADDITION

GARLAND RANCH REGIONAL PARK

An access permit is required on easement to trailhead parking
www.mprpd.org · 831-659-4488, then select option 5

Hiking distance: 4.6-mile loop
Hiking time: 2.5 hours
Configuration: loop
Elevation gain: 1,000 feet
Difficulty: moderate to strenuous
Exposure: shaded forest and exposed slope
Dogs: allowed
Maps: U.S.G.S. Carmel Valley · Garland Ranch Regional Park map

Kahn Ranch, a new addition to Garland Ranch Regional Park, sits at the southern end of the park in the hills above Carmel Valley Village. The ranch covers 1,100 acres and is open to bikes, horses, dogs, and hikers. The Hitchcock Loop climbs up Hitchcock Canyon (a stream-fed drainage), crosses Osborne Ridge, and returns via an open hillside slope with scenic mountain overlooks. En route, the trail visits Fern Falls, a 25-foot waterfall with two pools in a forested, rock-walled box canyon. Another spur trail leads to Stock Pond, a small pond in a ravine.

An access permit from the Monterey Peninsula Regional Park District is required to enter the ranch. Contact information is included above.

To the trailhead

From Highway 1 and Carmel Valley Road in Carmel, drive 11.9 miles east on Carmel Valley Road to Esquiline Road on the right. The turnoff is just past Carmel Valley Village. (Esquiline Road is located 2.2 miles east of Laureles Grade.) Turn right and drive 0.6 miles to Southbank Road. Turn right again and go 0.8 miles up the winding road to Hitchcock Road. Turn left and continue 0.6 miles to the signed Kahn Ranch entrance and parking area on the right.

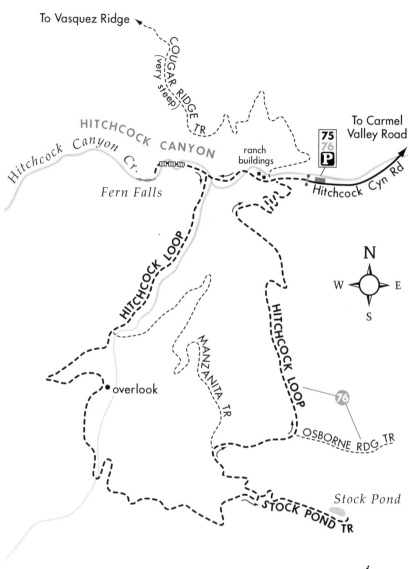

To Vasquez Ridge

COUGAR RIDGE TR
(very steep)

HITCHCOCK CANYON

Hitchcock Canyon Cr.

Fern Falls

HITCHCOCK LOOP

ranch buildings

75
76
P

To Carmel Valley Road

Hitchcock Cyn Rd

N
W · E
S

HITCHCOCK LOOP

overlook

MANZANITA TR

76

OSBORNE RDG TR

HITCHCOCK LOOP

STOCK POND TR

Stock Pond

REFERENCE MAPS
P. 186 · 216

75.
Rancho Loop
Cooper Ranch Addition
GARLAND RANCH REGIONAL PARK

The hike

Walk up the narrow, vehicle-restricted dirt road under the shade of oak trees. At 100 yards is a junction with the Hitchcock Loop Trail on the left. Begin the loop straight ahead, passing ranch buildings. Continue up canyon, crossing a seasonal fork of Hitchcock Canyon Creek to a posted junction. To the left is the Hitchcock Loop Trail, the main route.

For a short detour to Fern Falls, go right. Follow the footpath through the narrow, forested drainage alongside the creek to the right. Cross two bridges over the waterway, passing mossy tree trunks and a fern ground cover. Cross a third bridge, where the trail ends in a box canyon by the 25-foot cataract and two pools.

Return to the junction, and continue on the Hitchcock Loop Trail, now on the right. Head south on an easy uphill grade. Stay to the right of the ephemeral stream to a Y-fork. The Manzanita Trail veers left, shortening the loop by a half mile. Stay on the Hitchcock Loop Trail to the right and up to an overlook of the surrounding mountains. Descend back into the oak forest and cross the drainage. Switchback left and steadily climb the mountain at a moderate grade to a signed junction at a U-shaped left bend.

Detour right on the Stock Pond Trail. The 0.3-mile-long path climbs over the hill and drops down to the rock-walled seasonal pond tucked into a ravine.

Back at the main trail, continue uphill on the Hitchcock Loop, with vistas down canyon and of the mountainous backcountry. At the junction with the south end of the Manzanita Trail, go to the right, staying on the Hitchcock Loop Trail. Pass an overlook across Carmel Valley. At the ridge is a sitting bench on the right at another spectacular overlook. A short distance ahead is a posted junction with the Osborne Ridge Trail (Hike 76). Go to the left on the Hitchcock Loop and steeply descend, with alternating views of the forested backcountry and Carmel Valley. Wind down the mountain, completing the loop at the entrance trail. Walk 100 yards to the right, returning to the parking area. ■

76. Osborne Ridge

KAHN RANCH ADDITION

GARLAND RANCH REGIONAL PARK

An access permit is required on easement to trailhead parking
www.mprpd.org · 831-659-4488, then select option 5

Hiking distance: 6 miles round trip
Hiking time: 3 hours
Configuration: out-and-back
Elevation gain: 1,000 feet
Difficulty: moderate to strenuous
Exposure: shaded forest and exposed slope
Dogs: allowed
Maps: U.S.G.S. Carmel Valley · Garland Ranch Regional Park map

**map
page 223**

Osborne Ridge is a 1,600-foot ridge at the south end of Garland Ranch Regional Park in the Kahn Ranch addition. The ridge stretches over 2 miles between Hitchcock Canyon and the San Clemente Reservoir above Carmel Valley Village. This hike begins in Hitchcock Canyon and climbs up to Osborne Ridge. From the crest, the Sleepy Hollow Trail weaves through the forest to a bench and overlook of Carmel Valley. (Sleepy Hollow is a flat along the Carmel River at the base of the mountain. Unfortunately, access to Sleepy Hollow is off of San Clemente Drive, a private gated road.)

An access permit from the Monterey Peninsula Regional Park District is required to enter the ranch. Contact information is included above.

To the trailhead

From Highway 1 and Carmel Valley Road in Carmel, drive 11.9 miles east on Carmel Valley Road to Esquiline Road on the right. The turnoff is just past Carmel Valley Village. (Esquiline Road is located 2.2 miles east of Laureles Grade.) Turn right and drive 0.6 miles to Southbank Road. Turn right again and go 0.8 miles up the winding road to Hitchcock Road. Turn left and continue 0.6 miles to the signed Kahn Ranch entrance and parking area on the right.

The hike

Walk up the narrow, vehicle-restricted dirt road under the shade of oak trees. At 100 yards is a junction with the Hitchcock Loop Trail on the left. Bear left, leaving the road. Head up the south canyon wall on the Hitchcock Loop Trail. Wind up six switchbacks, climbing at a fairly steep grade. At the sixth bend, views open up into Hitchcock Canyon, Carmel Valley, and the surrounding mountains. Steadily gain elevation to a signed junction atop Osborne Ridge at 1.1 miles. The Hitchcock Loop Trail continues to the right (Hike 75).

Bear left on the Osborne Ridge Trail. Follow the easy rolling ridge south on a wide, grassy path under the shade of oak trees. At 1.5 miles, on a U-shaped left bend, is the old Osborne Loop Trail, now closed to public access. Gently descend on the Sleepy Hollow Trail, temporarily leaving the ridge. Traverse the steep hillside, then stroll along the scenic ridge to a bench and overlook at the end of the trail by the park boundary. Return along the same route. ■

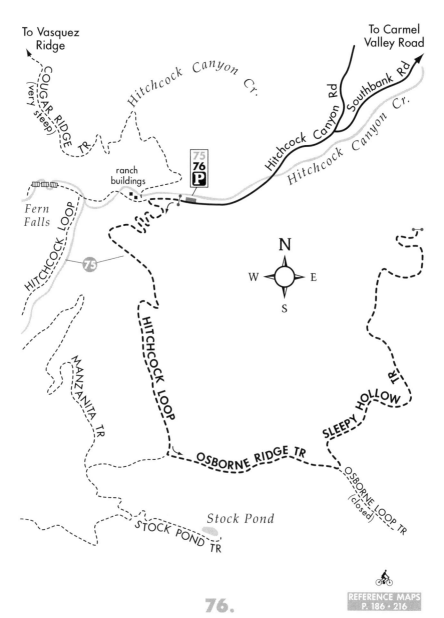

To Vasquez Ridge

To Carmel Valley Road

COUGAR RIDGE TR (very steep)

Hitchcock Canyon Cr.

Hitchcock Canyon Rd

Southbank Rd

Hitchcock Canyon Cr.

ranch buildings

75
76 P

Fern Falls

HITCHCOCK LOOP

75

N
W E
S

HITCHCOCK LOOP

MANZANITA TR

OSBORNE RIDGE TR

SLEEPY HOLLOW TR

OSBORNE LOOP TR (closed)

Stock Pond

STOCK POND TR

REFERENCE MAPS
P. 186 • 216

76.
Osborne Ridge
Cooper Ranch Addition
GARLAND RANCH REGIONAL PARK

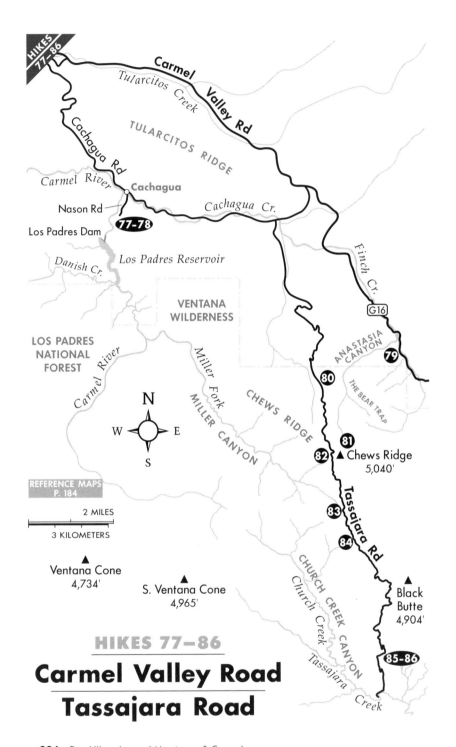

Carmel Valley Rd

Tularcitos Creek

TULARCITOS RIDGE

Cachagua Rd

Carmel River

Cachagua

Nason Rd

Cachagua Cr.

Los Padres Dam

77-78

Los Padres Reservoir

Danish Cr.

Finch Cr.

VENTANA
WILDERNESS

G16

LOS PADRES
NATIONAL
FOREST

Carmel River

Miller Fork

MILLER CANYON

ANASTASIA
CANYON

79

THE BEAR TRAP

CHEWS RIDGE

80

81
▲ Chews Ridge
5,040'

82

N
W   E
S

Tassajara Rd

83

84

REFERENCE MAPS
P. 184

2 MILES

3 KILOMETERS

CHURCH CREEK CANYON

Church Creek

Black
Butte
4,904'

▲
Ventana Cone
4,734'

▲
S. Ventana Cone
4,965'

Tassajara Creek

85-86

HIKES 77–86
Carmel Valley Road
Tassajara Road

77. Carmel River Trail to Danish Creek
LOS PADRES RESERVOIR

Hiking distance: 5.6 miles round trip
Hiking time: 2.5 hours
Configuration: out-and-back
Elevation gain: 300 feet
Difficulty: easy to moderate
Exposure: mostly shaded forest
Dogs: allowed
Maps: U.S.G.S. Carmel Valley and Ventana Cones
      Big Sur and Ventana Wilderness map
      Ventana Wilderness Los Padres National Forest map
      Los Padres National Forest Northern Section Trail Map

map
page 227

The Los Padres Reservoir is an 1,800-acre dammed lake along the Carmel River. The reservoir, nestled in a gorgeous valley surrounded by the forested mountains, lies adjacent to the Los Padres National Forest. The forested path contours the mountains along the western slope of the long reservoir from one end to the other, gaining little elevation. Be aware of ticks, which are prevalent along the trail during the winter season.

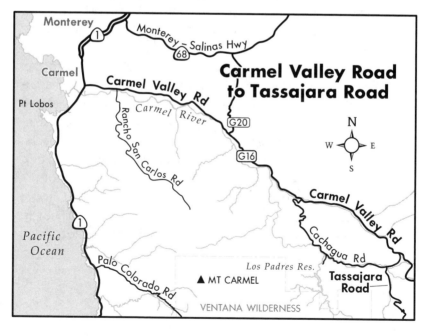

To the trailhead

From Highway 1 and Carmel Valley Road in Carmel, drive 16 miles east on Carmel Valley Road to the signed Los Padres Dam/Cachagua Road turnoff. Turn right and drive 5.8 miles on the winding road to the posted Nason Road turnoff in the community of Cachagua. Turn right and continue 0.6 miles to the large parking area at the end of the public road.

The hike

Walk through the trailhead gate. Follow the unpaved dam road (Carmel River Trail) up the Carmel River Canyon. Pass stately, twisted oaks to a large open flat with several forking side roads. Stay on the main road to the dam spillway in a granite gorge at a half mile. Cross the gorge on the bridge, and head up the road past the waterfall. Curve right to the Los Padres Dam and an overlook of the reservoir. Walk toward the hills on the west side of the reservoir. Curve sharply south (left) and traverse the hillside above the lake, enjoying a bird's-eye view of the lake and surrounding mountains. Several side paths on the left descend to the reservoir. The wide trail narrows to a single track and reaches a signed junction at 1.7 miles. The Carmel River Trail continues straight along the west side of the reservoir. The right fork is the Big Pines Trail (Hike 78).

Continue straight—on the Carmel River Trail—parallel to the reservoir. The trail alternates from shady forest to open chaparral as it follows the contours of the mountain on the cliff's narrow edge. Near the south end of the lake is an overlook of the snake-shaped reservoir. Gradually descend with the aid of switchbacks to Danish Creek, a tributary of the Carmel River. Follow the creek upstream to a rocky beach at 2.8 miles, the turn-around spot.

To continue, ford the creek and follow the Carmel River Canyon, reaching Bluff Camp at 4 miles. From Bluff Camp, the trail heads into Miller Canyon and up to China Camp off Tassajara Road. ■

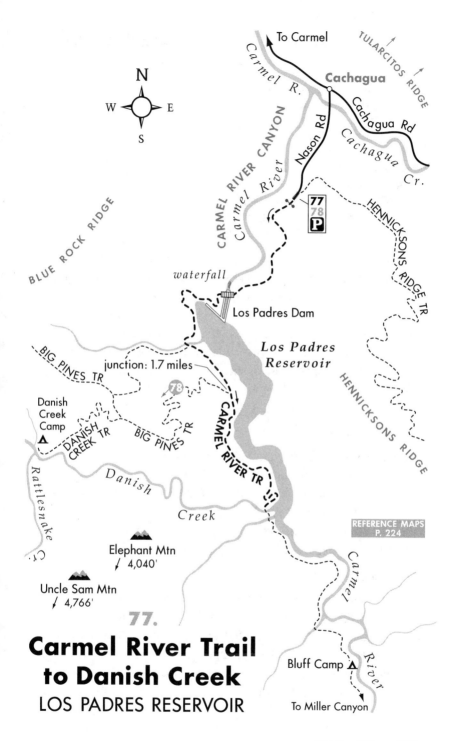

N
W · E
S

To Carmel

Carmel R.

Cachagua

TULARCITOS RIDGE

Cachagua Rd

Cachagua Cr.

CARMEL RIVER CANYON

Carmel River

Nason Rd

77
78
P

HENNICKSONS RIDGE TR

BLUE ROCK RIDGE

waterfall

Los Padres Dam

Los Padres Reservoir

BIG PINES TR

junction: 1.7 miles

78

CARMEL RIVER TR

HENNICKSONS RIDGE

Danish Creek Camp
△

DANISH CREEK TR

BIG PINES TR

Danish

Creek

REFERENCE MAPS
P. 224

Rattlesnake Cr.

Elephant Mtn
↓ 4,040'

Uncle Sam Mtn
↓ 4,766'

Carmel

River

77.

Carmel River Trail
to Danish Creek
LOS PADRES RESERVOIR

Bluff Camp △

To Miller Canyon

78. Big Pine Trail to Danish Creek Camp
LOS PADRES RESERVOIR

Hiking distance: 7 miles round trip
Hiking time: 3.5 hours
Configuration: out-and-back
Elevation gain: 1,300 feet
Difficulty: moderate to strenuous
Exposure: a mix of shaded forest and open meadow
Dogs: allowed
Maps: U.S.G.S. Carmel Valley · Big Sur and Ventana Wilderness map
Ventana Wilderness Los Padres National Forest map
Los Padres National Forest Northern Section Trail Map

The Big Pine Trail lies on the west side of the Los Padres Reservoir in a scenic mountain valley. Hikes 77 and 78 begin on the Carmel River Trail, curving around the dam and spillway along the western slope of the reservoir. While Hike 77 remains mostly level along the side of the reservoir, this hike switchbacks up to a ridge that overlooks the reservoir and surrounding wilderness area. A short spur trail drops into a small canyon at Danish Camp near the confluence of Danish and Rattlesnake Creeks. Be aware of ticks, which are prevalent during the wet season.

To the trailhead

From Highway 1 and Carmel Valley Road in Carmel, drive 16 miles east on Carmel Valley Road to the signed Los Padres Dam/Cachagua Road turnoff. Turn right and drive 5.8 miles on the winding road to the posted Nason Road turnoff in the community of Cachagua. Turn right and continue 0.6 miles to the large parking area at the end of the public road.

The hike

Walk through the trailhead gate. Follow the unpaved dam road (Carmel River Trail) up the Carmel River Canyon. Pass stately, twisted oaks to a large open flat with several forking side roads. Stay on the main road to the dam spillway in a granite gorge at a half mile. Cross the gorge on the bridge, and head up the road past the waterfall. Curve right to the Los Padres Dam and

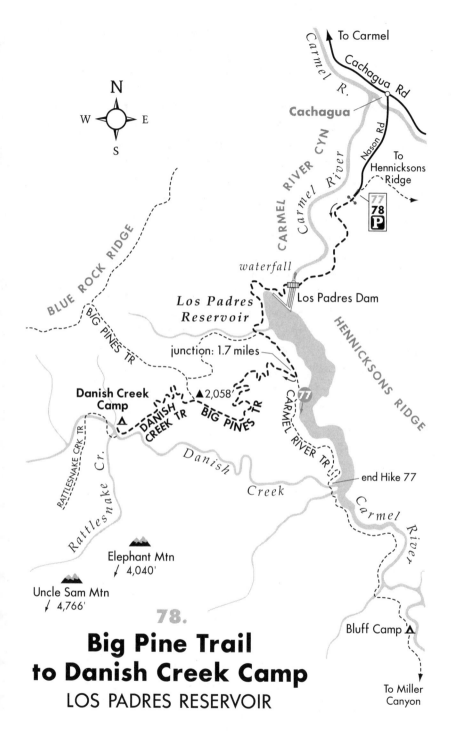

N
W · E
S

To Carmel

Carmel R.

Cachagua Rd

Cachagua

Nason Rd

To Hennicksons Ridge

CARMEL RIVER CYN

Carmel River

77
78 P

waterfall

Los Padres Reservoir

Los Padres Dam

BLUE ROCK RIDGE

BIG PINES TR

junction: 1.7 miles

HENNICKSONS RIDGE

Danish Creek Camp

▲ 2,058'

DANISH CREEK TR

BIG PINES TR

CARMEL RIVER TR

77

RATTLESNAKE CRK. TR.

Danish

Creek

end Hike 77

Rattlesnake Cr.

🏔 Elephant Mtn
✓ 4,040'

🏔 Uncle Sam Mtn
✓ 4,766'

Carmel River

78.

Big Pine Trail to Danish Creek Camp
LOS PADRES RESERVOIR

Bluff Camp △

To Miller Canyon

an overlook of the reservoir. Walk toward the hills on the west side of the reservoir. Curve sharply south (left) and traverse the hillside above the lake, enjoying a bird's-eye view of the lake and surrounding mountains. Several side paths on the left descend to the reservoir. The wide trail narrows to a single track and reaches a signed junction at 1.7 miles. The Carmel River Trail continues straight along the west side of the reservoir (Hike 77).

Take the right (west) fork on the Big Pines Trail up the narrow hillside path. Weave up the side canyon, steadily climbing to elevated views of the lake. The trail levels out on a saddle at the head of the canyon. Panoramic views extend west to Blue Rock Ridge, east to Hennicksons Ridge, and south to Elephant Mountain and Uncle Sam Mountain. Follow the ridge to a posted trail split at the high point of the hike at 2,058 feet.

Leave the Big Pines Trail and bear left on the Danish Creek Trail. Zigzag down the steep hillside for 0.7 miles to Danish Creek Camp. The camp is next to the creek on an open flat with a large live oak tree. The trail along Danish Creek is worth exploring. Rattlesnake Creek is a short distance upstream. ▪

79. Anastasia Trail—East Trailhead
Carmel Valley Road to Cahoon Spring

Hiking distance: 7 miles round trip
Hiking time: 4 hours
Configuration: out-and-back
Elevation gain: 600 feet
Difficulty: moderate
Exposure: mostly forested
Dogs: allowed
Maps: U.S.G.S. Chews Ridge · Big Sur and Ventana Wilderness map
Ventana Wilderness Los Padres National Forest map

The Anastasia Trail is a 2.8-mile-long trail connecting Carmel Valley Road with Tassajara Road. This hike follows the remote, stream-fed canyon floor through open valleys and a lush sycamore and black oak forest into Bear Trap Canyon. Cahoon Spring, a natural spring, is located in the canyon. The water flows out of a pipe into a watering trough in the shade of towering black oaks. This is a lightly traveled hiking and equestrian corridor, offering solitude.

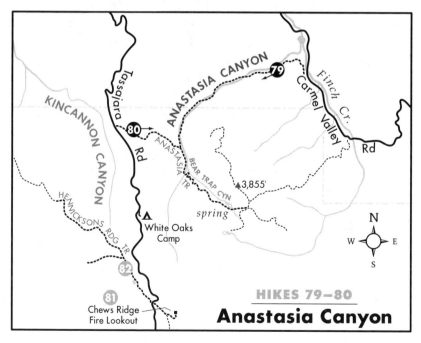

HIKES 79—80
Anastasia Canyon

To the trailhead

From Highway 1 and Carmel Valley Road in Carmel, drive 28.4 miles southeast on Carmel Valley Road, (passing through Carmel Valley Village at 11.5 miles) to the trailhead pullout on the right. The turnoff is 5.4 miles past Tassajara Road and 0.3 miles past mile marker 28.5. Park in the large dirt pullout on the right by the trail sign.

The hike

Pass through the gate by the wooden "Anastasia" sign. Follow the narrow dirt road, parallel to Finch Creek on the right. Climb the slope and drop down into the oak-filled, grassy meadows of Anastasia Canyon. Pass a seasonal hunter's cabin on the left, and continue up canyon on the grassy, single-track path. Rock-hop over Anastasia Creek and follow the canyon bottom, passing massive oaks. Hop over the creek two consecutive times, and enter the Los Padres National Forest and Ventana Wilderness. Steadily move up-stream, crossing the creek two more times. Bend to the left, following the curvature of the canyon, to an unsigned (and hard-to-spot) connection with the Anastasia Trail, which climbs up to Tassajara Road (Hike 80). Parallel the stream along the shaded canyon floor. Pass moss-covered tree trunks and rocks. Cross a tributary stream and gently ascend the hillside as the footpath becomes an old jeep road. Cross Anastasia Creek and ascend the east slope of the canyon, weaving up to the ridge.

Leave Anastasia Canyon and descend into Bear Trap Canyon. Curve sharply to the left, crossing a stream-fed draw. Continue downhill to Cahoon Spring in a shady oak grove. The spring flows from a pipe near a clawfoot bathtub used as an animal watering trough. Climb a quarter mile up the canyon to The Bear Trap, an open ridge with panoramic views and an unsigned junction. The left fork leads towards Carmel Valley Road, but the Cahoon Ranch, privately owned land, eliminates public access to the road. This is the turn-around spot. Return by retracing your steps. ■

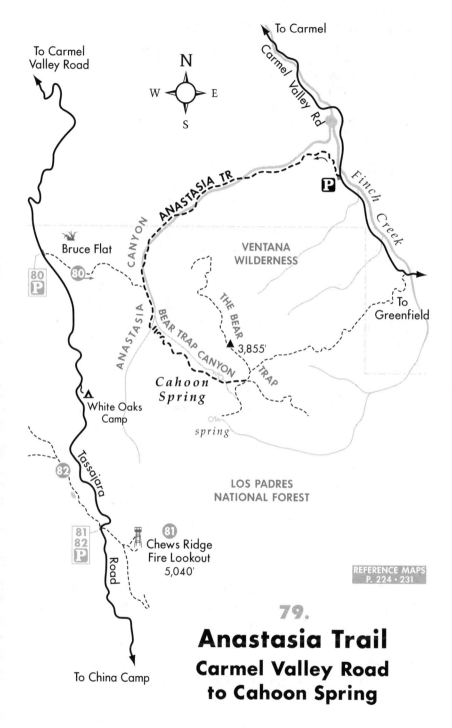

To Carmel

To Carmel
Valley Road

Carmel Valley Rd

N
W   E
S

P

Finch Creek

Bruce Flat

80
P

80

ANASTASIA TR

CANYON

VENTANA
WILDERNESS

To
Greenfield

ANASTASIA

BEAR TRAP CANYON

THE BEAR

3,855'

TRAP

*Cahoon
Spring*

spring

White Oaks
Camp

82

Tassajara

LOS PADRES
NATIONAL FOREST

81
82
P

Chews Ridge
Fire Lookout
5,040'

81

Road

REFERENCE MAPS
P. 224 · 231

79.

Anastasia Trail
Carmel Valley Road
to Cahoon Spring

To China Camp

80. Anastasia Trail—West Trailhead
Tassajara Road to Cahoon Spring

Hiking distance: 4.8 miles round trip
Hiking time: 2.5 hours
Configuration: out-and-back
Elevation gain: 900 feet
Difficulty: moderate
Exposure: mostly forested
Dogs: allowed
Maps: U.S.G.S. Chews Ridge · Big Sur and Ventana Wilderness map
Ventana Wilderness Los Padres National Forest map

The Anastasia Trail connects Carmel Valley Road with Tassajara Road. This hike begins from Tassajara Road in a large meadow known as Bruce Flat. The trail descends the mountain slope into the bucolic forest to the banks of Anastasia Creek. The path then follows the waterway into Bear Trap Canyon to Cahoon Spring, a natural spring under the shade of towering black oaks. Anastasia Canyon is lightly used, offering deep-forest solitude.

To the trailhead

From Highway 1 and Carmel Valley Road in Carmel, drive 23 miles southeast on Carmel Valley Road (passing through Carmel Valley Village at 11.5 miles) to Tassajara Road. Turn right and drive 1.3 miles to a signed Y-fork with Cachagua Road. Curve left, staying on Tassajara Road, and continue 5.1 miles to a cattle guard at the national forest boundary by barns and corrals on the right (west). Drive 0.2 miles farther to the second gate opening on the left at the south end of Bruce Flat, a flat grassy meadow. Park in the pullouts on either side of the road.

The hike

Pass through the signed trailhead gate, and cross the grassy meadow dotted with oaks, maples, and madrones. Traverse the rolling slope into the forested, east-facing slope of Anastasia Canyon. Descend the hillside, dropping 800 feet in the first 0.8 miles, to an unsigned junction. The junction is near the transient stream in bucolic Anastasia Canyon. The Anastasia Trail continues left to Carmel Valley Road (Hike 79).

For this hike, leave the Anastasia Trail and follow the shaded canyon floor to the right. Parallel Anastasia Creek, passing moss-covered tree trunks and rocks. Cross a tributary stream and gently ascend the hillside as the footpath becomes an old jeep road. Cross Anastasia Creek and ascend the east slope of the canyon, weaving up to the ridge. Leave Anastasia Canyon and descend into Bear Trap Canyon. Curve sharply to the left, crossing a stream-fed draw. Continue downhill to Cahoon Spring in a shady oak grove. The spring flows from a pipe near a clawfoot bathtub used as an animal watering trough. Climb a quarter mile up the canyon to The Bear Trap, an open ridge with panoramic views and an unsigned junction. The left fork leads towards Carmel Valley Road, but the Cahoon Ranch, privately owned land, eliminates access to the road. This is the turn-around spot. Return by retracing your steps. ■

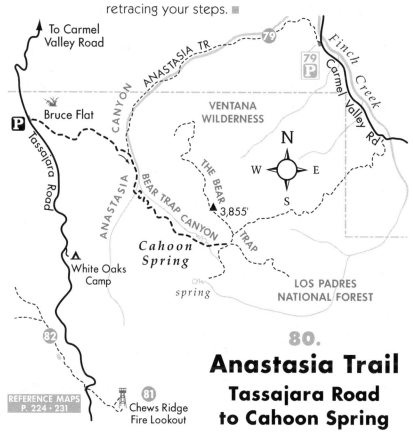

To Carmel Valley Road

ANASTASIA TR.

79

Finch Creek

79 P

Carmel Valley Rd.

CANYON

Bruce Flat

P

Tassajara Road

VENTANA WILDERNESS

N

W ⊕ E

S

ANASTASIA

BEAR TRAP CANYON

▲ 3,855'

THE BEAR TRAP

Cahoon Spring

▲ White Oaks Camp

spring

LOS PADRES NATIONAL FOREST

82

REFERENCE MAPS P. 224 • 231

81 Chews Ridge Fire Lookout

80.

Anastasia Trail

Tassajara Road to Cahoon Spring

81. Chews Ridge Fire Lookout

Hiking distance: 0.7 miles round trip
Hiking time: 30 minutes hours
Configuration: out-and-back
Elevation gain: 160 feet
Difficulty: easy
Exposure: mostly exposed
Dogs: allowed
Maps: U.S.G.S. Chews Ridge · Big Sur and Ventana Wilderness map
Ventana Wilderness Los Padres National Forest map

This trail hikes up a restricted dirt road to the Chews Ridge Fire Lookout. It is a short, but scenic, hike with little elevation gain. The abandoned fire lookout sits at an elevation of 5,040 feet and offers 360-degree vistas of the expansive Ventana Wilderness and across the Santa Lucia Range, from Salinas Valley to Monterey Bay. The trail winds through open woodland and chaparral. It is a great location to observe birds, including mountain quail, sparrow, owl, and western tanager.

Opposite the trailhead, going northwest, is the Hennicksons Ridge Trail (Hike 82), which follows Chews Ridge.

To the trailhead

From Highway 1 and Carmel Valley Road in Carmel, drive 23 miles southeast on Carmel Valley Road (passing through Carmel Valley Village at 11.5 miles) to Tassajara Road. Turn right and drive 1.3 miles to a signed Y-fork with Cachagua Road. Curve left, staying on Tassajara Road, and continue 7.7 miles to Chews Ridge. Park in the large dirt pullout on the right.

The hike

Cross Tassajara Road and walk around the left side of the vehicle gate atop 4,881-foot Chews Ridge. Head up the narrow, unpaved road among oaks and Coulter pines with their massive cones. At 0.2 miles is a fork. The right fork heads south towards the pine forest and leads to the MIRA Observatory (Monterey Institute for Research in Astronomy). Stay on the main trail towards the fire lookout, straight ahead. Curve left to the structure at the summit. From the lookout are vistas across the mountain peaks and canyons, spanning from Salinas Valley in the east to the Pacific Ocean in the west.

For a longer hike, take the Hennicksons Ridge Trail, following Chews Ridge to the northwest (Hike 82). ∎

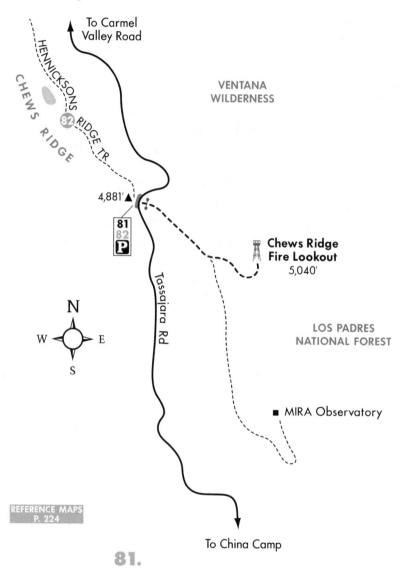

81.
Chews Ridge Fire Lookout

82. Chews Ridge
Hennicksons Ridge Trail from Tassajara Road

Hiking distance: 4 miles round trip
Hiking time: 2 hours
Configuration: out-and-back
Elevation gain: 600 feet
Difficulty: easy to moderate
Exposure: mostly exposed
Dogs: allowed
Maps: U.S.G.S. Chews Ridge · Big Sur and Ventana Wilderness map

Chews Ridge is a 4-mile-long spine in the Ventana Wilderness. The ridge sits at an average elevation of 3,500 feet, rising up to 5,000 feet at the fire lookout at its eastern tip. The easiest access to the ridge is from Tassajara Road, which crosses the ridge just west of the Chews Ridge Fire Lookout (Hike 81). The Hennicksons Ridge Trail follows the rolling ridge northwest between Miller Canyon and Kincannon Canyon. The first two miles of trail are maintained by volunteers, passing through open grassland and pockets of large black oak and grey pines. Along the ridge are views across the western ridges of the Ventana Wilderness and into the Carmel River watershed.

To the trailhead

From Highway 1 and Carmel Valley Road in Carmel, drive 23 miles southeast on Carmel Valley Road (passing through Carmel Valley Village at 11.5 miles) to Tassajara Road. Turn right and drive 1.3 miles to a signed Y-fork with Cachagua Road. Curve left, staying on Tassajara Road, and continue 7.7 miles to Chews Ridge. Park in the large dirt pullout on the right.

The hike

Walk around the left side of the vehicle gate and head northeast on an old jeep road. Follow the undulating ridge through groves of grey pines and mature twisted oaks. Pass a small pond on the left while strolling through the rolling landscape. Continue to an unmarked Y-fork. The left fork gently descends a half mile to an overlook into Miller Canyon, with panoramas of the coastal peaks. Beyond the overlook, the trail enters private land.

For this hike, veer right (north) and climb the hill to the ridge overlooking Kincannon Canyon. Curve left along the ridge to panoramas into Miller Canyon as the old dirt road narrows to a footpath. Meander among the oaks to a grassy knoll at two miles, with views across the mountains and across Monterey Bay to Santa Cruz. Beyond this point, the trail has become overgrown with brush and is obscured. This is a good turn-around spot. ■

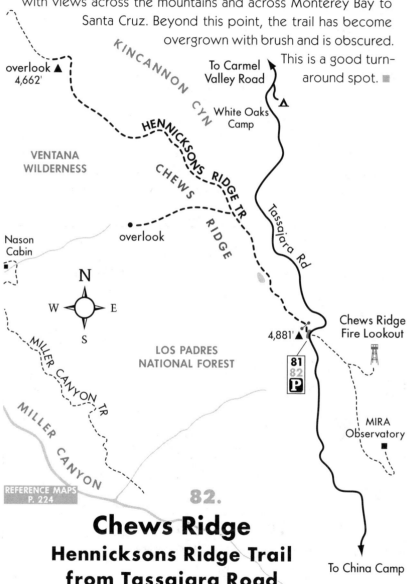

82.

Chews Ridge
Hennicksons Ridge Trail
from Tassajara Road

83. Church Creek Divide
Pine Ridge Trail from Tassajara Road

Hiking distance: 7.2 miles round trip
Hiking time: 3.5 hours
Configuration: out-and-back
Elevation gain: 1,200 feet
Difficulty: moderate to strenuous
Exposure: shaded forest and open grassy slopes
Dogs: allowed
Maps: U.S.G.S. Chews Ridge · Big Sur and Ventana Wilderness map
Ventana Wilderness Los Padres National Forest map

Church Creek Divide is a 1,000-foot-deep cleft below two ridges in the Ventana Wilderness. The 3,651-foot divide sits in a shady tree grove of stately black and tanbark oaks, ponderosa pines, and madrones. It is a major crossroad of wilderness trails.

This hike begins at the northeast end of the Pine Ridge Trail at Tassajara Road. The trailhead sits on a saddle above China Camp.

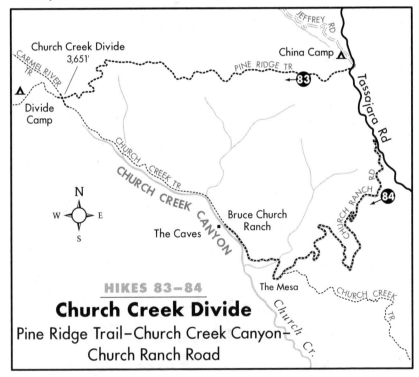

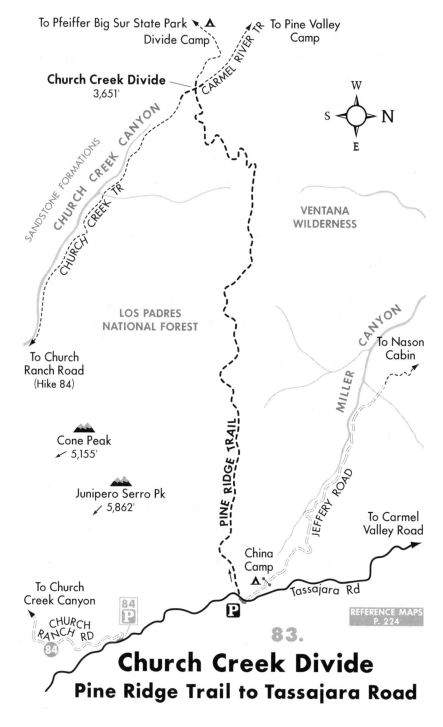

To Pfeiffer Big Sur State Park ▲
Divide Camp

To Pine Valley
Camp

Church Creek Divide
3,651'

CARMEL RIVER TR

SANDSTONE FORMATIONS

CHURCH CREEK CANYON

CHURCH CREEK TR

VENTANA
WILDERNESS

W
N
S
E

To Church
Ranch Road
(Hike 84)

LOS PADRES
NATIONAL FOREST

MILLER CANYON

To Nason
Cabin

Cone Peak
5,155'

Junipero Serro Pk
5,862'

PINE RIDGE TRAIL

JEFFERY ROAD

To Carmel
Valley Road

China
Camp ▲

To Church
Creek Canyon

Tassajara Rd

84 P

P

REFERENCE MAPS
P. 224

CHURCH
RANCH RD

84

83.

Church Creek Divide
Pine Ridge Trail to Tassajara Road

The path weaves through the remote and rugged wilderness along high ridges with open, grassy slopes. Panoramic views of the mountainous Ventana Wilderness extend to Cone Peak, Junipero Serra Peak, and down the Church Creek Canyon.

To the trailhead

From Highway 1 and Carmel Valley Road in Carmel, drive 23 miles southeast on Carmel Valley Road (passing through Carmel Valley Village at 11.5 miles) to Tassajara Road. Turn right and drive 1.3 miles to a signed Y-fork with Cachagua Road. Curve left, staying on Tassajara Road, and continue 9.2 miles (crossing Chews Ridge) to the signed China Camp turnoff on the right. Continue 50 yards past the turnoff to the parking area on the left (east).

The hike

Cross Tassajara Road to the posted Pine Ridge Trail. Climb the hillside above China Camp through native chaparral and brush. Burned oak and pine stumps remain from the 1977 Marble Cone Fire. After gaining 400 feet to a hilltop ridge, drop back down the hillside, losing the elevation gain on a long saddle in a stand of tanbark oaks. Cross a steep, sloping meadow just below the ridge and high above the Church Creek drainage to the south. Traverse the hillside, overlooking the sandstone formations in Church Creek Canyon to the left. Zigzag down the hillside to the canyon floor at Church Creek Divide. The divide sits in a pastoral forest by a posted 4-way junction. This is the turn-around spot.

To hike farther, the Pine Ridge Trail continues straight ahead to Divide Camp at a half mile and eventually to Pfeiffer Big Sur State Park (Hike 117). To the right (northwest), the Carmel River Trail leads 2 miles to Pine Valley Camp, a flat, grassy meadow lined with pines. To the left (southeast), the Church Creek Trail follows Church Creek, passing massive sandstone formations, to The Caves (2.5 miles ahead), Wildcat Camp (5.7 miles), and Tassajara Road (7 miles). ∎

84. Church Creek Canyon from Church Ranch Road

Hiking distance: 8 miles round trip
Hiking time: 4 hours
Configuration: out-and-back
Elevation gain: 2,100 feet
Difficulty: strenuous
Exposure: mostly exposed
Dogs: allowed
Maps: U.S.G.S. Chews Ridge · Big Sur and Ventana Wilderness map
    Ventana Wilderness Los Padres National Forest map

map
page 245

Church Creek Canyon is rich with massive sandstone formations, including caves, rock shelters, arching overhangs, and ancient pictographs from the Esselen people. This hike descends on Church Ranch Road, a gated dirt road overlooking the scenic canyon. The lightly traveled road, branching from Tassajara Road, winds down the brushy slope on an easy grade. The trail offers outstanding vistas but little shade. The road descends to Church Creek, a tributary of the Arroyo Seco that forms at Church Creek Divide. The 4-mile-long creek merges with Tassajara Creek on its journey to the ocean. A trail parallels Church Creek in an open forest of black oaks, Coulter pines, and Santa Lucia firs.

This out-and-back hike is downhill the entire way to Church Creek. Pace yourself accordingly for the strenuous hike back out.

To the trailhead

From Highway 1 and Carmel Valley Road in Carmel, drive 23 miles southeast on Carmel Valley Road (passing through Carmel Valley Village at 11.5 miles) to Tassajara Road. Turn right and drive 1.3 miles to a signed Y-fork with Cachagua Road. Curve left, staying on Tassajara Road, and continue 10.1 miles (crossing Chews Ridge) to the wide pull out on the right by a dirt road, also on the right. (The pullout is located 0.9 miles past the well-marked China Camp.)

The hike

Walk 30 yards up the dirt road and make a U-bend to the left. Pass through a metal vehicle gate and head downhill on Church Ranch Road (Forest Service Road 19S04). Traverse the mountain slope, overlooking Church Creek Canyon. The narrow dirt road, perched on the canyon cliffs, steadily descends while following the contours of the mountain. With every step are changing vistas of the rugged backcountry wilderness and sandstone formations. Near the bottom, pass pockets of oaks and pines. Head towards the base of the mountains on the floor of the canyon.

Pass the Church Creek Trail on the left, which is overgrown and hard to spot. Curve around The Mesa, a flat, unmarked, and nondescript knoll overlooking the canyon. Beyond The Mesa, the road/trail crosses Church Ranch Bridge, a wooden bridge crossing over a major fork of Church Creek. Stroll up canyon on the near-level path among massive sandstone outcrops. Parallel Church Creek from above, eventually reaching the sycamore-lined waterway. At 4 miles, the dirt road enters the private land of Bruce Church Ranch, located directly across the creek from The Caves, dramatic sandstone outcrops which are off-limits to the public. This is a good turn-around spot.

To extend the hike, the trail passes about a half mile along an easement through the private land. The dirt road then narrows to a footpath and leads 2.5 miles to the Pine Ridge Trail and Church Creek Divide (Hike 83). ▪

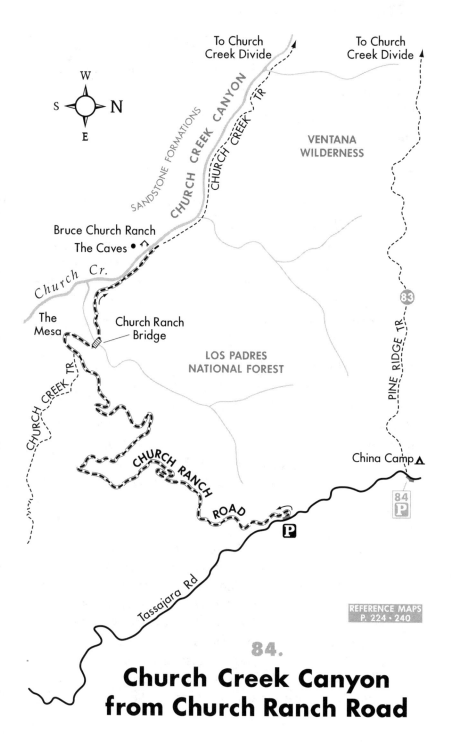

To Church
Creek Divide

To Church
Creek Divide

W N
S · E

SANDSTONE FORMATIONS

CHURCH CREEK CANYON

CHURCH CREEK TR

VENTANA
WILDERNESS

Bruce Church Ranch
The Caves •

Church Cr.

The
Mesa

Church Ranch
Bridge

LOS PADRES
NATIONAL FOREST

CHURCH CREEK TR

CHURCH RANCH

ROAD

P

83

PINE RIDGE TR

China Camp ▲

84
P

Tassajara Rd

REFERENCE MAPS
P. 224 · 240

84.
Church Creek Canyon
from Church Ranch Road

85. Horse Pasture Trail to Horse Pasture Camp

Hiking distance: 2.8 miles round trip
Hiking time: 1.5 hours
Configuration: out-and-back
Elevation gain: 400 feet
Difficulty: easy
Exposure: forested canyon and open grassland
Dogs: allowed
Maps: U.S.G.S. Tassajara Hot Springs · Big Sur and Ventana Wilderness map
Ventana Wilderness Los Padres National Forest map

Horse Pasture Trail is a lightly traveled trail off the far southern end of Tassajara Road. The trail leads to Willow Creek, linking Tassajara Road with Arroyo Seco. This hike along the first 1.4 miles of the trail leads to Horse Pasture Camp, a quiet, out-of-use campsite on the banks of seasonal Horse Pasture Creek. The camp sits on a beautiful creekside flat inside the Ventana Wilderness boundary.

To the trailhead

From Highway 1 and Carmel Valley Road in Carmel, drive 23 miles southeast on Carmel Valley Road (passing through Carmel Valley Village at 11.5 miles) to Tassajara Road. Turn right and drive 1.3 miles to a signed Y-junction with Cachagua Road. Curve left, staying on Tassajara Road, and continue 14.3 miles to the well-marked trailhead on the left (east) side. Park in the pullouts on either side of the road.

The hike

Take the signed Horse Pasture Trail into the oak forest and head uphill. Traverse the hillside on a ledge above Tassajara Road. Curving away from the road, cross open grasslands on the narrow path. The gentle grade gains 400 feet in 0.6 miles, reaching a saddle at the wilderness boundary. Descend the east-facing slope under a canopy of oaks and toyon. Switchbacks lead down the hillside into the forested canyon and to seasonal Horse Pasture Creek. Cross the creek and walk downstream a short distance to the abandoned Horse Pasture Camp on a grassy flat. After enjoying the area, return on the same trail. To make a 7-mile loop hike to Tassajara Creek, continue with Hike 86. ■

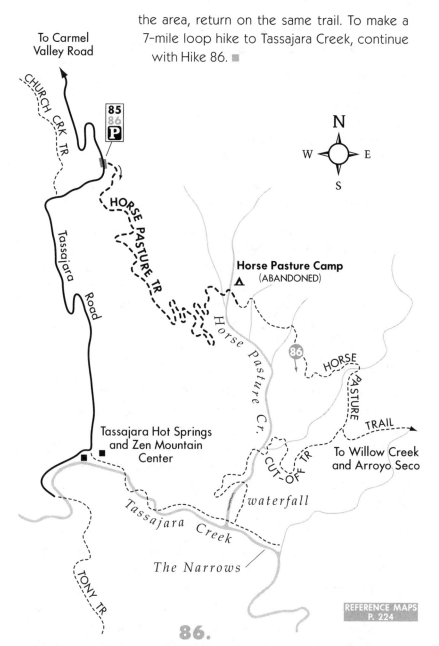

To Carmel Valley Road

CHURCH CRK TR

85
86
P

HORSE PASTURE TR

Tassajara Road

N
W — E
S

Horse Pasture Camp
▲ (ABANDONED)

Horse Pasture Cr.

86

HORSE PASTURE TRAIL

To Willow Creek and Arroyo Seco

Tassajara Hot Springs and Zen Mountain Center

CUT-OFF TR

Tassajara Creek

waterfall

The Narrows

TONY TR

REFERENCE MAPS
P. 224

86.
Horse Pasture Trail to Horse Pasture Camp

86. Horse Pasture Trail to the Narrows at Tassajara Creek

Hiking distance: 7-mile loop
Hiking time: 3.5 hours
Configuration: loop
Elevation gain: 1,200 feet
Difficulty: moderate to strenuous
Exposure: open grasslands and shaded forest
Dogs: allowed
Maps: U.S.G.S. Tassajara Hot Springs · Big Sur and Ventana Wilderness map
Ventana Wilderness Los Padres National Forest map

This hike leads to The Narrows on Tassajara Creek, a series of gorgeous pools and small waterfalls in a narrow canyon. This hike begins on the Horse Pasture Trail and descends down a side canyon, passing a waterfall in a rocky gorge. After exploring the cascades, the trail then loops upstream to Tassajara Hot Springs, located on the monastic Zen Mountain Center grounds at the very end of Tassajara Road.

To the trailhead

From Highway 1 and Carmel Valley Road in Carmel, drive 23 miles southeast on Carmel Valley Road (passing through Carmel Valley Village at 11.5 miles) to Tassajara Road. Turn right and drive 1.3 miles to a signed Y-junction with Cachagua Road. Curve left, staying on Tassajara Road, and continue 14.3 miles to the well-marked trailhead on the left (east) side. Park in the pullouts on either side of the road.

The hike

Take the signed Horse Pasture Trail into the oak forest and head uphill. Traverse the hillside on a ledge above Tassajara Road. Curving away from the road, cross open grasslands on the narrow path. The gentle grade gains 400 feet in 0.6 miles, reaching a saddle at the wilderness boundary. Descend the east-facing slope under a canopy of oaks and toyon. Switchbacks lead down the hillside into the forested canyon and to seasonal Horse Pasture Creek.

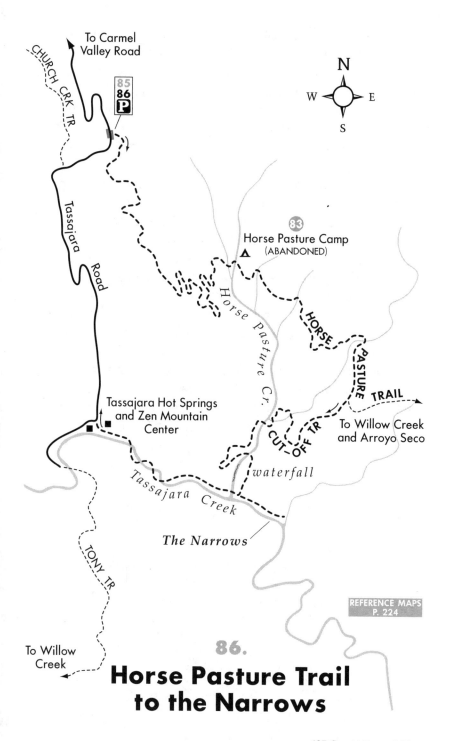

To Carmel
Valley Road

CHURCH CRK TR

N
W E
S

85
86
P

Tassajara

Road

Horse Pasture Camp
△ (ABANDONED)

83

Horse Pasture Cr.

HORSE PASTURE TRAIL

To Willow Creek
and Arroyo Seco

Tassajara Hot Springs
and Zen Mountain
Center

CUT-OFF TR

waterfall

Tassajara Creek

The Narrows

TONY TR

To Willow
Creek

REFERENCE MAPS
P. 224

86.
**Horse Pasture Trail
to the Narrows**

Cross the creek and walk downstream a short distance to the abandoned Horse Pasture Camp on a grassy flat.

Continue on the near-level path through grasslands with oak groves. Cross a shady stream-fed gully lined with ferns. Gradually ascend the hillside, curving right in the seasonal drainage at 2 miles. Continue 0.3 miles to a posted junction. The left fork continues on the Horse Pasture Trail to Willow Creek and Arroyo Seco.

Take the right fork on the Tassajara Cut-Off Trail. Descend into the lush draw, winding into the small side canyon. Cross a rocky streambed at 2.8 miles, and parallel the stream. Recross the stream and follow the watercourse along its left bank. Cross Horse Pasture Creek, passing large boulders to an overlook in a rocky gorge at the brink of a waterfall. The narrow, rocky path steeply descends along the canyon wall to a posted T-junction at Tassajara Creek. The left fork follows the creek 100 yards downstream, passing the series of pools and small waterfalls known as The Narrows.

After exploring The Narrows, take the path upstream along the creek past more pools. After several creek crossings, the trail ends at the Tassajara Zen Mountain Center near the south end of Tassajara Road. To make a loop, return along Tassajara Road. ■

87. Palo Corona Regional Park

A free access permit is required to hike the trail
www.mprpd.org · 831-659-4488, then select option 5

Hiking distance: 5 miles round trip
Hiking time: 2.5 hours
Configuration: out-and-back with a central loop
Elevation gain: 800 feet
Difficulty: easy to moderate
Exposure: exposed meadows and shaded forest
Dogs: not allowed
Maps: U.S.G.S. Monterey · Palo Corona Regional Park Trail Map

map
page 253

Palo Corona Regional Park sits at the northwest corner of the Santa Lucia Range, south of Carmel and above Monastery Beach and Point Lobos State Park. The 10,000-acre Palo Corona Ranch, stretching over 7 miles in length, was acquired by a collaboration between public agencies and conservation groups in 2004. The sprawling open-space park contains the headwaters to thirteen watersheds. It is a crucial wildlife corridor, protecting a diverse and endangered plant and animal species. The park's significant wildlife habitats include streamside riparian forests, redwood and madrone forests, coast live oak woodlands, a coastal terrace prairie, grasslands, native buckwheat, and vernal wetlands.

The 680-acre "Front Ranch" portion of the park, managed by the Monterey Peninsula Regional Park District, is open to the public. The park, bordered by the Carmel River to the north and Highway 1 to the west, has a trail system that crosses the grassy terrace and riparian corridor to Inspiration Point, an overlook on an oceanfront saddle. From the viewpoint is a bird's-eye view of the Carmel Coast, Point Lobos, Carmel, and Pebble Beach. The trail continues to Animas Pond, a secluded, reed-filled wetland.

Access is by permit only due to limited parking. Contact information is included above.

To the trailhead

From Highway 1 and Rio Road in Carmel, drive 0.6 miles south on Highway 1 to the signed Palo Corona Regional Park entrance on the left. It is located just after crossing the bridge over the

Carmel River. Park on the east (inland) side of the shoulder of Highway 1, just north of the trailhead gate.

The hike

Pass through the entrance gate and sign in. Walk east on the unpaved road, passing an old barn on the right. Continue on the Palo Corona Trail, or walk parallel to the dirt road. Pass the corrals and go through a cattle gate to a Y-fork near the base of the mountain. The right fork is the direct route to Inspiration Point, one mile ahead.

For this hike, go to the left on the Vista Lobos Trail. Walk 75 yards to a trail split. Veer right on the Laguna Vista Loop and head up the gentle slope. Curve around the south side of the knoll, where a side path leads 50 yards up to a bench atop the knoll by an oak grove. Descend and rejoin the Vista Lobos Trail. Go to the right a short distance, and veer left on the posted Oak Knoll Loop. As the name implies, the path loops through a gorgeous oak grove and rejoins the Vista Lobos Trail. Bear left (east) to a cattle gate and the Talus Trail on the right. Detour through the gate, straight ahead. Stay on the Vista Lobos Trail under the shade of the oaks. Drop down to the riparian corridor of the Carmel River among sycamores, willows, and cottonwoods. Stroll among the dense foliage, parallel to the south side of the river to the east gate. The Southbank Trail continues outside the gate on an old farm road. After the gate, the level, dog-friendly path leads 1.5 miles, parallel to the Carmel River, to Rancho San Carlos Road.

Return to the Talus Trail junction at the gate and take it to the left. Head south towards the vertical mountain wall to a T-junction back with the Palo Corona Trail. For an easy return, go to the right, completing the loop. To head to Inspiration Point and Animas Pond, bear left and traverse the north-facing slope. Steadily climb, slowly looping to the right. With every step, expanding views emerge of the Carmel River corridor and Carmel Valley. At the top is a grassland meadow surrounded by pines and a junction. Veer right and walk 250 yards to Inspiration Point. The point is located on a bluff overlooking the Carmel River, including the lagoon at the ocean, Carmel by the Sea, and Pebble Beach. After savoring the views, continue south on the Palo Corona Trail. Pass a second overlook on the right, and gently descend through open meadows to Animas Creek, the north fork of San Jose Creek. Cross a footbridge over the creek to Animas Pond on the left. As of this writing, public access beyond the point is prohibited. Return by retracing your steps. ■

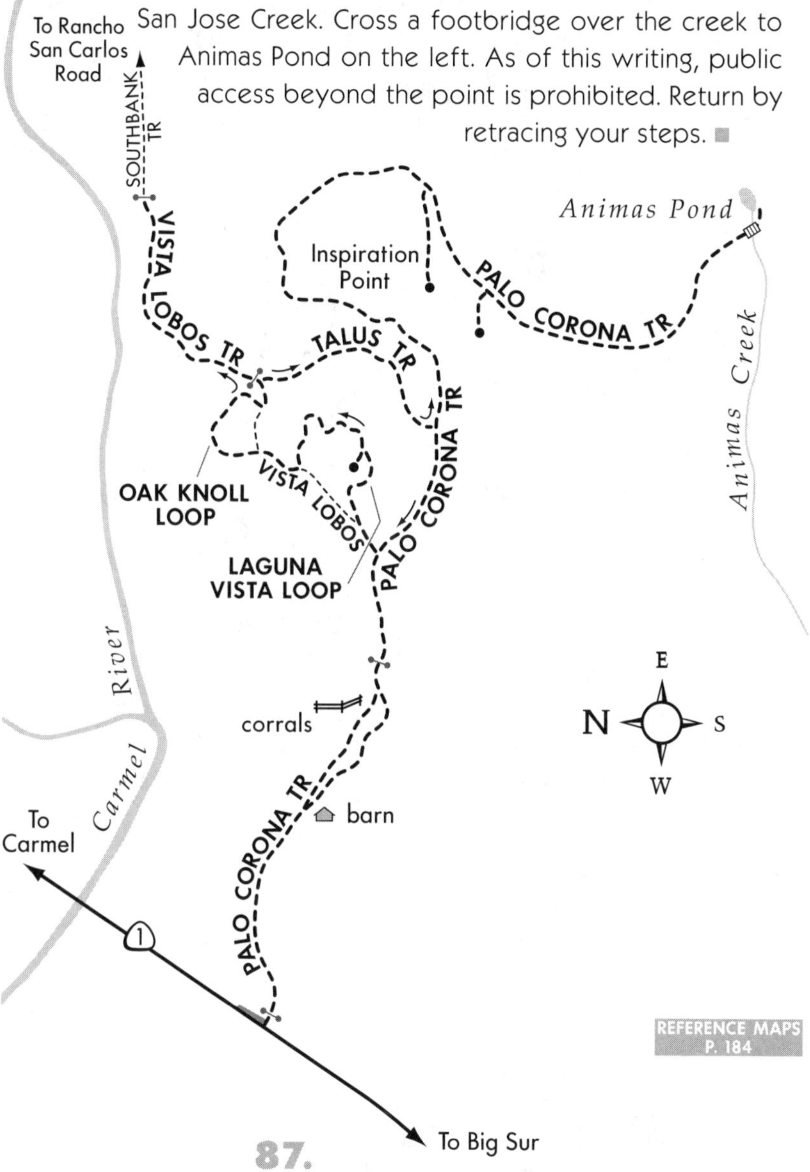

To Rancho San Carlos Road

SOUTHBANK TR

VISTA LOBOS TR

Inspiration Point

Animas Pond

PALO CORONA TR

TALUS TR

Animas Creek

OAK KNOLL LOOP

VISTA LOBOS

PALO CORONA TR

LAGUNA VISTA LOOP

River

Carmel

corrals

E

N

S

W

To Carmel

PALO CORONA TR

barn

REFERENCE MAPS P. 184

To Big Sur

87.
Palo Corona Regional Park

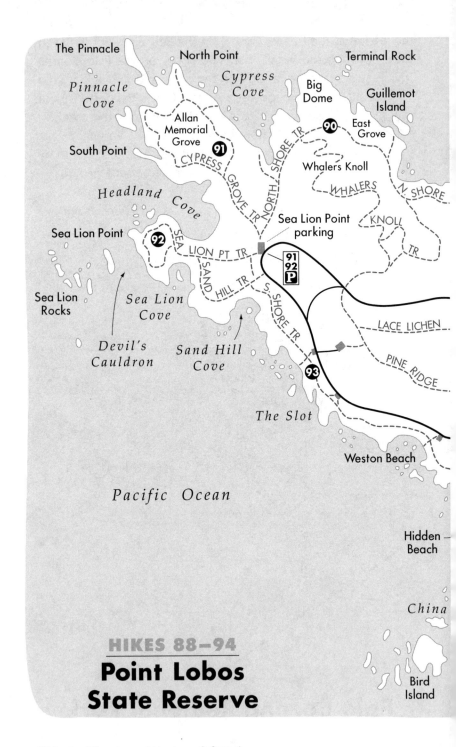

The Pinnacle

North Point

Terminal Rock

Pinnacle Cove

Cypress Cove

Big Dome

Guillemot Island

Allan Memorial Grove

91

South Point

CYPRESS GROVE TR

90

East Grove

Whalers Knoll

NORTH SHORE TR

Headland *Cove*

WHALERS

N SHORE

Sea Lion Point

92

Sea Lion Point parking

KNOLL

TR

SEA LION PT TR

SAND HILL TR

91 92 P

Sea Lion Rocks

Sea Lion Cove

S SHORE TR

LACE LICHEN

Devil's Cauldron

Sand Hill Cove

93

PINE RIDGE

The Slot

Weston Beach

Pacific Ocean

Hidden Beach

China

Bird Island

Point Lobos
State Reserve

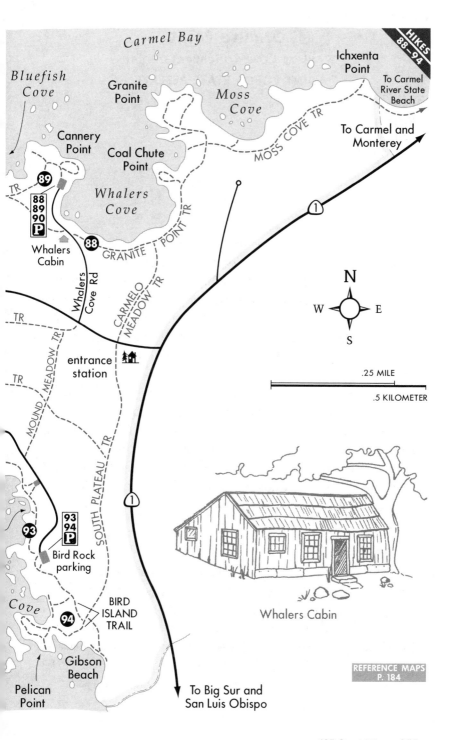

Carmel Bay

Bluefish Cove

Granite Point

Moss Cove

Ichxenta Point

To Carmel River State Beach

Cannery Point

Coal Chute Point

MOSS COVE TR

To Carmel and Monterey

Whalers Cove

TR

89

**88
89
90
P**

Whalers Cabin

88

GRANITE POINT TR

1

Whalers Cove Rd

CARMELO MEADOW TR

N
W   E
S

.25 MILE
.5 KILOMETER

TR

entrance station

MOUND MEADOW TR

TR

SOUTH PLATEAU TR

1

**93
94
P**

Bird Rock parking

93

BIRD ISLAND TRAIL

Cove

94

Gibson Beach

Pelican Point

To Big Sur and San Luis Obispo

Whalers Cabin

REFERENCE MAPS P. 184

88. Granite Point
Whalers Cove to Ichxenta Point
POINT LOBOS STATE RESERVE

Hiking distance: 2 miles round trip
Hiking time: 1 hour
Configuration: out-and-back
Elevation gain: near level
Difficulty: east
Exposure: open coastal bluffs and open fields
Dogs: not allowed
Maps: U.S.G.S. Monterey · Point Lobos State Reserve map

Point Lobos State Reserve is the crown jewel among California's state parks. It is located along the north end of the Big Sur coastline just south of Monterey and Carmel. The incredible 1,276-acre reserve has bold headlands, ragged cliffs, sculpted coves, large stands of Monterey cypress, rolling meadows, and many miles of hiking trails. The eroded inlets are home to tidepools, isolated beaches, craggy islets, and marine terraces. It is a great area to view oceanside wildlife.

The Granite Point Trail begins from Whalers Cabin, a historic cabin built by Chinese fishermen in the 1850s that is currently a history museum. The trail curves around Whalers Cove to coastal overlooks on Coal Chute Point and Granite Point. Views extend across Carmel Bay and its sandy beaches to the golf courses at Pebble Beach. The hike continues on the Moss Cove Trail across open fields to Ichxenta Point, a low granite headland overlooking Monastery Beach.

To the trailhead

CARMEL. From Highway 1 and Rio Road in Carmel, drive 2.2 miles south on Highway 1 to the signed Point Lobos State Reserve entrance. Turn right (west) to the entrance station. Continue 0.1 mile to the Whalers Cove turnoff. Turn right and drive 0.3 miles to the parking area at the end of the road. An entrance fee is required.

BIG SUR RANGER STATION. From the ranger station, drive 24 miles north on Highway 1 to the state park entrance and turn left.

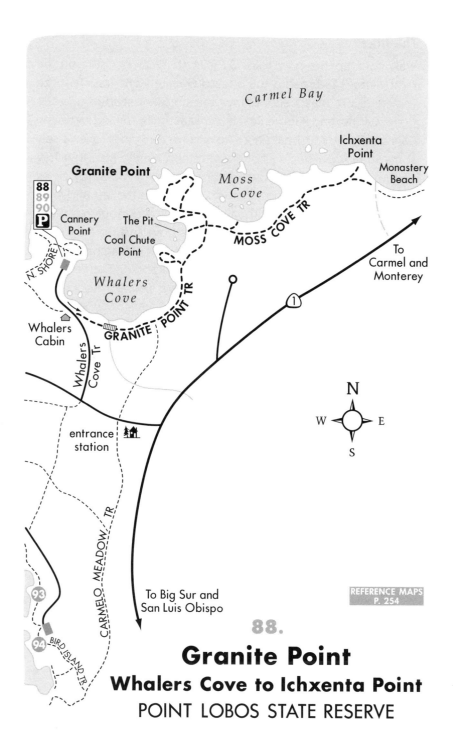

Carmel Bay

Ichxenta
Point

Monastery
Beach

Granite Point

*Moss
Cove*

88
89
90
P

Cannery
Point

The Pit

Coal Chute
Point

MOSS COVE TR

To
Carmel and
Monterey

N. SHORE

*Whalers
Cove*

GRANITE POINT TR

1

Whalers
Cabin

Whalers Cove Tr

GRANITE POINT TR

N

W ◆ E

S

entrance
station

CARMELO MEADOW TR

93

94

BIRD ISLAND TR

To Big Sur and
San Luis Obispo

REFERENCE MAPS
P. 254

88.

Granite Point
Whalers Cove to Ichxenta Point
POINT LOBOS STATE RESERVE

The hike

Walk back up the park road 0.1 mile to Whalers Cabin on the right. Across the road is the posted Granite Point Trail. Take the footpath left (east) and follow the crescent-shaped Whalers Cove. Carmel and Pebble Beach are beautifully framed between Cannery Point and Coal Chute Point. Cross a bridge over a seasonal stream, passing a junction with the Carmelo Meadow Trail. At the east end of the cove, enter a forest of Monterey pines, curving left to an unsigned trail fork. Detour to the left and loop around Coal Chute Point through wind-sculpted Monterey pines and cypress. The trail overlooks Whalers Cove and The Pit, a small sandy beach in a sculpted cove with natural rock arches. Return to the Granite Point Trail, and head north above The Pit. Drop over a small knoll to views of Moss Cove, Escobar Rocks, and Monastery Beach.

Descend steps to the Moss Cove Trail at a 4-way junction. The sharp left fork leads down a draw to The Pit. The middle fork climbs steps to a loop around Granite Point. The right fork continues east on the Moss Cove Trail and crosses Hudson Meadow, a flat, grassy marine terrace overlooking Moss Cove. Escobar Rocks forms a natural barrier to the beach cove. Carmelite Monastery can be seen peering out above the trees on the inland hillside. The trail ends at the northeast park boundary above Monastery Beach (Hike 47). Just before reaching the fenced boundary, a short path on the left ascends up to the rocky Ichxenta Point. ■

89. Whalers Knoll Trail
POINT LOBOS STATE RESERVE

Hiking distance: 2 miles round trip
Hiking time: 1 hour
Configuration: out-and-back with large loop
Elevation gain: 180 feet
Difficulty: easy
Exposure: a mix of open and shaded forest
Dogs: not allowed
Maps: U.S.G.S. Monterey · Point Lobos State Reserve map

**map
page 260**

Whalers Knoll was an historic lookout for spotting whales. The trail twists 200 feet up the hillside through an open Monterey pine forest draped with lace lichen to the exposed knob. At the summit is a bench and panoramic views of Big Dome, Carmel Bay, and the coastline to Pebble Beach. This hike begins from Whalers Cove and connects with Whalers Knoll via the North Shore Trail (Hike 90). The hike returns back down to Whalers Cabin, built by Chinese fishermen in the 1850s. The cabin now houses a museum.

To the trailhead

CARMEL. From Highway 1 and Rio Road in Carmel, drive 2.2 miles south on Highway 1 to the signed Point Lobos State Reserve entrance. Turn right (west) to the entrance station. Continue 0.1 mile to the Whalers Cove turnoff. Turn right and drive 0.3 miles to the parking area at the end of the road. An entrance fee is required.

BIG SUR RANGER STATION. From the ranger station, drive 24 miles north on Highway 1 to the state park entrance and turn left.

The hike

From the far north end of the parking area, take the signed North Shore Trail. Climb rock steps to an overlook of Cannery Point, Granite Point, Coal Chute Point, Whalers Cove, Carmel, Pebble Beach, Carmel Bay, and the Santa Lucia Mountains. Stay left up a long flight of wooden steps to a trail split. The right fork leads to an overlook of Bluefish Cove. Bear left on the North Shore Trail towards Whalers Knoll. The serpentine path curves around Bluefish Cove, passing the first junction with Whalers Knoll Trail, the return route.

Begin the loop to the right, staying on the coastal path along the jagged cliffs. Pass a side trail on the right that overlooks Guillemot Island. Cross the inland side of Big Dome to the posted Whalers Knoll Trail on the left. Climb up the hillside on the Whalers Knoll Trail, zigzagging through the Monterey pines to views of Sea Lion Point. Curve left, steadily climbing to the summit and a bench on the knoll. Savor the commanding views of Big Dome and Carmel Bay. Continue across the knoll and descend past two junctions with the Pine Ridge Trail on the right. Complete the loop back at Bluefish Cove on the North Shore Trail. Bear right to a signed junction on the right to the Whalers Cabin Trail, and descend through a native Monterey pine forest to the cabin at the park road. Take the park road 0.1 mile back to the left. ■

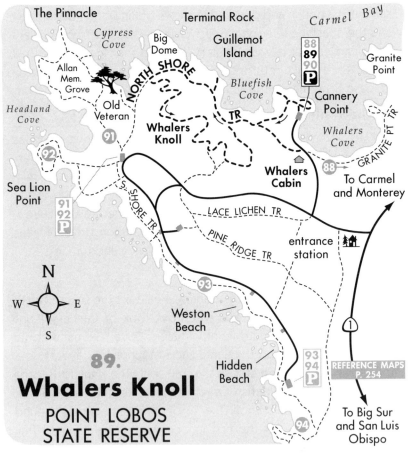

The Pinnacle
Terminal Rock
Carmel Bay
Cypress Cove
Big Dome
Guillemot Island
88 89 90 P
Granite Point
Allan Mem. Grove
NORTH SHORE
Bluefish Cove
Cannery Point
Headland Cove
Old Veteran
TR
Whalers Cove
GRANITE PT TR
91
Whalers Knoll
92
88
Sea Lion Point
91 92 P
S. SHORE TR
Whalers Cabin
To Carmel and Monterey
LACE LICHEN TR
PINE RIDGE TR
entrance station
N
W E
S
93
Weston Beach
1
89.
Whalers Knoll
POINT LOBOS
STATE RESERVE
Hidden Beach
93 94 P
REFERENCE MAPS P. 254
To Big Sur and San Luis Obispo
94

90. North Shore Trail
POINT LOBOS STATE RESERVE

Hiking distance: 2.8—3.2 miles round trip
Hiking time: 1.5—2 hours
Configuration: out-and-back
Elevation gain: 250 feet
Difficulty: easy
Exposure: shaded forest and open hillside
Dogs: not allowed

**map
page 263**

Maps: U.S.G.S. Monterey · Point Lobos State Reserve map

The North Shore Trail parallels the northern headlands of Point Lobos State Reserve at the southern end of Carmel Bay. The beautiful trail follows the exposed and rugged coast past sheer granite cliffs and coves. A spur trail leads to an overlook of Guillemot Island, a rocky offshore nesting site for seabirds. A second spur trail leads to Cypress Cove and Old Veteran, a windswept, gnarled Monterey cypress clinging to the cliffs of the cove. The main trail, perched above the rocky cliffs, winds through a canopy of Monterey pines and cypress draped with veils of lichen.

Additional side trips lead to vistas atop Whalers Knoll and to Whalers Cabin, an old cabin that now houses a museum.

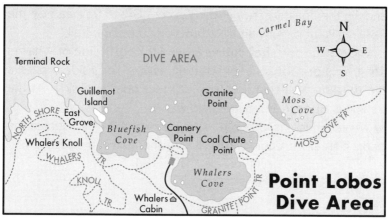

Diving is permitted only at Whalers Cove and Bluefish Cove. Proof of certification is required. Permission to dive is given when entering the reserve. Reservations are recommended and a must for weekends and holidays.

To the trailhead

CARMEL. From Highway 1 and Rio Road in Carmel, drive 2.2 miles south on Highway 1 to the signed Point Lobos State Reserve entrance. Turn right (west) to the entrance station. Continue 0.1 mile to the Whalers Cove turnoff. Turn right and drive 0.3 miles to the parking area at the end of the road. An entrance fee is required.

BIG SUR RANGER STATION. From the ranger station, drive 24 miles north on Highway 1 to the state park entrance and turn left.

The hike

Walk up the rock steps at the north end of the parking lot to a junction. The right fork loops around Cannery Point at the west end of Whalers Cove. Back at the first junction, ascend a long set of steps, and enter the forest to another junction. The short fork on the right leads to an overlook of Bluefish Cove. On the North Shore Trail, curve around the cove to a junction with the Whalers Knoll Trail on the left. Continue weaving along the coastal cliffs around Bluefish Cove to a short spur trail leading to the Guillemot Island overlook. Back on the main trail, continue northwest past a native grove of Monterey cypress in East Grove. Cross a saddle past Big Dome to a second junction with the Whalers Knoll Trail. At Cypress Cove, detour on the Old Veteran Trail to view the twisted Monterey cypress and the cove. The North Shore Trail ends in the coastal scrub at the Cypress Grove trailhead by the Sea Lion Point parking area. Return along the same trail.

The North Shore Trail curves around the north side of Whalers Knoll, a historic lookout for spotting whales. For a side trip, take the twisting Whalers Knoll Trail 200 feet up the hillside. At the summit is a bench and panoramic views.

Whalers Cabin is located on the park road 0.1 mile before the parking area. The cabin was built by fishermen in the 1850s. ▦

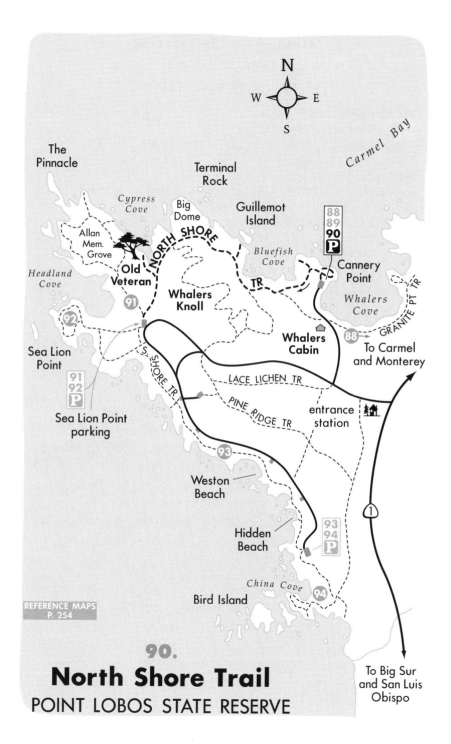

N
W E
S

The Pinnacle

Terminal Rock

Cypress Cove

Big Dome

Guillemot Island

Carmel Bay

88 89 **90** P

Allan Mem. Grove

NORTH SHORE

Bluefish Cove

Cannery Point

Old Veteran

Headland Cove

91

Whalers Knoll

TR

Whalers Cove

GRANITE PT TR

92

Whalers Cabin

88

To Carmel and Monterey

Sea Lion Point

91 92 P

S SHORE TR

LACE LICHEN TR

PINE RIDGE TR

entrance station

Sea Lion Point parking

93

1

Weston Beach

93 94 P

Hidden Beach

China Cove

94

Bird Island

REFERENCE MAPS P. 254

90.

North Shore Trail
POINT LOBOS STATE RESERVE

To Big Sur and San Luis Obispo

91. Allan Memorial Grove
Cypress Grove Trail
POINT LOBOS STATE RESERVE

Hiking distance: 0.8-mile loop
Hiking time: 30 minutes
Configuration: small loop with spur trails to coast
Elevation gain: 100 feet
Difficulty: east
Exposure: open coastal bluffs and shaded forest
Dogs: not allowed
Maps: U.S.G.S. Monterey · Point Lobos State Reserve map

The Cypress Grove Trail is a clifftop loop trail around Allan Memorial Grove in Point Lobos State Reserve. The trail passes through one of only two natural stands of Monterey cypress in the world. (The other occurs at Cypress Point on the west side of the Monterey Peninsula.) The hike loops around rugged, weathered cliffs with stunning views of Cypress Cove, Pinnacle Cove, South Point, Headland Cove, and The Pinnacle, a narrow peninsula at the northernmost point in the reserve.

To the trailhead

CARMEL. From Highway 1 and Rio Road in Carmel, drive 2.2 miles south on Highway 1 to the signed Point Lobos State Reserve entrance. Turn right (west) to the entrance station. Continue 0.7 miles to the Sea Lion Point parking area on the right side of the road. An entrance fee is required.

BIG SUR RANGER STATION. From the ranger station, drive 24 miles north on Highway 1 to the state park entrance and turn left.

The hike

Two well-marked trails begin on the north end of the parking lot. To the right is the North Shore Trail (Hike 90). Take the Cypress Grove Trail to the left through coastal scrub 0.2 miles to a trail split. Begin the loop around Allan Memorial Grove to the right. Follow the edge of Cypress Cove to a short spur trail on the right, leading to an overlook of Cypress Cove and Carmel Bay. Back on the loop, pass through an indigenous Monterey cypress grove. A spur trail at the north end of the loop leads to the North Point over-look and views of The Pinnacle. Back on the main trail, granite steps lead up to Pinnacle Cove on a rocky promontory, where there are stunning views of South Point and Headland Cove. Continue past South Point and Headland Cove, completing the loop. ▪

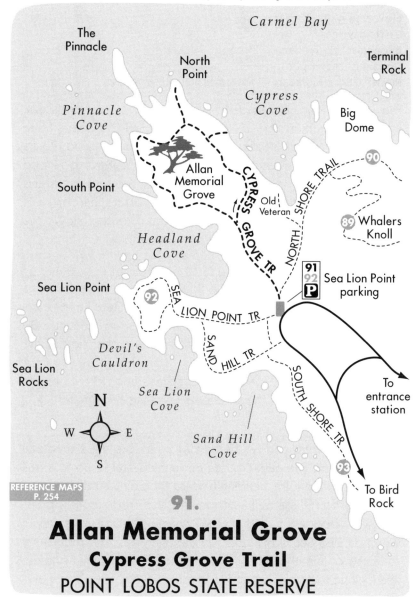

91.
Allan Memorial Grove
Cypress Grove Trail
POINT LOBOS STATE RESERVE

92. Sea Lion Point Trail
POINT LOBOS STATE RESERVE

Hiking distance: 0.7-mile double loop
Hiking time: 30 minutes
Configuration: two connected loops
Elevation gain: 50 feet
Difficulty: easy
Exposure: open coastal bluffs
Dogs: not allowed
Maps: U.S.G.S. Monterey · Point Lobos State Reserve map

The Sea Lion Point Trail leads to a spectacular, surreal landscape on the coastal bluff above Headland Cove in Point Lobos State Reserve. From the bluffs are vistas of Sea Lion Cove, Sea Lion Rocks, the churning whitewater at Devil's Cauldron, wave-pounded inlets, and sloping layers of rock. The offshore sea stacks and rocky coves are often abundant with sea otters, harbor seals, and barking California sea lions. The return route follows the eroded cliffs between Sea Lion Cove and Sand Hill Cove.

To the trailhead

CARMEL. From Highway 1 and Rio Road in Carmel, drive 2.2 miles south on Highway 1 to the signed Point Lobos State Reserve entrance. Turn right (west) to the entrance station. Continue 0.7 miles to the Sea Lion Point parking area on the right side of the road. An entrance fee is required.

BIG SUR RANGER STATION. From the ranger station, drive 24 miles north on Highway 1 to the state park entrance and turn left.

The hike

From the far west end of the parking area, take the signed Sea Lion Point Trail. The path crosses through coastal scrub to a trail split. Stay to the right, heading toward the point. At the crest of the rocky bluffs is a trail junction and an incredible vista point. The views include South Point, The Pinnacle, Sea Lion Cove, Devil's Cauldron, and Sea Lion Rocks. On the right, descend the natural staircase of weathered rock to the headland. From the lower level, circle the point around Headland Cove to close up views of Devil's Cauldron and Sea Lion Rocks. Loop back around by the sandy beach at Sea Lion Cove. Return up the steps to the over-look. Proceed south on Sand Hill Trail, following the cliffs above Sea Lion Cove and Sand Hill Cove. Pass the South Shore Trail on the right (Hike 92), and complete the loop at the parking area. ■

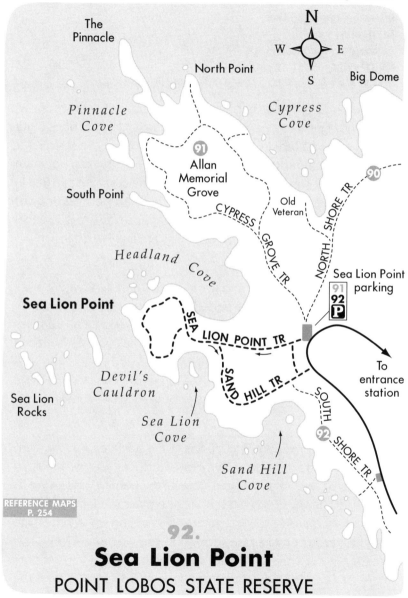

92.
Sea Lion Point
POINT LOBOS STATE RESERVE

93. South Shore Trail
POINT LOBOS STATE RESERVE

Hiking distance: 2 miles round trip
Hiking time: 1 hour
Configuration: out-and-back
Elevation gain: 30 feet
Difficulty: easy
Exposure: open coastal bluffs
Dogs: not allowed
Maps: U.S.G.S. Monterey · Point Lobos State Reserve map

The South Shore Trail explores the eroded sandstone terrain along the jagged southern ridges and troughs of Point Lobos State Reserve. The trail begins near Bird Island and ends by Sea Lion Point, weaving past tidepools and rocky beach coves tucked between the cliffs. The beach coves include rock-enclosed Hidden Beach and Weston Beach, covered with multi-colored pebbles and flat rock slabs. The trail continues past The Slot (a narrow channel bound by rock) and the 100-foot cliffs at Sand Hill Cove.

To the trailhead

CARMEL. From Highway 1 and Rio Road in Carmel, drive 2.2 miles south on Highway 1 to the signed Point Lobos State Reserve entrance. Turn right (west) to the entrance kiosk. Continue 1.6 miles to the Bird Rock parking area at the end of the road. An entrance fee is required.

BIG SUR RANGER STATION. From the ranger station, drive 24 miles north on Highway 1 to the state park entrance and turn left.

The hike

The signed South Shore Trail begins at the north end of the parking area overlooking China Cove. Head north (right), walking along the edge of the cliffs to a junction with the path to Hidden Beach on the left. Stone steps descend to the oval beach cove. Return to the main trail and follow the contours of the jagged coastline past numerous coves, tidepools, and rock islands. A few connector trails on the right lead to parking areas along the park road. At Sand Hill Cove, steps lead up to a T-junction with the

Sand Hill Trail—Hike 92. This is the turn-around spot. Return along the same trail. ■

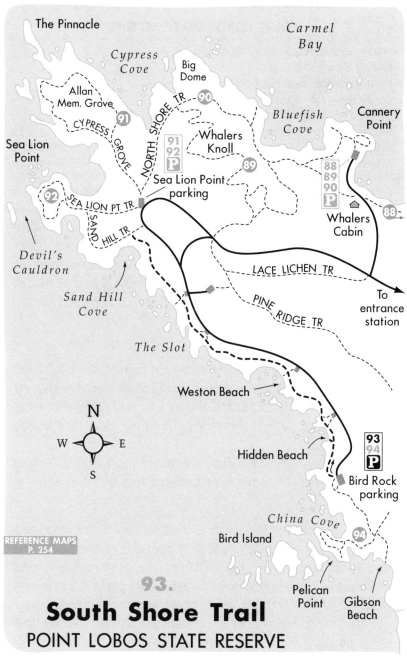

The Pinnacle

Carmel Bay

Cypress Cove

Big Dome

Allan Mem. Grove

CYPRESS GROVE

91

Bluefish Cove

Cannery Point

NORTH SHORE TR

90

Whalers Knoll

89

Sea Lion Point

91 92 P

Sea Lion Point parking

88 89 90 P

88

Whalers Cabin

SEA LION PT TR

92

SAND HILL TR

Devil's Cauldron

Sand Hill Cove

LACE LICHEN TR

To entrance station

PINE RIDGE TR

The Slot

Weston Beach

N
W   E
S

Hidden Beach

93 94 P

Bird Rock parking

China Cove

Bird Island

94

93.

Pelican Point

Gibson Beach

South Shore Trail
POINT LOBOS STATE RESERVE

94. Bird Island Trail
China Cove—Pelican Point—Gibson Beach
POINT LOBOS STATE RESERVE

Hiking distance: 0.8 miles round trip
Hiking time: 30 minutes
Configuration: out-and-back with small loop
Elevation gain: 20 feet
Difficulty: easy
Exposure: open coastal bluffs
Dogs: not allowed
Maps: U.S.G.S. Monterey · Point Lobos State Reserve map

The Bird Island Trail follows the rocky coastline through a Monterey pine forest along the clifftops overlooking the sea. The trail passes chasms, arches, sea caves, and the beautiful white sand beaches of China Cove and Gibson Beach. Both beach coves are surrounded by granite cliffs with staircase accesses. The hike then loops around Pelican Point, where off-shore Bird Island can be viewed. The island is inhabited by nesting colonies of cormorants and brown pelicans.

To the trailhead

CARMEL. From Highway 1 and Rio Road in Carmel, drive 2.2 miles south on Highway 1 to the signed Point Lobos State Reserve entrance. Turn right (west) to the entrance kiosk. Continue 1.6 miles to the Bird Rock parking area at the end of the road. An entrance fee is required.

BIG SUR RANGER STATION. From the ranger station, drive 24 miles north on Highway 1 to the state park entrance and turn left.

The hike

Ascend the steps at the south end of the parking lot, and head through a Monterey pine forest to an overlook of China Cove and Bird Island. Follow the cliffside path as it curves around the head of China Cove to a signed junction. A long set of stairs to the right descends the cliffs to the sandy beach and cave in China Cove.

After exploring the beach, return to the Bird Island Trail. Continue along the cliffs to a posted T-junction and overlook of

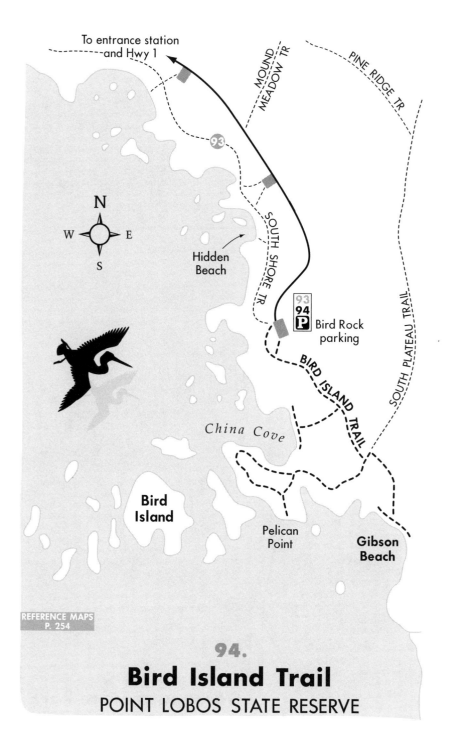

To entrance station
and Hwy 1

MOUND MEADOW TR

PINE RIDGE TR

93

N
W   E
S

SOUTH SHORE TR

Hidden
Beach

93
94 P Bird Rock
parking

BIRD ISLAND TRAIL

SOUTH PLATEAU TRAIL

China Cove

Bird
Island

Pelican
Point

Gibson
Beach

REFERENCE MAPS
P. 254

94.
Bird Island Trail
POINT LOBOS STATE RESERVE

the crescent-shaped Gibson Beach below the Carmel Highlands. For a short detour to Gibson Beach, bear left on the South Plateau Trail a few yards to the posted beach access on the right. Descend a long flight of steps to the sandy beach at the base of the cliffs.

Returning to the T-junction, head west towards Pelican Point through coastal scrub to a trail split. The paths loop around the flat bench, overlooking Bird Island, the magnificent offshore rock outcroppings, chasms, sea caves, and China Cove. Complete the loop and return along the same route. ■

HIKES 95—97
Garrapata State Park

95. Soberanes Canyon Trail
GARRAPATA STATE PARK

Hiking distance: 3 miles round trip
Hiking time: 1.5 hours
Configuration: out-and-back
Elevation gain: 900 feet
Difficulty: moderate
Exposure: shaded canyon
Dogs: not allowed
Maps: U.S.G.S. Soberanes Point · Garrapata State Park map
   Big Sur and Ventana Wilderness map

**map
page 275**

Just south of Point Lobos, the undeveloped Garrapata State Park stretches along four miles of scenic coastline and into the inland mountains. Soberanes Creek flows through the south end of the park and empties into the Pacific by the rocky headlands of Soberanes Point. The Soberanes Canyon Trail follows the creek up a wet, narrow canyon through magnificent stands of huge redwoods. The trail crosses the creek seven times before climbing up to the head of the canyon. At the top, the trail emerges onto the dry, chaparral-covered hillside with panoramic views.

If you wish to make the hike into a loop, it is recommended to start on the Rocky Ridge Trail—Hike 96—to avoid the steep climb from Soberanes Creek up to the ridge.

To the trailhead

CARMEL. From Highway 1 and Rio Road in Carmel, drive 6.8 miles south on Highway 1 to the unsigned parking turnouts on either side of the road. The turnouts are located by a tin roof barn behind a grove of cypress trees on the inland side of the highway.

BIG SUR RANGER STATION. From the ranger station, drive 19.4 miles north on Highway 1 to the parking turnouts.

The hike

From the inland side of the highway, walk past the trailhead gate, following the old ranch road through a cypress grove. Curve left around the barn and down to Soberanes Creek. Cross the bridge to a signed junction. The left fork leads to Rocky Ridge, the rounded 1,435-foot peak to the north—Hike 96.

Take the right fork and head up the canyon along the north side of the creek. Cross another footbridge and curve left, staying in Soberanes Canyon. Recross the creek on a third footbridge and head steadily uphill. Rock-hop over the creek, entering a beautiful redwood forest. Follow the watercourse through the redwoods to a lush grotto. The trail crosses the creek three consecutive times, then climbs a long series of steps. Traverse the canyon wall on a cliff ledge that climbs high above the creek. Switchbacks descend back to the creek. Climb up more steps to the head of the canyon. The lush canyon gives way to the dry sage-covered hills and an unsigned trail split, the turn-around point. Return down canyon along the same trail.

If you feel up for the climb, take the left fork up the steep slope towards Rocky Ridge and Doud Peak. The trail follows the dry, exposed hillside. The hike is strenuous, but the views of the ocean, coastline, and mountains are fantastic. Taking this return loop does not make the hike any longer, but it adds an additional 1,000 feet in elevation. ■

96. Rocky Ridge—
Soberanes Canyon Loop
GARRAPATA STATE PARK

Hiking distance: 6-mile loop
Hiking time: 3 hours
Configuration: loop
Elevation gain: 1,600 feet
Difficulty: strenuous
Exposure: open hillside and shaded canyon
Dogs: not allowed
Maps: U.S.G.S. Soberanes Point · Garrapata State Park map
Big Sur and Ventana Wilderness map

map page 277

Rocky Ridge is a 1,435-foot rounded grassy peak between Soberanes Canyon and Malpaso Canyon in Garrapata State Park. The steep trail up to Rocky Ridge follows a dry, exposed hillside. The rewards are sweeping views of the ocean, coastline and

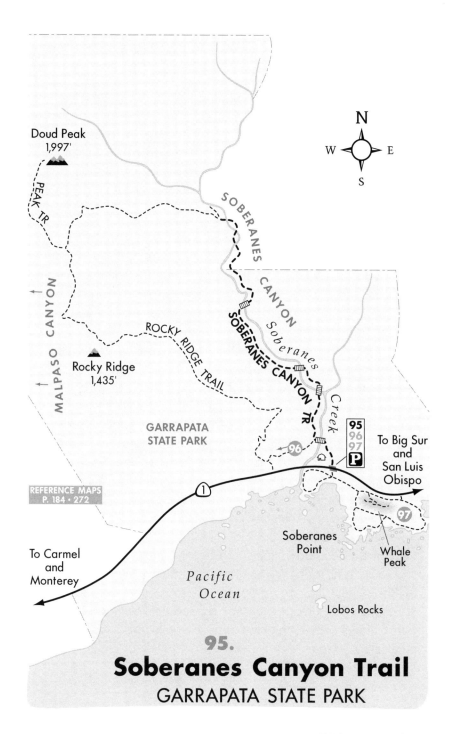

Doud Peak
1,997'

PEAK TR

N
W   E
S

SOBERANES

CANYON

MALPASO CANYON

ROCKY RIDGE TRAIL

Rocky Ridge
1,435'

SOBERANES CANYON TR

Soberanes Creek

GARRAPATA
STATE PARK

95
96
97
P

96

To Big Sur
and
San Luis
Obispo

REFERENCE MAPS
P. 184 · 272

1

97

To Carmel
and
Monterey

Soberanes
Point

Whale
Peak

*Pacific
Ocean*

Lobos Rocks

95.
Soberanes Canyon Trail
GARRAPATA STATE PARK

mountains, then a return hike down a cool, stream-fed canyon. This hike is strenuous and only recommended for serious hikers.

To the trailhead

CARMEL. From Highway 1 and Rio Road in Carmel, drive 6.8 miles south on Highway 1 to the unsigned parking pullouts on both sides of the road. The pullouts are located by a tin roof barn behind a grove of cypress trees on the inland side of the highway.

BIG SUR RANGER STATION. From the Big Sur Ranger Station, drive 19.4 miles north on Highway 1 to the parking pullouts.

The hike

From the inland side of the highway, walk past the trailhead gate, following the old ranch road through a cypress grove. Curve left around the barn down to Soberanes Creek. The rounded mountain peak straight ahead is Rocky Ridge. Cross the bridge to a signed junction. The right fork heads up Soberanes Canyon (Hike 95), the return route.

Bear left (north), parallel to the highway, on the lower grassy slopes of Rocky Ridge. Cross a couple of gullies to a trail split. The left fork returns to the highway. Take the right fork, which curves right and ascends the rugged, sage-covered slope to a ridge. Begin a much steeper ascent, reaching a knoll. After resting, cross a saddle, finally reaching Rocky Ridge at 1,435 feet. Continue uphill and around the ridge, overlooking the Malpaso Creek drainage to a junction with the Peak Trail (North Ridge Trail) at 3.3 miles. The 0.7-mile spur trail bears left, gaining 300 feet to the highest point in the state park at 1,977 feet.

Continue the loop on the right fork towards Soberanes Canyon. Descend down the south-facing ridge on the very steep and rocky trail, losing 1,000 feet in less than a mile. At the head of Soberanes Canyon, follow the north canyon wall down to Soberanes Creek along the cool, shaded canyon floor. The lush path follows the watercourse through a redwood forest with six creek crossings. ■

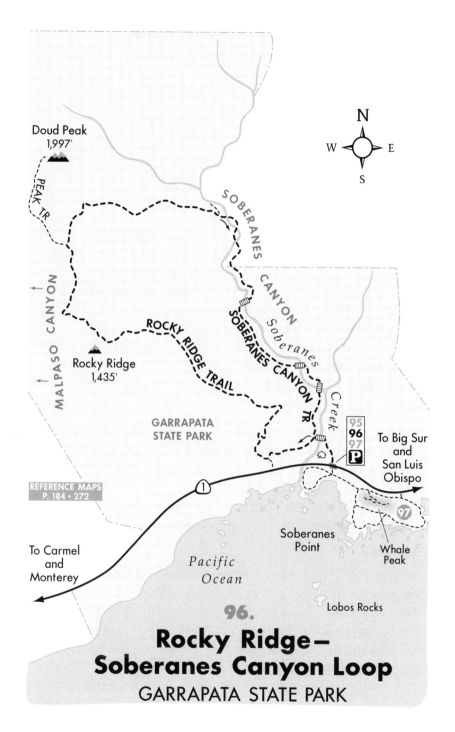

Doud Peak
1,997'

PEAK TR

N
W · E
S

SOBERANES

CANYON

Soberanes

Creek

MALPASO CANYON

ROCKY RIDGE TRAIL

SOBERANES CANYON TR

Rocky Ridge
1,435'

GARRAPATA
STATE PARK

95
96
97
P

To Big Sur
and
San Luis
Obispo

REFERENCE MAPS
P. 184 · 272

1

97

To Carmel
and
Monterey

Pacific
Ocean

Soberanes
Point

Whale
Peak

Lobos Rocks

96.

Rocky Ridge–
Soberanes Canyon Loop

GARRAPATA STATE PARK

97. Soberanes Point Trails
GARRAPATA STATE PARK

Hiking distance: 1.8 miles round trip
Hiking time: 1 hour
Configuration: loop
Elevation gain: 200 feet
Difficulty: easy
Exposure: open coastal bluffs
Dogs: allowed
Maps: U.S.G.S. Soberanes Point · Garrapata State Park map
       Big Sur and Ventana Wilderness map

Soberanes Point is a popular whale-watching spot in Garrapata State Park. The serrated headland is backed by Whale Peak, a 280-foot cone-shaped hill overlooking the Pacific. These coastal bluff trails along the point lead to a myriad of crenelated coves, hidden beaches, and rocky points. The trail circles the headland, overlooking sea caves, offshore stacks, and narrow inlets, then climbs Whale Peak. From the summit of the peak are 360-degree panoramic views, from Yankee Point in the north to Point Sur in the south.

To the trailhead

CARMEL. From Highway 1 and Rio Road in Carmel, drive 6.8 miles south on Highway 1 to the unsigned parking turnouts on both sides of the road. The turnouts are located by a tin roof barn on the inland side of the highway.

BIG SUR RANGER STATION. From the ranger station, drive 19.4 miles north on Highway 1 to the parking turnouts.

The hike

Walk through the trailhead gate on the ocean side of the highway, bearing left through a grove of cypress trees. Continue south towards Soberanes Point and Whale Peak, curving around the north side of the peak to an unsigned junction. The left fork circles the base of the hill. Take the right fork west along the coastal terrace to the northwest end of Soberanes Point. Follow the ocean cliffs to the southern point. From the south end, the trail returns toward Highway 1 by a gate. Stay on the footpath to the left, following the hillside trail to an unsigned junction. The left fork climbs a quarter mile up to the grassy ridge of Whale Peak. A trail follows the crest to the two summits. From the overlooks are coastal views north to Yankee Point and south to Point Sur. Return to the base of the hill, and continue to the north to complete the loop. ∎

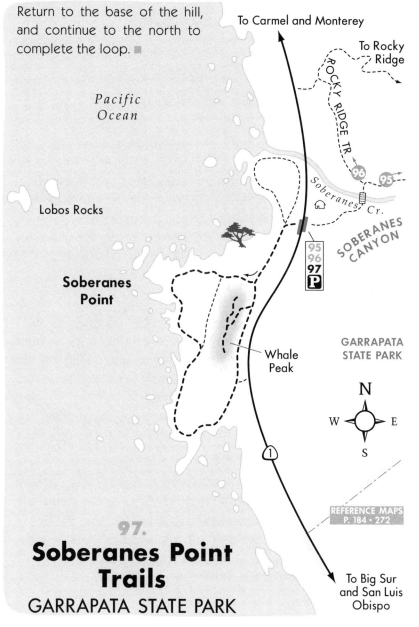

To Carmel and Monterey

To Rocky Ridge

ROCKY RIDGE TR.

Pacific Ocean

Soberanes Cr.

96

95

Lobos Rocks

95
96
97
P

SOBERANES CANYON

Soberanes Point

GARRAPATA STATE PARK

Whale Peak

N
W — E
S

1

REFERENCE MAPS
P. 184 · 272

97.
Soberanes Point Trails
GARRAPATA STATE PARK

To Big Sur and San Luis Obispo

98. Garrapata Beach and Bluff Trail
GARRAPATA STATE PARK

Hiking distance: 1—2.5 miles round trip
Hiking time: 1—1.5 hours
Configuration: out-and-back trail along the bluffs
Elevation gain: 50 feet
Difficulty: easy
Exposure: open coastal bluffs and beach
Dogs: allowed
Maps: U.S.G.S. Soberanes Point · Garrapata State Park map
Big Sur and Ventana Wilderness map

Garrapata Beach lies to the south of Soberanes Point along the coastal end of the 2,879-acre Garrapata State Park. The pristine beach is a half-mile crescent of white sand with rocky tidepools. At the south end, Garrapata Creek empties into the Pacific through a granite gorge. A trail follows the bluffs through an ice plant meadow above the beach. Stairways access the beach for a walk along the water. The beautiful sandy strand is an unofficial clothing-optional beach.

To the trailhead

CARMEL. From Highway 1 and Rio Road in Carmel, drive 9.6 miles south on Highway 1 to the unsigned parking turnouts on both sides of the highway. The turnouts are located between two historic bridges—1.2 miles south of the Granite Creek Bridge and 0.2 miles north of the Garrapata Creek Bridge.

BIG SUR RANGER STATION. From the ranger station, drive 16.6 miles north on Highway 1 to the turnouts.

The hike

Walk through gate 19 and descend a few steps. Follow the path to the edge of the oceanfront cliffs and a trail split. To the left, steps lead down the cliffs to the sandy beach. From the beach, head south (left) a short distance to Garrapata Creek and the jagged rocks at the point. Return north and beachcomb for a half mile along the base of the cliffs to the north point.

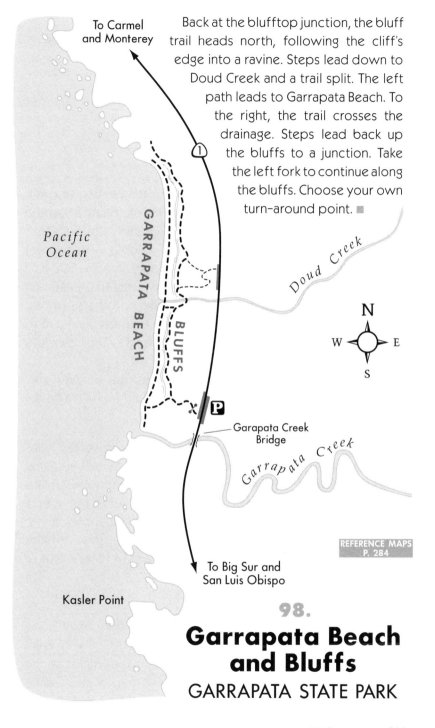

To Carmel
and Monterey

Back at the blufftop junction, the bluff trail heads north, following the cliff's edge into a ravine. Steps lead down to Doud Creek and a trail split. The left path leads to Garrapata Beach. To the right, the trail crosses the drainage. Steps lead back up the bluffs to a junction. Take the left fork to continue along the bluffs. Choose your own turn-around point. ■

Pacific
Ocean

GARRAPATA BEACH

BLUFFS

Doud Creek

N
W ⊕ E
S

X P

Garapata Creek
Bridge

Garrapata Creek

REFERENCE MAPS
P. 284

To Big Sur and
San Luis Obispo

Kasler Point

98.
Garrapata Beach
and Bluffs
GARRAPATA STATE PARK

99. Rocky Point

Hiking distance: 1.3 miles round trip
Hiking time: 30 minutes
Configuration: out-and-back with shoreline exploration
Elevation gain: 100 feet
Difficulty: physically easy but moderately technical
Exposure: open coastal bluffs
Dogs: allowed
Maps: U.S.G.S. Soberanes Point

Rocky Point is a dramatic rock formation jutting out to sea with powerful waves crashing against the rocks. The point is located just south of Kasler Point and is accessed directly from Highway 1. The point has a series of summits and overlooks with amazing coastal views that include Rocky Creek Bridge, spanning 500 feet and hovering 150 feet above the creek; the Point Sur Lightstation, jutting out to sea a few miles to the south; and the scalloped coastline and offshore rocks. This area can be hazardous due to large, sporadic waves and jagged rocky ledges. Step carefully and use extreme caution.

Parking is available at the trailhead for patrons of the Rocky Point Restaurant, cutting 0.8 miles off the round trip mileage.

To the trailhead

CARMEL. From Highway 1 and Rio Road in Carmel, drive 10.7 miles south on Highway 1 to the signed Rocky Point Restaurant entrance. Park in the large turnout on the right side of the highway, 0.2 miles south of the entrance. There is also a small turnout on the left (inland) side of the highway directly across from the entrance.

BIG SUR RANGER STATION. From the ranger station, drive 16 miles north on Highway 1 to Rocky Point, located 0.4 miles north of Palo Colorado Road.

The hike

Follow Highway 1 northbound 0.2 miles to Rocky Point Road. Follow the road west towards the ocean and the Rocky Point Restaurant. Curve left to the south end of the parking lot by the "Hazardous Waves" sign and a footpath at 0.4 miles. Walk towards the point and the first summit. Views open up to the numerous rock formations and crevices. Vistas of Rocky Creek Bridge and the jagged coastline continue to the south. Skirt around the right side of the summit to a trail split. Detour on the left fork to a point overlooking rock caves and crashing whitewater. Return to the junction and descend on the right fork down a grassy saddle to an overlook of the jagged rock fingers, water inlets, and a natural arch. Ascend to the west, climbing out of the saddle to the perch on the summit of Rocky Point. ■

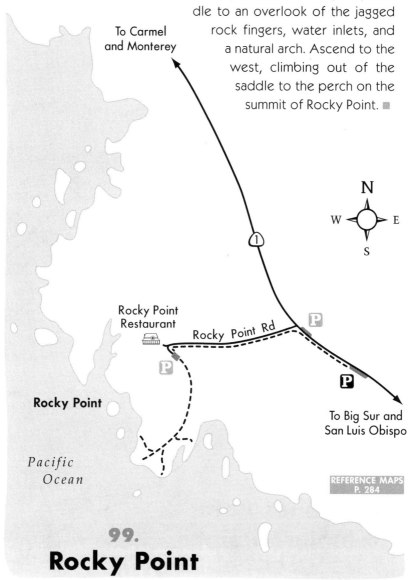

To Carmel and Monterey

N
W ← → E
S

Rocky Point Restaurant

Rocky Point Rd

Rocky Point

Pacific Ocean

To Big Sur and San Luis Obispo

REFERENCE MAPS
P. 284

99.
Rocky Point

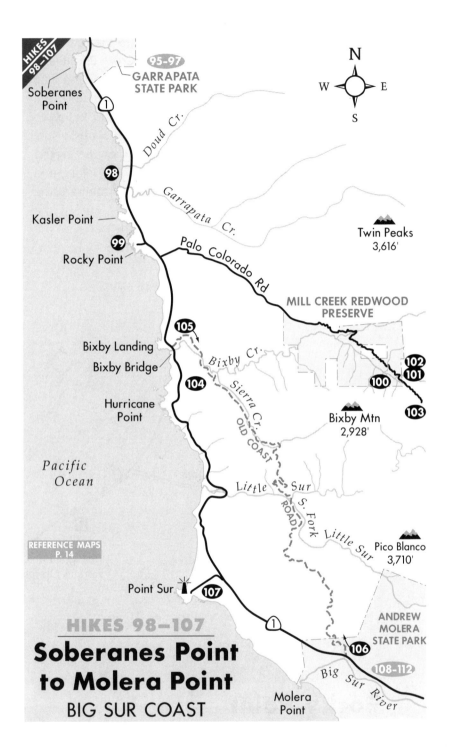

GARRAPATA
STATE PARK
95-97

Soberanes
Point

N
W E
S

1

98

Doud Cr.

Kasler Point

Garrapata Cr.

99

Rocky Point

Palo Colorado Rd

Twin Peaks
3,616'

MILL CREEK REDWOOD
PRESERVE

105

Bixby Landing

Bixby Cr.

Bixby Bridge

104

Sierra Cr.

OLD COAST

102
101

100

103

Hurricane
Point

Bixby Mtn
2,928'

Pacific
Ocean

Little Sur

S. Fork

ROAD

Little Sur

Pico Blanco
3,710'

REFERENCE MAPS
P. 14

Point Sur

107

1

ANDREW
MOLERA
STATE PARK

106

108-112

HIKES 98-107

Soberanes Point
to Molera Point
BIG SUR COAST

Molera
Point

Big Sur River

100. Mill Creek Redwood Preserve

A free access permit is required to hike the trail
www.mprpd.org · (831) 659-4488 then select option 5

Hiking distance: 5.5 miles round trip
Hiking time: 3 hours
Configuration: out-and-back
Elevation gain: 230 feet
Difficulty: easy to slightly moderate
Exposure: shaded forest
Dogs: allowed
Maps: U.S.G.S. Big Sur · Mill Creek Redwood Preserve Trail map

map page 287

The Mill Creek Redwood Preserve encompasses 1,534 acres in a richly atmospheric forest along the upper reaches of Palo Colorado Road, just shy of Bottchers Gap. The preserve sits in the shade of dense second-growth redwoods, sycamores, tanbark oaks, and maples on the northern slope of Bixby Mountain. Mill Creek flows through the forest and down the canyon, where it joins with Bixby Creek.

The area has a rich and storied logging history that dates from the 1800s through the 1980s. Homesteader Charles Bixby ran a timber logging business and sawmill along Mill Creek in the late 1800s. The area was later used for mining limestone. Remnants of the old logging operation and logging road are still evident. Holes in the trunks of redwoods, where planks were inserted for loggers to stand on while cutting the trees, can be spotted. The regional park was purchased in 1989 through the combined efforts of the Big Sur Land Trust and the Regional Park District.

A near-level trail through the length of the preserve was completed in 2007. The trail took 8 years to build and was constructed by hand. The beautifully terraced path winds through the canyon, following the curvature of the steep mountain slope. The trail ends on a panoramic coastal overlook atop a 1,986-foot exposed knoll, where there are views into the surrounding canyons and the ocean. En route, the serpentine footpath crosses several bridges and passes a waterfall, rock formations, and tree trunks blanketed in lichen. The path then ends with a wide open vista of the rugged Big Sur coastline and deep mountain canyons of the Santa Lucia Range.

Access is by a free permit, due to limited parking.

To the trailhead

CARMEL. From Highway 1 and Rio Road in Carmel, drive 11.1 miles south on Highway 1 to Palo Colorado Canyon Road, located 0.4 miles south of Rocky Point. Turn inland and drive 6.8 miles up the narrow, winding mountain road to the pullout on the right by the signed trailhead. The pullout is located 0.1 miles after crossing the bridge over Mill Creek.

BIG SUR RANGER STATION. From the ranger station, drive 15.1 miles north on Highway 1 to Palo Colorado Road.

The hike

Walk down the slope into the dense, shaded forest among tanbark oaks and redwoods. The old logging road can be spotted on the right by the massive redwoods. Cross a bridge over a seasonal tributary of Mill Creek. Traverse the hillside on the north-facing slope of Mill Creek Canyon. Cross a series of three more bridges over feeder streams among madrones and maples to a V-shaped view of the ocean. Cross a bridge over a stream by a small waterfall and pools. One hundred yards ahead is a view of a 50-foot waterfall below the trail. Continue westbound, passing limestone formations at a mostly level grade with a few minor dips and rises. Weave in and out of a redwood-filled drainage with a lush understory of ferns, crossing another footbridge. The trail breaks out of the trees and follows an open ridge, with Palo Colorado Canyon on the right and Beartrap Canyon (a box canyon) on the left. The trail ends on an overlook knoll with four benches at the end of the trail. From the 1,986-foot vista point are spectacular coastal panoramas and views into the surrounding canyons. ∎

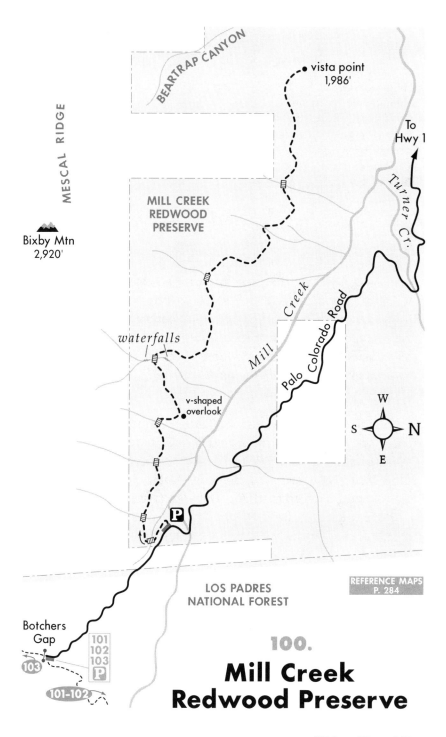

BEARTRAP CANYON

MESCAL RIDGE

Bixby Mtn
2,920'

vista point
1,986'

To
Hwy 1

Turner Cr.

MILL CREEK
REDWOOD
PRESERVE

Mill Creek

Palo Colorado Road

waterfalls

v-shaped
overlook

W

S — N

E

P

LOS PADRES
NATIONAL FOREST

REFERENCE MAPS
P. 284

Botchers
Gap

101
102
103
P

103

101-102

100.

Mill Creek
Redwood Preserve

101. Skinner Ridge Trail to Skinner Ridge Overlook

Hiking distance: 4.5 miles round trip
Hiking time: 2.5 hours
Configuration: out-and-back
Elevation gain: 1,400 feet
Difficulty: moderate
Exposure: shaded forest and open meadows
Dogs: allowed
Maps: U.S.G.S. Big Sur and Mt. Carmel · Ventana Wilderness Map

Skinner Ridge Trail begins from Bottchers Gap at the end of Palo Colorado Road, 2,000 feet above sea level. The trail follows the upper reaches of Mill Creek through the shade of oaks and madrones, reaching the crest of Skinner Ridge at the Ventana Wilderness boundary. From the 3,400-foot ridge are spectacular vistas southwest of the Little Sur watershed, Pico Blanco's white marble cone, the folded layers and ridges of the coast range, and the Pacific Ocean. The trail continues strenuously up to Devil's Peak and Mount Carmel (Hike 102).

To the trailhead

CARMEL. From Highway 1 and Rio Road in Carmel, drive 11.1 miles south on Highway 1 to the signed Palo Colorado Road, located 0.4 miles south of Rocky Point. Turn inland and drive 7.6 miles up the winding mountain road to the Bottchers Gap parking lot at the end of the paved road. A parking fee is required.

BIG SUR RANGER STATION. From the ranger station, drive 15.1 miles north on Highway 1 to Palo Colorado Road.

The hike

From the upper end of the parking lot, take the posted Skinner Ridge Trail into the forest, skirting the campground sites on the left. Pass through oak groves and chaparral. The northwest views extend into the Mill Creek drainage and across several ridges to the ocean. For a short distance, the trail parallels Mill Creek, then drops down to the creek. Ascend the hillside and wind through the woods, crossing a stream in a fern-lined gully. Cross two

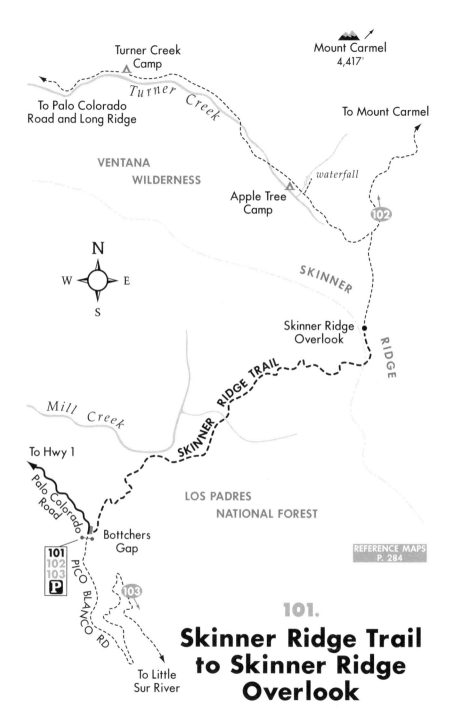

Mount Carmel
4,417'

Turner Creek
Camp

To Palo Colorado
Road and Long Ridge

Turner Creek

To Mount Carmel

VENTANA
WILDERNESS

waterfall

Apple Tree
Camp

102

N
W E
S

SKINNER

Skinner Ridge
Overlook

RIDGE

SKINNER RIDGE TRAIL

Mill Creek

SKINNER

To Hwy 1

Palo Colorado Road

LOS PADRES
NATIONAL FOREST

Bottchers
Gap

REFERENCE MAPS
P. 284

101
102
103
P

PICO BLANCO RD

103

To Little
Sur River

101.
Skinner Ridge Trail
to Skinner Ridge
Overlook

additional tributary streams, reaching Skinner Ridge on a sloping meadow at 2.2 miles. Curve left and head north up the grassy meadow to a knoll and a magnificent overlook. After savoring the views, return along the same trail.

To hike up to Mount Carmel, continue with the next hike. ■

102. Skinner Ridge Trail to Mount Carmel

Hiking distance: 9.6 miles round trip
Hiking time: 5 hours
Configuration: out-and-back
Elevation gain: 2,500 feet
Difficulty: very strenuous
Exposure: shaded forest and open ridge
Dogs: allowed
Maps: U.S.G.S. Big Sur and Mt. Carmel • Ventana Wilderness Map

Mount Carmel, at 4,417 feet, is the highest peak in the northwest reaches of the Ventana Wilderness. From the summit are endless vistas across the rugged mountainous interior to the Pacific Ocean, including prominent Pico Blanco, Ventana Double Cone, the Little Sur watershed, and Monterey Bay. This is a strenuous trail that climbs up to Skinner Ridge, skirts the twin summits of Devil's Peak, and continues the ascent up to Mount Carmel.

To the trailhead

CARMEL. From Highway 1 and Rio Road in Carmel, drive 11.1 miles south on Highway 1 to the signed Palo Colorado Road, located 0.4 miles south of Rocky Point. Turn inland and drive 7.6 miles up the winding mountain road to the Bottchers Gap parking lot at the end of the paved road. A parking fee is required.

BIG SUR RANGER STATION. From the ranger station, drive 15.1 miles north on Highway 1 to Palo Colorado Road.

N
W   E
S

Mount Carmel
4,417'

Turner Creek
Camp

Turner Creek

To Palo Colorado
Road and Long Ridge

Devil's Peak
4,158'

To Comings
Camp and
Big Pines

VENTANA
WILDERNESS

waterfall

Apple Tree
Camp

SKINNER

Skinner Ridge
Overlook
(end Hike 101)

RIDGE

SKINNER RIDGE TRAIL

Mill Creek

To Hwy 1

Palo Colorado Road

LOS PADRES
NATIONAL FOREST

REFERENCE MAPS
P. 284

Bottchers
Gap

101
102
103
P

PICO BLANCO RD

103

To Little
Sur River

102.
Skinner Ridge Trail
to Mount Carmel

The hike

From the upper end of the parking lot, take the posted Skinner Ridge Trail into the forest, skirting the campground sites on the left. Pass through oak groves and chaparral. The northwest views extend into the Mill Creek drainage and across several ridges to the ocean. For a short distance, the trail parallels Mill Creek, then drops down to the creek. Ascend the hillside and wind through the woods, crossing a stream in a fern-lined gully. Cross two additional tributary streams, reaching Skinner Ridge on a sloping meadow at 2.2 miles. Curve left and head north up the grassy meadow to a knoll and the magnificent Skinner Ridge Overlook.

After enjoying the views and a rest, walk along the ridge past oaks and madrones for 0.2 miles. Leave the ridge and descend along the path to a saddle and posted junction with the Turner Creek Trail on the left, which eventually leads back to Palo Colorado Road. Continue straight ahead and ascend the hillside through thick brush and spectacular vistas. Over the next mile, steadily climb up the steeper grade. Pass through oak, manzanita, and madrone groves to a sandy ridge near Devil's Peak. Follow the ridge to the left, viewing Mount Carmel to the north and Pico Blanco to the south. Curve around the right side of the second summit of Devil's Peak to a trail split. The right fork (straight ahead) leads to Comings Camp and Big Pines. Curve left 30 yards to a second fork. Curve to the left again and descend to a grassy saddle. Cross the saddle and follow the ridge through oak groves and dense oak scrub that crowd the trail. The path ends at the summit of Mount Carmel, crowned by a 10-foot granite rock outcropping and an old climbing pole. A survey pin in the rock marks the summit. Make one last climb up the rock for a 360-degree panorama. Return along the same trail. ▪

103. Pico Blanco Road to Little Sur River

Hiking distance: 7.2 miles round trip
Hiking time: 3.5 hours
Configuration: out-and-back
Elevation gain: 1,200 feet
Difficulty: moderate to strenuous
Exposure: mostly shaded forest
Dogs: allowed
Maps: U.S.G.S. Big Sur · Ventana Wilderness Map

map
page 295

Pico Blanco Road is an unpaved, vehicle-restricted road that winds through the mountains under the shadow of Pico Blanco. The road parallels and descends to the Little Sur River. En route are magnificent views of Pico Blanco's north face. The road is on private land with a right-of-way for hikers.

The hike begins on a mountain saddle at Bottchers Gap at an elevation of 2,050 feet. The road/trail descends 1,100 feet to a bridge crossing the river at Pico Blanco Boy Scout Camp. The camp was donated to the boy scouts by William Randolph Hearst in 1948. Redwoods planted between 1910 and 1921 surround the camp.

An optional two-mile side trip leads from the road to the Little Sur River Camp about half way into the hike.

To the trailhead

CARMEL. From Highway 1 and Rio Road in Carmel, drive 11.1 miles south on Highway 1 to the signed Palo Colorado Road, located 0.4 miles south of Rocky Point. Turn inland and drive 7.6 miles up the winding mountain road to the Bottchers Gap parking lot at the end of the paved road. A parking fee is required.

BIG SUR RANGER STATION. From the ranger station, drive 15.1 miles north on Highway 1 to Palo Colorado Road.

The hike

From the lower end of the parking lot, pass the locked gate and head down the unpaved Pico Blanco Road. Descend down the winding mountain road past several magnificent close-up views of Pico Blanco, Dani Ridge, and the Pacific Ocean. At 1.8 miles, on a left horseshoe bend, is the posted junction with the Little Sur River Camp Trail on the right. For a side trip to the camp, the narrow footpath descends one mile down eight switchbacks to the camp at the river, sitting amidst tanbark oak trees and towering redwoods.

On the main road, continue downhill through a redwood forest. Pass a tributary stream with a 15-foot waterfall dropping off a vertical rock ledge. After the stream, the road enters the boy scout property. Stay on the road parallel to the creek, passing a couple of cabins. Pass another group of cabins by the main lodge. At the river, cross the long wooden footbridge, and follow the trail signs to the posted Pico Blanco Trail at the camp crossroads. The Pico Blanco Trail leads up the hill to a trail fork with the Little Sur River Trail. This is the turnaround spot.

To extend the hike, the left fork leads 0.7 miles to Jackson Camp on the south bank of the Little Sur River, where the trail ends. The right fork climbs Pico Blanco and connects with the Mount Manuel Trail from Pfeiffer Big Sur State Park (Hike 116). ▣

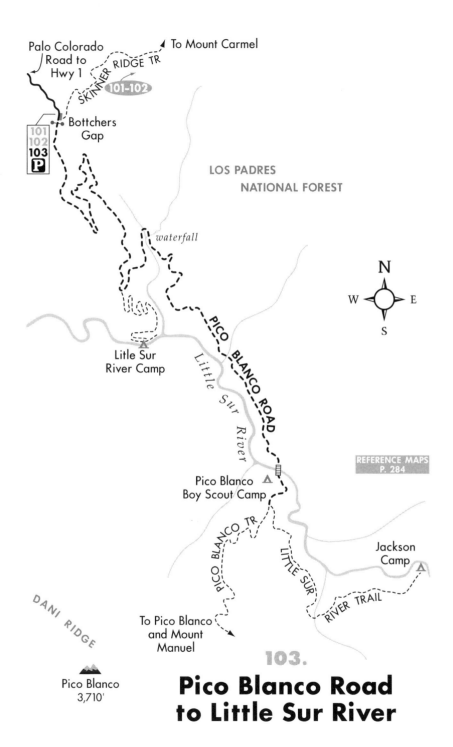

Palo Colorado
Road to
Hwy 1

To Mount Carmel

SKINNER RIDGE TR

101-102

Bottchers
Gap

101
102
103
P

LOS PADRES
NATIONAL FOREST

waterfall

N

W ⟵✦⟶ E

S

PICO BLANCO ROAD

Litle Sur
River Camp

Little Sur River

REFERENCE MAPS
P. 284

Pico Blanco
Boy Scout Camp

PICO BLANCO TR

LITTLE SUR

Jackson
Camp

RIVER TRAIL

DANI RIDGE

To Pico Blanco
and Mount
Manuel

Pico Blanco
3,710'

103.
**Pico Blanco Road
to Little Sur River**

104. Brazil Ranch

Hiking distance: 4.2 miles round trip
Hiking time: 2.5 hours
Configuration: out-and-back
Elevation gain: 1,100 feet
Difficulty: moderate
Exposure: exposed hillside and ridge
Dogs: allowed
Maps: U.S.G.S. Point Sur
　　　　 Big Sur and Ventana Wilderness map • Brazil Ranch map

Brazil Ranch stretches across 1,255 oceanfront acres along the Big Sur coast. The rocky shoreline includes the dramatic scalloped promontory of Hurricane Point. The old ranchland encompasses Sierra Hill, the 1,545-foot mountain that spans between Bixby Bridge to the north and the Little Sur River on the south. Tony and Margaret Brazil operated the ranch for nearly a century. In 1977 it was purchased by Allen Funt, creator of the television show *Candid Camera*. Funt developed the land and raised quarter horses and cattle. The U.S. Forest Service acquired the ranch in 2002.

This hike follows an old ranch road straight up the ridge of Sierra Hill to a series of flats with spectacular coastal and mountain vistas. The path follows the rolling grassy ridge to the summit.

To the trailhead

CARMEL. From Highway 1 and Rio Road in Carmel, drive 14.9 miles south on Highway 1 to the long, narrow pullout on the right, directly across the road from the gated, paved ranch road. The pullout is located 2.7 miles south of Palo Colorado Canyon Road and a half mile south of Bixby Bridge.

BIG SUR RANGER STATION. From the ranger station, drive 13 miles north on Highway 1 to the pullout on the left.

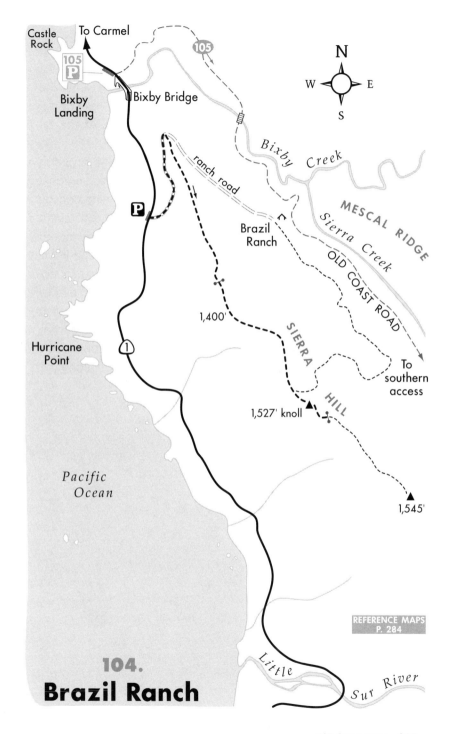

Castle Rock

To Carmel

105

P

Bixby Landing

Bixby Bridge

N

W E

S

Bixby Creek

ranch road

MESCAL RIDGE

Sierra Creek

P

Brazil Ranch

OLD COAST ROAD

1,400'

SIERRA HILL

To southern access

Hurricane Point

1

1,527' knoll

Pacific Ocean

1,545'

REFERENCE MAPS
P. 284

104.
Brazil Ranch

Little

Sur River

The hike

Pass through the trail gate and head up the old paved ranch road. Traverse the oceanfront slope overlooking Hurricane Point. At 0.45 miles is a U-shaped right bend. Round the bend into the interior mountains above Sierra Creek Canyon, with a view of the Brazil Ranch, Mescal Ridge, and the Old Coast Road. At the far end of the bend is a signed trail.

Bear right and take the grassy footpath up the spine of Sierra Hill. Steadily climb the ridge, with a few steep sections and past several false summits. With every step, the far-reaching coastal and mountain vistas expand. Pass through a trail gate, and climb to a 1,400-foot grassy flat. The coastal views include the mouth of the Little Sur River, the Point Sur Lighthouse, Hurricane Point, and mountain views into Sierra Creek Canyon and the surrounding ridges. Walk to a posted fork and take the designated trail to the right. Gently climb and cross over the rounded grassy knoll at 1,527 feet. Follow the rolling ridge to a gated fence at the end of the public access. Beyond the fence, the grassy road continues a half mile to the 1,545-foot summit of Sierra Hill. Return along the same route. ▇

105. Old Coast Road
NORTHERN ACCESS

Hiking distance: 11.5 miles round trip (or 10.2-mile shuttle)
Hiking time: 5.5 hours
Configuration: out-and-back with optional shuttle with Hike 106
Elevation gain: 2,000 feet
Difficulty: strenuous
Exposure: shaded forest and open grassland
Dogs: allowed
Maps: U.S.G.S. Point Sur and Big Sur
       Big Sur and Ventana Wilderness map

map page 302

The Old Coast Road was the original coastal route connecting Carmel with Big Sur before the Bixby Bridge was completed in 1932. The hike begins at the frequently photographed Bixby Bridge—at the north end of the Old Coast Road—and follows the twisting, unpaved back road through a shaded canyon dense with coastal redwoods and lush ferns. The trail parallels Bixby Creek and Sierra Creek and crosses two bridges over the Little Sur River. The road is open to the public but is bordered by private property. The hike may be combined with Hike 106 for a 10.2-mile shuttle hike with the road's southern access.

To the trailhead

CARMEL. From Highway 1 and Rio Road in Carmel, drive 12.7 miles south on Highway 1 to the Bixby Bridge. The parking pullout is at the north end of the bridge on the ocean side of the highway.

BIG SUR RANGER STATION. From the ranger station, drive 13.5 miles north on Highway 1 to the parking pullouts on the left, just after crossing Bixby Bridge.

The hike

From the north end of Bixby Bridge, take the signed Coast Road inland along the north side of Bixby Creek. At 0.3 miles, as the road curves right, is a great view down canyon of Bixby Bridge and the offshore rocks. Curve south and descend to the canyon floor. Cross a bridge over Bixby Creek. Gently ascend the lower reaches of Sierra Hill along the west wall of the canyon, passing homes tucked into the trees and numerous cliffside tributary streams. As the old road wends south through a lush redwood forest, Bixby Creek curves away to the east. The road continues parallel to Sierra Creek, a tributary of Bixby Creek. The road crosses the creek five consecutive times. At the sixth crossing, leave Sierra Creek on a hairpin right bend. Climb out of the shaded canyon to open rolling hillsides on the summit of the Sierra Grade. Descend 1,000 feet along the contours of the mountains on the chaparral slopes of the Sierra Grade. Pico Blanco, rising 3,710 feet, dominates the views to the southeast. At the bottom of the grade, walk through a stand of bishop pines to the Little Sur River. Two consecutive metal bridges cross the South Fork and Main Fork of the Little Sur River, just above their confluence.

Return along the same trail, or continue southward with the next hike for a one-way shuttle hike. ■

106. Old Coast Road
SOUTHERN ACCESS

Hiking distance: 9 miles round trip (or 10.2-mile shuttle)
Hiking time: 4.5 hours
Configuration: out-and-back with optional shuttle with Hike 105
Elevation gain: 1,650 feet
Difficulty: moderate to strenuous
Exposure: shaded forest and open grassland
Dogs: allowed
Maps: U.S.G.S. Big Sur
Big Sur and Ventana Wilderness map

map page 303

The Old Coast Road was the primary route of travel along this mountainous coastal stretch prior to 1932, when the 260-foot-high Bixby Bridge was opened. This hike begins at the Big Sur Valley in Andrew Molera State Park near the mouth of the Big Sur River—at the south end of the Old Coast Highway. The winding, breathtaking route curves along hillsides, offering panoramic vistas of the coastline and interior mountains. The road slowly descends into a shaded canyon to the Little Sur River, rich with lush ferns and coastal redwoods. The road is open to the public, but the adjacent land is privately owned. The hike may be combined with Hike 105 for a 10.2-mile shuttle hike with the road's northern access.

To the trailhead

CARMEL. From Highway 1 and Rio Road in Carmel, drive 21.4 miles south on Highway 1 to the signed Andrew Molera State Park entrance. Turn right and drive down to the entrance kiosk and parking lot. A parking fee is required.

BIG SUR RANGER STATION. From the ranger station, drive 4.8 miles north on Highway 1 to the Andrew Molera State Park entrance and turn left.

The hike

Walk back up to Highway 1, and cross the highway to the signed Coast Road. Head up the winding, unpaved road on a northern course to steadily improving coastal views. At 1.5 miles, weave through groves of oaks, sycamores, and redwoods, reaching a 942-foot summit. Views extend to the coastal marine terrace, Andrew Molera State Park, inland to the South Fork Canyon, and across Dani Ridge to the towering 3,710-foot Pico Blanco in the east. Slowly descend, passing a ranch on the left, and enter a lush redwood forest. Skirt around the west edge of Dani Ridge. Parallel the South Fork Little Sur River down the narrow, shaded canyon through oaks, maples, pines, redwoods, and an understory of ferns. At the canyon floor, two consecutive metal bridges cross the South Fork and Main Fork of the Little Sur River just above their confluence.

Return along the same trail or continue northward with Hike 102 for a one-way shuttle hike. ▪

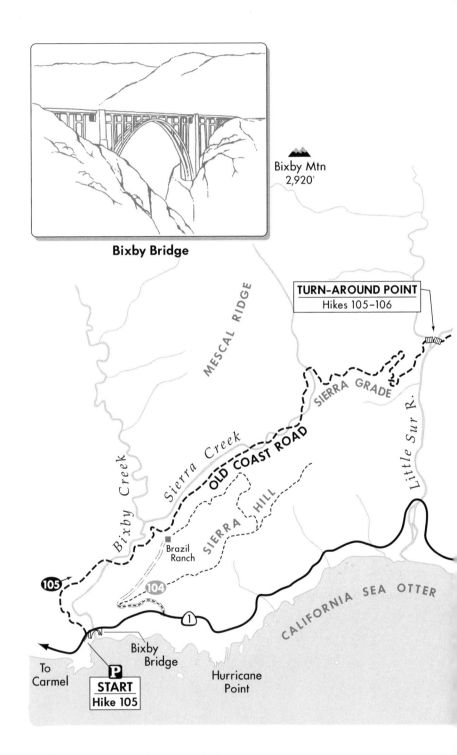

Bixby Bridge

Bixby Mtn
2,920'

MESCAL RIDGE

TURN-AROUND POINT
Hikes 105–106

SIERRA GRADE

Sierra Creek

OLD COAST ROAD

Bixby Creek

Little Sur R.

SIERRA HILL

Brazil Ranch

104

105

1

CALIFORNIA SEA OTTER

Bixby Bridge

Hurricane Point

To Carmel

P

START
Hike 105

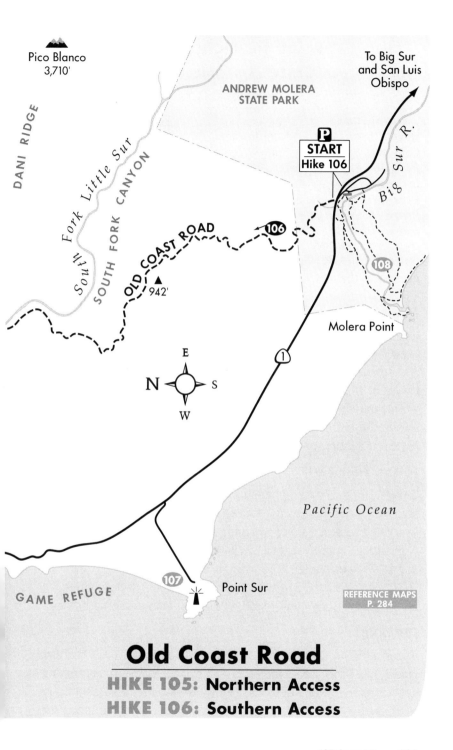

Pico Blanco
3,710'

DANI RIDGE

ANDREW MOLERA
STATE PARK

To Big Sur
and San Luis
Obispo

South Fork Little Sur

SOUTH FORK CANYON

START
Hike 106

Big Sur R.

OLD COAST ROAD 106

OLD 942'

108

Molera Point

E
N W S

Pacific Ocean

GAME REFUGE

107

Point Sur

REFERENCE MAPS
P. 284

Old Coast Road

HIKE 105: Northern Access
HIKE 106: Southern Access

107. Point Sur Lightstation State Historic Park

Docent led hike: call for scheduled tour times (831) 625-4419

Hiking distance: 1 mile round trip
Hiking time: 3 hours (docent-led hike)
Configuration: out-and-back with small loop
Elevation gain: 360 feet
Difficulty: easy
Exposure: exposed headland
Dogs: not allowed
Maps: U.S.G.S. Point Sur · Big Sur and Ventana Wilderness map

Point Sur is a 361-foot offshore metamorphic rock that is connected to the mainland by a sand bar called a tombolo. The El Sur Ranch owns the surrounding land except for the 34-acre volcanic rock. The Point Sur Lightstation atop the basaltic rock was built in 1889. This docent-led hike follows an old horse and buggy route used in the 1800s. The trail overlooks massive offshore rocks and crashing surf. The tour climbs the spiral staircase to the lamp tower at the top of the 38-foot stone lightstation, where there are magnificent views of the ocean and mountains from 270 feet above the water. Atop the point are intact sandstone buildings, restored historic barns, and a visitor center.

To the trailhead

CARMEL. From Highway 1 and Rio Road in Carmel, drive 18.6 miles south on Highway 1 to the signed Point Sur Lightstation entrance. Park in the pullout along the right side of the highway. A docent will lead a car caravan into the gated property. The base of Point Sur is 0.7 miles ahead. A tour fee is required.

BIG SUR RANGER STATION. From the ranger station, drive 7.6 miles north on Highway 1 to the Point Sur Lightstation entrance.

The hike

Ascend the hill on the paved lighthouse road, following the tour guide. The road steadily climbs and curves, overlooking the jagged coastline. Dramatic rocks with crashing whitewater are just offshore. Part of the trail follows an old railway route along the steep cliff. At the lightstation, a spiral staircase leads to the lamp and catwalk. A long set of wooden steps heads up to a ridge and an overlook of the light beacon. The old road leads past a blacksmith and carpenter shop, restored barn, two-foot-thick sandstone buildings (once home to lighthouse keepers), and a visitor center at the top of Point Sur. ■

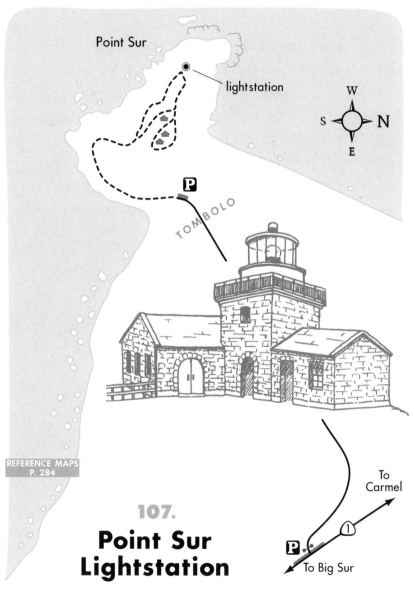

REFERENCE MAPS
P. 284

107.
Point Sur
Lightstation

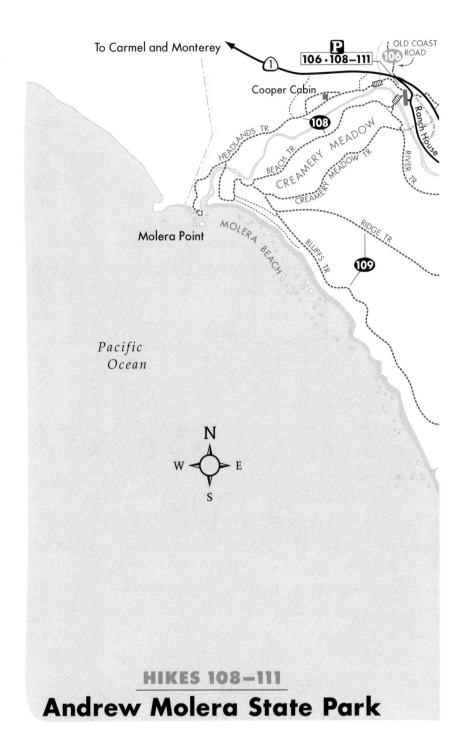

To Carmel and Monterey

① 106·108–111 P

OLD COAST ROAD 106

Cooper Cabin

108

HEADLANDS TR

BEACH TR

CREAMERY MEADOW

CREAMERY MEADOW TR

CREAMERY MEADOW TR

RIVER TR

Ranch House

Molera Point

MOLERA BEACH

BLUFFS TR

RIDGE TR

109

Pacific
Ocean

N
W — E
S

HIKES 108–111
Andrew Molera State Park

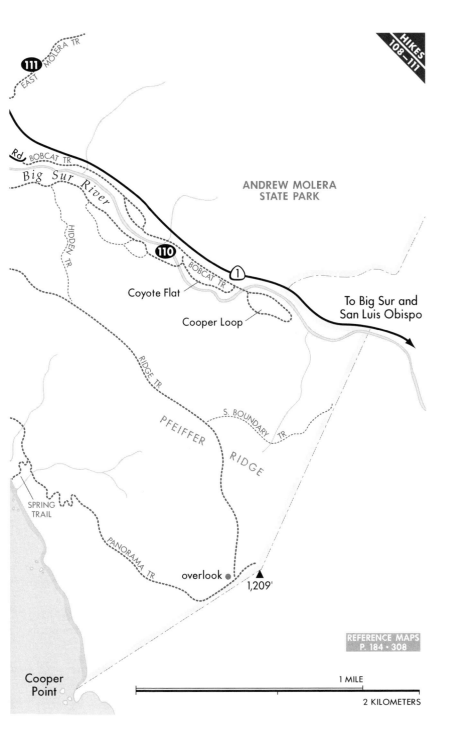

111

EAST MOLERA TR

Rd
BOBCAT TR

Big Sur River

HIDDEN TR

ANDREW MOLERA
STATE PARK

110

BOBCAT TR

1

Coyote Flat

Cooper Loop

To Big Sur and
San Luis Obispo

RIDGE TR

S. BOUNDARY TR

PFEIFFER

RIDGE

SPRING
TRAIL

PANORAMA TR

overlook

▲
1,209'

REFERENCE MAPS
P. 184 • 308

Cooper
Point

1 MILE

2 KILOMETERS

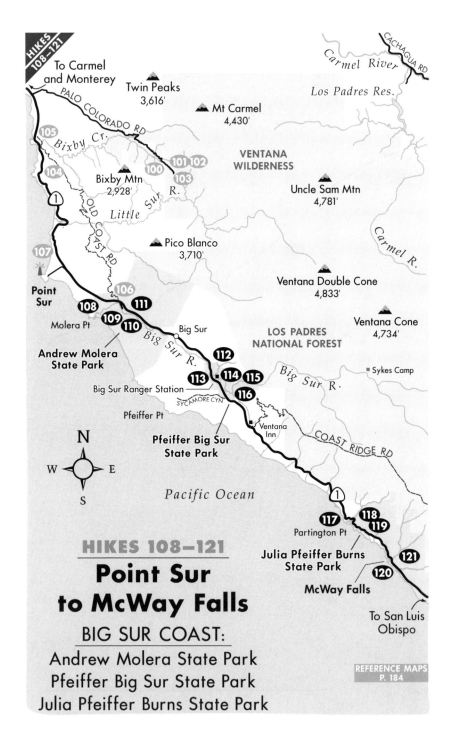

To Carmel
and Monterey

Carmel River

CACHAGUA RD

Twin Peaks
3,616'

Mt Carmel
4,430'

Los Padres Res.

PALO COLORADO RD

105

Bixby Cr.

VENTANA
WILDERNESS

104

100 **101** **102**

103

Bixby Mtn
2,928'

Uncle Sam Mtn
4,781'

1

Sur R.

Little

OLD COAST RD

Pico Blanco
3,710'

Carmel R.

107

Ventana Double Cone
4,833'

Point
Sur

106

108 **111**

Molera Pt

109 **110**

Big Sur

Big Sur R.

LOS PADRES
NATIONAL FOREST

Ventana Cone
4,734'

Andrew Molera
State Park

112

Big Sur R.

Sykes Camp

113 **114** **115**

Big Sur Ranger Station

SYCAMORE CYN

116

Pfeiffer Pt

Ventana
Inn

COAST RIDGE RD

N

Pfeiffer Big Sur
State Park

W ✦ **E**

1

S

Pacific Ocean

117

118
119

Partington Pt

HIKES 108–121

**Julia Pfeiffer Burns
State Park**

121

Point Sur
to McWay Falls

120

McWay Falls

To San Luis
Obispo

BIG SUR COAST:
Andrew Molera State Park
Pfeiffer Big Sur State Park
Julia Pfeiffer Burns State Park

REFERENCE MAPS
P. 184

108. Molera Point and Molera Beach
ANDREW MOLERA STATE PARK

Hiking distance: 2.5 miles round trip
Hiking time: 1.5 hours
Configuration: loop
Elevation gain: 70 feet
Difficulty: easy
Exposure: open marine terrace
Dogs: not allowed
Maps: U.S.G.S. Big Sur · Andrew Molera State Park map
Big Sur and Ventana Wilderness map

map page 311

Andrew Molera State Park, the largest state park on the Big Sur coast, encompasses 4,800 acres and extends along both sides of Highway 1. The park has mountains, meadows, a 2.5-mile strand of beach, and over 15 miles of hiking trails. The Big Sur River flows through the park to the Pacific Ocean.

This hike parallels the Big Sur River along ocean bluffs to Molera Point and Molera Beach at the coastline. From the ridge are views of this diverse park, its numerous hiking trails, Molera Beach, the Point Sur Lighthouse, and Cooper Point at the south end of the bay. A side trip leads to Cooper Cabin. Built with redwood logs in 1861, the cabin is the oldest surviving ranch structure in Big Sur. The return trail meanders through a grassy meadow lined with sycamores.

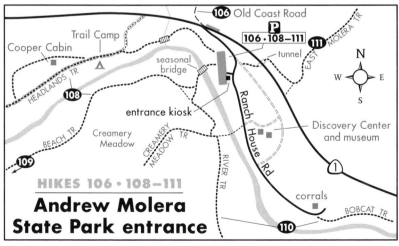

HIKES 106 · 108–111
Andrew Molera State Park entrance

To the trailhead

CARMEL. From Highway 1 and Rio Road in Carmel, drive 21.4 miles south on Highway 1 to the signed Andrew Molera State Park entrance. Turn right and drive down to the entrance kiosk and parking lot on the coast side of the highway. A parking fee is required.

BIG SUR RANGER STATION. From the ranger station, drive 4.8 miles north on Highway 1 to the state park entrance and turn left (towards the coast).

The hike

The signed trail is at the far northwest end of the parking lot. Walk past the Trail Camp sign and up into a shady grove. Cross a footbridge over a tributary stream, and parallel the Big Sur River. At 0.3 miles, the trail merges with an old ranch road. Bear left, entering Trail Camp, and walk through the campground past large oaks and sycamores. Cooper Cabin is to the south in a eucalyptus grove. After viewing the historic cabin, continue southwest on the ranch road, following the river to a signed junction and map at one mile. The left fork leads to a seasonal bridge crossing the Big Sur River to Molera Beach—the return route. First, continue on the right fork on the Headlands Trail, taking the wooden steps up to the ridge. Walk out to sea on the headlands, circling the point.

Return to the seasonal bridge, and head down to Molera Beach at the mouth of the Big Sur River. The beach extends south for two miles, but the tide often makes further access impossible. After exploring the beach, head to the back of the beach to the Beach Trail. Pass the Bluffs Trail and the Creamery Meadow Trail, both on the right. Stay left on the Beach Trail, and follow the river upstream a short distance. Soon the river veers left, and the footpath curves through the grassy meadow dotted with sycamore and cottonwood trees. The trail is separated from the river by dense willow thickets. Meander through Creamery Meadow to a junction with the River Trail and another seasonal bridge over the Big Sur River. Head left over the bridge, back to the parking lot. ■

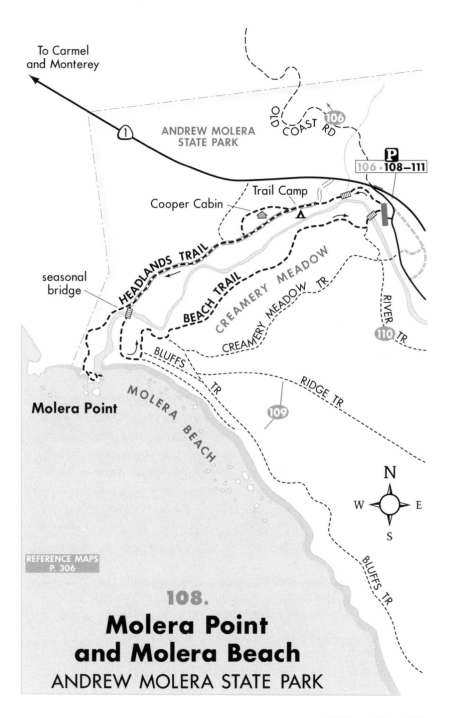

To Carmel
and Monterey

ANDREW MOLERA
STATE PARK

OLD COAST RD

106

P
106 · 108–111

Trail Camp

Cooper Cabin

HEADLANDS TRAIL

seasonal
bridge

BEACH TRAIL

CREAMERY MEADOW

CREAMERY MEADOW TR

RIVER TR

110

BLUFFS TR

MOLERA BEACH

RIDGE TR

109

Molera Point

N
W   E
S

REFERENCE MAPS
P. 306

BLUFFS TR

108.
Molera Point
and Molera Beach
ANDREW MOLERA STATE PARK

109. Bluffs — Panorama — Ridge Loop
ANDREW MOLERA STATE PARK

Hiking distance: 9-mile loop
Hiking time: 4.5 hours
Configuration: loop
Elevation gain: 1,100 feet
Difficulty: moderate to strenuous
Exposure: open bluffs and meadows, shaded forest
Dogs: not allowed
Maps: U.S.G.S. Big Sur · Andrew Molera State Park map
Big Sur and Ventana Wilderness map

This hike circles the western side of Andrew Molera State Park through a diverse cross-section of landscapes that include coastal bluffs, isolated beach coves, forested stream canyons, redwood forests, overlooks, meadows, and a river crossing. The long loop trail meanders for two miles on the flat marine terrace, then climbs up a ridge at the south park boundary to sweeping views of the coast and mountains. The trail descends along Pfeiffer Ridge through oak forests, massive redwood groves, and open grasslands with vistas of the Big Sur coastline.

To the trailhead

CARMEL. From Highway 1 and Rio Road in Carmel, drive 21.4 miles south on Highway 1 to the signed Andrew Molera State Park entrance. Turn right and drive down to the entrance kiosk and parking lot on the coast side of the highway. A parking fee is required.

BIG SUR RANGER STATION. From the ranger station, drive 4.8 miles north on Highway 1 to the state park entrance and turn left (towards the coast).

The hike

At the signed Beach Trail near the middle of the parking lot, cross the Big Sur River on the summer footbridge (or wade across if removed) to a trail fork. Stay to the left on the River Trail. Bear left again fifty yards ahead, staying on the River Trail to a posted junction at the base of the hillside. The River Trail curves left. Take

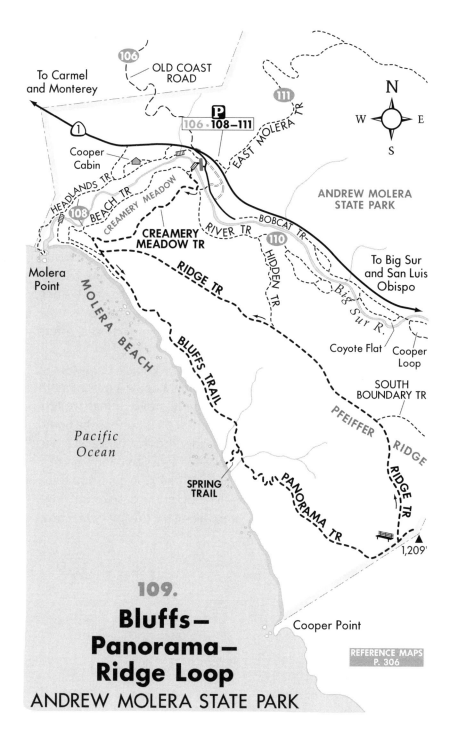

To Carmel
and Monterey

106 OLD COAST ROAD

111

P
106 • 108–111

EAST MOLERA TR

N
W E
S

Cooper
Cabin

HEADLANDS TR

BEACH TR

CREAMERY MEADOW

108

**CREAMERY
MEADOW TR**

RIVER TR

BOBCAT TR

ANDREW MOLERA
STATE PARK

110

To Big Sur
and San Luis
Obispo

Molera
Point

MOLERA BEACH

RIDGE TR

HIDDEN TR

Big Sur R.

Coyote Flat   Cooper
Loop

SOUTH
BOUNDARY TR

Pacific
Ocean

BLUFFS TRAIL

SPRING
TRAIL

PANORAMA TR

PFEIFFER RIDGE

RIDGE TR

1,209'

**109.
Bluffs–
Panorama–
Ridge Loop**
ANDREW MOLERA STATE PARK

Cooper Point

REFERENCE MAPS
P. 306

the Creamery Meadow Trail to the right, and contour southwest along the base of the hill, skirting the edge of the meadow. At 0.8 miles is a junction with the Ridge Trail on the left. Take the Ridge Trail and leave the meadow, heading up the ridge to an open flat and a trail fork a short distance ahead.

Begin the loop to the right on the Bluffs Trail. Cross the wide marine terrace between the jagged coastal cliffs and the inland hills. Pass several side paths that lead to the edge of the cliffs. Curve around a pair of eroding, spring-fed gullies. Dip in and out of another gulch to the end of the Bluffs Trail at a posted trail junction. The Spring Trail bears right and zigzags a short distance down a draw to a small pocket beach.

Continue on the Panorama Trail, dropping into a drainage. Climb out and steadily wind up the hillside to the park's south boundary and views of Pacific Valley and the Big Sur coast. Curve along the fenced boundary to the end of the Panorama Trail on the summit at 4.6 miles. A bench, set among the cypress trees, offers a respite with sweeping coastal views.

Take the posted Ridge Trail north, descending towards the towering redwoods ahead. The spongy, needle-covered path levels out and meanders through a shady grove of massive redwoods and twisted oaks draped with lace lichen. Pass the South Boundary Trail on the right, and follow Pfeiffer (Molera) Ridge across the exposed grass and chaparral. Cross two long, sweeping saddles to a junction with Hidden Trail. Continue down the seaward Ridge Trail, completing the loop at the base of the ridge at the Bluffs Trail. Retrace your steps along the Creamery Meadow Trail back to the parking lot. ▨

110. Bobcat Trail—River Trail Loop

ANDREW MOLERA STATE PARK

Hiking distance: 5 miles round trip
Hiking time: 2.5 hours
Configuration: inter-connecting loops
Elevation gain: 50 feet
Difficulty: easy to slightly moderate
Exposure: shaded forest and open meadows
Dogs: not allowed
Maps: U.S.G.S. Big Sur · Andrew Molera State Park map
Big Sur and Ventana Wilderness map

The Bobcat Trail and River Trail loop around the banks of the Big Sur River in Andrew Molera State Park. The route crosses four meadows, winds through numerous redwood groves and pockets of mature hardwood trees, passes a few swimming holes, and crosses the Big Sur River four times.

To the trailhead

CARMEL. From Highway 1 and Rio Road in Carmel, drive 21.4 miles south on Highway 1 to the signed Andrew Molera State Park entrance. Turn right and drive down to the entrance kiosk and parking lot on the coast side of the highway. A parking fee is required. The trail is also accessible from several gates along Highway 1, which may involve wading through the Big Sur River.

BIG SUR RANGER STATION. From the ranger station, drive 4.8 miles north on Highway 1 to the state park entrance and turn left (towards the coast).

The hike

Walk back to the entrance of the parking lot. Ten yards past the kiosk, take the unpaved Ranch House Road to the right. Follow the road southeast through oak and maple groves, passing a river crossing on the right and barns on the left. At the far (south) end of the corrals, the road ends at the posted Bobcat Trail on the right.

Take the footpath through a shady grove lush with ferns, poison oak, and towering redwoods. Weave through the forest between the Big Sur River and Highway 1, passing a trail access from Highway 1. Curve away from the highway to an open meadow. A path loops around the perimeter of the meadow. Take the right fork along the west edge. Beyond the meadow, the trail descends to a small, sandy beach by a rock cliff on the banks of the Big Sur River. Across the river is the River Trail—the return route. Continue following the watercourse upstream. Cross a tributary stream, and wind through a redwood grove to a Y-fork. Curve right and descend into Coyote Flat and a trail split. Again a trail circles the large meadow. Take the right fork along the southwest border of the meadow. A side path on the right leads to a large pool in the river. At the far end of Coyote Flat, the loop trail connects at a Y-junction. To the right is a wide river crossing.

Wade across the river to a trail fork at the beginning of the Cooper Loop. The Cooper Loop may be hiked in either direction. This route begins on the left fork, hiking clockwise. Wind through the thick forest to the banks of the river. Follow the river upstream to the far end of the loop. Curve right, leaving the river, and enter a dense redwood grove with lush ferns and mosses. Complete the 0.7-mile loop, and cross back over the river.

Return through Coyote Flat, now taking the right fork around the east end of the meadow. Pass a highway access trail on the right. Beyond Coyote Flat, descend through redwoods, crossing a tributary stream to a small pocket beach at the river by rock cliffs. Wade across the river to the west bank, and pick up the unsigned River Trail. Stay to the right on the route closest to the river, passing open meadows dotted with trees and views of the surrounding mountains. Skirt the west side of the meadow along the base of the cliffs. Curve left up a small rise, passing a junction with the Hidden Trail on the left. Gradually descend back to the meadow, and follow the hillside to the north end of the hill and a junction. Bear left 20 yards to the Creamery Meadow Trail. Curve right, staying on the River Trail to the signed parking lot junction. Cross the Big Sur River back to the parking lot. ▪

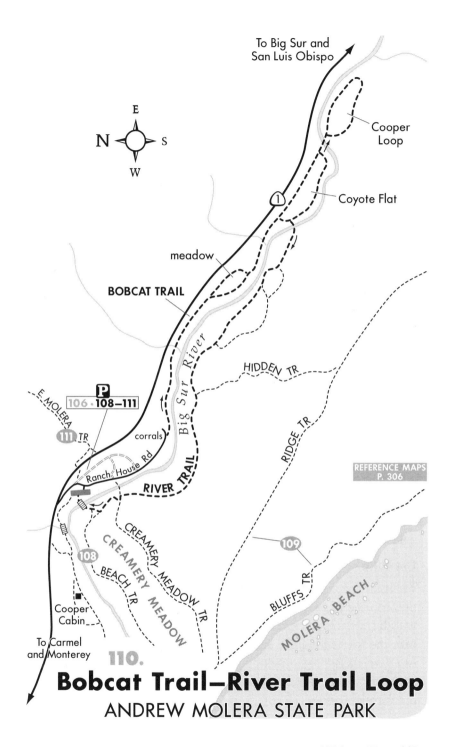

To Big Sur and
San Luis Obispo

E
N ✦ S
W

Cooper
Loop

1

Coyote Flat

meadow

BOBCAT TRAIL

Big Sur River

HIDDEN TR

E. MOLERA

P
106 · 108–111

111 TR

corrals

RIDGE TR

Ranch House Rd

RIVER TRAIL

REFERENCE MAPS
P. 306

CREAMERY MEADOW TR

109

CREAMERY MEADOW

108

BEACH TR

BLUFFS TR

MOLERA BEACH

Cooper
Cabin

To Carmel
and Monterey

110.
Bobcat Trail–River Trail Loop
ANDREW MOLERA STATE PARK

111. East Molera Trail

ANDREW MOLERA STATE PARK

Hiking distance: 4 miles round trip
Hiking time: 2 hours
Configuration: out-and-back
Elevation gain: 1,500 feet
Difficulty: moderate to strenuous
Exposure: open hillside
Dogs: not allowed
Maps: U.S.G.S. Big Sur · Andrew Molera State Park map
Big Sur and Ventana Wilderness map

Andrew Molera State Park encompasses 4,800 acres along both sides of Highway 1, with the majority of the acreage east of the highway. The East Molera Trail climbs up the coastal slope of the Santa Lucia Mountains to amazing vistas of the entire state park and up the coastline to the Point Sur Lightstation. The path crosses an old pasture to a ridge, where there is a beautiful grove of stately redwoods, backed by towering Pico Blanco. The views include Molera Beach, Molera Point, Creamery Meadow, the Big Sur River, Trail Camp, Pfeiffer Ridge, and the expansive coastline.

To the trailhead

CARMEL. From Highway 1 and Rio Road in Carmel, drive 21.4 miles south on Highway 1 to the signed Andrew Molera State Park entrance. Turn right and drive down to the entrance kiosk and parking lot on the coast side of the highway. A parking fee is required.

BIG SUR RANGER STATION. From the ranger station, drive 4.8 miles north on Highway 1 to the park entrance and turn left.

The hike

Walk past the entrance kiosk and up the road to the left bend. Bear right on the unpaved road, marked "Authorized Personnel Only." Walk a short distance to the signed East Molera Trail on the left. Take the footpath uphill and through the tunnel under Highway 1. At 0.2 miles is a signed junction. To the right is an access trail to Highway 1. Bear left uphill through a shady oak grove to an old ranch road. Follow the forested road to the left, passing a water tank on the right. The trail emerges from the forest canopy to the open, sloping grassland. Cross the slopes to the southern edge of the ridge. Veer left and traverse the west face of the mountain. Continue up two long, sweeping switchbacks. Wind around the south side of the mountain to the head of the canyon and a beautiful stand of redwoods on the ridge. Across the inland canyon is pyramid-shaped Pico Blanco and the South Fork Little Sur River canyon. A path follows the ridge in both directions. To the right are stately oaks and views up the Big Sur Valley. To the left is the summit and awesome coastal views. After marveling at the vistas, return along the same route. ■

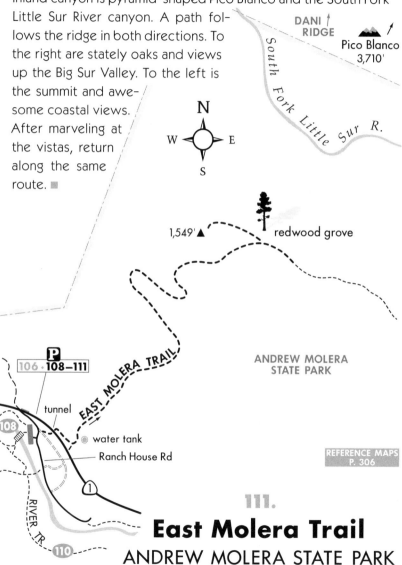

DANI RIDGE

Pico Blanco
3,710'

South Fork Little Sur R.

N
W ← → E
S

1,549' ▲

redwood grove

P
106 · 108–111

EAST MOLERA TRAIL

ANDREW MOLERA
STATE PARK

tunnel

108

water tank

Ranch House Rd

REFERENCE MAPS
P. 306

RIVER TR.

110

111.
East Molera Trail
ANDREW MOLERA STATE PARK

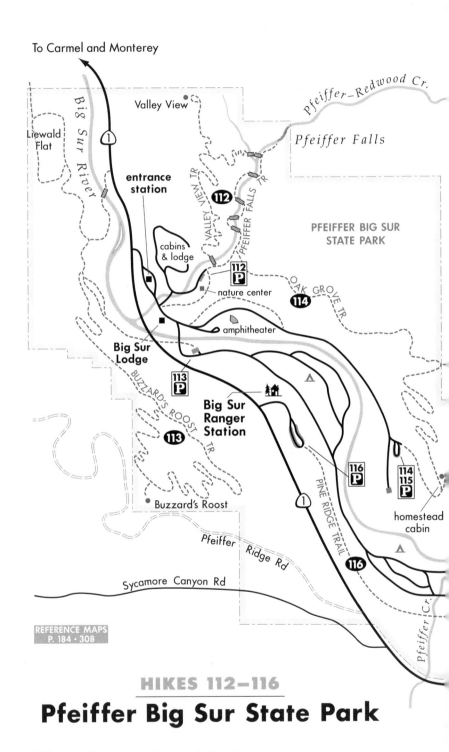

To Carmel and Monterey

Liewald Flat

Big Sur River

Valley View

1

entrance station

cabins & lodge

VALLEY VIEW TR

PFEIFFER FALLS TR

112

112 P

nature center

amphitheater

Big Sur Lodge

BUZZARD'S ROOST TR

113 P

113

Big Sur Ranger Station

Buzzard's Roost

Pfeiffer Ridge Rd

Sycamore Canyon Rd

Pfeiffer–Redwood Cr.

Pfeiffer Falls

PFEIFFER BIG SUR STATE PARK

OAK GROVE TR

114

116 P

114 115 P

homestead cabin

1

PINE RIDGE TRAIL

116

Pfeiffer Cr.

REFERENCE MAPS P. 184 • 308

HIKES 112–116
Pfeiffer Big Sur State Park

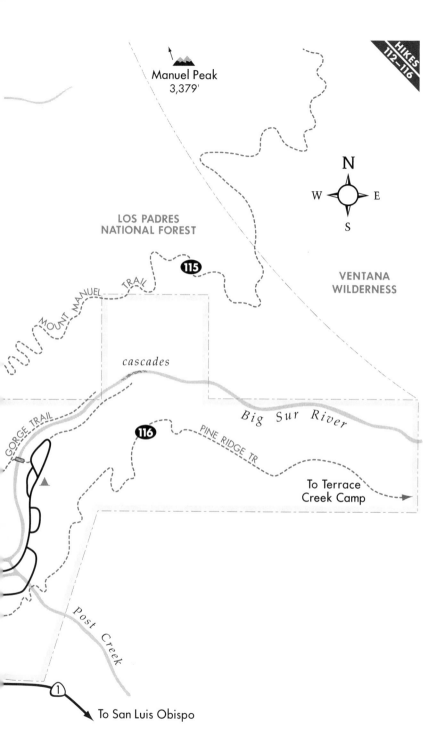

Manuel Peak
3,379'

LOS PADRES
NATIONAL FOREST

VENTANA
WILDERNESS

N
W E
S

115

MOUNT MANUEL TRAIL

cascades

Big Sur River

GORGE TRAIL

116

PINE RIDGE TR

To Terrace
Creek Camp

Post Creek

1

To San Luis Obispo

112. Pfeiffer Falls
Valley View Overlook
PFEIFFER BIG SUR STATE PARK

Hiking distance: 2.2-mile loop
Hiking time: 1 hour
Configuration: loop with short spur trail to overlook
Elevation gain: 500 feet
Difficulty: easy
Exposure: shaded forest
Dogs: not allowed
Maps: U.S.G.S. Big Sur · Pfeiffer Big Sur State Park map
Big Sur and Ventana Wilderness map

Pfeiffer Big Sur State Park is home to lush forests and open meadows surrounding the Big Sur River along Highway 1. This hike follows a moist, fern-lined trail along Pfeiffer-Redwood Creek up a steep-walled canyon through a redwood forest to the base of

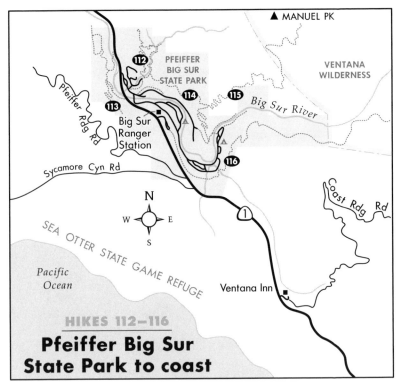

HIKES 112–116

**Pfeiffer Big Sur
State Park to coast**

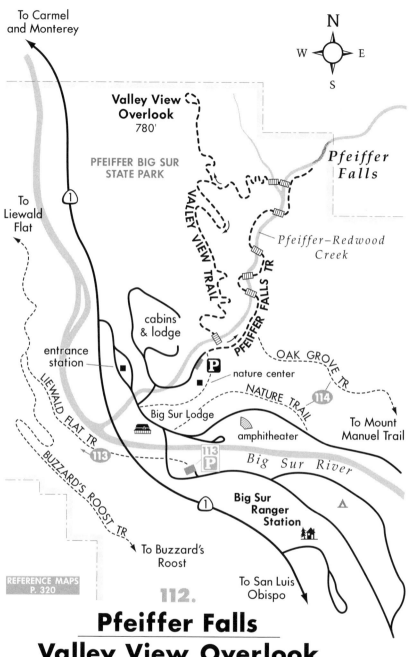

To Carmel
and Monterey

N
W   E
S

Valley View Overlook
780'

PFEIFFER BIG SUR
STATE PARK

Pfeiffer Falls

To
Liewald
Flat

VALLEY VIEW TRAIL

PFEIFFER FALLS TR

Pfeiffer–Redwood Creek

cabins
& lodge

entrance
station

P

nature center

OAK GROVE TR

Big Sur Lodge

NATURE TRAIL

114

To Mount
Manuel Trail

LIEWALD FLAT TR

amphitheater

113

113
P

Big Sur River

BUZZARD'S ROOST TR

Big Sur
Ranger
Station

To Buzzard's
Roost

REFERENCE MAPS
P. 320

To San Luis
Obispo

112.

Pfeiffer Falls
Valley View Overlook
PFEIFFER BIG SUR STATE PARK

Pfeiffer Falls. The waterfall spills 60 feet over granite rock in a small fern grotto with a pool. On the return, the Valley View Trail climbs out of the canyon into an oak and chaparral woodland. A spur trail to a 780-foot overlook offers sweeping views of the Santa Lucia Range, the Big Sur Valley, Point Sur, and the blue Pacific Ocean.

To the trailhead

From the Big Sur Ranger Station, located 27 miles south of Carmel, drive 0.5 miles north on Highway 1 to the signed Pfeiffer Big Sur State Park entrance. Turn right (inland) to the entrance station. Continue to a stop sign. Turn left and a quick right, following the trail signs 0.2 miles to the signed trailhead parking area on the right. An entrance fee is required.

The hike

Take the trail at the far northeast end of the parking area. Head gradually uphill through the redwood forest. Parallel Pfeiffer-Redwood Creek to the signed Valley View Trail on the left. Begin the loop to the right on the Pfeiffer Falls Trail. Ascend a long series of steps to a signed junction with the Oak Grove Trail on the right (Hike 114). Continue up the canyon towards Pfeiffer Falls as the path zigzags upstream over four wooden footbridges. After the fourth crossing is the second junction with the Valley View Trail on the left—the return route. Stay to the right to see Pfeiffer Falls, climbing two sets of stairs to a platform in front of the falls.

Return to the junction and take the Valley View Trail, crossing a bridge over the creek and another bridge over a tributary stream. Switchbacks lead up the south-facing slope to a signed junction. Bear right towards the Valley View Overlook. Ascend the ridge 0.3 miles to a short loop at the overlook. Return back downhill to the junction, and bear right to the canyon floor on the Valley View Trail. Cross the bridge over the creek, completing the loop on the Pfeiffer Falls Trail. Return to the trailhead on the right. ▪

113. Buzzard's Roost
PFEIFFER BIG SUR STATE PARK

Hiking distance: 2.5 miles round trip
Hiking time: 1.5 hours
Configuration: out-and-back with loop
Elevation gain: 800 feet
Difficulty: easy to moderate
Exposure: forested lowlands and open ridge
Dogs: not allowed
Maps: U.S.G.S. Big Sur and Pfeiffer Point · Pfeiffer Big Sur State Park map
        Big Sur and Ventana Wilderness map

**map
page 326**

The Buzzard's Roost Trail begins as a streamside stroll along the Big Sur River through groves of bay laurel, oak, and huge old-growth redwoods. Switchbacks wind up the forested hillside slope to Pfeiffer Ridge. The trail forms a 1.7-mile loop along the shrub-lined ridge. From the 1,050-foot Buzzard's Roost are far-reaching views of the Santa Lucia Mountains and the Pacific Ocean.

To the trailhead

From the Big Sur Ranger Station, located 27 miles south of Carmel, drive 0.5 miles north on Highway 1 to the signed Pfeiffer Big Sur State Park entrance. Turn right (inland) past the entrance station to the stop sign. Continue straight, through the intersection, and turn right after passing the Big Sur Lodge on the right. Drive 0.1 mile, crossing a bridge over the Big Sur River and curving left to the trailhead parking area on the left. An entrance fee is required.

The hike

Take the signed trail, crossing under the bridge that spans the Big Sur River. Follow the river downstream and under Highway 1. Gradually ascend the hillside past redwoods in the shade of the forest. The trail splits and rejoins a short distance ahead. Traverse the hillside to the signed Buzzard's Roost Trail on the left. The main trail leads to the campground and Liewald Flat. Instead, take the sharp left switchback, and climb up the hillside ledge to a trail split at 0.9 miles.

Begin the loop to the left. The path levels out and winds in and out of ravines along the contours of the mountain. Head up more switchbacks to Pfeiffer Ridge, overlooking the Big Sur Valley, Mount Manuel, and the Pacific Ocean. Steps lead up the eroded ridge to Buzzard's Roost. A short side path on the left (by the large antenna) detours to the 1,050-foot overlook. Return to the main trail, and descend the ridge into the forest. Continue weaving down the mountain, completing the loop. Bear left and retrace your steps to the trailhead. ■

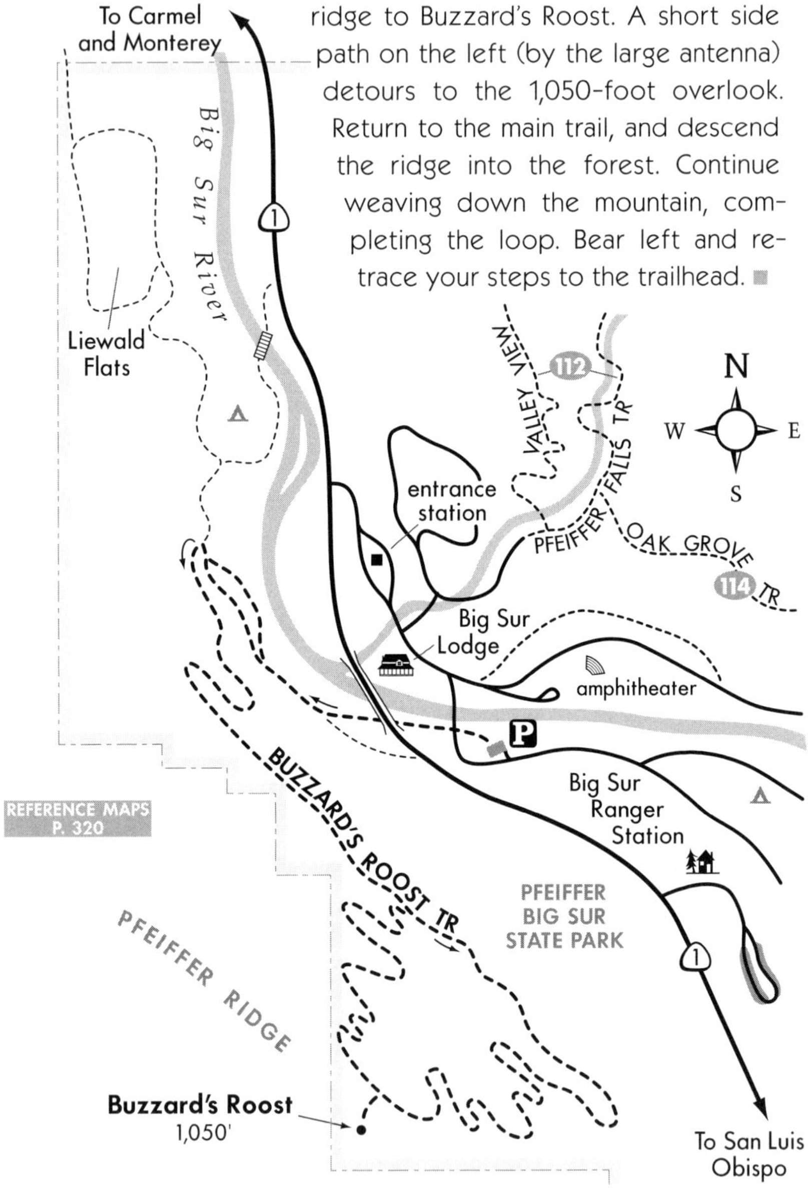

To Carmel
and Monterey

Big Sur River

①

Liewald
Flats

VALLEY VIEW

PFEIFFER FALLS TR

112

N

W ✦ E

S

entrance
station

PFEIFFER

OAK GROVE

114 TR

Big Sur
Lodge

amphitheater

P

Big Sur
Ranger
Station

REFERENCE MAPS
P. 320

BUZZARD'S ROOST TR

PFEIFFER RIDGE

PFEIFFER
BIG SUR
STATE PARK

①

Buzzard's Roost
1,050'

To San Luis
Obispo

113. **Buzzard's Roost**
PFEIFFER BIG SUR STATE PARK

114. Oak Grove Trail
PFEIFFER BIG SUR STATE PARK

Hiking distance: 2.8-mile loop
Hiking time: 1.5 hours
Configuration: loop (with park road)
Elevation gain: 350 feet
Difficulty: easy
Exposure: both shaded and open forest
Dogs: not allowed
Maps: U.S.G.S. Big Sur and Pfeiffer Point · Pfeiffer Big Sur State Park map
Big Sur and Ventana Wilderness map

map
page 328

The Oak Grove Trail traverses a beautiful, forested hillside through several natural ecosystems in Pfeiffer Big Sur State Park. The plant communities range from dry chaparral to hardwood forests with a mix of oaks and shady redwood groves. The path weaves in and out of numerous gullies, connecting Pfeiffer Falls Trail (Hike 112) with the Gorge Trail.

To the trailhead

From the Big Sur Ranger Station, located 27 miles south of Carmel, drive 0.5 miles north on Highway 1 to the signed Pfeiffer Big Sur State Park entrance. Turn right (inland) past the entrance station to the stop sign. Continue straight, through the intersection, passing Big Sur Lodge on the right. Quickly bear left, following the signs towards the picnic area. At 0.7 miles is the signed trailhead parking area on the left. An entrance fee is required.

The hike

Take the gated road past the trail sign into the shade of the old oak forest. At 0.1 mile is a junction at John Pfeiffer's homestead cabin on the left, built in 1884. The right fork follows the Big Sur River along the Gorge Trail to creekside cascades. Take the left fork on the Oak Grove Trail to the homestead cabin and a trail fork. Keep to the left (straight ahead) through the open coastal oak grove. Switchback up the hillside, alternating between shady oak woodlands to exposed scrub and chaparral. At 0.7 miles, the path levels out on a 560-foot saddle by a signed junction with the Mount Manuel Trail—Hike 115. Stay on the Oak Grove Trail to the left, curving down the oak-covered hillside. Descend into a small ravine, and cross the drainage on a wooden footbridge, reaching the west end of the trail at a T-junction with the Pfeiffer Falls Trail at 1.7 miles. Bear left through a grove of large redwoods, and parallel Pfeiffer-Redwood Creek to the paved park road. Follow the park road downhill and bear left at the lodge. Take the forested road 0.6 miles back to the parking lot. En route is a short nature trail to the left that parallels the road. ■

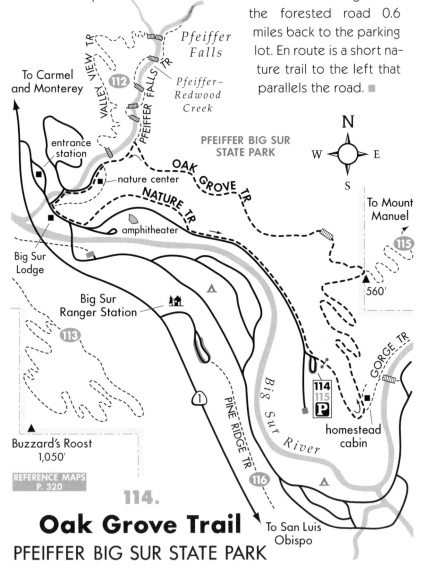

114.
Oak Grove Trail
PFEIFFER BIG SUR STATE PARK

115. Mount Manuel Trail
PFEIFFER BIG SUR STATE PARK

Hiking distance: 10.4 miles round trip
Hiking time: 5.5 hours
Configuration: out-and-back
Elevation gain: 3,200 feet
Difficulty: very strenuous
Exposure: mostly exposed hillside
Dogs: not allowed
Maps: U.S.G.S. Big Sur and Pfeiffer Point · Pfeiffer Big Sur State Park map
Big Sur and Ventana Wilderness map

map
page 330

Mount Manuel is the towering mountain that dominates Pfeiffer Big Sur State Park. This hike climbs to a vista point near the 3,379-foot summit. The sweeping 360-degree panoramic views extend across the entire Big Sur area, from the Santa Lucia Mountains to the expansive crenelated coastline and the sheer cliffs. The trail begins from the Oak Grove Trail and hikes up to the vista point on exposed, chaparral-covered hillsides that offer little shade.

To the trailhead

From the Big Sur Ranger Station, located 27 miles south of Carmel, drive 0.5 miles north on Highway 1 to the signed Pfeiffer Big Sur State Park entrance. Turn right (inland) past the entrance station to the stop sign. Continue straight, through the intersection, passing Big Sur Lodge on the right. Quickly bear left, following the signs towards the picnic area. At 0.7 miles is the signed trailhead parking area on the left. An entrance fee is required.

The hike

Take the gated road past the trail sign into the shade of the old oak forest. At 0.1 mile is a junction at John Pfeiffer's homestead cabin, built in 1884. The right fork follows the Big Sur River along the Gorge Trail to creekside cascades. Take the left fork to the homestead cabin and a trail fork. Keep to the left (straight ahead) through the open coastal oak grove. Switchback up the hillside, alternating between shady oak woodlands and exposed chaparral. At 0.7 miles, the path levels out on a 560-foot saddle by a signed junction with the Mount Manuel Trail.

Bear right up the steps, leaving the oak canopy. Begin zigzagging up the south flank of Mount Manuel above the Big Sur River Valley. Cross the arid, exposed mountainside amid low-growing scrub and forested gullies to a ridge. At 3 miles, the trail curves north and follows the ridge in the Ventana Wilderness, dipping in and out of more gullies. Views expand across Pfeiffer Ridge to the ocean. Cross a forested saddle to a reflector. A short distance ahead is the rocky summit and vista point at 3,379 feet above sea level. After enjoying the expansive views, return along the same trail.

The Mount Manuel Trail continues north to the Little Sur River drainage, connecting to Pico Blanco Road at Bottcher's Gap (Hike 103). ■

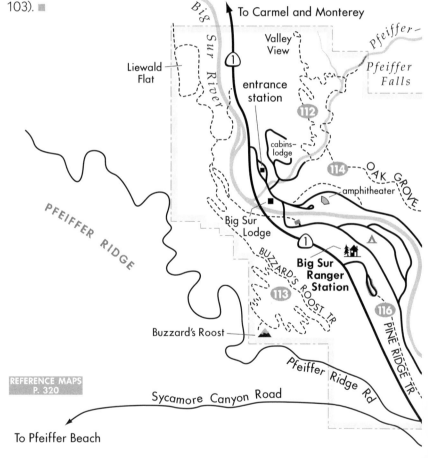

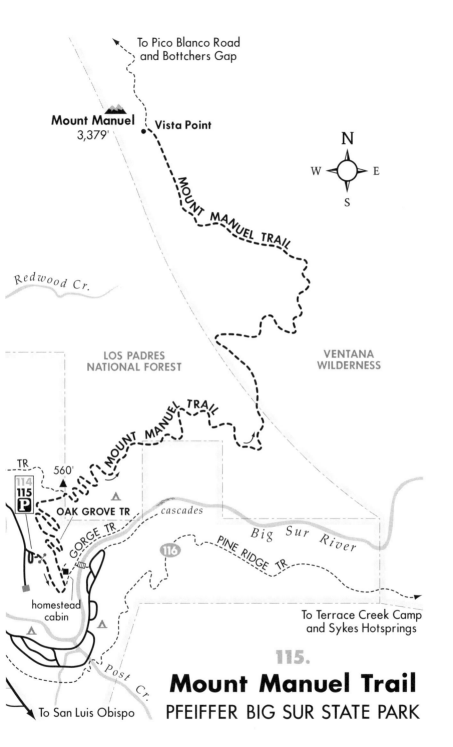

To Pico Blanco Road
and Bottchers Gap

Mount Manuel
3,379'

Vista Point

N
W E
S

MOUNT MANUEL TRAIL

Redwood Cr.

LOS PADRES
NATIONAL FOREST

VENTANA
WILDERNESS

MOUNT MANUEL TRAIL

TR
560'

114
115
P

OAK GROVE TR

cascades

Big Sur River

GORGE TR

116

PINE RIDGE TR

homestead
cabin

To Terrace Creek Camp
and Sykes Hotsprings

Post Cr.

To San Luis Obispo

115.

Mount Manuel Trail
PFEIFFER BIG SUR STATE PARK

116. Pine Ridge Trail to Terrace Creek
PFEIFFER BIG SUR STATE PARK to VENTANA WILDERNESS

Hiking distance: 10.6 miles round trip (or optional 12.5-mile loop)
Hiking time: 5.5 hours
Configuration: out-and-back (or optional loop)
Elevation gain: 1,000 feet
Difficulty: strenuous
Exposure: shaded forest and open hillside
Dogs: allowed
Maps: U.S.G.S. Pfeiffer Point, Partington Ridge, Ventana Cross
      Pfeiffer Big Sur State Park map
      Big Sur and Ventana Wilderness map

**map
page 334**

The Pine Ridge Trail is a key access route to numerous camps and trails throughout the expansive Ventana Wilderness. The trailhead begins at the Big Sur Ranger Station in Pfeiffer Big Sur State Park. The most popular destination from the Pine Ridge Trail is the ten-mile overnight hike to the hot springs at Sykes Camp. This hike takes in the first 5.3 miles of the trail to Terrace Creek, traveling along the Big Sur River Valley 600—800 feet above the river.

The hike can be made into a longer 12.5-mile loop by returning on the Terrace Creek Trail and the Coast Ridge Road. This route involves additional elevation gain and walking along Highway 1 back to the trailhead.

To the trailhead

The trail begins at the Big Sur Ranger Station in Pfeiffer Big Sur State Park. The turnoff is located 27 miles south of Carmel. Turn inland and drive 0.2 miles to the far end of the parking area.

The hike

Take the signed trail at the far end of the parking lot into the shaded forest. Cross the hillside above the Big Sur River through tanbark oak and redwood groves, skirting the edge of the Big Sur Campground to an unsigned trail split. The left fork descends into the campground. Stay to the right and cross a water-carved ravine along Pfeiffer Creek. Zigzag downhill and cross Post Creek. Climb out of the narrow canyon to vistas of the Big Sur River Valley.

Steadily gain elevation, traversing the cliffs above the valley. The path alternates from exposed chaparral to shady draws. The Mount Manuel Trail (Hike 115) is visible across the canyon.

At 2.5 miles, the trail leaves the state park and enters the Ventana Wilderness by a boundary sign. Continue up the river valley to a junction with the trail to Ventana Camp at 4 miles. The left fork descends 1.2 miles to the camp, situated in a horseshoe bend along the Big Sur River. Continue east on the Pine Ridge Trail for 1.2 miles to Terrace Creek and a signed junction with the Terrace Creek Trail. Terrace Creek Camp sits above and to the right, straddling the creek in a beautiful grove of redwoods. This is the turn-around spot. Retrace your steps along the same trail.

OPTIONAL RETURN LOOP HIKE: For a 12.5-mile loop, take the Terrace Creek Trail southeast, heading up through the lush, wooded canyon. At 1.6 miles from Terrace Creek Camp, the trail meets up with the unpaved Coast Ridge Road on a saddle. The road travels for miles along a ridge that runs parallel to the coast. Take the Coast Ridge Road right (west) past a gated side road on the right. The serpentine road begins descending across the rolling, grassy hills and several shady gullies, crossing a saddle with views into the Ventana Wilderness.

At two miles from the Terrace Creek Trail junction is a hairpin left bend along a ridge. Steadily descend down the open hillside trail while enjoying the commanding views of the Big Sur coast. Overlook a canyon filled with redwoods, then descend into a forest. Pass a narrow, 30-foot waterfall cascading off a vertical rock wall on the left. Curve sharply right, crossing the trickling headwaters of Post Creek. The wooded road continues winding down through the shaded oak, bay, and redwood forest. At 10.8 miles, near Highway 1, pass Ventana Inn and walk through a gate to a paved road. Walk 0.1 mile to the highway. Go right (north) along Highway 1 for 1.7 miles, back to the Big Sur Ranger Station. ▪

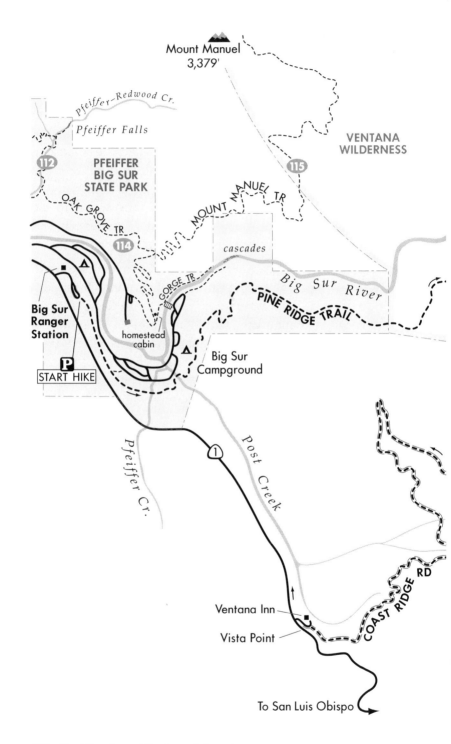

Mount Manuel
3,379'

Pfeiffer-Redwood Cr.

Pfeiffer Falls

112

PFEIFFER
BIG SUR
STATE PARK

OAK GROVE TR

114

MOUNT MANUEL TR

cascades

GORGE TR

homestead
cabin

Big Sur
Ranger
Station

P
START HIKE

Big Sur
Campground

Big Sur River

PINE RIDGE TRAIL

VENTANA
WILDERNESS

115

Pfeiffer Cr.

1

Post Creek

COAST RIDGE RD

Ventana Inn

Vista Point

To San Luis Obispo

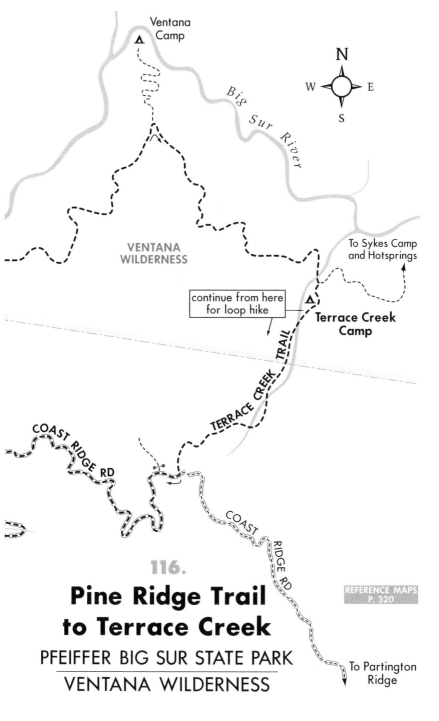

Ventana
Camp

N
W ← ☼ → E
S

Big Sur River

VENTANA
WILDERNESS

To Sykes Camp
and Hotsprings

continue from here
for loop hike

Terrace Creek
Camp

TERRACE CREEK TRAIL

COAST RIDGE RD

COAST RIDGE RD

REFERENCE MAPS
P. 320

To Partington
Ridge

116.
Pine Ridge Trail
to Terrace Creek
PFEIFFER BIG SUR STATE PARK
VENTANA WILDERNESS

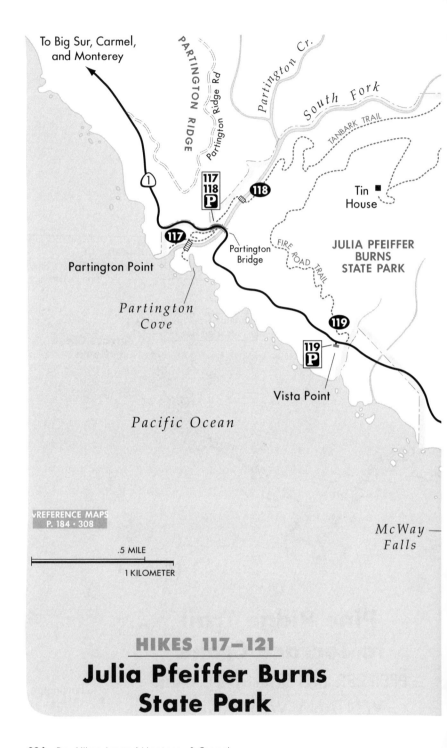

To Big Sur, Carmel,
and Monterey

PARTINGTON RIDGE

Partington Ridge Rd

Partington Cr.

South Fork

TANBARK TRAIL

1

117
118
P

118

Tin
House

117

Partington Point

Partington
Bridge

FIRE ROAD TRAIL

JULIA PFEIFFER
BURNS
STATE PARK

Partington
Cove

119

119
P

Vista Point

Pacific Ocean

REFERENCE MAPS
P. 184 · 308

McWay
Falls

.5 MILE

1 KILOMETER

HIKES 117–121
Julia Pfeiffer Burns
State Park

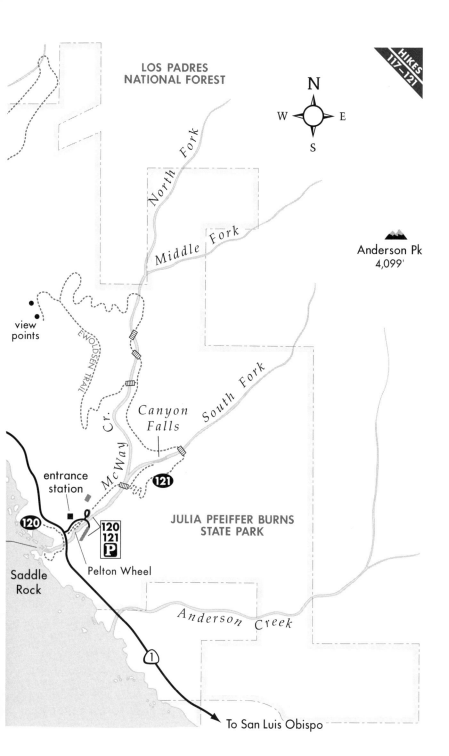

LOS PADRES
NATIONAL FOREST

HIKES 117–121

N
W — E
S

Anderson Pk
4,099'

North Fork

Middle Fork

South Fork

EWOLDSEN TRAIL

view
points

Canyon
Falls

McWay Cr.

121

entrance
station

120

120
121
P

Pelton Wheel

Saddle
Rock

JULIA PFEIFFER BURNS
STATE PARK

Anderson Creek

1

To San Luis Obispo

117. Partington Cove
JULIA PFEIFFER BURNS STATE PARK

Hiking distance: 1 mile round trip
Hiking time: 1 hour
Configuration: out-and-back
Elevation gain: 280 feet
Difficulty: easy
Exposure: open canyon wall; enclosed tunnel
Dogs: not allowed
Maps: U.S.G.S. Partington Ridge · Julia Pfeiffer Burns State Park map
       Big Sur and Ventana Wilderness map

Partington Cove sits at the northern boundary of Julia Pfeiffer Burns State Park along a pristine and rugged section of the Big Sur coastline. The trail to the enclosed cove descends down Partington Canyon on an old wagon route. The creek, which carved the canyon, empties into the ocean at the rocky west cove. A 120-foot manmade tunnel was cut through the cliffs over 100 years ago, leading to the east cove (an isolated, sheltered cove) and Partington Landing. The tunnel was a transit route to haul tanbark to the ships moored in Partington Cove. The historical landing was used as a shipping dock in the 1880s by homesteader John Partington.

To the trailhead

From the Big Sur Ranger Station, located 27 miles south of Carmel, drive 8.5 miles south on Highway 1 to the wide parking pullouts on both sides of the highway by Partington Bridge, where the road curves across Partington Creek and the canyon.

Heading north along Highway 1, the pullouts are 1.9 miles north of the signed entrance for Julia Pfeiffer Burns State Park.

The hike

Head west on the ocean side of Highway 1 past the trailhead gate. Descend on the eroded granite road along the north canyon wall, high above Partington Creek. The old road weaves downhill to the creek and a junction with an interpretive sign. The left fork follows Partington Creek upstream under a dense forest canopy.

Take the right fork 50 yards to a second junction. The left route crosses a footbridge over Partington Creek and leads to the historic tunnel carved through the granite wall. The tunnel emerges at the east cove, where remnants of Partington Landing remain.

Return to the junction by the bridge, and take the path that is now on your left. Follow the north bank of Partington Creek to an enclosed beach cove surrounded by the steep cliffs of Partington Point. Return along the same trail. ■

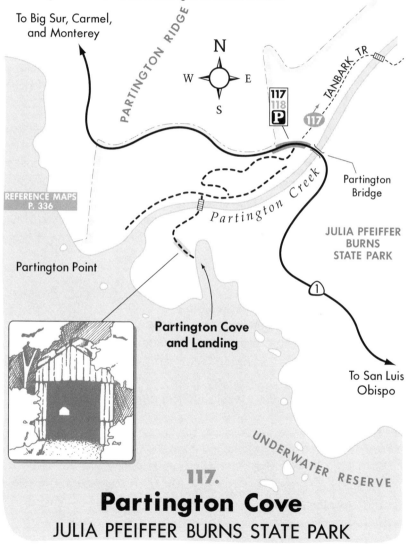

117.
Partington Cove
JULIA PFEIFFER BURNS STATE PARK

118. Tanbark Trail to Tin House
JULIA PFEIFFER BURNS STATE PARK

Hiking distance: 6.4 miles round trip (also 6.4 miles as a loop)
Hiking time: 4 hours
Configuration: out-and-back (or loop with Hike 119)
Elevation gain: 1,900 feet
Difficulty: strenuous
Exposure: shaded forest
Dogs: not allowed
Maps: U.S.G.S. Partington Ridge · Julia Pfeiffer Burns State Park map
      Big Sur and Ventana Wilderness map

The 3,762-acre Julia Pfeiffer Burns State Park lies along ten miles of beautiful Big Sur coast backed by 3,000-foot ridges. The Tanbark Trail is a steep climb up Partington Canyon to a grassy meadow with spectacular coastal views from the abandoned Tin House. The house was built during World War II on a 1,950-foot ridge. The path parallels Partington Creek through a dense forest of huge redwoods, tanbark oaks, and a lush understory of ferns. Switchbacks lead up the canyon wall to the ridge separating Partington and McWay Canyons in the heart of the park. The hike can be combined with the Fire Road Trail—Hike 119—for a 6.4-mile loop.

To the trailhead

From the Big Sur Ranger Station, located 27 miles south of Carmel, drive 8.5 miles south on Highway 1 to the wide parking pullouts on both sides of the highway by Partington Bridge, where the road curves across Partington Creek and the canyon.

Heading north along Highway 1, the pullouts are 1.9 miles north of the signed entrance for Julia Pfeiffer Burns State Park.

The hike

From the inland side of the road, take the path on the northwest (left) side of the bridge. Enter the forested canyon. Within a couple hundred yards, cross the wood footbridge over Partington Creek. Continue upstream on the Tanbark Trail along the east side of the creek, passing huge rock formations, redwood groves,

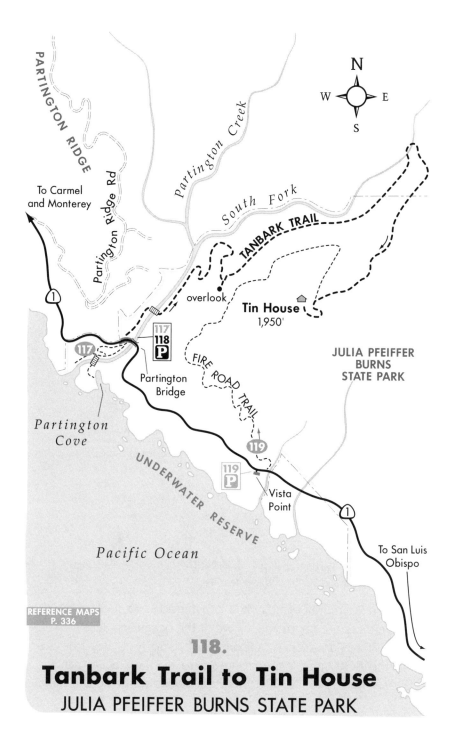

PARTINGTON RIDGE

Partington Creek

Partington Ridge Rd

Partington Ridge

To Carmel
and Monterey

South Fork

TANBARK TRAIL

N
W   E
S

overlook

Tin House
1,950'

1

117
118
P

117

Partington
Bridge

FIRE ROAD TRAIL

JULIA PFEIFFER
BURNS
STATE PARK

Partington
Cove

UNDERWATER RESERVE

119

119
P

Vista
Point

1

To San Luis
Obispo

Pacific Ocean

REFERENCE MAPS
P. 336

118.
Tanbark Trail to Tin House
JULIA PFEIFFER BURNS STATE PARK

pools, cascades, waterfalls, ferns, and mossy boulders. Cross a tributary stream by McLaughlin Grove, and head up the canyon wall on a few switchbacks, leaving the creek and canyon floor. Weave up the mountain to a sharp left switchback. A short detour to the right leads to a ridge overlooking Partington Point.

Return to the trail and traverse the canyon wall through tanbark oaks and redwoods. Cross planks over the South Fork of Partington Creek. Sharply switchback to the right, and recross the creek by a bench in a redwood grove. Continue uphill towards the south, reaching the high point of the hike at a trail sign. Descend to a T-junction with the Fire Road Trail (Hike 119). Bear left on the unpaved road, and descend a short distance, curving to the right to the abandoned Tin House, perched on a ridge. Below the rusty ruins is a grassy meadow with inspiring views of the Big Sur Coast.

Retrace your steps along the same trail, or return along the Fire Road Trail—Hike 119—for a 6.4-mile loop. The loop requires returning 0.9 miles along Highway 1 back to the trailhead. ▪

119. Fire Road Trail to Tin House
JULIA PFEIFFER BURNS STATE PARK

Hiking distance: 4.6 miles round trip (also 6.4 miles as a loop)
Hiking time: 2.5 hours
Configuration: out-and-back (or loop with Hike 118)
Elevation gain: 1,600 feet
Difficulty: moderate to strenuous
Exposure: shaded forest
Dogs: not allowed
Maps: U.S.G.S. Partington Ridge · Julia Pfeiffer Burns State Park map
Big Sur and Ventana Wilderness map

The Fire Road Trail climbs up a coastal ridge to the Tin House, where there are panoramic views of the ocean and Julia Pfeiffer Burns State Park from an elevation of 1,950 feet. This trail is a shorter and slightly easier route up to the Tin House than the Tanbark Trail (Hike 118). The wide trail begins on the coastal cliffs

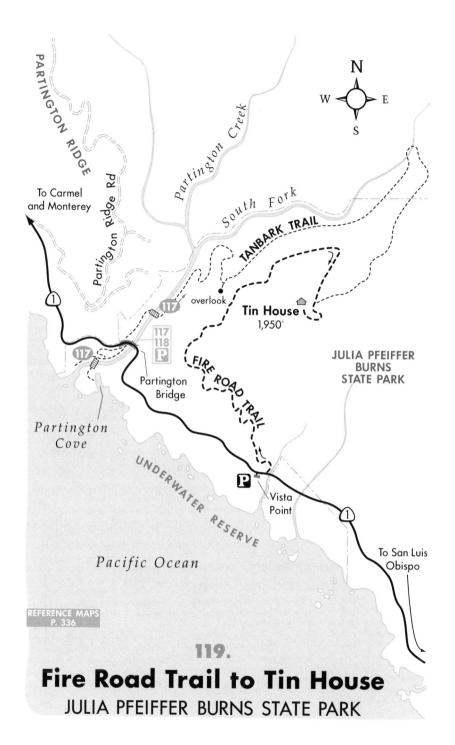

N
W   E
S

PARTINGTON RIDGE

Partington Creek

Partington Ridge Rd

To Carmel
and Monterey

South Fork

TANBARK TRAIL

overlook

117

117
118
P

117

Tin House
1,950'

JULIA PFEIFFER
BURNS
STATE PARK

FIRE ROAD TRAIL

Partington
Bridge

Partington
Cove

UNDERWATER RESERVE

P

Vista
Point

1

Pacific Ocean

To San Luis
Obispo

REFERENCE MAPS
P. 336

119.
Fire Road Trail to Tin House
JULIA PFEIFFER BURNS STATE PARK

across from Vista Point and heads inland, weaving in and out of gullies to Partington Canyon. The path contours the east wall of the canyon, rich with coastal redwoods, tanbark oaks, and shade-loving plants. The trail ends at the Tin House, a boarded up tin building on the high ridge separating Partington and McWay Canyons. Below the building is a grassy meadow with great coastal vistas. This hike can be combined with the Tanbark Trail—Hike 118—for a 6.4-mile loop.

To the trailhead

From the Big Sur Ranger Station, located 27 miles south of Carmel, drive 9.3 miles south on Highway 1 to the signed Vista Point parking pullout on the right (coastal) side.

Heading north along Highway 1, the pullout is 1.1 miles north of the signed entrance for Julia Pfeiffer Burns State Park.

The hike

Head 75 yards southbound on Highway 1 to the gated Fire Road on the inland side of the highway. Walk around the trail gate into a shady redwood grove, paralleling a trickling stream on the right. Curve left, emerging from the trees, and climb to an overlook of the coast and offshore rocks. The trail follows the coastal cliffs along the oceanfront mountains. As you near Partington Canyon, a thousand feet above Partington Cove, curve right and enter the canyon. The views extend across the canyon to homes on the south-facing cliffs. Curve along the contours of the mountain, winding uphill on the serpentine path through redwoods and tanbark oaks. A few switchbacks aid in the climb through the shady forest. The road tops out at a signed junction with the Tanbark Trail on the left. Continue straight ahead and gently descend for a short distance, looping to the right. The trail ends at the abandoned Tin House, perched on a ridge, and the grassy meadow overlook just below the building.

From the landmark structure, retrace your steps along the same trail, or return on the Tanbark Trail (Hike 118) for a 6.4-mile loop. The loop requires returning 0.9 miles along Highway 1 back to the Vista Point pullout. ∎

120. McWay Falls and Saddle Rock
JULIA PFEIFFER BURNS STATE PARK

Hiking distance: 0.7 miles round trip
Hiking time: 30 minutes
Configuration: out-and-back
Elevation gain: 50 feet
Difficulty: easy
Exposure: a mix of shaded forest and open hillside
Dogs: not allowed
Maps: U.S.G.S. Partington Ridge · Julia Pfeiffer Burns State Park map
Big Sur and Ventana Wilderness map

**map
page 346**

McWay Falls pours 80 feet onto a sandy pocket beach along the edge of the Pacific at the mouth of McWay Canyon (back cover photo). The incredibly scenic waterfall drops off the granite bluff in a wooded beach cove lined with offshore rocks. A handicap accessible trail leads to a viewing area of McWay Cove and the cataract on the 100-foot-high bluffs. The pristine beach itself is not accessible. On the south side of the bay is a footpath to a scenic overlook at a cypress-shaded picnic area adjacent to Saddle Rock.

To the trailhead

From the Big Sur Ranger Station, located 27 miles south of Carmel, drive 10.4 miles south on Highway 1 to the signed Julia Pfeiffer Burns State Park. Turn left (inland) and park in the day-use parking lot.

The hike

Descend the steps across the road from the restrooms. At the base of the steps, bear right and head southwest on the signed Waterfall Trail. Follow the north canyon wall above the creek, and walk through the tunnel under Highway 1 to a T-junction. The left fork leads to the Saddle Rock Overlook. For now, take the right fork along the cliffs. Cross a wooden footbridge, with great views of McWay Falls pouring onto the sand. Beyond the bridge is an observation deck with expansive coastal views.

After enjoying the sights, return to the junction and take the footpath towards the south end of the bay. Walk through a canopy of old-growth eucalyptus trees high above the falls. Descend to the trail's end at the 206-foot Saddle Rock Overlook in a cypress grove by a picnic area. ■

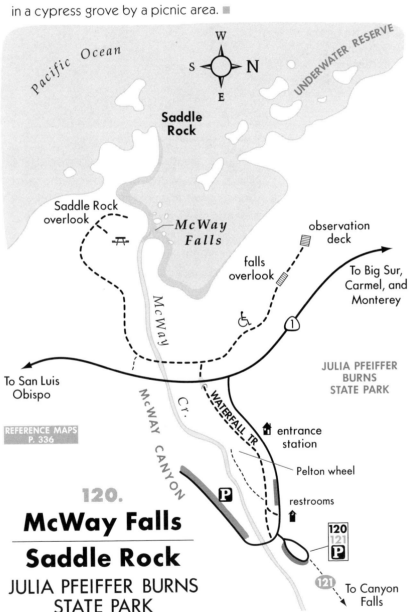

120.
McWay Falls
Saddle Rock
JULIA PFEIFFER BURNS STATE PARK

121. Ewoldsen Trail
to Canyon Falls and Overlook

JULIA PFEIFFER BURNS STATE PARK

Hiking distance: 4.5 miles round trip
Hiking time: 3 hours
Configuration: out-and-back with large loop
Elevation gain: 1,600 feet
Difficulty: moderate to strenuous
Exposure: shaded forest
Dogs: not allowed
Maps: U.S.G.S. Partington Ridge · Julia Pfeiffer Burns State Park map
Big Sur and Ventana Wilderness map

**map
page 349**

The Ewoldsen Trail in Julia Pfeiffer Burns State Park leads through a dense coastal redwood forest in McWay Canyon. The trail crosses several bridges as it heads up to the steep ridge separating McWay and Partington Canyons. From the grassy coastal cliffs are amazing overlooks perched on the edge of the cliffs. The views extend across the park and far beyond, showcasing the jagged coastline and endless mountain ridges and valleys. En route to the ridgetop overlooks is Canyon Falls, a long, narrow, two-tiered waterfall on the South Fork of McWay Creek. The 70-foot cataract cascades off fern-covered rock cliffs in a lush grotto at the back of a serene canyon.

To the trailhead

From the Big Sur Ranger Station, located 27 miles south of Carmel, drive 10.4 miles south on Highway 1 to the signed Julia Pfeiffer Burns State Park. Turn left (inland) and park in the day-use parking lot.

The hike

From the upper end of the parking area, take the signed Canyon and Ewoldsen Trails into a dark redwood forest. Follow McWay Creek upstream past the picnic area. Cross a wooden footbridge over the creek to the east bank, just below the confluence of the South Fork and Main Fork of McWay Creek. A short distance upstream is a posted junction. Take the left fork on the Canyon Trail, staying close to the creek. The narrow, cliffside path ends at the base of Canyon Falls.

Return back to the junction, and continue on the Ewoldsen Trail up the switchbacks, leaving the canyon floor and creek. Zigzag up the south wall of the canyon, and cross another foot-bridge over the South Fork. Traverse the hillside up the mountain contours, and rejoin the main fork of McWay Creek, where views extend down canyon to the sea. Follow the watercourse above the creek to a signed junction at one mile, beginning the loop. Take the right fork along the east bank of the creek. Cross two bridges over the creek, passing cascades, small waterfalls, pools, outcroppings, and moss-covered boulders. Cross a log bridge over the creek, and ascend the west canyon wall. Enter an oak woodland and follow the hillside path to a signed junction. Detour to the right a quarter mile to the view points on the 1,800-foot oceanfront cliffs. Take a break atop the ridge and enjoy the vistas.

Return to the junction and continue on the loop. The winding path descends along the oceanfront ridge, then curves left into the forested canyon. Complete the loop at the bridge over McWay Creek, and retrace your steps back to the right. ■

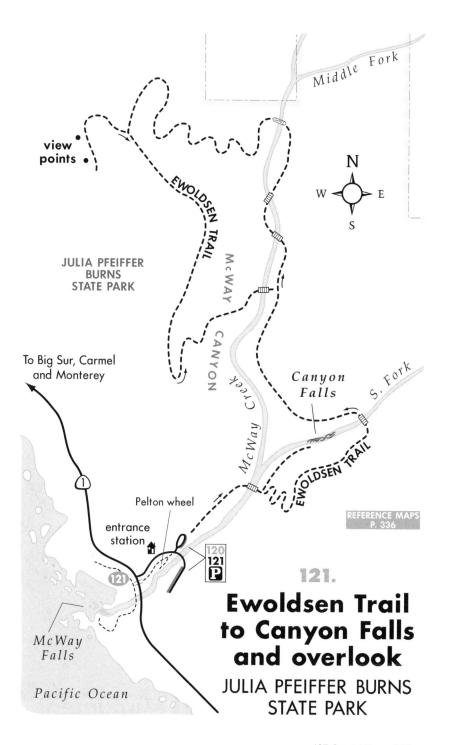

Middle Fork

view
points

N
W   E
S

EWOLDSEN TRAIL

JULIA PFEIFFER
BURNS
STATE PARK

McWAY CANYON

To Big Sur, Carmel
and Monterey

*Canyon
Falls*

S. Fork

McWay Creek

EWOLDSEN TRAIL

REFERENCE MAPS
P. 336

Pelton wheel

entrance
station

120
121
P

121.
Ewoldsen Trail
to Canyon Falls
and overlook
JULIA PFEIFFER BURNS
STATE PARK

1

121

*McWay
Falls*

Pacific Ocean

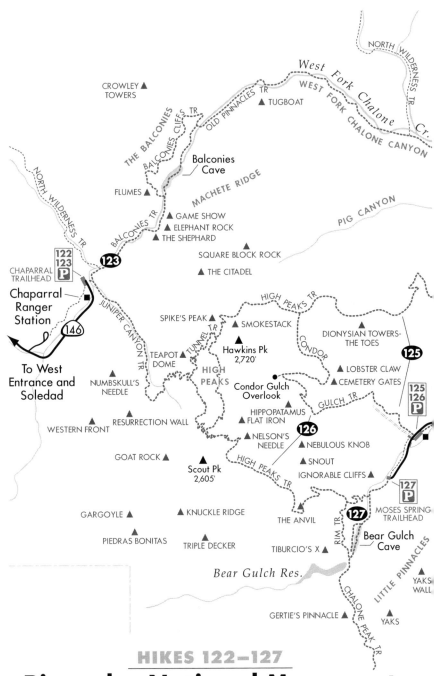

CROWLEY ▲
TOWERS

West Fork Chalone Cr.

NORTH WILDERNESS TR

WEST FORK CHALONE CANYON

▲ TUGBOAT

THE BALCONIES

BALCONIES CLIFFS TR

OLD PINNACLES TR

Balconies
Cave

NORTH WILDERNESS TR

FLUMES ▲

MACHETE RIDGE

PIG CANYON

BALCONIES TR

▲ GAME SHOW
▲ ELEPHANT ROCK
▲ THE SHEPHARD

SQUARE BLOCK ROCK ▲

122
123
P

CHAPARRAL
TRAILHEAD

123

▲ THE CITADEL

Chaparral
Ranger
Station

JUNIPER CANYON TR

HIGH PEAKS TR

146

SPIKE'S PEAK ▲

▲ SMOKESTACK

CONDOR

DIONYSIAN TOWERS-
THE TOES

125

To West
Entrance and
Soledad

TEAPOT
DOME

TUNNEL TR

Hawkins Pk
2,720'

HIGH
PEAKS

Condor Gulch
Overlook

GULCH TR

▲ LOBSTER CLAW
▲ CEMETERY GATES

125
126
P

NUMBSKULL'S
NEEDLE

HIPPOPOTAMUS
▲ FLAT IRON

WESTERN FRONT ▲

RESURRECTION WALL

▲ NELSON'S
NEEDLE

126

▲ NEBULOUS KNOB

GOAT ROCK ▲

HIGH PEAKS TR

▲ SNOUT

Scout Pk
2,605'

IGNORABLE CLIFFS ▲

127
P

GARGOYLE ▲

▲ KNUCKLE RIDGE

RIM TR

127

MOSES SPRING
TRAILHEAD

PIEDRAS BONITAS ▲

▲ TRIPLE DECKER

THE ANVIL

TIBURCIO'S X ▲

Bear Gulch
Cave

LITTLE PINNACLES

Bear Gulch Res.

YAKS
WALL

CHALONE PEAK TR

GERTIE'S PINNACLE ▲

▲ YAKS

HIKES 122–127
Pinnacles National Monument

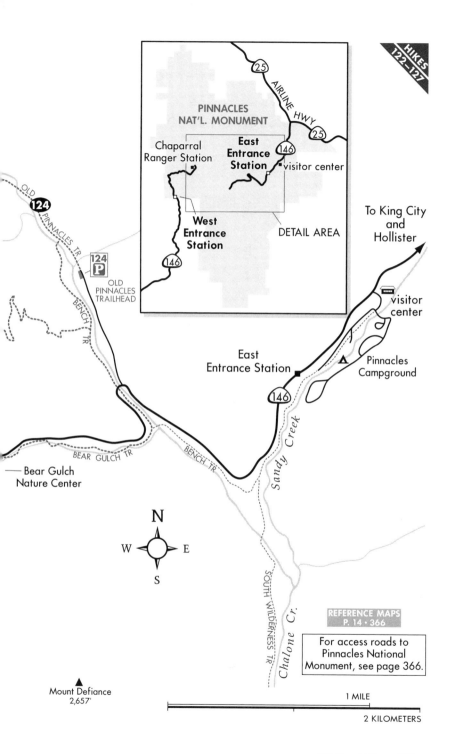

124 P
OLD PINNACLES TRAILHEAD

PINNACLES NAT'L. MONUMENT

Chaparral Ranger Station

East Entrance Station

visitor center

West Entrance Station

DETAIL AREA

To King City and Hollister

visitor center

East Entrance Station

Pinnacles Campground

Bear Gulch Nature Center

BEAR GULCH TR

BENCH TR

Sandy Creek

N
W E
S

SOUTH WILDERNESS TR

Chalone Cr.

Mount Defiance
2,657'

REFERENCE MAPS
P. 14 • 366

For access roads to Pinnacles National Monument, see page 366.

1 MILE
2 KILOMETERS

122. High Peaks—Tunnel Trail Loop via Juniper Canyon

WEST ENTRANCE

PINNACLES NATIONAL MONUMENT

(831) 389-4485

Hiking distance: 4.3 miles round trip
Hiking time: 2.5 hours
Configuration: out-and-back with loop
Elevation gain: 1,150 feet
Difficulty: strenuous (with some technically challenging sections)
Exposure: mostly exposed with semi-shaded canyon
Dogs: not allowed
Maps: U.S.G.S. North Chalone Peak · National Park Service: Pinnacles
     Tom Harrison Maps: Pinnacles National Monument Trail Map

map page 355

Established in 1908, Pinnacles National Monument contains more than 26,000 acres in the low rolling hills of the Gabilan Range. The monument is tucked away east of Salinas Valley near Soledad and King City. The oddly shaped geological formations, remnants of an ancient volcano, rise abruptly from the rolling, grassy hills. The Pinnacles landscape is composed of sheer rock walls and tall spires that rise and twist in exotic configurations and surrealistic forms, creating a natural statue garden.

The park is divided into two districts: east and west. Both districts are accessible by car, but a road does not make a continuous route across the park—the volcanic peaks form a barrier between the two entrances. Only footpaths link the east and west sides of the park. The area is a hiker's and climber's park.

The High Peaks Trail is the premier trail at Pinnacles National Monument. The breathtaking trail winds up, over, and around the landscape's namesake pinnacles. Built by the Civilian Conservation Corps (CCC) in the 1930s and early 1940s, the trail takes the hiker through a rocky, geological wonderland. The circuitous route winds around giant knobs and towers of volcanic, weather-sculpted formations known as The Pinnacles. The trail travels along a narrow ledge etched into the side of the smooth rock face, up a steep staircase hand-chiseled out of the solid rock, under overhanging rocks, and across sheer ledges. The looming rock spires along the precipitous trail change with every step.

This hike begins from the end of the west access road and winds up to the High Peaks Trail via Juniper Canyon, a stream-fed canyon named for the native juniper trees. The trail follows the waterway up the forested canyon among California juniper, blue oaks, and live oaks. From the trail are picture-perfect vistas of the sculpted towers of rock along the mountain crest. The trail climbs to the ridge and forms a loop through the heart of the park. The loop returns along the Tunnel Trail, passing through a 106-foot-long tunnel blasted into the flank of the mountain and crossing a 25-foot-long concrete bridge built into the rock.

To the trailhead

SOLEDAD—DRIVING SOUTHBOUND: WEST ENTRANCE
Soledad is located 25 miles south of Salinas, 100 miles north of San Luis Obispo, and 21 miles north of King City. From Highway 101 in Soledad, take Highway 146/Exit 302. Turn left on Front Street, and drive 0.3 miles to East Street. Turn right on East Street, and go 0.2 miles to Metz Road (Highway 146). Turn right on Metz Road, and continue 2.7 miles to the signed Pinnacles National Monument turnoff on the left. Turn left (east), staying on Highway 146, and go 7 miles to the west entrance station and visitor center. Continue 2.3 miles to the Chaparral Ranger Station and trailhead parking lot at the end of the road.

SOLEDAD—DRIVING NORTHBOUND: WEST ENTRANCE
From Highway 101 in Soledad, take Highway 146/Exit 302. Drive 0.6 miles straight ahead on Front Street to East Street. Turn right on East Street, and go 0.2 miles to Metz Road (Highway 146). Turn right on Metz Road, and continue 2.7 miles to the signed Pinnacles National Monument turnoff on the left. Turn left (east), staying on Highway 146, and go 7 miles to the west entrance station and visitor center. Continue 2.3 miles to the Chaparral Ranger Station and trailhead parking lot at the end of the road.

KING CITY: WEST ENTRANCE
King City is located 46 miles south of Salinas and 77 miles north of San Luis Obispo. From Highway 101 in King City, take Exit 281. Turn

east and drive 1.4 miles on First Street (Monterey County Road G-15) to a junction with Metz Road on the left. Turn left, staying on G-15, and continue 17 miles to Highway 146. Turn right and go 7 miles to the west entrance station and visitor center. Continue 2.3 miles to the Chaparral Ranger Station and trailhead parking lot at the end of the road.

The hike

From the trailhead kiosk, walk 30 yards to a junction. The left fork leads to Balconies Cave (Hike 123). Take the right fork, heading directly towards the mesmerizing High Peaks. Follow the floor of Juniper Canyon southeast among massive boulders with caves and a picture-perfect view of the craggy peaks. Cross the drainage two times, then traverse the east canyon wall among blue oaks, live oaks, and California juniper. Cross the seasonal waterway a third time, and begin climbing the canyon wall. The footpath winds through the towers of rock, imposing rock spires, and giant knobs with the aid of 19 switchbacks. The picnic area and ranger station can be seen below.

At 1.2 miles is a signed Y-fork with the Tunnel Trail. The loop can be hiked in either direction. For this hike, veer right, staying on the Juniper Canyon Trail. Continue uphill, passing under eroding overhangs and between rock walls amongst the scenic views. Continue zigzagging up the rocky landscape while constantly in awe of the ever-changing formations. At 1.8 miles is a T-junction with the High Peaks Trail in a saddle on the ridge. The vistas span in every direction. On the saddle is a sitting bench and a stone restroom. To the right, the High Peaks Trail descends two miles to Bear Gulch and the eastern trailheads (Hikes 125–127).

Bear left and follow the mountain crest among manzanita and scattered pines. Meander along the undulating rocky ridge—with numerous twists and turns—along the shoulder of Hawkins Peak. Weave through a natural rock garden with towering monoliths on the stretch of the High Peaks Trail that is known for a myriad of protruding rock pinnacles. Wind through channels cut into the rock, climb natural rock steps, and continue up a steep staircase chiseled out of the solid rock. This memorable section of the trail traverses the vertical rock walls, climbing up and around over-hanging rock, sheer ledges, and jagged spires. A steel handrail helps safeguard this section of the trail. At 2.5 miles is a junction with the northern end of the Tunnel Trail.

Leave the High Peaks Trail, and bear left on the Tunnel Trail. Zipper down the mountain, weaving through more stunning formations. Cross a rocky gorge on a 25-foot-long concrete bridge built into the rock, then pass through a 106-foot-long tunnel bored through the rock below the High Peaks. Complete the loop at 3.1 miles. Retrace your steps to the right, descending back into Juniper Canyon. ■

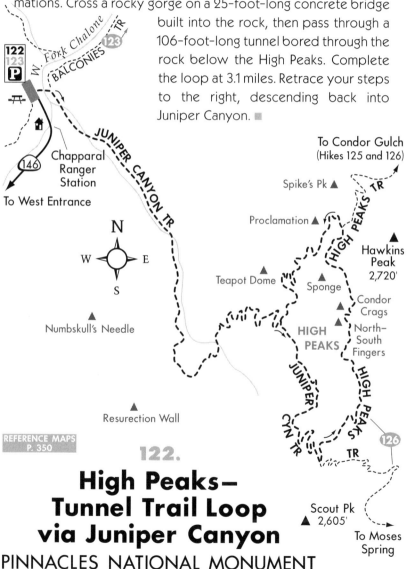

REFERENCE MAPS
P. 350

122.

High Peaks–
Tunnel Trail Loop
via Juniper Canyon

PINNACLES NATIONAL MONUMENT

123. Balconies Cave
via Balconies Trail

WEST ENTRANCE

PINNACLES NATIONAL MONUMENT

(831) 389-4485

Hiking distance: 2.4 miles round trip
Hiking time: 1.5 hours
Configuration: out-and-back with loop
Elevation gain: 200 feet

**map
page 359**

Difficulty: easy to moderate (with some technically challenging
  sections)
Exposure: mostly exposed (except in the cave)
Dogs: not allowed
Note: To hike through the cave, a flashlight is required.
Maps: U.S.G.S. North Chalone Peak and Bickmore Canyon
  Tom Harrison Maps: Pinnacles National Monument Trail Map
  National Park Service: Pinnacles

Balconies Cave is not a typical subterranean cavern but rather a
talus cave created from a rock-roofed passage. The tunnel-like
cavern was formed from a jumble of huge boulders that toppled
into the narrow stream-fed canyon, creating a cave-like ceiling
with a dark passage below. The passageway can be walked from
one end to the other.

  Balconies Cave can be accessed from either the west or east
ends of Pinnacles National Monument. This hike follows the
Balconies Trail from the end of the west entrance road, paralleling the seasonal West Fork of Chalone Creek to the mouth of
the cave. Weaving through the maze-like cave includes climbing,
ducking, squeezing, and scrambling in a dark and narrow passage with low ceilings. (A flashlight is required as you work your

---

Notes about Highway 146: Both the east and west entrances to
Pinnacles National Monument are accessed from Highway 146. However,
Highway 146 is not a through road. There is not a road that crosses
continuously through the park. For access roads, see page 366.

---

way through the pitch-black darkness.) The loop returns along the Balconies Cliff Trail, which traverses the soaring, near-vertical cliffs of the Balconies formation above the cave. From the trail are views of the spectacular pinnacles and Machete Ridge.

To the trailhead

SOLEDAD—DRIVING SOUTHBOUND: WEST ENTRANCE

Soledad is located 25 miles south of Salinas, 100 miles north of San Luis Obispo, and 21 miles north of King City. From Highway 101 in Soledad, take Highway 146/Exit 302. Turn left on Front Street, and drive 0.3 miles to East Street. Turn right on East Street, and go 0.2 miles to Metz Road (Highway 146). Turn right on Metz Road, and continue 2.7 miles to the signed Pinnacles National Monument turnoff on the left. Turn left (east), staying on Highway 146, and go 7 miles to the west entrance station and visitor center. Continue 2.3 miles to the Chaparral Ranger Station and trailhead parking lot at the end of the road.

SOLEDAD—DRIVING NORTHBOUND: WEST ENTRANCE

From Highway 101 in Soledad, take Highway 146/Exit 302. Drive 0.6 miles straight ahead on Front Street to East Street. Turn right on East Street, and go 0.2 miles to Metz Road (Highway 146). Turn right on Metz Road, and continue 2.7 miles to the signed Pinnacles National Monument turnoff on the left. Turn left (east), staying on Highway 146, and go 7 miles to the west entrance station and visitor center. Continue 2.3 miles to the Chaparral Ranger Station and trailhead parking lot at the end of the road.

KING CITY: WEST ENTRANCE

King City is located 46 miles south of Salinas and 77 miles north of San Luis Obispo. From Highway 101 in King City, take Exit 281. Turn east and drive 1.4 miles on First Street (Monterey County Road G-15) to a junction with Metz Road on the left. Turn left, staying on G-15, and continue 17 miles to Highway 146. Turn right and go 7 miles to the west entrance station and visitor center. Continue 2.3 miles to the Chaparral Ranger Station and trailhead parking lot at the end of the road.

The hike

From the trailhead kiosk, walk 30 yards to a junction. The right fork heads up Juniper Canyon to the imposing, weather-sculpted High Peaks (Hike 122). Bear left on the Balconies Trail, and go 200 yards to a junction with the North Wilderness Trail on the left. Continue straight ahead, staying on the Balconies Trail. Parallel the West Fork of Chalone Creek northeast. Follow the canyon bottom towards the amazingly gorgeous rock formations and soaring cliffs of Machete Ridge. Weave in, through, and around the weather-sculpted volcanic formations and huge boulders while marveling at their grandeur. Cross bridges over the seasonal drainage to the mouth of the Balconies Cave. At the last bridge is a fork with the Balconies Cliffs Trail on the left—the return route—and a rock climbers path on the right. Continue along the canyon floor to the mouth of Balconies Cave.

With flashlight in hand, enter the cave and climb, duck, squeeze, and weave through the dark and narrow rock-roofed passage. When in doubt of the route, arrows painted on the walls point the way. At the far north end, emerge from the darkness and pass through the cave gate. Descend through the narrow, moss-filled canyon down rock steps to a posted junction in the Chalone Creek Canyon. The Old Pinnacles Trail goes to the right, down canyon (Hike 124).

For this hike, go to the left on the Balconies Cliffs Trail and climb the canyon wall. Traverse the northwest wall high above the Balconies Cave, with expansive views of the surrounding terrain. Descend to the canyon floor, and complete the loop at the bridge. Return by retracing your route to the right. ■

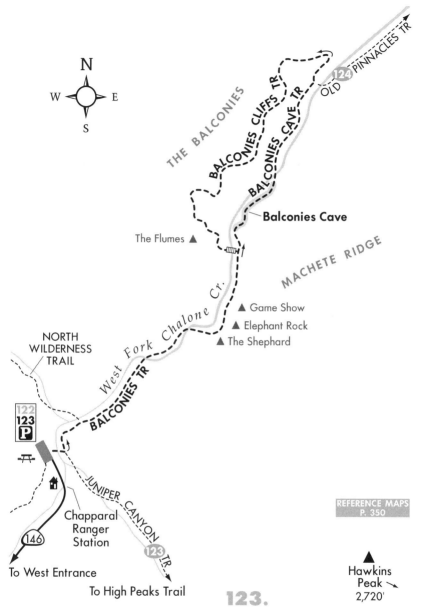

The Flumes ▲

Balconies Cave

MACHETE RIDGE

THE BALCONIES

BALCONIES CLIFFS TR

BALCONIES CAVE TR

OLD PINNACLES TR

124

West Fork Chalone Cr.

BALCONIES TR

▲ Game Show
▲ Elephant Rock
▲ The Shephard

NORTH
WILDERNESS
TRAIL

122
123
P

Chapparal
Ranger
Station

JUNIPER CANYON TR.

123

146

To West Entrance

To High Peaks Trail

REFERENCE MAPS
P. 350

▲
Hawkins
Peak
2,720'

123.

Balconies Cave
via Balconies Trail
PINNACLES NATIONAL MONUMENT

124. Balconies Cave via Old Pinnacles Trail

EAST ENTRANCE

PINNACLES NATIONAL MONUMENT

(831) 389-4485

Hiking distance: 5.2 miles round trip
Hiking time: 3 hours
Configuration: out-and-back with loop
Elevation gain: 400 feet
Difficulty: moderate
Exposure: mostly exposed (except in the cave)
Dogs: not allowed
Note: To hike through the cave, a flashlight is required.
Maps: U.S.G.S. North Chalone Peak and Bickmore Canyon
Tom Harrison Maps: Pinnacles National Monument Trail Map
National Park Service: Pinnacles

map page 362

Balconies Cave can be accessed from either the west or the east sides of Pinnacles National Monument. This hike accesses the cave from the east entrance via the Old Pinnacles Trail, which is the easiest route between the east and west sections of the park. The scenic route follows the West Fork of Chalone Creek up the canyon on a gentle grade. En route, the footpath crosses several bridges over the drainage while traveling through an open forest of gray pines, live oaks, willows, buckeye, and streamside vegetation. The trail ends at Balconies Cave.

Balconies Cave is not a typical subterranean cave. It is actually a talus cave. The tunnel-like cavern was formed when massive rocks fell into a narrow, stream-cut canyon. The boulders, loosened by erosion and earthquakes, formed a ceiling over the canyon. The passageway can be walked from one end to the other. Weaving through the cave includes climbing, ducking, squeezing, and scrambling in a dark and narrow passage with low ceilings. (A flashlight is required as you work your way through the pitch-black cave.) After climbing through the cave, the trail makes a return loop on the Balconies Cliffs Trail, clambering up and over the cave below while traversing the mountainside. The picturesque views include Machete Ridge and the sheer rock walls of the Balconies.

To the trailhead

KING CITY: EAST ENTRANCE
King City is located 46 miles south of Salinas and 77 miles north of San Luis Obispo. From Highway 101 in King City, take Exit 281. Turn east and drive 1.4 miles on First Street (Monterey County Road G-15) to a junction with Metz Road on the left. Drive straight ahead on Bitterwater Road (Monterey County Road G-13), and continue 14.2 miles to a T-junction with Highway 25 (Airline Highway). Turn left (north) and go 14 miles to Highway 146 on the left. Turn left (west) and continue 1.9 miles to the ranger station and pay station. Continue 1.9 miles to the turnoff for the Old Pinnacles Trailhead. Veer to the right and drive 0.6 miles to the trailhead parking lot at the end of the road.

HOLLISTER: EAST ENTRANCE
From the town of Hollister, take Highway 25 (Airline Highway) south for 32 miles to Highway 146 on the right. Turn right (west) and drive 1.9 miles to the ranger station and pay station. Continue 1.9 miles to the turnoff for the Old Pinnacles Trailhead. Veer to the right and drive 0.6 miles to the trailhead parking lot at the end of the road.

The hike

From the far end of the parking lot, follow the trail past the information kiosk. Enter the Chalone Creek drainage, and follow the east side of the canyon. Bear right at a posted fork with the Bench Trail. Continue up canyon along the northeast side of seasonal Chalone Creek among oaks, pines, and multi-colored rock formations. Cross a wooden footbridge over the waterway to a signed junction with the North Wilderness Trail on the right at 0.7 miles. The North Wilderness Trail follows the main valley of Chalone Creek. Stay on the Old Pinnacles Trail in the West Fork Chalone Creek drainage, crossing the drainage four times. As the canyon narrows, pass eroded rock formations pocked with caves and overhangs. Cross the creekbed a fifth time to a posted junction at two miles.

Begin the loop on the Balconies Cave Trail, straight ahead. Pass massive formations and stunning views of the High Peaks. Ascend rock steps among the formations in the narrow, moss-filled canyon. Climb up and around boulders to the gated cave entrance. With flashlight in hand, enter the cave and climb, duck, and weave through the dark and narrow rock-roofed passage. At the far south end, emerge from the darkness on the canyon floor. Head south a short distance to a bridge and a junction.

▲ Crowley
  Towers

OLD PINNACLES TR

▲ Tugboat

BALCONIES CLIFFS TR

THE BALCONIES

BALCONIES CAVE TR

Balconies Cave

The Flumes

MACHETE RIDGE

123 BALCONIES TR

▲ Game Show
▲ Elephant Rock
▲ The Shephard

To Chaparral
Ranger Station and
West Entrance

124.

Balconies Cave
via Old Pinnacles Trail
PINNACLES NATIONAL MONUMENT

The Balconies Trail continues along the drainage to the Chaparral Picnic Area and trailhead (Hike 123).

For this hike, bear right on the Balconies Cliffs Trail, and climb up the canyon wall. Traverse the northwest wall of the Balconies, high above the cave, with views of the surrounding terrain. The imposing 400-foot spires of Machete Ridge rise to the southeast. Descend to the canyon floor, and complete the loop at the junction with the Old Pinnacles Trail. Return by retracing your route two miles back down canyon. ▩

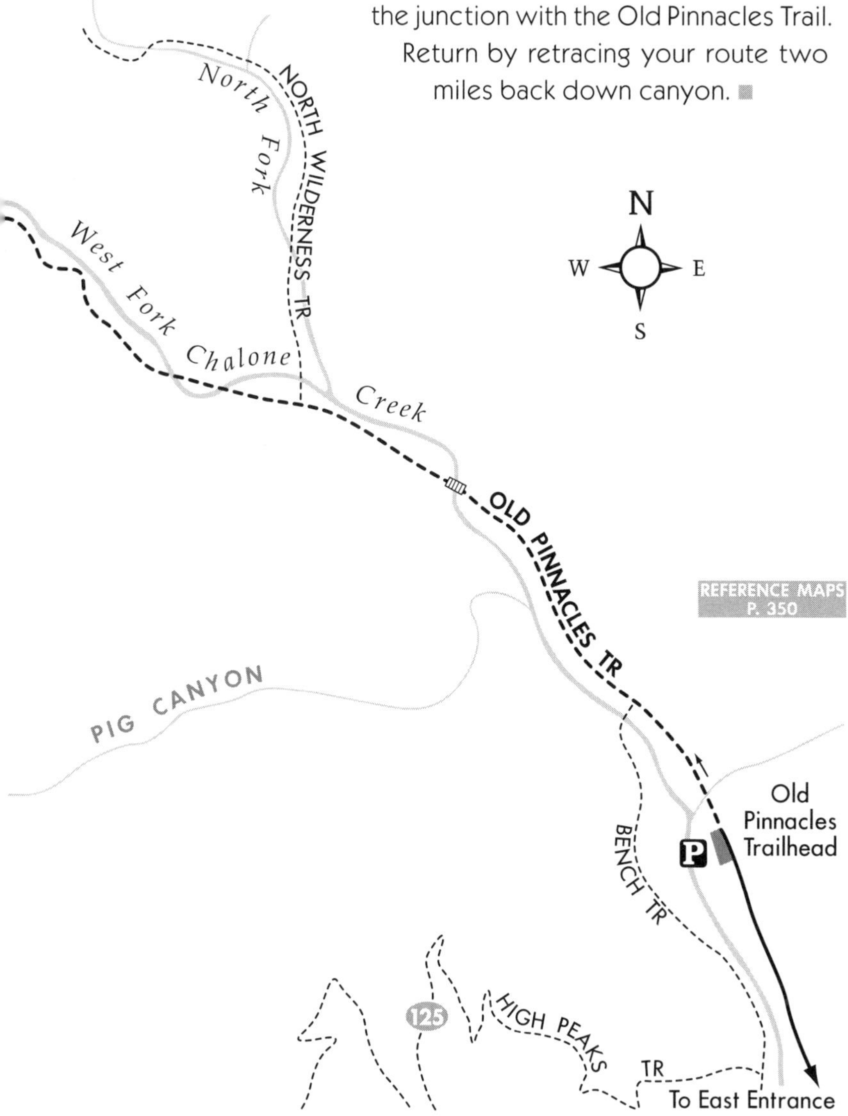

North Fork

NORTH WILDERNESS TR

West Fork Chalone

Creek

OLD PINNACLES TR

N
W — E
S

REFERENCE MAPS
P. 350

PIG CANYON

BENCH TR

P Old Pinnacles Trailhead

125

HIGH PEAKS

TR

To East Entrance

125. Condor Gulch and the High Peaks Trail: EAST LOOP

High Peaks Trail—Bear Gulch Loop

EAST ENTRANCE
PINNACLES NATIONAL MONUMENT
(831) 389-4485

Hiking distance: 5.2-mile loop
Hiking time: 3 hours
Configuration: loop
Elevation gain: 1,060 feet
Difficulty: moderate to strenuous
Exposure: a mix of shaded forest and open chaparral
Dogs: not allowed
Maps: U.S.G.S. North Chalone Peak · National Park Service: Pinnacles
   Tom Harrison Maps: Pinnacles National Monument Trail Map

map
page 367

Condor Gulch, in the heart of Pinnacles National Monument, is home to the endangered California condors. The rocky canyon on the south slope of the High Peaks is a nesting and roosting site for the scavenger bird. Part way up the canyon is the Condor Gulch Overlook, offering a unique opportunity to spot the condors soaring on warm updrafts.

This large loop hike climbs up the Condor Gulch Trail from the Bear Gulch Nature Center to the overlook and the High Peaks Trail atop the mountain. En route, the scenic path passes through chaparral vegetation, live oak, and gray pine. Throughout the climb are breathtaking views of the massive red rock formations. From the ridge, the hike follows the High Peaks Trail east, crossing the grassy ridges high above the West Fork Chalone Canyon back down to the canyon floor. The return through Bear Gulch is a cool streamside stroll under the shade of oaks, sycamores, willows, cottonwoods, live oaks, and a beautiful display of ferns. The trail crosses the tumbling Bear Gulch Creek on a series of footbridges.

To the trailhead

KING CITY: EAST ENTRANCE

King City is located 46 miles south of Salinas and 77 miles north of San Luis Obispo. From Highway 101 in King City, take Exit 281. Turn east and drive 1.4 miles on First Street (Monterey County Road G-15) to a junction with Metz Road on the left. Drive straight ahead on Bitterwater Road (Monterey County Road G-13), and continue 14.2 miles to a T-junction with Highway 25 (Airline Highway). Turn left (north) and go 14 miles to Highway 146 on the left. Turn left (west) and continue 1.9 miles to the ranger station and pay station. Continue 3 miles to the Bear Gulch Nature Center on the left. Park in the lot by the nature center.

HOLLISTER: EAST ENTRANCE

From the town of Hollister, take Highway 25 (Airline Highway) south for 32 miles to Highway 146 on the right. Turn right (west) and drive 1.9 miles to the ranger station and pay station. Continue 3 miles to the Bear Gulch Nature Center on the left. Park in the lot by the nature center.

The hike

Cross the park road to the posted Condor Gulch Trail. Traverse the oak-dotted hillside on the northeast slope of Condor Gulch. Straight ahead is a picture-perfect view of the High Peaks, located in the direction of the hike. Continue up canyon, over-looking the oak- and pine-filled canyon and, farther ahead, the south wall of Hawkins Peak. Near the base of the sculpted rock formations, climb four switchbacks to a junction with the Condor Gulch Overlook at one mile. Detour twenty yards left to the can-yon lookout atop a massive boulder. After enjoying the views, continue uphill on the main trail. At 1.7 miles, the trail ends atop the barren ridge at a T-junction with the High Peaks Trail. The left fork climbs into the heart of the High Peaks amidst the maze of pinnacles (Hike 122).

For this hike, bear right and cross the saddle with 360-degree vistas. Skirt around the east flank of a knoll and steadily descend, perched on the east-facing slope. Curve past two rounded summits high above the West Fork Chalone Canyon. Return to the grassy ridge and continue downhill, passing scattered oaks and pines. Follow the contours of the mountain through the chaparral, consisting mainly of manzanita, buckbrush, and chamise. At 3.7 miles, the trail ends on the canyon floor at a signed junction with the Bench Trail. The left fork leads 2.7 miles to Balconies Cave on the Old Pinnacles Trail (Hike 124).

Go to the right and head down canyon. Follow the west edge of the seasonal, rocky drainage. Cross under the park road, and stroll through the pine and oak forest, well below the road. At 4.3 miles is a junction with the Bear Gulch Trail. Take a right and follow the canyon bottom. Traverse the north canyon slope that showcases a beautiful display of rock outcrops. Cross a 40-foot-long bridge over the stream in a mixed forest, including maples and ferns. Cross a second bridge and stroll through the shade of the forest, passing small pools. Climb past caves on the left. Cross two more bridges over the drainage and the paved driveway of a private residence. Cross another two bridges, completing the loop at the nature center and trailhead parking lot. ■

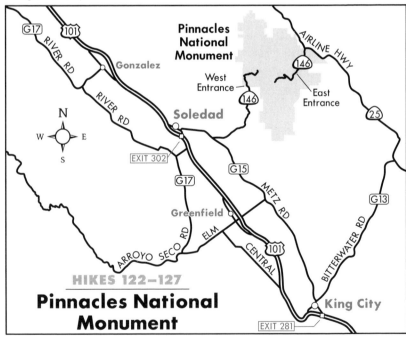

HIKES 122–127

Pinnacles National Monument

To Balconies Cave

OLD PINNACLES TR

N
W E
S

PIG CANYON

124

124 P

Old Pinnacles Trailhead

BENCH TR

HIGH PEAKS TR

Hawkins Pk
▲ 2,720'

Dionysian Towers–
The Toes ▲

CONDOR

To East Entrance

HIGH PEAKS

▲ Lobster Claw

▲ Cemetery Gates

Condor Gulch Overlook
1,840'

GULCH TR

CONDOR GULCH

BEAR GULCH TR

▲ Nebulous Knob

Bear Gulch
Nature Center

126

▲ Snout
Ignorable Cliffs ▲

125
126 P

HIGH PEAKS

TR

DISCOVERY WALL

127

127 P

The Anvil ▲

Moses Spring Trailhead

REFERENCE MAPS
P. 350

Bear Gulch
Reservoir

Bear Gulch
Cave

LITTLE PINNACLES

▲
Mount Defiance
2,657' ↓

To North Chalone Peak

125.

Condor Gulch and the
High Peaks Trail: EAST LOOP

High Peaks Trail–Bear Gulch Loop

PINNACLES NATIONAL MONUMENT

126. Condor Gulch and the High Peaks Trail: WEST LOOP

High Peaks Trail—Hawkins Peak Loop

EAST ENTRANCE
PINNACLES NATIONAL MONUMENT
(831) 389-4485

Hiking distance: 5-mile loop
Hiking time: 3 hours
Configuration: loop
Elevation gain: 1,250 feet
Difficulty: strenuous (with some technically challenging sections)
Exposure: a mix of shaded forest and open chaparral
Dogs: not allowed
Maps: U.S.G.S. North Chalone Peak · National Park Service: Pinnacles
Tom Harrison Maps: Pinnacles National Monument Trail Map

map
page 371

Condor Gulch is a rocky gorge on the south flank of the volcanic High Peaks. The canyon is a favorite haunt of the endangered California condors, which nest in the rock faces and forage for food in the oak woodlands. Part way up the canyon is the Condor Gulch Overlook, offering a unique opportunity to spot the endangered birds riding the air thermals.

The hike begins from the Bear Gulch Nature Center and climbs up the Condor Gulch Trail through the rocky gorge, passing chaparral vegetation, live oak, and gray pine. The trail traverses the steep side hill above the canyon bottom to the mountain ridge, with views of the massive red rock formations throughout the climb. The High Peaks Trail follows the ridge along the flank of 2,720-foot Hawkins Peak, winding between the knobs and sculpted towers of rock. The amazing trail was built by the Civilian Conservation Corps (CCC) in the 1930s and early 1940s, taking the hiker through a stony wonderland of giant knobs and towers of weather-sculpted formations. The trail follows along a narrow ledge etched into the side of the smooth rock face, up steep steps hand-chiseled into the rock, under overhanging rocks, and across sheer ledges. The looming reddish-rock spires along the precipitous trail change with every step.

To the trailhead

KING CITY: EAST ENTRANCE
King City is located 46 miles south of Salinas and 77 miles north of San Luis Obispo. From Highway 101 in King City, take Exit 281. Turn east and drive 1.4 miles on First Street (Monterey County Road G-15) to a junction with Metz Road on the left. Drive straight ahead on Bitterwater Road (Monterey County Road G-13), and continue 14.2 miles to a T-junction with Highway 25 (Airline Highway). Turn left (north) and go 14 miles to Highway 146 on the left. Turn left and continue 1.9 miles to the ranger station and pay station. Continue 3 miles to the Bear Gulch Nature Center on the left. Park in the lot by the nature center.

HOLLISTER: EAST ENTRANCE
From the town of Hollister, take Highway 25 (Airline Highway) south for 32 miles to Highway 146 on the right. Turn right (west) and drive 1.9 miles to the ranger station and pay station. Continue 3 miles to the Bear Gulch Nature Center on the left. Park in the lot by the nature center.

The hike

Cross the park road to the posted Condor Gulch Trail. Traverse the oak-dotted hillside on the northeast slope of Condor Gulch. Straight ahead is a picture-perfect view of the High Peaks, the destination for this hike. Continue up canyon, overlooking the oak- and pine-filled canyon and, farther ahead, the south wall of Hawkins Peak. Near the base of the sculpted rock formations, climb four switchbacks to a junction with the Condor Gulch Overlook at one mile. Detour twenty yards left to the canyon lookout atop a massive boulder. After enjoying the views, continue uphill on the main trail. At 1.7 miles, the trail ends atop the barren ridge at a T-junction with the High Peaks Trail. The right fork (Hike 125) makes a loop around the east end of the High Peaks Trail, descending to the Chalone Creek drainage.

For this hike, bear left on the north-facing rocky path. Meander along the undulating rocky crest along the shoulder of Hawkins Peak. Weave through a natural rock garden with towering monoliths to a posted junction with the Tunnel Trail. Both routes connect up ahead. For this hike, continue straight, staying on the stretch of the High Peaks Trail that is known for its myriad of protruding rock pinnacles. Wind through channels cut into the rock, climbing natural rock steps and a steep staircase chiseled out of the solid rock. This memorable section of the trail climbs up, around, and over the vertical rock walls, passing overhanging rock, sheer ledges, and jagged spires. A steel handrail helps safeguard this section of trail. At 3 miles is a junction with the Juniper Canyon Trail (Hike 122) in a saddle on the ridge, with remarkable vistas in every direction. Walk 15 yards ahead and bear left, remaining on the High Peaks Trail. Descend beneath the towering rocks, zigzagging down the canyon past jagged Scout Peak to the right. Steadily descend to a Y-fork at 4.5 miles. The Rim Trail to Bear Gulch Reservoir goes to the right.

Stay to the left, passing moss-encrusted boulders to another fork. To the right, the Moses Spring Trail leads to the Bear Gulch Cave (Hike 127). Walk straight ahead to the Moses Spring Trailhead parking lot at the end of the park road. Cross the road and follow the trail through the oak-filled picnic area. Complete the loop at the nature center and trailhead parking lot. ▪

The Citadel ▲

N
W · E
S

▲ Spike's Pk

HIGH PEAKS TR

▲ Smokestack

Dionysian Towers–
The Toes

126

TUNNEL TR

Hawkins Pk
2,720'

**Condor
Gulch
Overlook
1,840'**

▲ Lobster Claw

Sponge ▲

Condor
Crags ▲

North–South
Fingers

▲ Cemetery Gates

122

JUNIPER CYN TR

HIGH

PEAKS

The Hippopotamus ▲

CONDOR GULCH TR

CONDOR GULCH

To East
Entrance

Flat Iron ▲

Nelson's Needle ▲

▲ Nebulous Knob

125

126
P

Bear
Gulch
Nature
Center

HIGH PEAKS TR

▲ Snout

Ignorable Cliffs ▲

Scout Peak
2,605'

TOURIST TRAP

127
P

▲ Knuckle Ridge

The Anvil ▲

DISCOVERY WALL

RIM TR

127

MOSES SPRG TR

Moses Spring
Trailhead

Bear Gulch
Cave

▲ Triple Decker

Tiburcio's X ▲

*Bear Gulch
Reservoir*

REFERENCE MAPS
P. 350

Bear Cr.

To North
Chalone Peak

126.

Condor Gulch and the
High Peaks Trail: WEST LOOP

High Peaks Trail–Hawkins Peak Loop
PINNACLES NATIONAL MONUMENT

127. Bear Gulch Cave
Moses Spring—Bear Gulch Reservoir—Rim Trail Loop

EAST ENTRANCE
PINNACLES NATIONAL MONUMENT
(831) 389-4485

Hiking distance: 1.5-mile loop
Hiking time: 1 hour
Configuration: loop
Elevation gain: 300 feet
Difficulty: easy to moderate
Exposure: a mix of shaded forest, dark cave, and exposed hillside
Dogs: not allowed
Note: To hike through the cave, a flashlight is required.
Maps: U.S.G.S. North Chalone Peak · National Park Service: Pinnacles
 Tom Harrison Maps: Pinnacles National Monument Trail Map

**map
page 375**

This popular loop hike is the easiest and shortest hike in Pinnacles National Monument, yet it is a fascinating and diverse journey. Bear Gulch Cave is another talus cave that was formed by giant boulders falling into a narrow canyon, wedging themselves together to form a ceiling. The winding cave passage, which can be walked from one end to the other, is pitch black in places, naturally spooky, and can induce claustrophobia. The cave is home to a colony of Townsend's big-eared bats. The shy bats, numbering over 350, is one of the largest colonies in the state. The bats use the cave for roosting, hibernating, and raising their young. The trail emerges from the cave at Bear Gulch Reservoir, a manmade reservoir in a boulder-filled gorge on Bear Creek. The picturesque, rock-walled reservoir sits upstream from the cave at an elevation of 1,600 feet. The loop returns on the Rim Trail, a short but scenic route perched on Discovery Wall, the west wall of Bear Gulch. The path overlooks the gulch and Bear Gulch Cave.

The hike begins at the lower end of Bear Gulch among moss-covered rocks. The trail climbs through the shaded forest to the cave. Weaving through the cave includes climbing, ducking, squeezing, and scrambling in a dark and narrow passage with low ceilings. (A flashlight is required as you work your way through the pitch-black cave.) The path ascends stairs carved into the reddish volcanic rock, exiting the cave to the scenic Bear Gulch Reservoir.

Some sections of Bear Gulch Cave are closed seasonally to protect the bat species. Check with the ranger station or website for the status of the cave.

To the trailhead

KING CITY: EAST ENTRANCE
King City is located 46 miles south of Salinas and 77 miles north of San Luis Obispo. From Highway 101 in King City, take Exit 281. Turn east and drive 1.4 miles on First Street (Monterey County Road G-15) to a junction with Metz Road on the left. Drive straight ahead on Bitterwater Road (Monterey County Road G-13), and continue 14.2 miles to a T-junction with Highway 25 (Airline Highway). Turn left (north) and go 14 miles to Highway 146 on the left. Turn left (west) and continue 1.9 miles to the ranger station and pay station. Continue 3.3 miles to the Moses Spring Trailhead and parking lot at the end of the road.

HOLLISTER: EAST ENTRANCE
From the town of Hollister, take Highway 25 (Airline Highway) south for 32 miles to Highway 146 on the right. Turn right and drive 1.9 miles to the ranger station and pay station. Continue 3.3 miles to the Moses Spring Trailhead and parking lot at the end of the road.

The hike

From the information kiosk, head up the signed trail surrounded by moss-covered boulders, weather-carved rock formations, stately oaks, California buckeye, and toyon. At 0.1 mile is a Y-fork with the High Peaks Trail on the right. Stay to the left on the Moses Spring Trail, beginning the loop. Gently climb, weaving through the lush forest. Pass through a tunnel cut through a huge rock in the 1930s to another Y-fork. The right fork bypasses the cave and traverses the canyon, perched on the rocky cliff wall.

To walk through the cave, stay to the left on the Bear Gulch Cave Trail. Pass through a narrow corridor between imposing vertical rock walls to the cave entrance. With flashlight in hand, enter the cave and snake up canyon beneath the tumble of boulders which form the ceiling. Duck, squeeze, and climb many steps through the dark and narrow rock-roofed passage. Gaps in the boulders overhead allow some light into the cave. Metal walkways and stairs aid in some of the steepest sections of the cave. Look for white arrows painted on the walls to help with navigation. At the south end of the water-sculpted cavern, emerge from the darkness and climb the steps that lead out of the cave, carved out of the solid rock. Emerge at the east corner of Bear Gulch Reservoir to a gorgeous view across the lake. Cross the bridge to the left and detour along the scenic, rock-lined reservoir on the Chalone Peak Trail. To extend the hike, the Chalone Peak Trail leads 3.2 miles southwest along the exposed chaparral hillsides to 3,304-foot North Chalone Peak, the high point in the parklands.

For the return loop, take the Rim Trail to the right. The trail traverses Discovery Wall, the rocky west canyon wall of Bear Gulch, offering far-reaching canyon views. The Rim Trail ends at a signed junction with the High Peaks Trail. Bear sharply to the right, and weave down the mountain along five switchbacks. Pass moss-covered rocks into the tree-shaded forest. Complete the loop at the Moses Spring Trail junction. Bear left, returning to the trailhead. ▪

N
W · E
S

▲ Nebulous Knob

▲ Snout

Ignorable Cliffs ▲

Bear Gulch Nature Center

125-126

125 126 P

CONDOR GULCH TR

TOURIST TRAP TR

126

HIGH PEAKS

The Anvil ▲

DISCOVERY WALL

RIM TR

Moses Spring

127 P

Moses Spring Trailhead

MOSES SPRING TR

Bear Gulch Cave

Tiburcio's X ▲

The Monolith

Upper Crust

▲ Yaks Wall

Bear Gulch Reservoir

CHALONE PEAK TR

LITTLE PINNACLES

Gertie's Pinnacle ▲

To North Chalone Peak

▲ Yaks

REFERENCE MAPS
P. 350

127.

Bear Gulch Cave

Moses Spring–Bear Gulch Reservoir–
Rim Trail Loop

PINNACLES NATIONAL MONUMENT

DAY HIKE BOOKS

Day Hikes On the California Central Coast	978-1-57342-058-7	17.95
Day Hikes On the California Southern Coast	978-1-57342-045-7	14.95
Day Hikes In the Santa Monica Mountains	978-1-57342-065-5	21.95
Day Hikes Around Sonoma County	978-1-57342-053-2	16.95
Day Hikes Around Napa Valley	978-1-57342-057-0	16.95
Day Hikes Around Monterey and Carmel	978-1-57342-067-9	19.95
Day Hikes Around Big Sur	978-1-57342-041-9	14.95
Day Hikes Around San Luis Obispo	978-1-57342-051-8	16.95
Day Hikes Around Santa Barbara	978-1-57342-060-0	17.95
Day Hikes Around Ventura County	978-1-57342-062-4	17.95
Day Hikes Around Los Angeles	978-1-57342-061-7	17.95
Day Hikes Around Orange County	978-1-57342-047-1	15.95
Day Hikes In Yosemite National Park	978-1-57342-059-4	13.95
Day Hikes In Sequoia and Kings Canyon N.P.	978-1-57342-030-3	12.95
Day Hikes Around Sedona, Arizona	978-1-57342-049-5	14.95
Day Hikes On Oahu	978-1-57342-038-9	11.95
Day Hikes On Maui	978-1-57342-039-6	11.95
Day Hikes On Kauai	978-1-57342-040-2	11.95
Day Hikes In Hawaii	978-1-57342-050-1	16.95
Day Hikes In Yellowstone National Park	978-1-57342-048-8	12.95
Day Hikes In Grand Teton National Park	978-1-57342-046-4	11.95
Day Hikes In the Beartooth Mountains Billings to Red Lodge to Yellowstone N.P.	978-1-57342-064-8	15.95
Day Hikes Around Bozeman, Montana	978-1-57342-063-1	15.95
Day Hikes Around Missoula, Montana	978-1-57342-066-2	15.95

These books may be purchased at your local bookstore or outdoor shop. Or, order them direct from the distributor:

The Globe Pequot Press

246 Goose Lane • P.O. Box 480 • Guilford, CT 06437-0480
on the web: www.globe-pequot.com

800-243-0495 DIRECT   800-820-2329 FAX

DAY HIKES ON THE
California Central Coast

120 COASTAL HIKES FROM
SANTA CRUZ TO SANTA BARBARA
Robert Stone

DAY HIKES ON THE
California Southern Coast

100 GREAT HIKES
Robert Stone

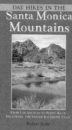

DAY HIKES IN THE
Santa Monica Mountains

FROM LOS ANGELES TO POINT MUGU
INCLUDING THE ENTIRE BACKBONE TRAIL
Robert Stone

DAY HIKES AROUND
Sonoma County

95 GREAT HIKES
Robert Stone

DAY HIKES AROUND
Napa Valley

88 GREAT HIKES
Robert Stone

DAY HIKES AROUND
Monterey & Carmel

125 GREAT HIKES
Robert Stone

DAY HIKES AROUND
Big Sur

80 GREAT HIKES
Robert Stone

DAY HIKES AROUND
San Luis Obispo

Robert Stone

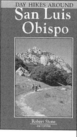

DAY HIKES AROUND
Santa Barbara

115 GREAT HIKES
Robert Stone

DAY HIKES AROUND
Ventura County

116 GREAT HIKES
Robert Stone

LOS ANGELES TIMES BESTSELLER
DAY HIKES AROUND
Los Angeles

135 GREAT HIKES
Robert Stone

DAY HIKES AROUND
Orange County

108 GREAT HIKES
Robert Stone

DAY HIKES IN
Yosemite NATIONAL PARK

80 GREAT HIKES
Robert Stone

DAY HIKES IN
Sequoia & Kings Canyon NATIONAL PARKS

Robert Stone

DAY HIKES AROUND
Sedona ARIZONA

100 GREAT HIKES
Robert Stone

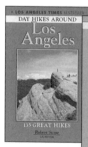

DAY HIKES IN
Yellowstone NATIONAL PARK

82 GREAT HIKES
Robert Stone

DAY HIKES IN
Grand Teton NATIONAL PARK

72 GREAT HIKES
Robert Stone

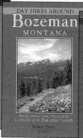

DAY HIKES IN THE
Beartooth Mountains

BILLINGS TO RED LODGE & YELLOWSTONE
THROUGH VALLEY PARADISE VALLEY
Robert Stone

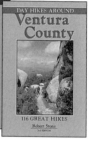

DAY HIKES AROUND
Bozeman MONTANA

INCLUDING THE GALLATIN
CANYON AND PARADISE VALLEY
Robert Stone

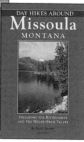

DAY HIKES AROUND
Missoula MONTANA

INCLUDING THE BITTERROOTS
AND THE SEELEY-SWAN VALLEY
Robert Stone

Day Hikes Around Big Sur

Big Sur is an amazing stretch of beautiful coastline in central California where the Santa Lucia Mountains rise over 5,000 feet from the ocean The area is character-ized by craggy coastal headlands backed by mountains and carved canyons. The area's topography, as well as its wilderness and national forest designations, have kept Big Sur unspoiled.

Day Hikes Around Big Sur includes a cross-section of 80 memorable hikes found along the coastline and throughout the parallel mountain range. Hikes range from beach strolls to ele-vated climbs with far-reaching views. Undoubtedly, the trails reveal some of the best scenery in Big Sur and California.

184 pages • 80 hikes • 1st Edition 2003 • ISBN 978-1-57342-041-9

Day Hikes On the California Central Coast

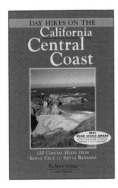

The Central California coast has some of the most spec-tacular scenery in the state. Rugged coastal terraces are backdropped by mountain ranges that run parallel to the Pacific coastline. Picturesque communities dot a landscape abundant with valleys, white sand beaches, cool forests, and natural preserves. The surf crashes onto weather-sculpted headlands and carved canyons along the Big Sur stretch of coast.

This guide includes 400 miles of coastline between San Francisco and Los Angeles. The hike descriptions include how and where to access the best trails and geographical features from Highway 1, offering many opportunities to explore the beautiful landscape.

320 pages • 120 hikes • 2nd Edition 2009 • ISBN 978-1-57342-058-7
BEST BOOK SERIES AWARD: Rocky Mountain Outdoor Writers and Photographers

INDEX

DEBRA COFFEY

About the Author

Since 1991, Robert Stone has been writer, photographer, and publisher of Day Hike Books. He is a Los Angeles Times Best Selling Author and an award-winning journalist of Rocky Mountain Outdoor Writers and Photographers, the Outdoor Writers Association of California, the Northwest Outdoor Writers Association, the Outdoor Writers Association of America, and the Bay Area Travel Writers.

Robert has hiked every trail in the Day Hike Book series. With 24 hiking guides in the series, many in their fourth and fifth editions, he has hiked thousands of miles of trails throughout the western United States and Hawaii. When Robert is not hiking, he researches, writes, and maps the hikes before returning to the trails. He spends summers in the Rocky Mountains of Montana and winters on the California Central Coast.